Performative monuments

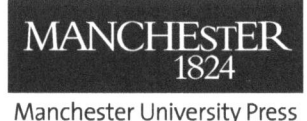

Manchester University Press

rethinking
art's histories

SERIES EDITORS
Amelia G. Jones, Marsha Meskimmon

Rethinking Art's Histories aims to open out art history from its most basic structures by foregrounding work that challenges the conventional periodisation and geographical subfields of traditional art history, and addressing a wide range of visual cultural forms from the early modern period to the present.

These books will acknowledge the impact of recent scholarship on our understanding of the complex temporalities and cartographies that have emerged through centuries of world-wide trade, political colonisation and the diasporic movement of people and ideas across national and continental borders.

Also available in the series

Art, museums and touch   Fiona Candlin

The 'do-it-yourself' artwork: Participation from fluxus to relational aesthetics   Anna Dezeuze (ed.)

After the event: New perspectives in art history
Charles Merewether and John Potts (eds)

Photography and documentary film in the making of modern Brazil   Luciana Martins

Women, the arts and globalization: Eccentric experience
Marsha Meskimmon and Dorothy Rowe (eds)

After-affects|after-images: Trauma and aesthetic transformation in the virtual Feminist museum   Griselda Pollock

Vertiginous mirrors: The animation of the visual image and early modern travel   Rose Marie San Juan

The newspaper clipping: a modern paper object
Anke Te Heesen, *translated by* Lori Lantz

Screen/space: The projected image in contemporary art   Tamara Trodd (ed.)

Performative monuments

The rematerialisation of public art

Mechtild Widrich

Manchester University Press

The right of Mechtild Widrich to be identified as the author of this work has been asserted by her in accordance with the Copyright, Designs and Patents Act 1988.

Published by Manchester University Press
Altrincham Street, Manchester M1 7JA
www.manchesteruniversitypress.co.uk

A catalogue record for this book is available from the British Library

ISBN 978 0 7190 9163 6 hardback
ISBN 978 0 7190 9591 7 paperback

First published 2014

The publisher has no responsibility for the persistence or accuracy of URLs for any external or third-party internet websites referred to in this book, and does not guarantee that any content on such websites is, or will remain, accurate or appropriate.

Typeset in Minion with Myriad display
by Koinonia, Manchester

To Laurens and Andrei

Contents

List of illustrations

Acknowledgements

This book has grown out of my doctoral research in the History, Theory and Criticism of Art and Architecture (HTC) Program at MIT. I would first of all like to thank my advisors, Caroline Jones, Martha Buskirk, and Mark Jarzombek, who have guided me through the twists and turns of the project with admirable patience and continuous support. Among HTC faculty, Nasser Rabbat, Arindam Dutta and Erika Naginski have offered perceptive advice and criticism that shaped the early trajectory of this work, as have my former colleagues at HTC, Lucia Allais, Zeynep Çelik-Alexander, Anneka Lenssen, Ana María León Crespo, Fabiola López-Durán, Ijlal Muzaffar, Michael Osman and Rebecca Uchill. Beyond HTC, I have learned from the scholarship and teaching of Ewa Lajer-Burcharth, Elaine Scarry, and Carrie Lambert-Beatty at Harvard University. As postdoctoral fellow at the Chair of the History of Art and Architecture at ETH (Swiss Federal Institute of Technology) Zurich, I was able to thoroughly rework the manuscript. I would like to thank Philip Ursprung and my colleagues Martino Stierli, Emily Scott, Nina Zschocke, Anette Freytag and Sabine von Fischer for their intellectual support and for their encouragement, and Dora Imhof additionally for her critical feedback on the manuscript.

My archival research would not have been possible without the help of many. I would like to thank the artists who patiently answered my questions: Peter Hassmann, Hermann Hendrich, VALIE EXPORT, Jochen Gerz, and Marina Abramović. The following scholars helped me locate much-needed material, and surprised me with new evidence and directions for study: at the archive of the Institute for the History and Theory of the Architecture, ETH, Bruno Maurer, at the Solomon R. Guggenheim Museum Archive, New York, Francine Snyder; at the Museum of Contemporary Art in Belgrade, curator Zoran Erić and archivist Una Popović; at the Student Cultural Centre in Belgrade, Ljubinka Gavran; at the Generali Foundation Archive, Vienna, Doris Leutgeb and Michael Punzengruber; at the Charim Galerie Vienna, Kurt Kladler; at the Historisches Museum, Vienna, Gudrun Ratzinger; at the Galerie Krinzinger, Vienna, Ursula Krinzinger; at the Museum Moderner

Kunst, Vienna, Sophie Haase and Matthias Michalka; at the Office for Cultural Affairs in Hamburg, Achim Könneke and Anne-Kathrin Reinberg; at the documenta Archive, Kassel, Karin Stengel and Petra Hinck. My work in Belgrade would not have been possible without Vukan Vujević, my enterprising and generous research assistant and translator of Serbian texts.

Valuable comments on particular parts of this study came from Ivan Drpić, Amelia Jones, Gabriele Mackert, Asja Mandić, Hilde van Gelder, Joyce Tsai, Tijana Vujosević, and Helen Westgeest. Crucial information and advice also came from Eva Badura-Triska, Benjamin Buchloh, Harry Cooper, Thomas DaCosta Kaufmann, Lorraine Daston, Konstanze Sylva Domhardt, Werner Hanak-Lettner, Christine Mehring, Hanno Millesi and Krzysztof Wodiczko. Finally, Andrei Pop has supported this project from the very start, emotionally and intellectually, and I would like to express my gratitude for his encouragement.

Essays related to this study were published at various stages of my work in: Viktor Kittlausz, Gabriele Mackert, Winfried Pauleit, eds., *Blind Date. Zeitgenossenschaft als Herausforderung*. Nuremberg: Institut für Moderne Kunst, 2008; Hilde van Gelder and Helen Weestgeest, eds, *Photography between Poetics and Politics*. Leuven: University Press Leuven, 2008; Amelia Jones and Adrian Heathfield, eds, *Perform, Repeat, Record: A Critical Anthology of Live Art in History*. Bristol: intellect, 2012, *Grey Room*, no. 47 (April 2012), and *TDR-The Drama Review* (February 2013).

I would like to thank Marsha Meskimmon and Amelia Jones for including me in their exciting series. Editorial director Emma Brennan made the production process a very pleasant experience. I also would like to thank Judith Oppenheimer for copy-editing the manuscript so carefully.

Unless otherwise noted, all translations are mine. All translations from Serbo-Croatian are by Vukan Vujević.

Holidays in the Sun, 1977 by Paul Cook, Steve Jones, Johnny Rotten, Sid Vicious, published by Careers Music, Inc. BMI/WB Music Corp.

Introduction:
what is a performative monument?

There is an aphorism by Robert Musil, first printed in his 1936 *Posthumous Papers of a Living Author*, to the effect that 'there is nothing in the world as invisible as monuments'.[1] We simply overlook traditional monumental sculpture in public space. The statues of great heroes and formerly famous poets have mysteriously fallen silent. Worse, we throw the famous deceased, with a stone monument around their necks, into a sea of forgetting. Musil's text, especially the sentence cited above, is quoted often in defence of contemporary public art. The brief essay, originally delivered as a talk on 10 December 1927, puts great emphasis on the monument's need for attention from an audience.[2] And that is because this audience is itself the monument's target. The job of monuments, according to Musil, is to kick-start commemoration (*ein Gedenken erst zu erzeugen*), to 'grab our attention and give our feelings a pious direction; and at this their main business monuments fail always'.[3] Musil uses the German term *Denkmal*, usually translated as monument, but literally a mark to think.[4] The Austrian writer and critic sees the function of the monument as social through and through, a function obscured by undue focus on a few great artistic monuments of the past that people seek 'with Baedeker in hand', like the Venetian Colleoni and the Paduan Gattamelata. These 'energetic monuments' have nothing to do with the dullness of the equestrian statues still commissioned in Musil's day. These pale in comparison with advertisement, which knows very well how to meet its audience. At least, Musil suggests innocently, statues could clap their eyes open and shut, or carry slogans like 'Goethe's *Faust* is the best!' Thus they could avoid the 'oil on water effect', wherein our attention slides off them like water off a duck's back as we make our way through the city.[5] Why do we do this? It is not malice on our part, but the plain need to orient ourselves in public, free of the encumbrance and individual attention that political art demands of its subjects. 'The arm points forward imperiously, but no one thinks to obey it.'[6] No one fears the drawn sword of the hero, no one steps out of the way of his charging steed. 'By God! Monument figures make no step forward, and yet they're always making a *faux pas*.'[7] What Musil has put his finger on here is not the comic inadequacy of immortalized action. Of course a cavalry charge does not go on forever: what strikes him is that it does not even go on for a moment for the pedestrian with his hot dog (*Wurstbrot*). The social function of the monument, explicit in the general's barked command, does not touch its target. In a way, the story of this book is the story of Musil's monuments: a shift from seeing them as outdated authoritarian machines to harnessing their social potential – the involvement of the audience in a social bond intended to instil historical consciousness.

Today's monuments often enough have, and flaunt, an event character. They are 'temporary', 'precarious', small, they 'engage', 'act on' and 'with' their audience. Take for example the work of Swiss artist Thomas Hirschhorn. Hischhorn showed his *Bataille Monument* on the outskirts of Kassel during the eleventh documenta (documenta 11) in 2002. In order to see the monument, visitors had to take a detour to a neighbourhood known for a high proportion of immigrants, high unemployment, and desolate grey social housing (Figure 1). In fact, the titular monument itself was just one among eight elements of this expansive project: besides the sculpture, resembling a tree stump, a Georges Bataille Library invited visitors to browse books arranged by keywords like 'word', 'image', and 'sex'; a didactic display presented Bataille's life and work; various workshops were open to all comers; a kebab stand run by a Turkish couple served fast food; a television studio allowed locals as well as philosophers to broadcast on topics however loosely connected to Bataille; a free shuttle service brought visitors to the site, and locals to the main art venues downtown; a webcam and website expanded access to the site for viewers outside Kassel. The project, funded by documenta, was built and overseen by the young members of a local boxing club. Hirschhorn explained the work as a critique of the monument genre:

> The Bataille monument is a precarious, temporary art project in public space, which is erected and looked after by the youth and by inhabitants of a quarter. The Bataille Monument wants to pose questions and wants to open space and time for discussions and ideas through the site, its materials, and the duration of the exhibition. The Bataille Monument is a critique of the existing monument; the Bataille Monument comes from below, it does not want to intimidate anyone, it is not indestructible, it is not defined for eternity.[8]

Hirschhorn's negations reveal a post-war consensus on the monument: authoritatively installed 'from above', intimidating, permanent, oblivious to its site, and, one might add with Musil, socially dysfunctional or ineffective. Hirschhorn's monument, in contrast, was meant to turn visitors into participants. 'He does not want to work for an exclusive public. He wants to include and connect people. A noble thought (*ein herrlicher Gedanke*)', concluded a regional newspaper, not without a hint of irony.[9]

If the *Bataille Monument* itself consists in part in the selling of kebab, lending videos, and broadcasting amateurs, in short, in the social connections and press that the work generates, it follows that the monument is a temporally and physically distributed event. Following this idea, one could consider Hirschhorn's statement, the newspaper interview and the resulting article, and other such acts and objects, as themselves parts of the monument, since they partake in the creation and maintenance of its social goals. Indeed, such a way of reading the publicity around the monument can hardly be seen as against the grain, since the statements in question fit the requirements for a 'monument from below' that Hirschhorn himself articulated. These strategies are more familiar from ephemeral urban performance art than from monumental sculpture.[10] But they are not the end of the story. After the 'precarious', 'ephemeral' exhibition has ended, there remain individuals who remember having participated in or encountered the work, and documents and artefacts that recorded its presence. The public statements and press clips that seemed so 'action-like' a moment ago immortalize the project as

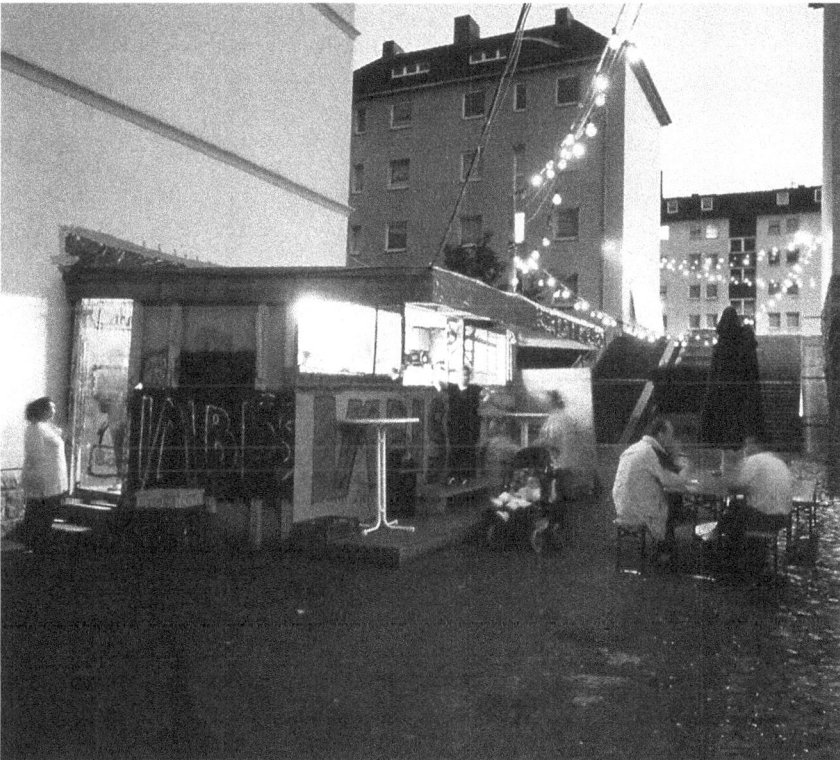

Thomas Hirschhorn, *Bataille Monument*, 2002 (snack bar), documenta 11, Kassel, 2002   **1**

they enter libraries and archives, and are cited by historians. This element of permanence, or at least extended duration, brings back with it some of the function and authority of the classic monument. At the very least, it tells us how to see monuments, Kassel, and Hirschhorn's intervention there, whose print discourse defines it, if not for eternity, for long enough.

Must the *Bataille Monument* be read as an ephemeral performance or as a lasting monument? These seemingly contradictory genres are in fact intertwined; work like Hirschhorn's is unthinkable apart from a historical process of rapprochement dating back to the 1960s at least. In the chapters that follow, I will show how the live art of that era, with its anarchic but carefully planned and documented street actions, provided the impetus for new ways of addressing the past in 1980s Europe and beyond. Performance, the supposed antipode to the monument in its temporality and embodiment, in fact held the key to its revival as 'democratic' community-builder. Under the force of performance, made durable and rhetorically powerful through photographic documents, the monument became a practice that involved audiences explicitly in actions with binding social force. This book thus rethinks both the supposed one-time encounter of performance art and the orthodoxy that commemorative art of the post-war period 'turned against itself' by divesting its 'countermonuments' of any marks of authority. Without authority, public art can claim no agency. How it can have this without being authoritarian is the tricky issue.

To begin answering the question, I draw attention to a remarkable and puzzling historical fact about post-war European art: young, oppositional performance artists of the 1960s and 1970s became the foremost monument designers of the 1980s and 1990s (and remain so, to some extent, in the early twenty-first century). A majority of the artists I discuss are women: it is women who posed some of the most unsettling questions about the historical depth of supposedly immediate experience in performance art, and it is the same women who most dramatically manifest the historical, commemorative direction of contemporary performance. This means a shift not simply in gender, but in focus: away from the implicitly male authority of the hero, whether architect or action painter, to the challenging analysis of historical consciousness and of the built environment. And yet, some of the most prominent architects of the new monuments are men. But their own background as performers, in the relevant cases, attuned these male artists to issues neglected in the sculpture, painting, and architecture of their time. The shift is one from 'making' history, experiencing it 'first hand', to reconstructing it, experiencing it at a remove: through the body, by thinking about it and past events, and in general by drawing connections between body, site, and time.

Performance is itself a form of public art. As such, it encounters social forces, and causes social reactions, that, in their visibility and documentation, acquire monumental authority. My larger claim is that performance artists, in working in public space, came not just to resemble monuments in their performances but to be interested in just those problems of political representation and its relation to the spectator that drove Musil's questions about monuments. They thus reoriented public art around an intersection of performance and the monument, of which Hirschhorn is only a recent manifestation. There are many varieties of this engagement, which in its paradigmatic form I call the *performative monument*. Their common denominator, audience participation, is an inheritance of performance art. Some are ephemeral objects in a literal sense – like the *Bataille Monument*, dismantled after documenta closed. This might suggest ephemerality as their practice, and main affinity to performance, but this suggestion is deceptive. For instance, the cars used for the shuttle service of the *Bataille Monument* were auctioned on eBay – signed by the artist, no less (Figure 2). Does that mean that a part of Hirschhorn's monument persists in some collector's home, or, plies the streets of Europe? I should say not: there is no medium-specific law of ephemerality of objects in play, endangering the 'precariousness' of Hirschhorn's temporary monument. What I see, rather, is the paradoxical situation that the temporal limitation of the monument has given it a retrospective interest issuing in such actions as the auction. In any case, an interest in a past event, not in a present artefact, motivated the sale and other extensions of the *Bataille Monument*. And that, however marginally, makes that summer's event in Kassel – not the tree stump, not the car – into a performative monument.

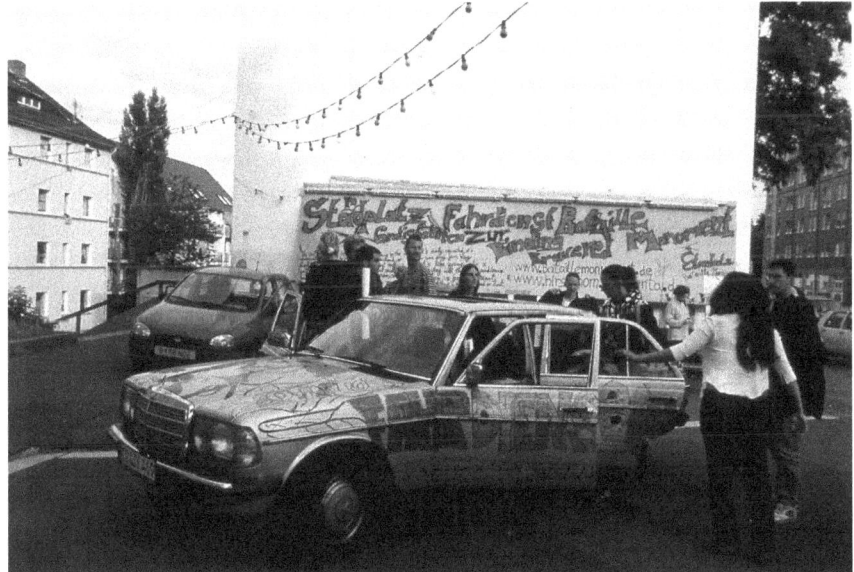

Thomas Hirschhorn, *Bataille Monument*, 2002 (car service), documenta 11, Kassel, 2002   **2**

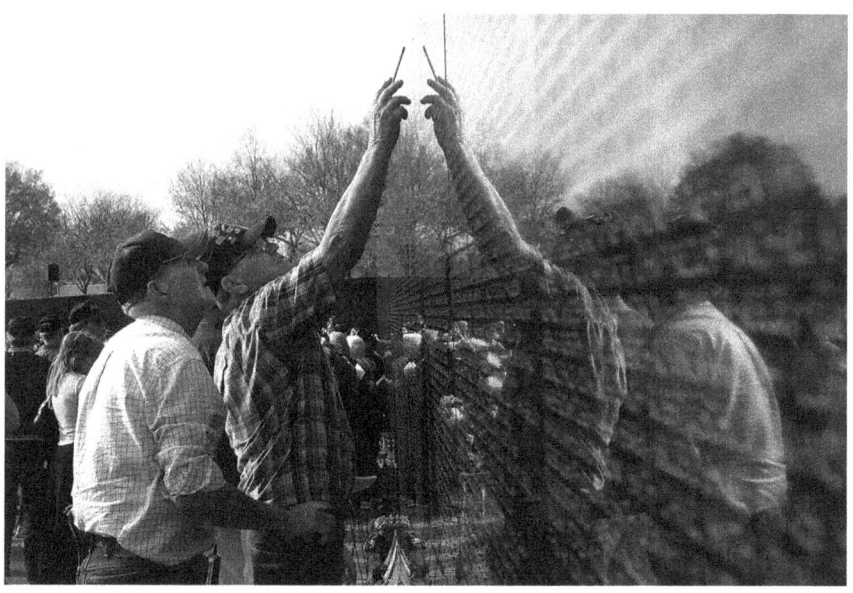

3   Maya Lin, *Vietnam Veterans Memorial*, Washington, D.C., 1982

What is crucial to the performative monument, then, cannot be imper-manence as such, but the temporal interaction with an audience that itself is no eternal public, but a succession of interacting subjects. Ephemerality of objects is one strategy among others in making concrete this temporality of the work. Could a monument consisting of two 75 meter-long granite walls function as a performative monument? It does. Visitors to Maya Lin's *Vietnam Veterans Memorial* in Washington trace the names engraved into the stone on pieces of paper to take home (Figure 3). Indeed, the volunteers organized by the National Park Service hand out pencil and tracing paper, cementing what was at first a spontaneous and personal (if foreseeable) mode of interaction.

The behaviour of visitors to Lin's memorial may not add up to a new practice as such – the Renaissance knew similar funerary rituals, and German architect and theorist Gottfried Semper declared the pomp of victory proces-sions the origin of monumental objects.[11] What is new in Lin's work is that interaction with the audience has become so much part of the work that most printed photographs of the monument show some sort of engaged visitor, touching the stone and being reflected in the polished granite; most are busy tracing, though of course one seldom sees photos of the Park Service volun-teers.[12] Yet the photographs invariably reproduce a person's action before the monument. In this sense the monument is also always a performance. In being photographed, the private ritual becomes a public act of commemoration for a wider public to see: it is part and parcel of the monument's 'success story'.

Historical and theoretical aims

The artists I discuss in this study developed in a period during which monuments were largely discredited as authoritarian. This has been the case for some time.

Musil's literary account is in a way matched by the efforts of the architectural avant-garde of the 1930s, from conservative modernist Peter Meyer to Congrès internationaux d'architecture moderne founder and technophile Sigfried Giedion. These critics initiated an international debate about the status of monumentality, hoping to produce an alternative to the 'pseudo-monumentality' of fascism and Stalinism, a new form of monumentality responsive to the needs of communities, not governments.[13] The debate went largely unheard within art circles. Architecture became important in artistic practice of the 1960s, however, both in the abstract discourse of minimalist spatial experience and as a marker of a vaguely threatening public sphere. The 'monumentality' of architecture stood for authority in general, and while avant-garde architects such as Superstudio in Italy and Robert Venturi in America redefined highway ramps and fast-food stands as the 'real' contemporary monument, artists started experimenting with historical and social aspects of public space, reconsidering their own involvement in the production and mediation of Öffentlichkeit (publicness).[14] Often, they used their own physical presence to trip the hidden wires of power that they saw in monumental architecture. The turning point is the early 1970s, when a counter-cultural rhetoric of revolutionary presence cooled into works experimenting with the collaboration between act and mediation. To trace a shift from confrontational performance to media performance in public space, and finally performative monuments, and link these to long-running debates on what public art is, while showing the political breadth of the monument, is the historical aim of this book.

Theoretically, my task is to understand the combination of political needs and aesthetic solutions proposed for them that comprise the performative monument. The historical bookends of this development are the Second World War and 1989, the much-repressed memory of the Holocaust in the decades after 1945 and the politics of the Cold War. Not all artworks I discuss deal explicitly with history, but all can be read in tension between the individual and the (mass-) political in Europe after 1945, where so much stress lay on memory and its suppression. These circumstances provide us with a necessary footing for understanding how the performative monument became a privileged mode of reckoning with the past. The ascendancy of the new monument coincides with the memory boom – and debate – of the 1990s. By taking into consideration the more recent problematization of audience participation in both architecture and performance, and by acknowledging the historical heterogeneity of public space and experience, I strive to go beyond a study of 'memorial art' and 'art in the public interest'. The subject of this book, in other words, is not given with either one art discourse – be it memorials, performance, or photography – or historical milieu. My approach is more conceptual, thinking through the notion of a temporally extended audience. Such a delayed audience can, but need not, comprise a community, just as its acts of commemoration need not be acts of memory. An act of commemoration does not relive the past but is itself a present fact of public conduct. The insistence on real presence and experience is thus radically ambiguous, pointing to the past while carrying its political and aesthetic effects into the future.

To show how this functions in practice, I have to identify several distinct possible relationships between performance and the monument, and explore them in historical contexts where their engagement with political questions can emerge. In Chapter 1, *Documents*, I first connect performance with history through the recent phenomenon of re-performance, reconstructing the different temporal layers of the audience of one act.

The second chapter, 'Audiences', turns to the Austrian avant-garde since the 1960s, whose contradictory, elaborate staging of visceral acts already play their part in the first chapter. The Viennese Actionists and VALIE EXPORT in particular stage a confrontation with patriarchal society through closely photographed events allegorizing a state of radical mediation. On this principle EXPORT went on to examine authoritarian patterns in state architecture by photographing a body in space. She later designed memorials that took up these strategies of bodily mediation: the realized *Transparent Cube* and her proposal for the Holocaust Monument Vienna (won by Rachel Whiteread) show how glass can mediate spectator bodies in a performance of history.

In the move from photography to architecture, the performance shifts from artist to spectator. To see how spectators can enter the complex set of circumstances in which they become collaborators in public art, in Chapter 3 I examine art in the former Yugoslavia. I start with early works by Marina Abramović wherein she politically marks the city through acts of erasure and projection. Abramović's confrontation with Belgrade in her early slide work *Freeing the Horizon* is comparable to EXPORT's work in Vienna, but brings to light contexts of censorship and indoctrination in which to view her work is construed as itself a political act. To explain this, I sharpen the theoretical tools of site, insisting on its temporal specificity. Abramović has since used her body as a political marker of nationhood and region to be read in a global context, undertaking grandiose theatrical productions and memorials. These works, of which I discuss recent examples in Salzburg and Basel, paradoxically invite spectators to reflect on their relative insignificance and inability to participate in the making of history.

The mobilization of spectators as performers leads me to the means by which artists and theorists in Germany dealt with their national past, and the contested notion of nation in general, trying to arrive at a democratic model of 'citizens' rather than national subjects. Chapter 4 begins with the Venice Biennale of 1976, remarkable for contributions by Joseph Beuys, Jochen Gerz, and Reiner Ruthenbeck that circle around the monument as metaphor for national identity. Gerz's 1986 *Monument against Fascism*, a column that visitors signed as a protest against fascism and that was lowered into the ground when enough signatures had accumulated, is key to this development. Against the orthodox view of this work as blandly permitting a stand for or against fascism, I show how Gerz, who came out of performance, used the force of monumental speech-acts developed in Venice to arrive at a public art that aims at contractually binding its spectators as agents.

The subject matter of the book is thus geographically and temporally distributed, addressing artists and spectators on both sides of the Second World War and the Cold War, in geographically and culturally adjacent stretches of Central Europe. Given this focus, a few words are required on the method and terminology of my study. I have discussed 'performance' and 'monument', and will further historicize these terms, but it is worth stating right away that I do not use 'performative' simply as the adjective of performance. Performance art is sometimes but not always performative, as, I claim, are monuments. What these works have in common that is of interest to me is their performative *force*, the fact that through conventional gestures they effect changes in social reality.[15] The model I employ to extract these social implications is speech-act theory, itself a philosophical product of the period under study. This will involve a particular modification of speech-acts or 'performatives', as defined by the English philosopher J.L. Austin in lectures of the mid-1950s, to works of art, in particular though not exclusively photographs. Though my reading of Austin is informed by later criticisms, notably Jacques Derrida's claim that the frame of communication can never be exactly determined, and thus, that effects are unpredictable, I think that Austin's texts anticipate most objections. A careful reading of his texts shows an awareness of the instabilities of communication, instabilities that are even more acute in artistic contexts (Austin himself tended to exclude 'art' speech from his preliminary analysis). It is revealing that Austin's theory was adapted by the German post-war philosopher Jürgen Habermas, who has made the performative central to his reconstruction of democratic political theory and, less successfully, commemoration.

The speech-act model, which I will describe in detail later, is concerned with acts of representation that bring about what they represent. Analogously, I will show how the contemporary monument does not 'tell' political facts, but engages audiences in forming new ones. Herein lies their political appeal, but also their danger. Can political art deal with the past, when its results are not representations of the past but new historical facts? Here we must rethink art's function, which is not that of bearer of information, however theoretical or abstract. Performative monuments work to establish a political relation to a history that the performer has not personally experienced. The attitude to the past of the spectator of a performative monument is conventionalized and made public, and thus becomes an object of public inquiry. Is the new relation more politically responsible than traditional spectatorship? Is performative public art in a sense politically compulsory or manipulative? These questions can only be assessed – but not homogeneously answered – in specific cases.

The aesthetic and political practice that issues in performative monuments takes as its starting point the principle that symbolic acts have social consequences. Acting on this principle binds together bodily presence, documentation, and historical discourse in intimate and sometimes uncomfortable ways. It is appropriate that the flowering of the new performative monuments corresponds to the renewed call, during the last years of the Cold War and beyond, for political discussion of the relationship of the individual to the state. In the decades that form the main focus of the book, there is a sea change from a general distrust of the very idea of monument in the 1960s, to a conscious involvement of the person and its architectural surrogates in remembrance since the 1980s, just as personal memory and oral history become officially accepted, seemingly democratic models of commemoration. Performance practice has in many ways followed suit: from violent actions to the staging of objects and bodies in installations, from the messy presence of the artist to delegate performance, from performance for the camera to a complex mixing of mediated layers of reality, performance has from its inception been rethinking the relationship between artistic production and its environment, be it the built environment or the social life of audiences. The shift from seeing the monument as authoritarian colossus to harnessing its concrete social force is the story of this book.

Notes

1 'Es gibt nichts auf der Welt, was so unsichtbar wäre wie Denkmäler.' Robert Musil, 'Denkmale', *Nachlass zu Lebzeiten*, in *Gesammelte Werke*, ed. Adolf Frisé, vol. 7 (Reinbek bei Hamburg: Rowohlt, 1978), 506–9. The German title, which Musil explains, is more literally *Legacy in My Lifetime*. The paraphrase above, which better conveys the joke, is from the English translation by Peter Wortsman, *Robert Musil, Posthumous Papers of a Living Author* (Hygiene, Colorado: Eridanos Press, 1987).

2 Musil, 'Denkmale', 604–10. The lecture contains details that Musil left out in 1936, notably enthusiastic praise for the *Siegesallee*, a marble gallery of Prussian rulers installed by Kaiser Wilhelm II in Berlin Tiergarten (605).

3 Ibid., 507.

4 Ibid. In German 'monument' is applied to works of art regardless of function: thus a series of postcards of Musil's era, recording Catholic cloisters and their

contents, bears the Latin title *Monumenta Photographica Austriae*, and, in German, *Geschichts- und Kunstdenkmale Österreichs*.

5 Musil, 508.

6 Ibid.

7 Ibid.

8 Thomas Hirschhorn, '"Bataille Monument" für documenta 11 Kassel 2002', statement dated February 2002, reprinted in Thomas Hirschhorn, *Bataille Maschine* (Berlin: Merve, 2003), 42. See also the catalogue on the occasion of Hirschhorn's contribution to the 2011 Venice Biennale: Thomas Hirschhorn (ed.), *Establishing a Critical Corpus*. With essays by Claire Bishop, Hal Foster, Sebastian Egenhofer, and others (Zurich: Ringier Kunstverlag, 2011).

9 Martin Scholz, 'Mehr ist mehr; weniger ist weniger. Martin Scholz über das "Bataille Monument"', *Hessische/Niedersächsische Allgemeine* (15 June 2002).

10 Notice of this is impaired by Hirschhorn's occasional claims that he is a formalist sculptor. Benjamin Buchloh, for instance, builds a historical arc from Hirschhorn to the classical avant-garde, Fluxus, and post-minimalist sculpture in 'Cargo and Cult. The Displays of Thomas Hirschhorn', *Artforum*, 40:3 (November 2001), 109–15. Against this, it may be noted that the 'precariousness' of Hirschhorn's work has more to do with the actual relationships he enters into in assembling his monuments than with visual commitments: see Sebastian Egenhofer, *Produktionsästhetik* (Zurich: Diaphanes, 2010), 133. Hirschhorn himself cites Joseph Beuys as his precursor.

11 Triumphal arches, Semper argued, needed to be executed in more solid material than processional architecture only, so that memory of the victory could be passed on to later generations. Semper's role in the debate on monumentality in architecture is well explained in Ákos Moravánszky, 'Monumentalität', in *Architekturtheorie im 20. Jahrhundert. Eine kritische Anthologie*, edited by Ákos Moravánszky and Katalin M. Gyöngy (Vienna/New York: Springer, 2002), 366.

12 See Geraldine A. Johnson, 'Sculpture, Photography, and the Politics of Public Space. Serra's *Tilted Arc* and Lin's *Vietnam Veterans Memorial*', in Geraldine A. Johnson (ed.), *Sculpture and Photography. Envisioning the Third Dimension* (Cambridge: Cambridge University Press, 1998), 213ff. Kirk Savage calls Lin's project 'the nation's first "therapeutic" memorial' in 'The Conscience of the Nation', *Monument Wars. Washington D.C., the National Mall, and the Transformation of the Memorial Landscape* (Berkeley/London/Los Angeles: University of California Press, 2009), chapter 6.

13 See Sigfried Giedion, José Luis Sert, and Fernand Léger's 1943 'Nine Points on Monumentality'. Of this manifesto, Giedion recalls that all had been asked by the American Abstract Artists Group (AAA) to write on the topic, and decided to pool their resources. Sigfried Giedion, *Architecture, You and Me. A Diary of a Development* (Cambridge, Mass.: Harvard University Press, 1958), 22. See also Peter Meyer, 'Überlegungen zum Problem der Monumentalität' [1938] in Moravánszky, *Architekturtheorie*, 427–33. The debate in architectural circles persisted for a decade: in 1948, the *Architectural Review* held a symposium under the title 'In Search of a New Monumentality', published in *Architectural Review*, 104 (1948), 117–28.

Central to this debate is architectural and social critic Lewis Mumford, from 'Death of the Monument' [1937] in Mumford, *The Culture of Cities* (New York: Praeger, 1938), 433–40, to 'Monumentalism, Symbolism and Style', *Architectural Review*, 105 (1949), 173–80. On the debate and its effect on planning, in particular public gardens, see Andrew M. Shanken, 'Planning Memory: Living Memorials in the United States during World War II', *Art Bulletin*, 84:1 (March 2002), 130–47.

14 On monumentality in postmodern architecture, see Martino Stierli, *Las Vegas im Rückspiegel. Die Stadt in Theorie, Fotografie und Film*, (Zürich: gta Verlag, 2010), and Annette Urban and Carsten Ruhl (eds), *Mythos Monument. Urbane Strategien in Architektur und Kunst seit 1945* (Bielefeld: Transcript, 2011).

15 This model is distinct from theatricality, which concerns only experience. I thus omit the protracted debate over minimalism, on which see Michael Fried, 'Art and Objecthood', *Artforum* 5 (June 1967), 12–23, reprinted in Fried, *Art and Objecthood: Essays and Reviews* (Chicago: University of Chicago Press, 1998), 148–72; Yves-Alain Bois, 'A Picturesque Stroll around Clara-Clara', *October*, 29 (Summer, 1984), 32–62, and Anna Chave, 'Minimalism and the Rhetoric of Power', *Arts Magazine*, 645 (January 1990), 44–63.

'Presence', in its dual significance of immediacy and of being in a particular place at a particular time, has become the major theme in recent performance practice and theory. The intense interest in the status of the documentation of performances – be they photographs or films – set in motion a search for new means of immediacy, but also a scepticism concerning the existence of authentic presence.[1] In the last decade, many artists have rethought and questioned the one-time experience of performance art by re-enacting their own work or that of colleagues. Mike Kelley and Paul McCarthy's libidinal tour of the 1970s in their *Fresh Acconci Portfolio* of 1995 (in which they hired aspiring Hollywood actors to redo well-known Acconci works), Dan Graham's reflection on his own 1975 videotaped performance *Performer/Audience/ Mirror* under the title *Video/Architecture/Performance* in 1995, and Yoko Ono's revival of her most famous performance, the mid-1960s *Cut Piece*, in a small theatre in Paris in 2003 as a protest against the war in Iraq, are examples of this trend.[2] These mature artists posed new and forceful questions concerning the status of performance, its historicization and the role of the document, decades after they themselves began their artistic production, bringing to the surface questions that were already problematic but had been concealed by more pressing political issues in the 1960s and 1970s.[3]

Entering performance art through the looking-glass of re-performance requires a form of historical writing beginning in the present and working its way back. Through this, I will ask new questions about the concern with history in performance art. For beyond the self-reflexive concern with the history *of* performance, there is a growing interest in the historical dimension of all performance, in the ability of performance to confront political history in actions at once symbolic and concretely literal. Re-performance can help us see how history plays a role in performance art as such, for it strikes at the foundation of performance by challenging what used to be considered the core value of the medium: its dependence on the 'authentic' encounter between artist and audience. If we want to do justice to performance art as it is being re-performed, we need to reconsider this foundation as an art form the life of which does not simply 'end' with its taking place, but one which allows us belatedly to refer back to this event, to think and argue about it – in short to re-imagine it by exercising one's memory.[4]

The insistence on the ephemeral value of performance art can be found at the very beginning of its historiography in the late 1970s, when scholars like RoseLee Goldberg began to publish, tracing performance back to the endeavours of that segment of the 1920s European avant-garde concerned with theatre, particularly Futurism, which she presented as a 'manifesto' of performance long preceding its practice. The plays of the Austrian artist Oskar Kokoschka, the Dadaists at the Cabaret Voltaire, and Bauhaus theatre feature prominently in a trajectory that in her view is taken up in the United States by Black Mountain College, run by by European émigrés since the late 1930s.[5] Goldberg criticized conventional art history for ignoring ephemeral practices of the avant-garde:

> Despite the fact that most of what is written today about the work of the Futurists, Constructivists, Dadaists, or Surrealists continues to concentrate on the art objects produced by each period, it was more often than not the case that these movements found their roots and attempted to resolve problematic issues in performance.[6]

This focus on the immateriality of performance art, and its basis in work of the early twentieth century was groundbreaking, but in advocating performance as purely a 'live art', Goldberg smoothed over the fact that she herself had to reach her conclusions with the help of historical sources: texts and grainy images and recordings.

Performance scholars working since the mid-1990s have painted a rather different picture. They focus on the document more self-consciously to trace performance art back to object-based art practices, such as action painting, and the polemics of a post-Second World War art world discursively severed from the classic European avant-garde. Great prominence is given to art critic Harold Rosenberg's 1952 interpretation of the New York School painting as 'arena in which to act', and Allan Kaprow's reading of Jackson Pollock as precursor of happenings in the 1958 manifesto 'The Legacy of Jackson Pollock': both readings nurtured by Hans Namuth's famous photographs of Pollock working in his studio.[7] As different as the conclusions stemming from this trajectory might be – ranging from psychoanalytical discussions of desire to critiques of capitalist consumption of images – they usually include a strong reading of performance *documents* as essential components in the development of performance *art*, consciously reflecting on the demands of the art world that the action be productive, i.e. leave a trace in the form of an object that can be sold and exhibited, or at the least interpreted and productively misunderstood by the next generation of practitioners and scholars.

Apart from any generational divergence, the crucial distinction between these positions is their assertion of divergent ideological bases for performance: the live event, developing out of theatre and discounting the document, versus the document-laden performance, emerging out of a postmodern *reading* of painting itself as an audience-directed performance. This second position does not necessarily disavow the force of live performance, but emphasizes that the document features prominently both as precursor to and in the after-life of the event, constituting its event character in the manner of a witness or piece of evidence.[8]

Can the two views find common ground? On one hand, performance scholar Peggy Phelan insists on the one-time encounter of performance from a deconstructivist standpoint: because, according to her, signs are repeat-able by their nature, performance, which is unrepeatable, does not consist of signs.[9] And in the German-speaking context, media philosopher Dieter Mersch, starting from the Derridean thesis that signs are both repeatable and different each time they occur, sees in their repeated occurrence an unpredict-able, contextually unique 'event' [*Ereignis*], whose strong claims of presence typify aesthetic experience, whether in language, art, or science.[10] From these cases it appears that the disagreement, far from being unbridgeable, is a matter of emphasis: events have both differences and similarities to previous events (as would be reasonable to expect in our case of re-enactments). The decision to regard them, then, as essentially the same performance or artwork, must rest on a way of approaching the evidence: in the case of performance art, primarily photographic documentation.

Documentation has been the 'faithful' companion of performance since the grainy image of Hugo Ball reciting his poetry in Marcel Janko's cardboard costume (an image hanging near the stage of the Cabaret Voltaire in Zurich to this day), and it has turned up in gallery exhibitions as well as on the art market since the 1960s.[11] But it was not until the self-conscious acts of *reading of the document* by the current generation of American performance scholars, comfortable with the poststructuralist suspicion of all forms of 'authenticity', that performance art was systematically related to or even reduced to its mediation. This interest in the document brought with it new questions: in which ways do these documents play their part in historicization? This book proposes that their main function, indispensable to performance as tradition-ally envisioned as an 'ephemeral' practice with critical ambitions, is to extend the performance in time for an ever-widening audience. But before this argument and the subsequent question of how this might work can be voiced, the status of documentation *within* performance must be established. Are documents incidental to the performance, necessary correlates in practice, or are they even somehow theoretically constitutive of it? If these stronger claims about performance documents are true, do they imply that the possibility of repetition is part of the very idea of performance art, once it is documented or mediated in any form – or should we remain content with thinking of documents as by-products, however inevitable?

Both approaches, that which sees performance as essentially an event that happens to be documented, and that which sees performance as essentially a documented event that happened to take place, show strain under the pressure of re-performance. For, whether one takes re-performance as a return to liveness or an elaborate mediation – it is also a new performance that is in a way *about* an older performance. How can scholars committed to one-time encounters account for this? And why should it interest scholars who insist that the mediation is all that matters? The answer to both questions is the same: re-performance concerns both presence *and* history. And it is becoming obvious that artists of the 1960s were aware of the force of the document, even as they insisted on direct encounter between performer and audience: a paradox only if presence and mediation are considered as mutually exclusive. This dualism is untenable, and it may be that, with its loss, the individual poles of the dualism will also lose their appeal. I shall argue that the most interesting questions being posed by contemporary re-performance are issues of history and memory.[12] Recent scholarship, particularly Rebecca Schneider's *Performance Remains* (2011) has begun addressing the '*theatricality* of time' in re-performance and re-enactment, troubling received views of history through the claim that 'live art and media of mechanical and technological reproduction, such as photography, cross-identify, and, more radically, cross-constitute, and 'improvise' each other'.[13] I welcome this work, but do not see the historicity of performance as a subjective invention of the past, for reasons that will emerge directly. Let me state my issue concretely: how is an art form ostensibly resting on a 1960s emphasis on embodied 'experience' and participation in the socio-political landscape of the United States, Europe, and Japan reconfigured for a later global audience in terms of historiography? Do audience and history need each other, and what role does the document play in this relationship? And, what happens to the 'site' of performance with the migration of the document? 'The document' as concept and as concrete cases of photographic, film, and other media, will surface prominently in the performances I am discussing. I hope to show how it holds bodily presence in suspension between an event in the past and a monument constituted in the act of remembering.

Reappearances

In my first case study, a 1969 'action' by Austrian artist VALIE EXPORT that was re-performed by Marina Abramović in 2005, I shall neither advocate presence nor attempt to efface all differences between mediated and unmediated modes of interaction.[14] Rather, I want to show how an ephemeral art practice creates more than one performance situation. We need to differentiate discrete levels of mediation, without simply favouring one of them a priori. Even the 'zero-level' of the live event is mediated through seeing, hearing, the air that circulates around the performer, the lighting, the architectural space, and the audience, to say nothing of the art institution that is often its setting, and the culture in which certain bodily movements are interpreted as actions of one kind or another. Modern media like photography, radio, television, and closed-circuit video carry traces of the action into an indefinite future, introducing performance to later audiences as well as making possible (and at times refuting) more elusive social means of mediation such as gossip, hearsay, legends, and interviews, and explicitly historical media such as articles, exhibition catalogues, lectures, and finally re-performances. What connects all of these is a flexible concept of memory and forgetting, distributed more or less socially or privately in accordance with the degree of direct involvement: one's memory of an event seen is different from one's memory of an event heard about in an undergraduate lecture course. For this reason, considerations of medium specificity do not play a prominent role in my discussion – though photographic practice is important – because the same medium functions differently in different contexts of use, and because newly minted labels for the practices I discuss, such as 'photo-performance' and 'performance for the camera', tend to prematurely encapsulate the difficulty of explaining an action that unfolds over time and between media.[15] Instead of medium I draw upon another set of specificities, namely reception, history, and memory. These terms are neither interchangeable nor strictly analogous, although they fuse at times to play their part in representation. Because of its centrality to the historical reception of live art, the document resurfaces in all of these settings – and with it the question of whether it is self-contained or discursive in its effects, and to what extent it can be said to have an audience of its own.

First, let me address the reconstruction of presence where it is most emphatically asserted: in a catalogue text on Marina Abramović, RoseLee Goldberg plausibly finds 'presence' to be the artist's 'overriding obsession'.[16] Abramović has been known since the 1970s for challenging and even endangering her body in uncomfortable and often daring performances, some of which depended on direct audience participation – for example *Rhythm 0*, 1974, in which the spectators were asked to use tools, among them knives, a loaded gun, and scissors, on the artist, in a process with no fixed endpoint, which ended in disarray. The tension between objectification, institutional placement of performance, and an insistence on personal experience came to the forefront in late 2005. Abramović re-staged six performances of the 1960s and 1970s, five of which were not initially her own, together with a newly conceived performance, under the heading *Seven Easy Pieces*. Among the works chosen were Joseph Beuys's 1965 *How to Explain Pictures to a Dead Hare*, Bruce Nauman's 1974 *Body Pressure*, and EXPORT's *Genital Panic*.[17] If one reads the re-enactments along the lines suggested by Goldberg, Abramović replaced the body of the original performer with her own, painstakingly redoing the action decades after the fact in order to overcome (for herself and the audience) the most obvious limitation of performance art, namely the unavailability of the 'original' experience to those not present at the earlier event. But things are not so simple. An investigation of the relocations of *Genital Panic*, from its first occurrence in 1969 to Abramović's re-enactment in the rotunda of the Guggenheim Museum in 2005, will allow us to interrogate the assumption that the live act provides unmediated access to the *performance* in question through the artist's body.

It is said that, in 1969, VALIE EXPORT went into a cinema in Munich wearing jeans with a triangular cut-out aimed to reveal the pubic area. Once inside the auditorium, she walked slowly through the rows, with her 'cunt and [the audience's] nose on the same level'.[18] The intention of this 'action', the word EXPORT herself favours, was to confront the voyeuristic male movie-goer with a 'real' female body, instead of the mediated one that could be consumed clandestinely – thus anticipating and inverting Laura Mulvey's famous 1975 feminist manifesto 'Visual Pleasure and Narrative Cinema' by several years.[19]

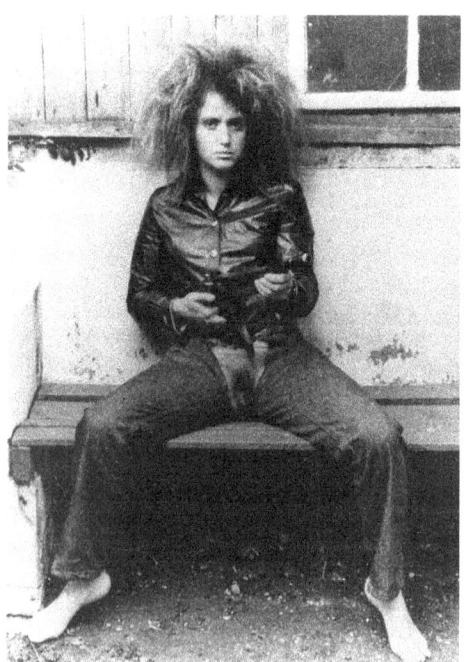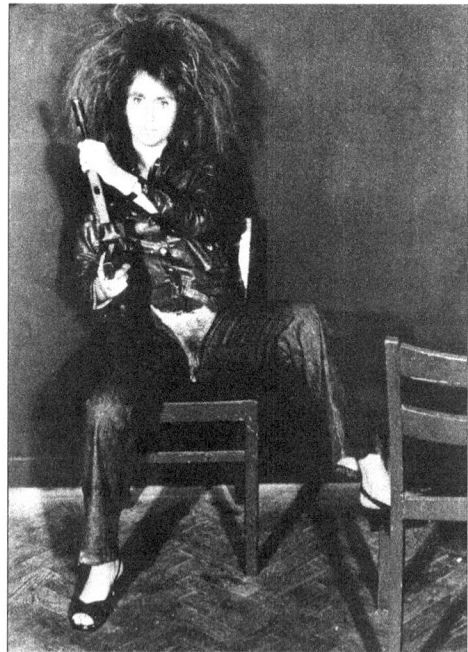

4 & 5   VALIE EXPORT, *Action Pants: Genital Panic*, 1969

'People in the back of the cinema got up and fled the situation, because they were afraid I would come up to them as well,' EXPORT stated in a recent interview, thereby confirming that the titular 'panic' had in fact taken place and stressing the presence of the real woman as pivotal to the audience reaction.[20]

Let us examine the images associated with EXPORT's action more closely. Two of them, taken in 1969, became the stand-ins for *Genital Panic* in surveys of post-war art throughout Europe and the United States. One photograph shows EXPORT, with teased hair, seated on a bench outside what looks like a house in rural Austria, with bare feet, her exposed crotch in the centre of the composition, pointing a machine gun in the general direction of the camera (Figure 4). In a second photograph we see EXPORT inside what must be the same building, sitting with one leg propped aggressively on the wooden cross-beam of a second, apparently empty, chair (the cropping reveals only the left edge of the seat), thus emphasizing her pubic area and suggesting a confrontation, the gun's barrel directed at the ceiling (Figure 5). A third image, also shot outside, with EXPORT standing legs apart before the bench, has been widely published in recent years.[21]

None of the photographs is a document taken during the performance EXPORT described. None tries to restage the ostensible setting of the performance, though the indoor setting has at times been mistaken for the theatre. On the contrary, all three focus on the carefully posed artist, exchanging the cinema in the metropolis for a suburban milieu – in fact the studio of the photographer Peter Hassmann, on the northern outskirts of Vienna. The compositions resemble publicity posters, while the grainy texture links them to the mid-twentieth-century practice of documentary photography.[22] They seem to be a distillation of the *idea* of the action, rather like film stills. Given the iconic nature of the images, it is no surprise that Hassmann had become locally known at the time for political posters commissioned by the Austrian Socialist Party.

Because the photographs are detached from the reputed location of the original performance, they raise a question of how we know what took place in Munich. This particular case reflects larger issues attendant on any study of live art: how does one link textual or verbal descriptions of the event, which often circulate in conflicting versions, with the few documentary images or films that remain? What does the *picture* have to do with the *narrative* of the event? Accounts of *Genital Panic* around the time of its reputed execution are sparse; the first seems to be the 1970 publication *Bildkompendium Wiener Aktionismus and Film*, which EXPORT collaborated on with fellow artist Peter Weibel, and from which I quoted the initial description. This is surprising, given the extensive, often outraged, press coverage EXPORT enjoyed for some contemporaneous actions, such as *Touch Cinema* in 1968. EXPORT's own extant accounts come a few years later. Take the following interview from 1979, in which EXPORT tells the story in a way that closely follows the photographs in some respects (supplying a gun) while elaborating on other aspects of the 1969 performance (the movie theatre):

> Genital Panic was performed in a Munich theatre that showed pornographic films. I was dressed in a sweater and pants with the crotch completely cut away. I carried a machine gun. Between films I told the audience that they had come to this particular theatre to see sexual films. Now, actual genitalia was available, and they could do anything they wanted to it.[23]

Twenty years later, EXPORT renounced this combative stance, stating: 'I never went in a cinema in which pornographic movies are shown, and NEVER with a gun in my hand', a position she confirmed in an interview with me in February 2007, contradicting her own 1979 description of the event and expressing bafflement about who had first described the theatre as 'pornographic'.[24] Almost parenthetically, EXPORT remarked that if she had actually entered the theatre with a gun, '[t]he security would have shot me'.[25] The weapon in the photograph – confirmed by Hassmann to have been an actual firearm – seems unlikely indeed to have been wielded in public, given the politically tense German climate of the time, with the terrorist Red Army Faction on the eve of its first attacks, and above all in conservative Bavaria.[26]

What are we to make of these revisions, besides the commonplace that historians should not trust the oral accounts of artists or interviewers, or, more generally, the memory of eyewitnesses? Most conspicuous in this case is the correlation of EXPORT's 1979 interview with the photographs featuring the machine gun, a prop that appeared also in Abramović's re-performance in 2005. If EXPORT could not have used the gun in public, then is Abramović's gun an '*Ergänzung*' (addition, supplement) to the 1969 work, as EXPORT explained it to me when asked about Abramović's re-enactment?[27]

Truth and performative utterances

I shall return to the significance of the machine gun in a moment. First, however, I want to propose that EXPORT's 1979 account of her work is not simply a true or false statement, though of course it is one as well, and one can imagine circumstances in which this aspect would dominate. But in the context of an interview carried out in the journal *High Performance*, where the border between performance and its historiography was hardly a pressing issue, indeed one which 'operating on an open submission policy ... published any artist who could provide black-and-white photographic documentation, dates, and a description of the performance', other goals of speech predominated.[28] EXPORT's statement is an accomplice in the performative establishment of its object, or, to put the manner in historical terms, the interest-laden verification of a past event.[29] The pornographic cinema, the weapon, in short, EXPORT's role as the feminist warrior, is a performance in its own right, detached from the bodily presence of any performer and audience in the 'here and now' (and ten years later, the 'there and then') of the Munich theatre. The performance, insofar as there is one, took place in the interview.

The interview becomes performative in re-instantiating the earlier, perhaps non-existent, performance. The English verb 'to perform', derived from French *perfourir*, is richly polysemic, but its two main uses are roughly 'to accomplish a task' (as in finance, or the technophilic usage 'high performance', on which the title of the magazine plays), and 'to carry out a pre-scripted action in public', e.g. in a theatrical or musical context. Note that the two senses diverge: the first implies effective results in the real world (stocks or auto engines that perform well), while the second, neutral as to success or failure, implies an artistic event, bracketed by being a performance from the world around it. The adjective 'performative', on the other hand, quite self-consciously implies both. When philosopher J.L. Austin introduced it as a piece of new philosophical jargon in the 1950s, he wished to draw attention to a specific relationship between speech and action, that is, simply put, to speech *as* action. To this end he pointed to a performative dimension in all practical language (acts like promising, convincing, and threatening, but also wordless gestures, signs, etc.), which *always* shares the stage with a descriptive function which tells us how the world is.[30] Having pointed this out, Austin tried to identify the core of the phenomenon, those utterances that represent something and, in doing so, bring it about ('I apologize', but not 'I'll kill you!').[31] His most famous examples are wedding vows ('I hereby take you to be my husband') and the baptism of a ship, that is, utterances that constitute a change in the social situation due to conventions, often tied to certain rituals (the rings, the champagne bottle), and not comprehensible outside this context (you must be familiar with the idea of baptizing a boat). It is no coincidence that Austin, who had decoded German messages for the British government during the war and thus had first-hand experience of the force of words, should become interested in the circumstances in which words constitute action in the real world. In a post-war context, these concerns with actionable words may be seen as a philosophical counterpart for social psychological studies of coercion, such as Stanley Milgram's obedience experiments at Yale University in 1961.[32] Milgram's interest in the question whether participants could be coerced to hurt or even kill others simply by the verbal force of an authority was provoked by the Eichmann trials, as he expressly wrote.[33]

What really can words do, and how? As mentioned, Austin initially distinguished performatives from factual ('constative' or descriptive) statements that have the property of being true or false. But he found that he needed to complicate this distinction and introduced locutionary (act *of* saying something), perlocutionary (act achieved *through* saying something), and illocutionary (act set in motion by saying something, under which performatives fall) acts in order to account for the fact that every form of speech contains both normative and descriptive elements, so that the transition is a gradual one.[34] For my reading, it is important that constitutive and descriptive statements need not be exclusive of one another, as they seldom are in an artistic context that wants to be both political and imaginative, or which involves an interaction between performer and audience.

In a legal sense EXPORT's statements about *Genital Panic* appear dubious, being unverified by witnesses and contradicted by her own later accounts. Yet she is not simply narrating the performance truthfully or untruthfully, nor are we dealing with a 'faked' work of art – for if we were, where precisely is the fake? And where the original? The traditional definition of performance as ephemeral action already excluded the photos that EXPORT produced (which never made any bones about their separation from the action) from counting as the performance itself. If, on the traditional view plus EXPORT's interview, the work consisted of an encounter in a Munich theatre in 1969, which none of the readers has experienced, the performance as thus imagined 'took place' inside readers' heads, whether it really took place in Munich or not. And so EXPORT's statements in the 1979 interview must be considered what Austin calls a 'happy performative', namely a representation that, because all necessary circumstances are met, is taken for the very fact that it represents.[35]

A requirement that Austin sets for every 'happy performative', that is, simply, a performative that *works*, is 'appropriate circumstances', or a 'situation' that makes possible the concrete consequences of the performative, combining with the actual physical actions to form the 'total speech act'.[36] These may be the conventions and formulas for performing a certain ritual ('I do'), corresponding artefacts, the correct and complete execution of a procedure, and even the 'feelings' of the participants that a ritual has succeeded. These requirements, as even this brief summary indicates, are flexible, in part subjective, and vary from case to case. In our case, the situation encompasses the public nature of the magazine in which the interview was printed and the willingness of members of the art world to historicize the event in the reassuring form of the pictures and the artist's retrospective account, and also, through experience of these pictures or words or both, to forget that they were not present at the 'original' event.

Given the missing action in Munich, the photographs, and the various interviews concerning *Genital Panic*, what should we say constitutes the performance? A pure 'event' interpretation might conclude sadly that there is nothing to investigate; a pure 'document' interpretation would be forced to treat the photos as ... well, as nothing but photos. But the speech-act model allows us to give a more satisfying account of the proceedings. First off the bat, can an image, as opposed to a piece of language, be performative? Intuitively, there seems to be no reason to exclude the force of *making it so* in cases exactly parallel to familiar speech-acts, such as Jan van Eyck's *Arnolfini Wedding*: as Erwin Panofsky and Linda Seidel divergently interpret it, the painting serves as a binding document either for Giovanni Arnolfini or his spouse, Giovanna Cenami.[37] But how *could* it do so, given that a painting can just as easily represent a fantastic state of affairs? Well, the context of the commission and the understanding of spectators that a real event is being commemorated would determine this: if, as Lorne Campbell has more recently argued, the wedding took place *thirteen years* after the portrait was taken, its act character disappears, and we are dealing with a double portrait and nothing more.[38] Or if, as another contemporary historian has it, the spouses are *another* Giovanni Arnolfini, Giovanni di Nicolao Arnolfini, a cousin of the first, and his wife, who died in 1433, the work becomes a memorial portrait.[39] Act character in a picture, then, as in a piece of language, depends on the total speech-act, on things outside the picture or the utterance: but it would not have that act character at all if the picture or language did not have a performative component, which by connecting with its context in a meaningful way comes to constitute and not just represent a historical event. The performative dimension of some images, then, points to a feature they share with speech-acts: in marking and making an occurrence, they are historical through and through.[40]

Returning to photography, I want to note that such features of van Eyck's oil painting that, within his total speech-act, were particularly suited to the impression of a documented event (the legible signature, the likenesses, the feeling of real space) are intrinsic to our social interaction with photographs, whether in colour or black and white. The total speech-act in the case of EXPORT's *Genital Panic* amounts to an assertion that the titular panic took place. Its context ranges over the seemingly embodied act in 1969 that the photographs at least allude to, the 1970 *Bildkompendium* with its concise description in the context of Actionism, the 1979 interview, and later interviews like my own, Abramović's re-enactment, and beyond. In this sense, the 1979 interview, in its mediated condition, as it was received at the time or as we read it today (for example, through my citation of it here), draws its authority from, but also itself *enacts* the belief in, the bodily presence of the artist, which is retrospectively projected back into the perhaps imaginary event. The interview, along with other articulations of the work, thus creates a new form of audience to which EXPORT's body is imaginatively present, a *reading audience*.[41] Readers in 1979 could thus connect the event to the photographs, affirming or even producing a new historical version of the performance ten years after it was said to have been done: an audacious and aggressive act in public.

Is it appropriate to apply Austin's theory, which is concerned with concrete actions in everyday life, to the context of artistic practice? Over the two decades since the 1990s, the notion of the performative has been extended to relate cultural practice to linguistic usage, and specifically in the realm of theatre and performance scholarship. In particular, Judith Butler's extension of Austin's concept has dominated the reception of speech-act theory in cultural and visual studies. Butler deserves this prominence in particular for arguing that many phenomena of a seemingly private or introspective nature, above all, sexual identity, are linked with explicit social acts that are symbolic in character. This insight, which Butler took from Erving Goffman rather than Austin, has suggested a general 'performativity' driving the construction of subjects.[42] This sense that everything we do is performative, together with the etymological closeness of the adjective to the noun 'performance', might be responsible for the recent indiscriminate application of the term 'performative' to all kinds of performance, usually without much discussion of the difference of the two concepts. Art historian Dorothea von Hantelmann has attacked the merging of 'performativity' and 'performance art', which she considers a profound misunderstanding of the linguistic phenomenon.[43] I understand her impatience with indiscriminate uses of the term in performance, but have to register reservations in turn about her sweeping identification of 'performative' with art that she considers socially effective.[44] Paying attention to the idea of 'doing through saying' does shed light on *some* performance and its documents. In a discussion of Yves Klein's *Saut dans le vide* (*Leap into the Void*, 1960) and Chris Burden's *Shoot* (1971), American performance theorist Philip Auslander employs speech-act theory to conclude provocatively: 'The act of documenting an event as a performance is what constitutes it as such.'[45] Burden was actually shot in the arm by a friend, an act artfully recorded through depth of field and a long exposure that captures the movement of the bullet and Burden's wounded body in one image. The photograph, Auslander argues, makes this rather irresponsible act a work of art, specifically of performance art. Auslander does *not* mean that a live event that is photographed is performance and one that is not photographed is not: for there can be a performance where *no* single event has been documented. Klein's dangerous-looking jump out of the window is a photomontage, substituting the view of an empty street for the safety net held by Klein's assistants. In the case of such modified documents, Auslander's interpretation shows its force: the performance is not in Klein's acrobatic leap, which required a net for it not to end in suicide. The performance is rather his 'leap into the void', possible first and only through the doctored photograph.

Auslander says the 'act of documenting' constitutes a performance, but given the Klein example, he must in fact mean that it *is* the performance.[46] Taking Auslander at his word, in our case the contradictory versions of *Genital Panic* would be irrelevant, since a photograph constitutes the performance: it would be of no interest that EXPORT's photos are not taken at a public performance, nor that the gun is present in the pictures and then reported in her 1979 interview but disclaimed in later publications and statements of the artist. It would be of equally little interest whether the artist ever went into a cinema with her 'Action Pants'. The photographs have all the ingredients of a performative, and they even approximate EXPORT's oral utterance (or verbal performance) of the piece in the 1979 interview. Yet it should be clear from this attempt to apply Auslander's argument to EXPORT that it leaves out the tension between acts and performance documents. A 'document-only' model cannot account for what is interesting here, namely that the oscillations between different instances of the performative reveal the different audiences that are being produced. At best, it leaves us with an indifferent series of unrelated *Genital Panics*.

Auslander's disregard for original context is not unintentional: it follows Derrida's generalization and criticism of Austin, according to which, due to the iterability (roughly, repeatability) of linguistic signs, an infinite number of contexts can crop up, leading to wildly divergent interpretations. While this is true, and indeed a main concern of Austin's, Derrida concludes sceptically that context is *never* determinate, that it is not fully shared by the performer and the receiver, let alone practical questions of how we could know what's on everyone's mind. As a result, the use of the performative turns out to be a species of fiction that we believe in.[47] According to this view, context, being inexhaustible, is unmanageable: if we can never be sure that a performative has succeeded (because some fact unknown to us intervenes), how can we know that one is even possible? Here we must admit that Austin errs by lumping together internal and social criteria for unhappy performatives: for instance, he cites bigamy as one cause of failure to marry, but this fact results in the acts being deemed a failure only if one applies a traditional model of marriage in Western legal contexts, and only if others *know* it. If performatives are social facts, then a social context comprising the act as a whole is all that is required. The 'total speech act', as Austin called it, does not require mastery of an infinite context; it creates or delimits its own range of relevant contexts, and this seems to be enough to assure us that life is not just one interminable performance.[48]

Whatever we make of such generalizing claims, Auslander's application of them works only partially even for his carefully chosen examples. The fascinating aspect in the Klein photomontage is exactly the tension between that which we see and that which might or might not have happened, i.e. the artist's play with the athletic performance (the bold leap) and the introduction of doubt about 'faking' it, his ironic heroism in erasing the safety net, and his self-conscious staging and self-promotion. Auslander flattens the different layers of the performative as regards medium (corporeal and documented, simple or composite) and temporality (the difference between Klein publishing the jump in his own newspaper, *Dimanche*, on 27 November 1960 and our uses of it today). I should argue that only by minutely examining and historicizing these moments of the performative relay can we disclose the historically specific notions of public art and of the audience they produce, and thus arrive at a general theory of performance.[49]

Performatives, performance, and the past

What if, instead of favouring either the document or the event, we were to locate the interest of performance art precisely in its ability to bridge bodily presence and its representation? Amelia Jones has described this double aspect of performance as follows:

> Precisely by using their bodies as primary material, body or performance artists highlight the 'representational status' of such work rather than confirming its ontological priority. The representational aspects of this work – this 'play within the arena of the symbolic,' and, I would add, its dependence on documentation to attain symbolic status within the realm of culture – expose the impossibility of attaining full knowledge of the self through bodily proximity.[50]

In other words, body and documents are not mutually exclusive elements, and there is no reason why they cannot interact in producing meaning: by being one about the other, for instance. Jones also points to the role that documentation plays in 'enacting the artist as public figure', and acknowledges that documentation is the moment of the performance where cultural representation, and thus history, begins.[51] One could add that history continues to be built through palimpsests of discourse and image making that flow inexorably from this moment – including reviews, interviews and artist's statements, art historical texts, exhibitions and catalogue essays, and a range of performative utterances and images, from the artist's documents of the supposed original event to later uses of these images and re-enactments. But such heterogeneity has its price: for how do we bind this reception history to the performative force of the images, to *the* performance in question?

In our particular case, the question of motivation helps to clarify the relationship between image and event. Why would EXPORT insist on the shock value of the real in a planned *Genital Panic* 'action' and produce an image of it, only to question the visual 'facts' she thus established in her later reminiscences about the piece? Why does the gun enter the picture at all, and why does EXPORT then dispute its presence in the original performance in later statements? If we followed Auslander, we might try to conflate all early interviews and images into one 'constructed' performance, or else declare that various independent performances had taken place, due to the multiplicity of documents. Neither view is appealing, since the documents differ significantly from one another, yet *propose to refer to the same historical event*, however ambiguously or inconsistently. They act as performative relays, maintaining the force of EXPORT's performance as something that took place for us in the present. The shifts they represent are shifts in reception and in the history of the work, which suggests that we must pay attention to changes in context instead of declaring its irrelevance to a general performativity.

The cause for the shifts in narrative and imagery seems to me a historical one: EXPORT needed to alter the set-up of the planned action in the photographs in order to achieve a functioning speech-act. The photographs in fact circulate under a slightly different title, namely *Aktionshose: Genitalpanik* (*Action Pants: Genital Panic*), not the mere *Genitalpanik* of the performance, as if EXPORT were presenting only the prop or remnant of that action. The most conspicuous addition, the machine gun, is crucial to the effect of the photographs: it must be seen, in the artist's parlance, as an apt 'substitute' for the most prominent loss in the photographic version of the work, namely the absent bodies of her presumed male audience in an encounter outside the art world – hence also the porn theatre instead of the art cinema, which functions in language just as the addition of the gun does visually. The gun brings the potential aggression of the encounter with the audience in public space into the image, appropriating the signs of sexual aggression (presumed male) for the female protagonist. EXPORT returns the putative male gaze directed toward her genitals with a feminist appropriation of an obvious phallic symbol. For the reading audience this prop was and remains a necessary cue, providing the tension within the picture that refers to the unavailable event and thereby refers to the movie-theatre action. EXPORT had to transfer the gender conflict, and, indeed, the mythic audience of the live act, into the photograph in order for the confrontation to remain legible at all.

At the same time, however, the machine gun redirects the gaze away from the genitals, transforming the genital panic into a perhaps terrorist one, replenishing the effect of original performance by introducing fresh circumstances, such as the somewhat mysterious rural architecture.[52] The performative utterance can, Austin thought, be conveyed in written form or through a gesture, and also, I would argue, be transposed from a gesture into a photograph, as long as the narrative conventions and the situational cues enable one to make sense of the action. In fact, photography must be a privileged medium of the performative dimension of performance, not because there is nothing outside of it, as Auslander implies, but through its dual capacity of acting as quasi-legal document of the past (a convention applicable even when the photographs are staged) and of offering an experiential re-enactment for the viewer in the present.

Indeed, the balance of autonomy and reference in the photograph has underwritten the long history of *Genital Panic*. EXPORT's aim in producing the photographs was to disseminate the bench image as a poster in public space in Vienna. Silkscreen posters of this photograph showing EXPORT on the bench, stamped with EXPORT's name logo, were printed by Kari Bauer the same year that the photos were made. EXPORT claimed in a 2007 interview, plausibly enough, that after having the posters made she was not able to get permission from the city to distribute the posters publicly, nor did she have the means and the workforce to put them up; she recalls 'giving them to friends'.[53] She had a similar poster displayed in the streets of Berlin as a contribution to the 1994 exhibition *Gewalt/Geschäfte* (*Violence/Business*) of the Neue Gesellschaft für Bildende Kunst.[54] Both of the well-known photographs were sold as photo editions, shown in exhibitions, and disseminated as stand-ins for the performance, with photograph captions in books and wall texts providing the necessary narrative link to the live event.

In short, these images have acquired historical significance, even if they cannot be regarded as documentary proof of the performance. This historical substance of the images, their use in later performances, raises again the problem of the 'original performance'. Are the photos still dependent upon it, their meaning inherently linked to the original 'action', or are they self-sufficient artworks? EXPORT experimented much with photographic self-staging of the kind taken up by the *Pictures* artists a decade later, notably the *Identitätstransfer I* (*Identity Transfer I*) of 1968, in which she presents herself in a stereotypical male posture for the camera (Figure 6). From the beginning of her career, photography was never simply a medium for documenting her actions, but one that self-reflexively opened up complex social interactions – in performances expressly for the camera.[55] EXPORT's deft use of photography might suggest that she privileges the document over the actual performance. And yet, given the repeated emphasis on *Genital Panic* as a performance in public, and its need to be envisioned as having taken place in the cinema, Auslander's argument that performative force belongs solely to the document, that there is no collaboration between the live action and its documentation, does not hold. It does not hold even in this ideal situation, where we lack all evidence of the performance's having taken place in public space.

I am making the case that, though performance photographs are not always the mechanical reproduction of the appearance of a first version of a performance, they do almost always *refer* to it. They are images of an imaginary performance that sometimes has taken place and sometimes not, but which is always identified discursively as the object of interest through descriptions, citations, and reproductions in the public sphere.[56] The photograph provides the imaginary performance with an image, one that is completed in our heads, so that we can think that the event has taken place. I insist on the verbs 'think' and 'imagine' here, for of course photographs, like Klein's or EXPORT's, do not always tell the truth. This should not be confused with the view that performance is always a fiction, to which scholars and spectators assent in

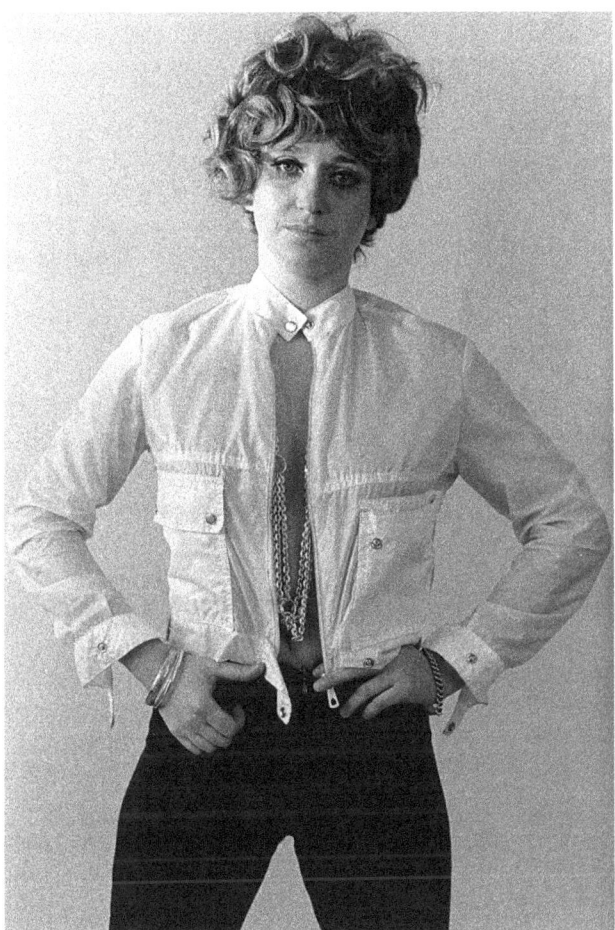

VALIE EXPORT, *Identity Transfer 1*, 1968   **6**

'performatively' attributing to it social effectiveness. Such a theory copes with real and imaginary performances by making all performances imaginary. My view, on the contrary, is that photographs *always* refer to the past, even if the past events they refer to did not always take place. Amelia Jones's attempt to balance live experience with the constructive force of documentation in fact came to similar conclusions: 'The body art event needs the photograph to confirm its having happened; the photograph needs the body art event as an ontological "anchor" of its indexicality.'[57] This claim is accurate, but the trouble lies in the index. Whether one takes indexicality to mean physical proximity, or, as Peirce did, causation of the sign by its object, there is no indexical relation to imaginary objects.[58] Fascinatingly, Jones develops her claim in response to myths concerning a Viennese peer of EXPORT's:

> Kristine Stiles has brilliantly exposed the dangers of using the photograph of a performative event as 'proof' in her critique of Henry Sayre's book *The Object of Performance*. Sayre opens his first chapter with the now-mythical tale of Rudolf Schwarzkogler's suicidal self-mutilation of his penis in 1966, a story founded on the circulation of a number of 'documents' showing a male torso with bandaged penis (a razor blade lying nearby). Stiles, who has done primary research on the artist, points out that the photograph, in fact, is not even of Schwarzkogler but, rather, of another artist (Heinz Cibulka) who posed for Schwarzkogler's entirely fabricated ritual castration.[59]

Stiles deserves recognition for clearing up this error, which, ironically, marks a book that emphasizes the constitutive role of photographs in performance.[60] Sayre in fact tries to do this *through Schwarzkogler*: 'The photographic record asserted itself most horribly in the documentation, exhibited in Kassel in 1972, of Rudolf Schwarzkogler's 1969 piece by piece amputation of his penis.'[61] Sayre is right when we take him literally: the image as misunderstood is a forceful if false assertion. But how is it an index? Jones might say that it is an index of the 1966 performance – or more likely 1965, for Schwarzkogler ceased all performances, including his 'penis washings' (*Penisbespülungen*) in early 1966.[62]

My point in drawing attention to this convoluted history, so like that of *Genital Panic*, yet stemming from misidentification rather than absence of causes, is not so much that it marks, as Stiles nicely puts it, 'the contingency of the document not only to a former action but also to the construction of a wholly fictive space'.[63] Rather, I claim that performance documents are neither indexes, which can't lie, nor fictive spaces, which can't contain real actions, but assertions of the 'reality' of a past state of affairs, as Sayre inadvertently reveals when he writes that 'the photographic record asserted itself most horribly'.

The past reference of photography forms part of the context that we need for the speech-act to work on us in the present as the record of a past performance. Naturally, the assertions that 'this has taken place' may be false. But for a performative to work, its factual content need not be true. What is needed is a context in which the evidence is taken as decisive: in our cases, the image taken as historical evidence. This context is not a supplement, but the medium within which performative action unfolds. The social effect of performance art – its Austinian 'making it so' – depends neither exclusively on the force of live action nor on documentation, but on documentation as the historical bearer of action into the future.

A monument to performance art

The historical structure of documentation marks performance as a profoundly time-based art. When Marina Abramović re-performed *Genital Panic*, she based her seven-hour-long performance consciously on the photographic documents she knew (Figure 7).[64] The body she 'brought back' was yet another imaginative constitution of presence for a viewing public, informed by mediated historical fragments that ensure no 'authentic' return to bodily presence, but at best an intention to achieve this. Almost every aspect of the '1969 action' was reformulated or newly specified: the unknown original duration (given rather oddly as '10 minutes' in the Guggenheim catalogue) became a seven-hour marathon, the male German cinema public became an urbane, mixed New York audience.[65] And yet Abramović herself wrestled with the problem of revisionism, as we can gather from retrospective statements concerning the motivation of *Seven Easy Pieces*:

> I'm one of these artists of the 70s and I'm just fed up with the copying of not just my work – of all the artists of the 70s in different ways in MTV, in theatre, in dance, in fashion, in young artists, I'm also fed up with young critics who actually evaluate the young artists' work and tell us they are original, without referring to the past works at all. They deny history.[66]

Abramović's attention to history is a model to artists and scholars, and yet, her suggestion that there is an authentic version of the performance waiting to be excavated for history, and that this version can be retrieved through re-enactment, elides the fact that circumstances have changed since the original performance.[67] If she wanted above all historical accuracy, why re-perform? Also, Abramović's claim that amnesia has removed these originals from consciousness is not convincing, since the works she re-enacted in 2005 are among the most historically visible in performance. Rather, it seems to me that the dual insistence on accuracy and liveness is meant precisely to activate the speech-act component of performance, an experiment to determine what these performances *were* by seeing what they will *do* now. At least, that is the ideal case, since history has already transformed and re-contextualized these pieces. For the effect of canonical 1960s performances in 2005 depends not only on themselves, but also on the audience's prior knowledge (or supposed knowledge) of these works.

Abramović's 2005 project shifts our historical understanding of re-enacted works such as EXPORT's *Genital Panic*. First, there is the issue of reconstruction of the 'original'. The organizers of *Seven Easy Pieces* ran into various difficulties while trying to unearth the original course of events. The confusion reached a climax when EXPORT wrote in a 2005 email to curator Nancy Spector that she 'did it [*Genital Panic*] two times, one time in a Art Cinema in München and second for the poster', with the weapon featured only the second time.[68] This doubling already anticipates the idea of re-performing *Genital Panic* and the possibility of inaugurating performance relays in place of the demand for lost presence, but also reveals a readiness to equate performance and photography which we hardly associate with the 1960s. In 2007 Abramović herself recalled

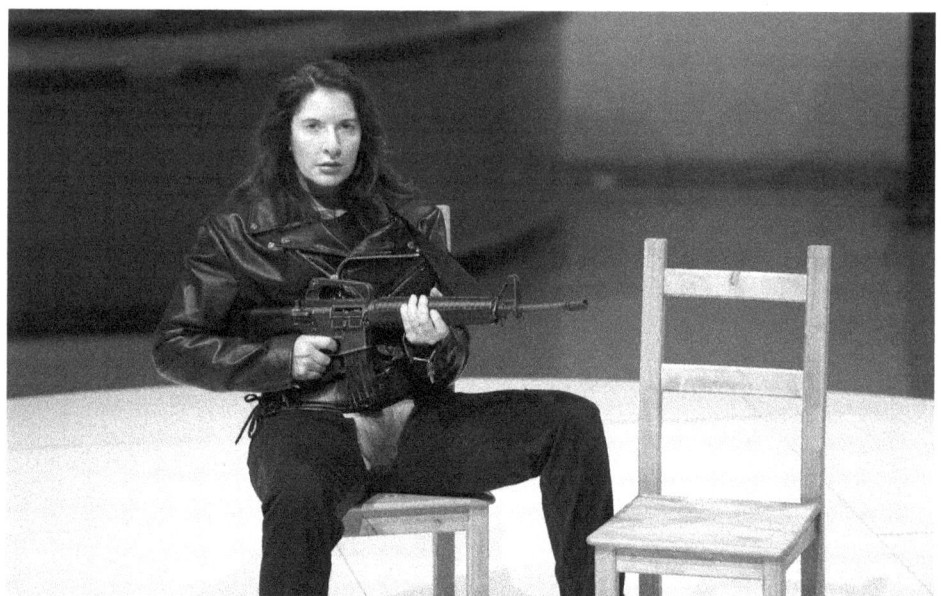

7   Marina Abramović, *Seven Easy Pieces: Action Pants: Genital Panic*, 11 November 2005, Solomon R. Guggenheim Museum New York

the difficulty of accessing the performance through EXPORT's oral account:

> I was the most critical and most careful about this piece because in reality she stated that she originally performed the piece in this theatre at the erotic film festival in Vienna, but at the same time she made the poster as well. *Genital Panic* is a great contradiction […] because she also made the photograph in her studio and there are lots of different images of that poster.[69]

On the basis of this uncertainty, Abramović decided in her re-enactment not to give up the gun, thus indicating that the images had become central to the historical imagining of *Genital Panic*. The solution at the Guggenheim was to title the evening *Action Pants: Genital Panic* after the photographic work, but to cite the Munich action as historical reference both on the website and in the catalogue.[70]

The complex and often inconsistent history of *Genital Panic* made it clear to Abramović that spectators approaching performance must mobilize a version of history not based on investigation-transcendent facts, but on hearsay and tradition concerning the 'original' performance, and its subsequent discussion and documentation. Abramović *was* concerned with historical truth, as she claimed, but also with the impossibility of perfectly re-enacting the pieces. For what would be a perfect re-enactment of *Genital Panic*? Abramović knew that she performed her *Seven Easy Pieces* for a new public, and the irony in the title, with its allusion to repetitive exercises in music, already suggests her awareness of an appropriation in a new context.[71] The – by now historical – sources were therefore made more prominent than they would have to be in a re-enactment: this was also evident in Abramović's talk of the original performances as 'scripts'. The performance consisted of her posing statically, as if she were doing a *tableau vivant* – using the props of the chairs, the gun, and the cut-out pants, mostly sitting in the position of EXPORT's seated photos, and sometimes – every hour or so – getting up slowly, walking to the edge of the platform, posing upright in the posture of the third photograph, walking back, and sitting down again. The 'action' became a set of slowly shifting photographic stills, enacted with care so as not to overstep the bounds of the formative documentation.

Abramović's re-enactment of history is an embodiment of the performative document, an artefact that points to the past without simply having been part of it. In its distillation of reception and memory, Abramović proposed a new, more self-consciously canonical status for the performances she staged. The weapon in *Genital Panic* – according to the files at the Guggenheim, a replica of an American M16 rifle (quite different visually from the smaller semiautomatic EXPORT had used) – played a particular role for Abramović.[72] It externalized the potentially violent gender conflict that the photographs had staged – since the Guggenheim public was also not the aggressive male audience of the fabled porn theatre. Additionally, the fact that the gun in the Guggenheim show was a replica removes any doubt that the context of the new work was the art world and not an imagined revolutionary public sphere of 1960s Europe. The crucial question thus becomes not 'is this a new work or an interpretation of EXPORT?' but, 'given the radical change in context, how does the work function in relation to EXPORT?' Roughly so: Abramović as the female protagonist becomes the re-enactor of history and the guarantor of recollection, one that changes the 'original' as she must in making it anew.

In the European culture of commemoration, female bodies have always played an important part, most manifestly in the monument as abstract personification of virtues or nation.[73] Is Abramović monumentalizing EXPORT's performance, or performance art in general? After all, she decided to restage the performances in the Guggenheim Museum, an institution supremely effective in canonizing works of art. Aside from the choice of venue, the obvious particularity of the re-performance – apart from the props approximating those in the photographs – was Abramović's bodily presence, a presence tempered by the use of a tall white cylindrical platform serving as base. Instead of the close encounter between the audience's faces and EXPORT's crotch – which, EXPORT had argued, constituted the work's shock value – Abramović was visible from all sides but untouchable. The audience walked freely, as in any museum setting, and Abramović's operational zone was additionally demarcated as 'forbidden' by a circle of black tape on the floor around the platform. At one point a young man with a ponytail tried to climb on stage, and was promptly removed by security personnel.[74] This attempted interaction did not stir Abramović in the least. She sat in her chair, impassive as a statue – or a photograph. In my reading, she had to, because the intruder did not understand the recreated piece, which was not, as in EXPORT's case, about real encounter, about the acting out and inverting real gender relations. Rather, Abramović made herself into what we might call a monument – a *Denkmal*, a mark for thinking.[75] A monument cannot ensure 'authentic' remembering, since it addresses spectators with divergent experiences of the past, some indeed with no relevant experience. What a monument makes possible is, rather, social *commemoration*: rituals establishing new relations to the past event. In this view, there is no need for monuments to be massive, or to give an impression of permanence.[76] What I shall call *performative monuments* are monuments that do not necessarily come in the form of performances, but which work by provoking public acts of commemoration.

With *Action Pants: Genital Panic*, as with each of the other *Seven Easy Pieces*, Abramović mediated through her body both documents and imagined historical actions. Although she did not interpret all *Seven Easy Pieces* in as static a manner as she did *Genital Panic*, the extension in time – every piece was performed for seven hours, no matter its original length – led to a deliberate aesthetic distance and exhaustion on the side of the viewer.[77] The performances were meditative, infused with Abramović's own memory, fed mostly on relics, since Abramović had not been present at any performance she reproduced, excepting of course her own *Lips of Thomas*. Is there a change in context even in this performance, or was the original re-performed 'faithfully' in the privileged case of the performing of her own act? *Thomas Lips*, as the 1975 performance in Innsbruck, Austria was originally called, was radically modified for the Guggenheim Museum. It is plausible that Abramović's own history gave her a particular amount of freedom to 'recreate' the past. The artist split the complex actions of the 1975 event into smaller units that were repeated several times, as if fragmented pieces of memory were being dredged up obsessively.[78]

The last evening of *Seven Easy Pieces* made explicit Abramović's ambition that the performances should be taken as a monument to performance art. Abramović titled her single new work *Entering the Other Side*, with the telling subtitle *The Artist is Present Here and Now*. Astonishingly, given this activist rhetoric, she described the static event as 'an installation' (Figure 8).[79] Abramović appeared high above the platform wearing a gigantic blue dress, serving in her own words as a 'projection screen' for the public.[80] For seven hours, she confined herself to several small gestures, such as turning her upper body from one side to the other and extending her arms; at some point a

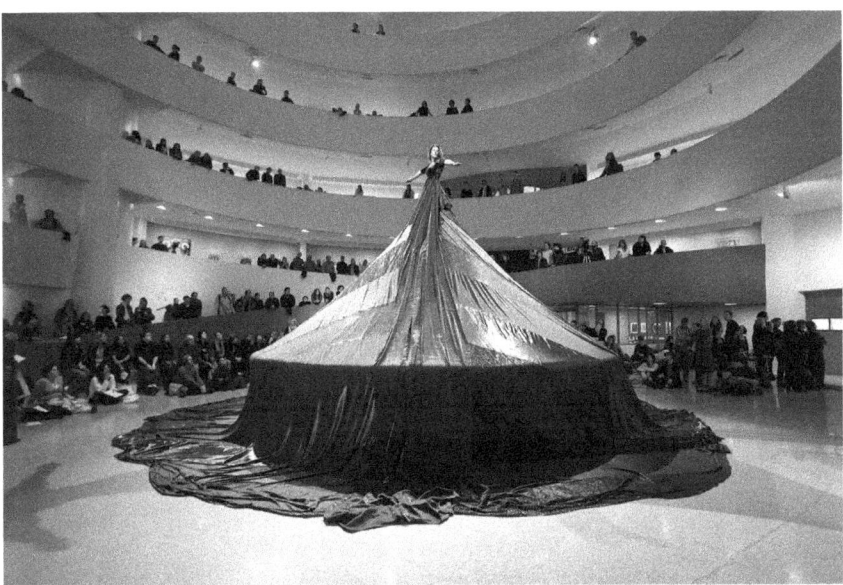

Marina Abramović, *Seven Easy Pieces: Entering the Other Side*, 15 November 2005,   **8**
Solomon R. Guggenheim Museum New York

Slavic song was played on tape. This monumental inactivity, interrupted by a recorded bit of the past, indicates that Abramović was not just 'present' as a personification of performance art. She was present and distant at the same time, a sublime marker for performance, comprehensible as both image and embodied landmark. What remained implicit in the other performances was openly treated here: though the performance premiered at the Guggenheim and was no re-enactment, the audience was invited to form and cultivate a memory rather than experience an action.

In the Guggenheim series as a whole, if not on each individual evening, document and act merged into performative monument, which refers to the past by having spectators reflect on it in the present. Abramović acted for a historically informed public, not because its members might have been present at EXPORT's, Beuys's or Abramović's performance thirty years earlier, but precisely because, though they had not been, they had heard or read about it (or *would* have heard or read about it as a result of the Guggenheim event). History and memory, or, to be more exact, cultural memory based on access to mediated experience, were embodied equally in the performer and the audience that came, went, and returned.

To be sure, to thus treat mediated and unmediated performance as exemplifying the same logic requires a significant shift from 1960s ideologies of authentic and inauthentic experience. In 1961, American historian Daniel

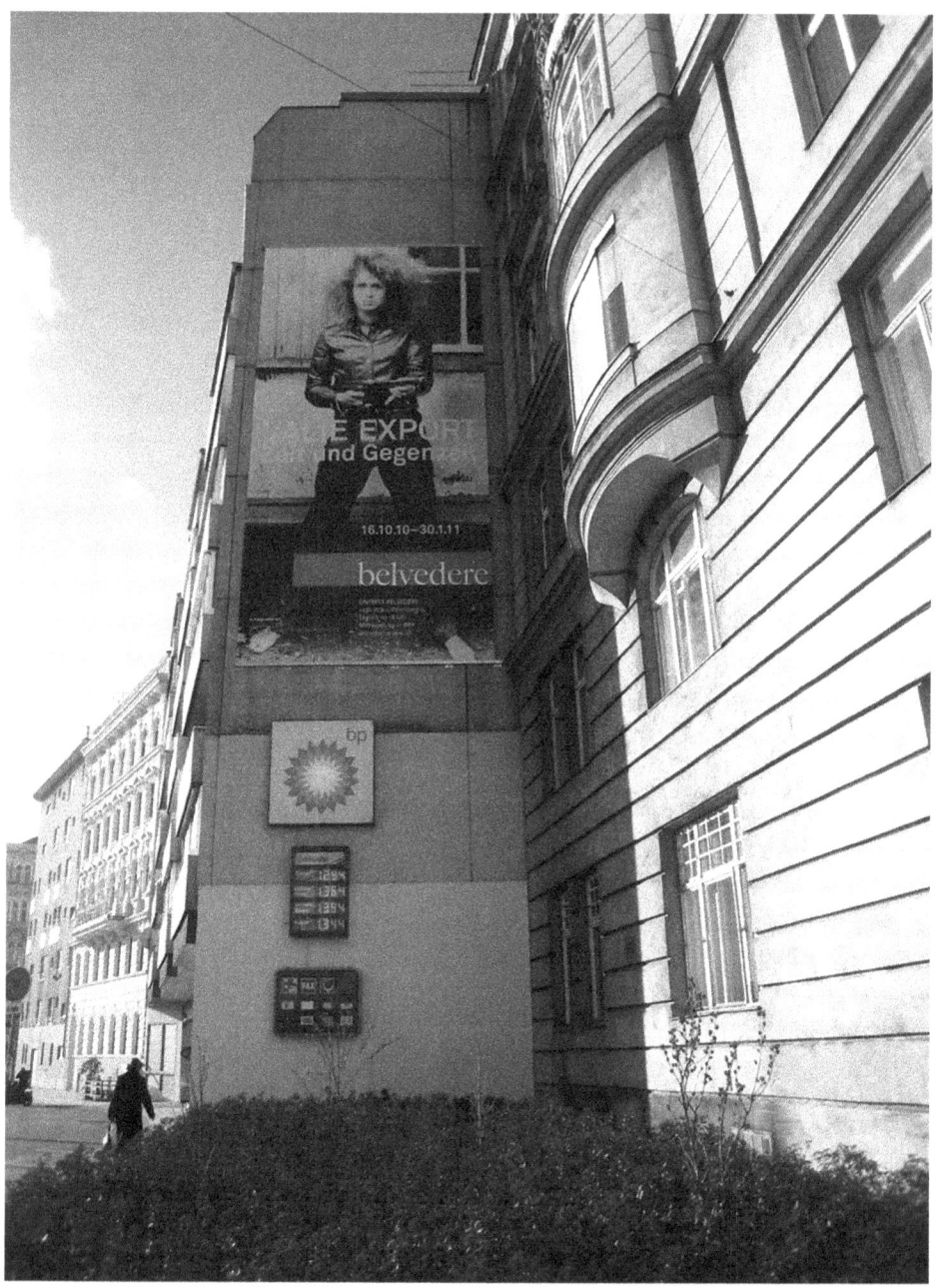

9   Poster for VALIE EXPORT's retrospective *Time and Countertime* in Vienna, 2010

Boorstin coined the term 'pseudo-event' for occurrences that existed solely for the media or for mediation, anticipating concepts such as the spectacle of Guy Debord or the simulacrum of Jean Baudrillard.[81] While from today's point of view the value judgement that rates mediated lower than authentic experience may be questioned, Boorstin exemplifies a general fear of losing authentic experience in the post-war period, and a political worry that such a loss would result in a society of alienated spectators, that also played into the development of practices such as Nouveau Réalisme, Fluxus, Situationism, Viennese Actionism, and various forms of performance. EXPORT's *Genital Panic* makes the problematic nature of the concept obvious even at its high tide.

It should be added, as is the case with EXPORT, that the opponents of mediation, far from being naïve, were among its most perceptive observers. Boorstin coined a definition of the celebrity as someone 'well-known for being well-known', a formula with obvious ties to the self-fulfilling character of the performative; in a late preface to his book, he noted that it too was well-known for being well-known. The interest in unmediated experience is paradoxical insofar as *any* interest, whether exemplified in texts concerning an event, photographic documentation, memory, and imagination, is a form of mediation. Self-conscious gestures toward mediation in 1960s performance are often obscured by the mediation itself – the discourse around performance art that would disguise that the artists operated within a paradoxical view of authentic experience. Abramović is marked by the era Boorstin inhabited, and remains committed to notions of performance as authentic experience, to which she credits the impulse to carry out *Seven Easy Pieces*: 'The unreliability of the documents and the witnesses led to the total mystification and misrepresentation of the actual performance.'[82] Yet, she incorporated historiography and myth in her re-performances in ways that one hopes do not mystify but reveal the historical structure of performance.[83]

The apparent contradiction between an interest in presence and mediation can be resolved by returning to our speech-act definition of performance. Recall that in Austin, to speak (a mediation) was to do something (an event, 'presence'). With this in mind, we can come back to the root of our inquiry: did EXPORT's *Genital Panic* ever take place as a performance? Certainly: there is a thirty-year paper trail indicating that it has done so. But there are indications that the act of the artist in a movie theatre in Munich might have remained in the planning stage: the entry on the piece in the anthology of Actionism co-edited by EXPORT in 1970, which printed the bench photograph for the first time with a text, uses the modal auxiliary verb 'I should' (*sollte*) to qualify the encounter between EXPORT's crotch and the spectators' heads.[84] However we interpret this passage, it is consistent with the thesis that the performance had, in 1970, not (yet?) taken place, even though there might have been, of course, a gap between written text and published book.

EXPORT's 'I should' in fact indicates a future tense aiming at eventual realization, or it could mean what *should have* taken place; these two readings equivocate over time, but both are descriptions of plans not carried out. The utterance, however, could also be taken as an imperative, as 'I ought'. The ambiguity between the descriptive and the normative, and past and future, is at the centre of the piece. The 'should happen' is a description that can become an Austinian 'it is so', in the minds of spectators whose sole criterion for a performance having taken place is that it is presented to them as past. Indeed, this has happened in the brief but eventful history of this work. In her retrospective in Austria in the fall of 2010, *Action Pants: Genital Panic* reappeared as giant poster in public space in Vienna, with the title of the exhibition printed over her private parts (Figure 9). In the show, the work was shown in yet another configuration: as a photograph on canvas, recently for sale in a contemporary art auction at Christie's.[85] And so the 'original' continues to work in our heads, and even in such a firmly art historical context as 'a Genital Panic on canvas' remains inseparable from the past act which performance presupposes.

That we cannot here distinguish the 'truth' from 'myth' is a truism, as it is in the case of many historical events. This is in part so for a simple empirical reason: 'myth' is itself the form we give to those facts as a coherent historical narrative, which goes beyond those facts which we have incontrovertibly, but itself becomes a historical fact shaping our attitude to the past. Hans Blumenberg has defined myth as a narration of highest consistency, comparable to the 'theme and variations' in music.[86] In the history of performance, what is forgotten or distorted, but also what is remembered, exaggerated, or straightforwardly invented, adds up to myths as complex as EXPORT's, with which facts intertwine. For past facts, even in such a case as mine, where the textual record is strong, remain inconclusive. The myths, on the other hand, are indisputably effective, however fuzzy their borders, and their story needs to be repeated, carried on, changing yet consistent. Given this temporal predicament, and its relevance beyond performance, it should be no surprise that a wide array of historians have in the last decades devoted themselves to what they call mnemohistory, investigating neither political history nor its delimitation from myth, but on the contrary the more or less manifest role of mythical rethinking in shaping tradition and political history via commemoration. Jan Assmann, together with Aleida Assmann one of the pioneers of mnemohistory, describes his own agenda in words that could apply to the *Seven Easy Pieces*: 'The task of mnemohistory consists in analyzing the mythical elements in tradition and discovering their hidden agenda.'[87] The practice of mnemohistory consists in applying a reception theory to historical transmission: essentially, what I have been doing for performance.[88] The audience, be it a contemporary one or one contemporary to Moses or the

October Revolution, always mediates the event by perceiving and discussing it, without even taking political pressure into account – which is always present, of course. Similarly, historical truth is, in practice, always inflected by memory, historiography, and myth making, and, in a stronger thesis, perhaps, is only of interest when so inflected.[89] Mnemohistory is ambivalent about myth: it wants to record its force objectively, but finds it valuable in itself. The speech-act approach to performance history outlined here can help us to see why this is so. The past is not simply whatever we want it to be: a narcissistic subjectivism rather like that of Abramović's intruder.[90] But past proposals to act which are taken by later spectators to have taken place have *in that sense and that sense only* taken place. Their place is in the past, and their reality, though not always material, is the stuff of history. As a consequence of this, performance, with its emphasis on specificity of place and time, is always implicitly a historical medium. And re-performance is explicitly historical, less an investigation than an aesthetic mode of remembering or of drawing attention to the past. And while I do not think that performance of the 1960s differs essentially from re-performance in this regard, we can see why only through a closer look at the relationship between document and history as formulated at the time.

In the wider context of historical writing as knowledge production and political action, Michel Foucault sketched in the late 1960s a relationship of the document to the monument that is important to my approach:

> [H]istory, in its traditional form, undertook to 'memorize' the monuments of the past, transform them into documents, and lend speech to those traces which, in themselves, are often not verbal, or which say in silence something other than what they actually say; in our time, history is that which transforms *documents* into *monuments*.[91]

Foucault writes this in a discourse on historical method, where it is clear that the aim is normative rather than descriptive: he is contrasting an older practice of history which consisted in constructing subjective, human 'documents' out of inhuman historical fragments ('monuments') through an introspective procedure of 'memory' or 'memorizing'. On the other hand, Foucault welcomes and practises a kind of history in which anthropomorphic traces (Foucault's 'documents', the mnemohistorians' 'myth') are dissected in their purely systematic relations, set out without anthropomorphism as fragments of discourse (Foucault's 'monuments'). Foucault claims that it was a mistake to make the historical monument function as a document (i.e., to make old records speak to people in the present about people in the past). He sees the document as pointing to an enclosing theoretical discourse freed of human referents, what he calls a monument, to which it may be reduced by a critical history.

An immediate question arises whether Foucault's use of the terms 'monument' and 'document' are idiosyncratic, or whether they point to deeper tendencies within these bodies of discourse that remain pertinent to our problem. The *Archaeology of Knowledge* is concerned with systems of knowledge in their peculiar autonomy, and emphasizes the self-referentiality of historical knowledge, the fact that grasping an obsolete discourse may not mean believing it.[92] Even if we do not want to do away with individual agency in the anti-humanist style of French 1960s theory, it is worth importing into our context Foucault's idea of a symbiotic connection between the document and the monument (encompassing the idea of discourse as an 'artefact', and also as a ruin or landmark) and the importance of a directionality in their relationship. Whether truthful or misleading, photographic or frankly manufactured, documents refer to the past. I will expand on this argument to show how commemoration requires performance, arguing that it is not embodiment as such that makes performance into a monument, but the socially binding (potentially performative) act of representing the past in public. How this is possible within the vantage point of embodied, conspicuously gendered subjects struggling with unseen political forces is the subject of the next chapter, which treats the remarkably assured photographic documents and performances of VALIE EXPORT in 1960s Vienna and beyond. The relationship between presence and mediation in 1960s art became, I argue, the Janus-faced prerequisite for performance to become a paradigmatic public art, able to handle the historical persistence of the past in the present at the moment of bodily encounter – an encounter that is documented and simulated, experienced and imagined. It is via the document and its self-location in the past that the here and now of performance becomes the there and then of recollection.

Notes

1 RoseLee Goldberg has argued the radical ephemerality of performance since the 1970s: see *Performance: Live Art, 1909 to the Present* (New York: Abrams, 1979), especially 9ff; revised as *Performance Art. From Futurism to the Present* (London: Thames & Hudson, 1988). Amelia Jones discusses means of accessing performance otherwise than through 'presence' in *Body Art: Performing the Subject* (Minneapolis: University of Michigan Press, 1998), and problematizes the access to performance granted by the document in '"Presence" in Absentia. Experiencing Performance as Documentation', *Art Journal*, 56:4 (Winter 1997), 11–18; the essay is reprinted with a 2010 commentary in 'Temporal Anxiety/"Presence in Absentia"', in Gabriella Giannachi, Nick Kaye and Michael Shanks (eds), *Archaeologies of Presence* (London/New York: Routledge, 2012), 197–221. Nick Kaye devoted much of his research to the tension between presence and documentation: see *Postmodernism and Performance* (Basingstoke: Macmillan, 1994), *Site-Specific Art: Performance, Place and Documentation* (London/New York: Routledge, 2000), and the aforementioned edited volume. Philip Auslander has theorized performance art as radically mediated in *Presence and Resistance: Postmodernism and Cultural Politics*

in Contemporary American Performance (Ann Arbor: University of Michigan Press, 1992), *Liveness: Performance in a Mediatized Culture* (London/New York: Routledge, 1999), and especially 'The Performativity of Performance Documentation', *Performing Arts Journal*, 84, 28:3 (September 2006), 1–10. Martha Buskirk's discussion of 'delay' in *The Contingent Object of Contemporary Art* (Cambridge: Mass.: MIT Press, 2003) informed my early thinking on this topic. Though often cited in other contexts, there is a brilliant, neglected passage on the relation of photography to performance in Mary Kelly, 'Re-viewing Modernist Criticism', *Screen*, 22:3 (Autumn 1981), 41–62, reprinted in Brian Wallis (ed.), *Art after Modernism: Rethinking Representation* (New York: New Museum/Boston: Godine, 1984), 87–103. See also Philip Ursprung, Mechtild Widrich, and Jürg Berthold (eds), *Presence*. forthcoming.

2 *Cut Piece* was performed several times in the 1960s. See Kevin Concannon, 'Yoko Ono's Cut Piece. From Text to Performance and Back Again', *Performing Arts Journal*, 90, 30:3 (September 2008), 81–93. In recent years, reenactments of historical events as well as restagings of post-war art have also attracted enormous attention. See Rebecca Schneider, *Performing Remains: Art and War in Times of Theatrical Reenactment* (London: Routledge, 2011), chapter 1 for the challenges these pose to historiography. Exhibitions such as *A Little Bit of History Repeated* (Berlin: Kunstwerke, 2001), *A Short History of Performance* (Whitechapel Gallery, London, 2002/03), *Life once More: Forms of Reenactment In Contemporary Art* (Rotterdam: Witte de With, 2005), *Ahistoric Occasion: Artists Making History* (North Adams: Massachusetts Museum of Contemporary Art, 2006), *Now Again the Past: Rewind, Replay, Resound* (New York: Carnegie Art Center, 2006), and *History Will Repeat Itself. Strategien des Reenactment in der zeitgenössischen (Medien-)Kunst und Performance* (Dortmund and Berlin 2007) are symptomatic of this interest. That these issues remain current, and will probably continue to do so for a while, can be seen from the 2012 show at San Francisco Museum of Modern Art, *Staged Presence*, the 2011 theme of the Performance Studies International (psi) Conference 2011 in Utrecht: 'memory' and psi 2013 at Stanford: 'now-then'.

3 A second generation of performance artists, including Tino Sehgal, has entered this context with different aims. Sehgal's 'constructed situations' are encounters between audience and 'interpreters' who initiate an often verbal, choreographed performance. Photography is strictly forbidden. See Caroline Jones, 'Staged Presence', 48, 9 (May 2010), 274, notes 6 and 12, and Dorothea von Hantelmann, *How to Do Things with Art. The Meaning of Art's Performativity* [2007] (Paris: Les presses du réel, 2010), chapter 3.

4 Rebecca Schneider has recently argued that 'to read "history" then, as a set of sedimented acts that are not the historical acts themselves but the act of securing any incident backward – the repeated act of securing memory – is to rethink the site of history in ritual repetition'. 'Performance Remains Again', in Giannachi et al. (eds), *Archaeologies of Presence*, 74.

5 Goldberg, *Live Art from 1909 to the Present*, 79f on Black Mountain College; at 85f, the Judson Dance Group is discussed, establishing a lasting canon. Cf. Claire Bishop, *Artificial Hells: Participatory Art and the Politics of Spectatorship* (London: Verso, 2012), whose second chapter, on the 'Historic Avant-garde' rehearses

Goldberg, as Bishop has noted in an interview with Julia Bryan-Wilson.

6 Goldberg, 'Performance: A Hidden History', in Gregory Battcock and Robert Nickas (eds), *The Art of Performance. A Critical Anthology* (New York: E.P. Dutton, 1984), 26.

7 Harold Rosenberg, 'American Action Painters', [1952] in *The Tradition of the New* (New York: McGraw-Hill, 1965). Kaprow's radical conclusion from Pollock's work is a breakdown of medium specificity: 'Young artists of today need no longer say, "I am a painter" or "a poet"; or "a dancer". They are simply "artists". All of life will be open to them.' Allan Kaprow, 'The Legacy of Jackson Pollock', [1958] in *Essays on the Blurring of Art and Life* (Berkeley/Los Angeles/London: University of California Press, 1993), 9. Amelia Jones devotes one whole chapter to 'the Pollockian performative' in *Body Art: Performing the Subject* (Minneapolis: University of Michigan Press, 1998), 53–102, while the most influential exhibition catalogue on the subject begins with Hans Namuth's photos. See Paul Schimmel (ed.), *Out of Actions: Between Performance and the Object, 1949–1979*, Museum of Contemporary Art, Los Angeles (London/New York: Thames & Hudson, 1998).

8 Indeed, these authors often go further, drawing sceptical conclusions about the possibility of live art and its dependence on mediation or documentation to first register as 'live' in the first place.

9 Peggy Phelan, *Unmarked: The Politics of Performance* (London/New York: Routledge, 1993).

10 Dieter Mersch, *Was sich zeigt. Materialität, Präsenz, Ereignis* (Munich: Wilhelm Fink Verlag, 2002), and, more concisely, 'Performativität und Ereignis. Überlegungen zur Revision des Performanz-Konzeptes der Sprache', in Jürgen Fohrmann (ed.), *Rhetorik. Figuration und Performanz, Schriftreihe Germanistische Symposien, Berichtband 25* (Metzler: Stuttgart, 2004), 502–35.

11 See Sven Lütticken, 'An Arena in which to Reenact', in Sven Lütticken (ed.), *Life, Once More. Forms of Reenactment in Contemporary Art.* (Rotterdam: Witte de With Center for Contemporary Art, 2005), 17–60.

12 See also Jane Blocker's *Seeing Witness: Visuality and the Ethics of Testimony* (Minneapolis: University of Minnesota Press, 2009). Building on her earlier *Where is Ana Mendieta?* (Durham: Duke University Press, 1999), Blocker sees in performance and its study a melancholic longing after a lost material body.

13 Schneider, *Performing Remains*, 7. The passage addresses some ideas of Fred Moten.

14 VALIE EXPORT is the artist's stage name, to be spelled in capital letters. See Chapter 2.

15 This is not a criticism of the valuable scholarship linking performance to other post-war art practices, e.g. Frazer Ward, 'Some Relations between Conceptual and Performance Art', *Art Journal*, 56:4 (Winter 1997), 36–40. Of Christ Burden's 'Shoot', Ward writes: 'it now exists primarily as documentation (and what Burden refers to as "relics"), so that its material existence, as with much performance art, somewhat resembles the characteristic forms of Conceptual art' (39). On the issues raised by performance in video art, see Anne M. Wagner, 'Performance, Video, and the Rhetoric of Presence', *October*, 91 (Winter 2001), 59–80, and Mechtild Widrich, 'Stars and Dilettantes: On the Voice in Video Art', in *Sounding the Subject* (Cambridge, Mass.: MIT List Visual Arts Center, 2007), 24–32.

16 RoseLee Goldberg, 'Here and Now', in Chrissie Iles (ed.), *Marina Abramović. Objects Performance Video Sound* (Oxford: Museum of Modern Art Oxford, 1995), 11.

17 Originally, Abramović had the following selection and sequence in mind: Marcel Duchamp, *Marcel Duchamp playing chess with a nude female model* (1963), Bruce Nauman, *Body Pressure* (1974), Vito Acconci, *Seedbed* (1972), VALIE EXPORT, *Genital Panic* (1968 [*sic*]), Gina Pane, *Self-Portrait(s)* (1973), Chris Burden, *Trans-Fixed* (1974), and Marina Abramović, *Crossing to the Other Side* (2005). Due to copyright and other issues, the seven events finally re-performed were: Bruce Nauman, *Body Pressure* (1974), Vito Acconci, *Seedbed* (1972), VALIE EXPORT, *Action Pants: Genital Panic* (1969), Gina Pane, *The Conditioning, first action of Self-Portrait(s)* (1973), Joseph Beuys, *How to Explain Pictures to a Dead Hare* (1965), Marina Abramović, *Lips of Thomas* (1975), Marina Abramović, *Entering the Other Side* (2005). Exhibition files, *Seven Easy Pieces*, The Solomon R. Guggenheim Museum Archive, New York.

18 Peter Weibel in collaboration with VALIE EXPORT (eds), *Bildkompendium Wiener Aktionismus und Film* (Frankfurt am Main: Kohlkunstverlag, 1970), 290.

19 Mulvey describes the use of psychoanalysis in her essay as a 'political weapon, demonstrating the way the unconscious of patriarchal society has structured film form'. Laura Mulvey, 'Visual Pleasure and Narrative Cinema', [delivered as a paper in 1973], *Screen* 16:3 (1975), 6–18.

20 VALIE EXPORT, interview by author, New York, 19 February 2007.

21 This photograph of EXPORT standing can be found in Roswitha Mueller, *VALIE EXPORT. Fragments of The Imagination* (Indiana University Press: Bloomington and Indianapolis, 1994), 18, in Giovanna Zapperi, 'VALIE EXPORT', *le journal*, 20 (2003), Centre national de la photographie, Paris, 2–3, in Hedwig Saxenhuber (ed.), *VALIE EXPORT*. Exh. Cat. National Centre for Contemporary Art and Ekaterina Foundation, Moskow (Vienna/Bolzano: Folio, 2007), 32, and in Agnes Husslein-Arco, Angelika Nollert, and Stella Rollig (eds), *VALIE EXPORT. Zeit und Gegenzeit/Time and Countertime*, Exh. Cat. Belvedere Wien and Lentos Kunstmuseum Linz (Cologne: Walther König, 2010), 147. An even rarer standing interior pose can be found in *REAL SEX*, Exh. Cat. Salzburger Kunstverein (Klagenfurt: Verlag Ritter, 1993), 80.

22 The outdoor photos were taken in the secluded courtyard of a house in the 22nd district of Vienna that *had* been used for film screenings by the previous owner. Hassmann used a Pentax 35mm camera, accounting for the grain when blown up to poster size. Peter Hassmann, interview by author, Vienna, 13 August 2007.

23 'VALIE EXPORT interviewed by Ruth Askey in Vienna 9/18/79', *High Performance Magazine* (Spring 1981), 80. On the journal, which in its 1978 issue prominently featured Viennese Actionist Hermann Nitsch, see Jenni Sorkin, 'Envisioning High Performance', *Art Journal*, 62:2 (Summer 2003), 36–51.

24 Kristine Stiles, 'Corpora Vilia. VALIE EXPORT's Body', in *VALIE EXPORT. Ob/De+Con(Struction)* (Philadelphia: Moore College of Art and Design, 1999), note 7, and VALIE EXPORT, interview by author. EXPORT described the theatre as an art cinema. This is consistent with the account in Abramović's Guggenheim catalogue, taken from an interview with EXPORT by Nancy Spector (October 2005): 'the performance took place in an art cinema in Munich, where I was invited with

other filmmakers to show my films'. Marina Abramović, *Seven Easy Pieces* (Milano: Edizione Charta, 2007), 118.

25 VALIE EXPORT, interview by author, New York, 19 February 2007.

26 While Hassmann did not remember the details, Hermann Hendrich, photographer of EXPORT's *Body Configuration* series as well as producer of some of her films, recalled that the gun was acquired from Udo Proksch, businessman and weapon collector, who was later convicted of murder in the course of one of the greatest insurance frauds in Austria's history, the shipwreck of the *Lucona* in 1977. Hermann Hendrich, interview by author, audio file, Vienna, 29 January 2008.

27 VALIE EXPORT, interview by author, Vienna, 29 January 2008.

28 Sorkin, 'Envisioning *High Performance*', 38. The open submission policy, due to founder Linda Frye Burnham, set aside a section, 'The Artist's Chronicle', which ran until winter 1983, when it was dropped in favour of a reviews section.

29 This doesn't mean that EXPORT brought a past event into being: merely that, in describing an event which may not have occurred, she instantiated the (non-occurring) event in her discussion.

30 J.L. Austin, *How to Do Things with Words* [1955, first printed 1962], 2nd edn (Cambridge, Mass.: Harvard University Press, 1975) Lecture XI, and 'Performative-Constative', trans. Geoffrey Warnock, in Charles E. Caton (ed.), *Philosophy and Ordinary Language* (Urbana: University of Illinois Press, 1963), 22–53.

31 Austin calls these 'explicit performatives'. *How to Do Things with Words*, Lecture VI. See also John R. Searle, 'How Performatives Work', *Linguistics and Philosophy*, 12:5 (October 1989), 535–58.

32 Stanley Milgram, 'Behavioral Study of Obedience', *Journal of Abnormal and Social Psychology*, 67:4 (October 1963), 371–8. The experiment is well known, so I simply summarize: subjects were told by an experimenter to give electric shocks to their partners (really actors) if these failed to repeat a word pair. The voltage of the shocks increased in intervals. The participants knew at which point the shock would be painful or even deadly; more than 60 per cent could be coerced into giving supposedly fatal shocks. Subjects were more willing to shock when assured that the responsibility rested with the experimenter. The Milgram experiment has, as one might expect, been re-performed by a contemporary artist, Rod Dickinson, in Glasgow in 2002. See Steve Rushton, *The Milgram Re-Enactment* (Maastricht: Eyck Academie, 2004).

33 Stanley Milgram, *Obedience to Authority: An Experimental View* (New York: Harper and Row, 1974), Preface, 8–11, and passim. Austin refers to the classes on legal philosophy that he taught with H.L.A. Hart, and the legal statements they examined. See Austin, 'A Plea for Excuses', *Philosophical Papers* (Oxford: Oxford University Press, 1979), 195–7.

34 A characteristic Austinian example of how fact shades into interpretation is 'France is hexagonal' (Austin, *How to Do Things with Words*, 143).

35 Lying is a perlocutionary act in Austin, as it gets the hearer to do something (believe a falsehood), rather than establishing the truth of its own descriptive contents in the manner of real performatives like the vow.

36 Austin distinguishes between 'happy' and 'unhappy', because, as he explains, much can go wrong in a speech-act. An unhappy performative may be one of various

kinds of failures, not all of which result in the act not having taken place. A vivid example of a ritual that fails for no clear reason (or for many) is the attempt to baptize penguins, which Austin takes from Anatole France. See Austin, 'Performative-Constative', 23. On the 'total speech act' and its context, see *How to Do Things with Words*, 52.

37 Erwin Panotsky, 'Jan van Eyck's Arnolfini Portrait', *Burlington Magazine* 64 (1934): 117–27, Linda Seidel, '"Jan van Eyck's Arnolfini Portrait": Business as Usual?' *Critical Inquiry*, 16:1 (Autumn, 1989), 54–86.

38 Lorne Campbell, *Fifteenth-Century Netherlandish Paintings* (London: National Gallery, 1998), 174–211.

39 Margaret L. Koster, 'The Arnolfini Double Portrait: A Simple Solution', *Apollo*, 158:499 (September 2003), 3–14. Aside from the factual dispute, the spectator-oriented nature of the painting's symbolism is well brought out in John Ward, 'Disguised Symbolism as Enactive Symbolism in Van Eyck's Paintings', *Artibus et Historiae*, 15:29 (1994), 9–53. Horst Bredekamp's 2007 Adorno Lectures, *Theorie des Bildakts* (Frankfurt am Main: Suhrkamp, 2010), despite similar terminology, do not in fact deal with pictures as speech-acts, but with imaginative acts undertaken by spectators faced with pictures presenting an 'I-form', for instance, portraits in which the sitter seems to address the spectator.

40 One could approach the performativity of images from an angle more congenial to poststructuralists by noting the pictorial quality of written language: a printed receipt records a sale and sets up obligations (for the buyer to pay, for the seller to hand over goods). Yet it persists and is not a 'one-time act', though it commemorates one. On Austin's own, interesting theory of contracts and other documents, see Chapters 2 and 4. Liz Kotz, *Words to be Looked At: Language in 60s Art* (Cambridge, Mass.: MIT Press, 2010), chapters 5 and 6, shows how conceptual art's interest in the pictorial aspect of writing informed a 'performative and operational' mode (150) in the writings and actions of Lawrence Wiener, Bruce Nauman, and others.

41 Cf. Jane Blocker, *What the Body Cost: Desire, History, and Performance* (Minneapolis: University of Minnesota Press, 2004), 80, on the 'audience of readers' who imaginatively takes up performance.

42 See Erving Goffman, *The Presentation of Everyday Life* (New York: Anchor, 1959), and Judith Butler, 'Performative Acts and Gender Constitution: An Essay in Phenomenology and Feminist Theory', *Theatre Journal* 49:1 (December 1988), 519–31, which does not yet mention Austin, Derrida, or the performative, but quotes Goffman approvingly. Carl Ginet may have in fact coined the noun form in his 'Performativity', *Linguistics and Philosophy*, 3 (1979), 245–65. Butler's books *Bodies That Matter: On the Discursive Limits of 'Sex'* (New York: Routledge, 1993) and *Excitable Speech: a Politics of the Performative* (New York: Routledge, 1997) deal more explicitly with performatives. For a good overview, see the introduction to Sybille Krämer (ed.), *Performativität und Medialität*, (Munich: Wilhelm Fink, 2004).

43 Dorothea von Hantelmann's approach is concisely set out in 'Performativity', in Brigitte Franzen, Kasper König and Carina Plath (eds), *Sculpture Projects Muenster 07* (Cologne: Walther König, 2007), 415, and in detail in her *How to Do Things with Art*.

44 See the detailed criticisms in Sven Lütticken, 'Progressive Striptease', in Amelia Jones and Adrian Heathfield (eds), *Perform Repeat Record: Live Art in History* (Bristol: Intellect, 2012), 187–98.

45 Auslander, 'The Performativity of Performance Documentation', 5. Auslander makes it clear that he is discussing performance *qua art*, and does not object to ethnologists being more interested in live events.

46 In a 2010 lecture at the Academy of Fine Arts, Vienna, Auslander admitted that the initial act should not be completely ignored. Citing Gadamer's hermeneutics, he explained that an artwork is always seen from a contemporary context with its own 'truth', so that we cannot assume a permanent 'truth' established at the time of its making. As earlier, Auslander compared performances to recorded music. A heated discussion between Auslander and the curator for performance art at the Museum of Modern Art Vienna, Eva Badura-Triska, followed, in which she insisted that the different levels of documentation (snapshots, staging, action for the camera) were essential for interpretation. Conference discussion at *This Sentence is Now Being Performed*, Akademie der bildenden Künste Wien, 9 November, 2010. A publication edited by Carola Dertnig and Felicitas Thun-Hohenstein is in preparation.

47 'For a context to be exhaustively determinable, in the sense demanded by Austin, it at least would be necessary for the conscious intention to be totally present and actually transparent for itself and others, since it is a determining focal point of the context'. Jacques Derrida, 'Signature, Event, Context', in *Margins of Philosophy*, translated by Alan Bass (Chicago: University of Chicago Press, 1982), 327. This conclusion has been criticized often, and Austin would have distrusted it: 'we should not despair too easily and talk, as people are apt to do, about the *infinite* uses of language. Philosophers will do this when they have listed as many as, let us say, seventeen; but even if there were something like ten thousand uses of language, surely we could list them all in time' (Austin, *Philosophical Papers*, 234). Austin denied the need for 'inner performances'. See *How to Do Things with Words*, chapter 1, and the discussion following the lecture 'Performative-Constative'.

48 'An exceedingly important aid is the circumstances of the utterance. Thus we might say "coming from *him*, I took it as an order, not as a request."' Austin does – here I agree with Derrida – assume this too easily: 'But in a way these resources are over-rich: they lend themselves to equivocation and inadequate discrimination; and moreover, we use them for other purposes, e.g. insinuation. The explicit performative rules out equivocation and keeps the performative fixed, relatively' (Austin, *How to Do Things with Words*, 76 [his italics]). But Austin is surely right that the performative can work even in unstable situations.

49 On live and later audiences, see Mechtild Widrich, 'The Informative Public of Performance: A Study of Viennese Actionism, 1965–1970', in *TDR. The Drama Review*, 217 (February 2013), 137-51.

50 Amelia Jones, '"Presence" in Absentia', 13; with 'play within the arena of the symbolic', Jones cites Kathy O'Dell, *Toward a Theory of Performance Art: An Investigation of its Sites* (PhD dissertation, City University of New York, 1992), 43–4. O'Dell draws on a Freudian and Lacanian model of subjectivity to illuminate the social bond between performer and spectator. See also Jane Blocker, *What the Body Cost*, and Amelia Jones, '"The Artist is Present". Artistic Re-enactments and

the Impossibility of Presence'. *TDR. The Drama Review*, 209 (Spring 2011), 16–45, here 18. In this recent reflection on the nature of performance, Jones argues against any ascription of presence on the basis of her own disenchanted experience of Abramović's 2010 *The Artist is Present*: In an email exchange, Jones clarified her objections to presence as 'self-justification on the part of artists', the 'mystifying language by critics, curators, and art historians who want an easy way to justify-ing the exhibition of "live" art in museums', as part of the 'gloss[ing] over all of the social, political, and economic specificities of the situation (of the "original" performances, as well as of the apparatuses of critical discourse and display)'. Email to the author, 23 March 2011.

51 Amelia Jones, *Body Art: Performing the Subject*, 6.

52 One could of course argue that EXPORT, unable to use the gun in the cinema, or take photographs in that darkened space, produced photographic and verbal supplements of how she imagined her own piece to function under ideal circum-stances. If so, the question remains why she did not recreate the setting, or at least the cinema.

53 VALIE EXPORT, interview by author. The Museum of Modern Art acquired some of the silk screen posters in 2011. On its website, it repeats the myth about an actual performance (now absurdly dated 1968), mixing the story of the art cinema with the claim that the audience was mostly male (probably a reference to the porn cinema version), but at least making clear that the photograph was taken later: www.moma.org/audio_file/audio_file/2108/381.mp3 (accessed 14 December 2011).

54 *Gewalt/Geschäfte Eine Ausstellung zum Topos Gewalt in der künstlerischen Ausein-andersetzung*, Exh. Cat. (Berlin: Neue Gesellschaft für Bildende Kunst, 1994).

55 This trend is finely exemplified in Jens Hoffmann and Joan Jonas (eds), *Art Works Perform* (New York: Thames and Hudson, 2005), and the exhibition Camera/Action: Performance and Photography at the Museum of Contemporary Photog-raphy, Chicago, 2004. On EXPORT as a performer of technological media, see Mechtild Widrich, 'Location and Dislocation. VALIE EXPORT's Media Perfor-mances', *Performing Arts Journal*, 99 (September 2011), 53–9.

56 Cf. Auslander: 'Although I have stated that the relationship between the live and the mediated is one of competitive opposition at the level of cultural economy, I do not see that opposition as deriving from the intrinsic characteristics of live and mediatised forms but, rather, as determined by cultural and historical contingen-cies', *Liveness*, 11.

57 '"Presence" in Absentia', 16. Jones has just praised Rosalind Krauss for noticing (in her 'Notes on the Index') 'the philosophical reciprocity of photography and performance, situating the two as different kinds of reciprocity'. Jones adds the Derridean insight that the index in both cases is 'supplementary', a necessary but fallible stabilization of contingent signs. The concluding passage I quoted in the body text is, perhaps appropriately for this 'supplementarity' reading, enclosed in parentheses.

58 See Charles Sanders Peirce, *Collected Papers*, vol. 2, ed. Charles Hartshorne and Paul Weiss (Cambridge, Mass.: Harvard University Press, 1960), 147–9 and 304. I myself speak of the *Genital Panic* photograph as 'a metaphorical version of an indexical sign' in my 'Can Photographs Make It So?' in Amelia Jones and Adrian

Heathfield (eds), *Perform Repeat Record: Live Art in History* (Bristol: Intellect, 2012), 89–103, here 98. I regard that text as correct but verbally confusing.

59 Jones, "'Presence" in Absentia', 16. Kristine Stiles' relevant publications, both of which appeared in 1990, are 'Performance and Its Objects', *Arts Magazine*, 65:3 (November 1990), 35–47, and 'Notes on Rudolf Schwarzkogler's Images of Healing', *White Walls: A Magazine of Writings by Artists* 25 (Spring 1990), 13–26, the latter reprinted in *Rudolf Schwarzkogler*, Exh. Cat. (Vancouver: University of British Columbia, 1993), 29–39.

60 Stiles traces the myth to Robert Hughes, 'The Decline and Fall of the Avant-Garde', *Time* (18 December 1972), 111. On the occasion of a 1996 Schwarzkogler exhibition at the Hirschhorn, Hughes replied that his myth 'was in circulation before I got to it', adding: 'Unfortunately, there's no way to put the toothpaste back into the tube.' Murray White, 'Schwarzkogler's Ear', *The New Yorker* (11 November 1996), 36.

61 Henry M. Sayre, *The Object of Performance: The American Avant-Garde since 1970* (Chicago: University of Chicago Press, 1989), 2. The further reference to Schwarzkogler's 'amputation piece' (15) makes it clear that Sayre encountered the work in the context of Harald Szeeman's *documenta 5* (1972). Sayre does not cite Hughes, but his 'piece by piece amputation' does sound like Hughes's 'inch by inch'.

62 See Hubert Klocker, *Der zertrümmerte Spiegel: Wien, 1960–1971* (Klagenfurt: Ritter, 1989), 92, which gives the date for the series as 1964–65 and in addition claims that photographs were taken by Heinz Cibulka's wife. In Hubert Klocker and Eva Badura-Triska (eds), *Rudolf Schwarzkogler: Leben und Werk* (Klagenfurt: Ritter, 1992), 186, 194, photographs of the summer 1965 actions are credited to Ludwig Hoffenreich. Kristine Stiles, 'Performance', in Robert S. Nelson and Richard Schiff (eds), *Critical Terms for Art History* (Chicago: University of Chicago Press, 2003), 87, exaggerates in claiming that 'Höffenreich's [*sic*] black-and-white photographs of Cibulka performing in Schwarzkogler's sets duped critics and historians alike'. The myth, whether originating with Hughes or more likely *documenta 5*, is not to be found in Austrian books on Actionism, and would not survive a glance at Heinz Cibulka's own book, *Mein körper bei aktionen von Nitsch und Schwarzkogler. 1965–1975* (Napoli: Edizioni Morra, 1977).

63 Stiles, 'Performance and its Objects', 37. The passage is quoted in Jones, "'Presence" in Absentia', 16.

64 In the Guggenheim catalogue, both Sandra Umathum and Erika Fischer-Lichte note how the re-enactment followed the photograph (which appeared after the event). Umathum perceptively denies that the image literally documents the live act (50), whose occurrence she does not question. Sandra Umathum, 'Beyond Documentation, or the Adventure of Shared Time and Place. Experiences of a Viewer', 47–55, in Marina Abramović, *Seven Easy Pieces* (Milan: Charta, 2007) and Erika Fischer-Lichte, 'Performance Art – Experiencing Liminality', in Abramović, *Seven Easy Pieces*, 33–45. Fischer-Lichte insists on the 'co-presence' of performer and audience as central to performance (41). She goes further in *Archaeologies of Presence*, 103–18, where, beside 'a weak and a strong' conception of presence she defines a 'radical' one, to be spelled 'PRESENCE': this consists in the revelation of the performer as another embodied mind beside our own. This discovery is an everyday one (116), which connects great performance to daily life.

65 Jessica Santone describes the alterations of Nauman's *Body Pressure* and of *Genital Panic* nicely as 'recreating authentic experience from the sum of fragments'. Santone, 'Marina Abramović: Seven Easy Pieces. Critical Documentation Strategies for Art's Histories', *Leonardo*, 41 (February 2008), 145–52, this quote 150. One wishes to know what 'authentic' means here: surely aesthetically valid, rather than historical.

66 Marina Abramović, Q&A Session at the conference *Feminist Future* at the Museum of Modern Art (New York, 26 January 2007). Audio file archived online at www.wps1.org/include/shows/moma.html (accessed 1 April 2007).

67 Schneider, *Performing Remains*, 4–6, criticizes Abramović's 'linear' historiography, offering instead a temporal 'cross-hatch' of memories and associations. It seems to me that both approaches are justified.

68 Email from VALIE EXPORT to Nancy Spector, 3 January 2005. The Solomon R. Guggenheim Museum Archive, New York. In 2007, EXPORT re-performed *Up+Down+On+Off* (1968) in expanded form at the Austrian Cultural Forum, New York.

69 Abramović in dialogue with Amelia Jones, 'The Live Artist as Archaeologist (New York, August 5, 2007)', in Amelia Jones and Adrian Heathfield, eds., *Perform, Repeat, Record: A Critical Anthology of Live Art in History* (Bristol: Intellect, 2012), 550. Note the inconsistencies that abound in the recent statements: Vienna vs. Munich, EXPORT's studio vs. the photographer's, art vs. pornographic cinema.

70 Abramović, *Seven Easy Pieces*, 118, and www.guggenheim.org/exhibitions/Abramović/ (accessed 23 July 2008). The ostensible date of the performance is unclear. The Guggenheim and other recent sources date the action 22 April 1969. EXPORT performed *Touch Cinema* as well as *Publikumsauspeitschung* (together with Peter Weibel) in Munich on 15 April 1969 – not for the first time – which is well-documented, e.g. in 'Exhibitionisten an die Front', *Der Spiegel* (21 April 1969), 194, and Wolfgang Kudrnofsky, 'Dem Publikum die Peitsche', *action. Filmzeitschrift*, 5 (Mai–June 1969), 21. She performed *Touch Cinema* again in Zurich on 18 and 25 April (Archive of the Generali Foundation, Vienna), making an appearance in Munich on 22 April just possible but unlikely. The Guggenheim catalogue gives the theatre as Augusta Lichtspiele (118). But the 2010 retrospective of VALIE EXPORT's work in Vienna vaguely listed a Stadtkino in its wall text. The catalogue, and, as of November 2011, EXPORT's website, do not mention *Genital Panic* under 'Aktionen/Performances', but only as a photograph titled *Aktionshose Genitalpanik*: www.valiexport.at (accessed 10 November 2011).

71 *Easy Pieces*, like Études is a generic title for elementary musical compositions, e.g., by Ferdinando Carulli, Niccolo Paganini, and Ernst Krenek. They are often used to instruct beginners, so Abramović might be alluding ironically to herself as both beginner and instructor. Abramović also lists Richard P. Feynman, *Six Not So Easy Pieces: Relativity, Symmetry and Space-Time*, 1997, based on the physicist's lectures at Caltech in the 1960s, as influential for her work, in a questionnaire that appeared in *Frieze* 100, reprinted in Lioba Reddeker (ed.), *ACA Art Critics Award. Lesebuch* (Vienna: basis wien, 2007). Note the 'not' in Feynman's title. Bob Rafelson's film *Five Easy Pieces* from 1970 might be another reference.

72 The M16 has been the US infantry rifle since the 1960s and featured prominently

in the Vietnam War. Abramović simply requested a 'machine gun' as prop without specifications. Exhibition file *Seven Easy Pieces*, The Solomon R. Guggenheim Museum Archive, New York.

73 See Marina Warner, *Monuments and Maidens* (New York: Atheneum, 1985).

74 An interview or, rather, transcript of a conversation with the anonymous man is printed in the *Seven Easy Pieces* catalogue, 153–5. He claims self-indulgently that he wanted to show Abramović his genitals in a 'non-violent' manner, interpreting the empty chair as invitation to sit and expose himself.

75 In addition, Abramović decided to show the video documentation (done with a static camera) of the previous evening on screens in the vicinity of her performance. The audience was thus confronted with presence turning into mediation over the course of a day. Experimental filmmaker Babette Mangolte produced a 90-minute film of the whole event (USA, 2006). Erika Fischer-Lichte discusses a similar 'misunderstanding' on behalf of Peter Handke's theatre piece *Publikumsbeschimpfung*, a dialogue with the audience. When it was first performed in 1966 in Frankfurt, individual audience members climbed the stage and were pushed back by the actors. Eventually, director Claus Peymann interrupted the performance, because the audience did not 'interact' through language as expected. Erika Fischer-Lichte, *Ästhetik des Performativen* (Frankfurt am Main: Suhrkamp, 2004), 27–8, translated by Saskya Iris Jain as *The Transformative Power of Performance: A New Aesthetics* (New York: Routledge, 2008), 20–2.

76 Cf. Roland Barthes: 'Earlier societies managed so that memory, the substitute for life, was eternal, and that at least the thing which spoke Death should itself be immortal: this was the Monument. But by making the (mortal) Photograph into the general and somehow natural witness of "what has been", modern society has renounced the Monument. A paradox: the same century invented History and Photography.' *Camera Lucida. Reflections on Photography* (New York: Hill and Wang, 1981), 93. The ephemerality of the photograph is not absolute: in a competent archive it can survive much like any other physical monument.

77 Acconci's *Seedbed* is the only performance shortened in the *Seven Easy Pieces*. The original supposedly stretched over two weeks, taking place '2 times a week. 6 hours each day'. Abramović, *Seven Easy Pieces*, 70.

78 *Lips of Thomas* had already also been incorporated into Abramović's *The Biography* (1992), while the iconography of the communist star already features in earlier performances such as *Rhythm 5* (Belgrade, 1974). At the Guggenheim, the Russian song 'Slavic Souls' was played, and the text was made available to the audience. It is reprinted in Abramović, *Seven Easy Pieces*, 202. Despite this, little of the 1975 context was presented: the fact that Thomas Lips was a person, for instance. See Chapter 3.

79 'The last piece was different, because it was an installation, and I liked the demystification that at midnight I could disappear through the dress and change, and then come out … because when you do performances, you are the object and subject of the work … it was important that kind of ending, it was detached'. Abramović in a discussion with Nancy Spector, 18 November 2005, at the Guggenheim Museum. Video document, The Solomon R. Guggenheim Museum Archive, New York.

80 Ibid.

81 Daniel Boorstin, *The Image. A Guide to Pseudo-Events in America* [1961] (New York, Harper & Row, 1964). Baudrillard sees his difference from Debord (and implicitly Boorstin) in his discarding of any concept of the unmediated.

82 Marina Abramović, 'Reeneactment. An Introduction by Marina Abramović', in *Seven Easy Pieces*, 10.

83 Even more openly combining the conflicting ideas of historical truth and interpretation, Abramović described her idea of re-enacting performances from the 1960s and 1970s in an interview almost ten years earlier: 'There's the structure of the performance that you can see, and then you can make your own interpretation and have your own experience. You absolutely have to respect the originality of the piece and ask the living artist for the permission. You can do whatever you want after that.' Janet Kaplan, 'Deeper and Deeper: Interview with Marina Abramović', *Art Journal*, 58:2 (Summer 1999), 14. Abramović must be credited with raising the question of intellectual property in performance art; lately she has been criticized for insisting on it.

84 '… anstelle einer vorführung sollte ich mich mit entblösster fut (an der hose ausgeschnitten) durch die zuschauerreihen drängen, ergo fut und nase in gleicher höhe, indirekter sexueller kontakt mit dem publikum. valie export.' [Instead of a screening I should push through the rows of the audience with exposed cunt (cut out of the pants), ergo cunt and nose on the same level; indirect sexual encounter with the audience. valie export.] Text printed in Weibel and EXPORT, *Bildkompendium*, 290. The project is dated 1969. But identified as 'planned' (*geplant*) rather than executed.

85 See Cat. *VALIE EXPORT, Time and Countertime*, 147, and the list of exhibited works, 296. See also the cover of the Christie's auction catalogue *Post-war and Contemporary Art* (London, 7 April 2013; England: Christies, Manson & Woods Ltd., 2013). One almost wonders whether the canvas is an ironic reference to the cinema screen (also *Leinwand* in German). The retrospective was shown simultaneously in two locations, as if to emphasize EXPORT's mediation: the Austrian Gallery Belvedere in Vienna and the Lentos Museum Linz. It travelled to the Museion in Bolzano. The live performance of *Genital Panic* in a cinema has not been questioned in the literature: Mueller, *VALIE EXPORT. Fragments*, 18, describes the performance briefly in the context of 'sexual liberation', without mentioning the gun. The porn cinema is revived by Doris Guth, 'Aktionshose Genitalpanik von VALIE EXPORT', in Carola Dertnig and Stefanie Seibold (eds), *Let's Twist Again: Performance in Wien von 1960 bis heute* (Gumpoldskirchen: DEA, 2006), 72–75. Bojana Pejić points towards the staged nature of the photographs in calling the photograph an 'artist poster'. Yet her otherwise excellent text does not question the public event, concluding that EXPORT sought agonistic confrontation in the sense of Chantal Mouffe and Rosalyn Deutsche. Bojana Pejić, 'On Pants, Panics and Origins', in Hedwig Saxenhuber (ed.), *VALIE EXPORT*. Exh. Cat. National Centre for Contemporary Art and Ekaterina Foundation, Moskow (Vienna/Bolzano: Folio, 2007), 54–63.

86 Hans Blumenberg, *Arbeit am Mythos (Work on Myth)* (Frankfurt am Main: Suhrkamp, 1979).

87 Jan Assmann, *Moses the Egyptian: The Memory of Egypt in Western Monotheism*

(Cambridge, Mass.: Harvard University Press, 1999), 10. Aleida Assmann, whose work will be highly relevant for the German context in Chapter 4, has recently rethought memory on a global scale. Aleida Assman and Sebastian Conrad (eds), *Memory in a Global Age. Discourses, Practices and Trajectories* (Houndmills, UK/ New York: Palgrave Macmillan, 2010). The texts were first presented at a conference in Vienna in 2008.

88 Jan Assmann, 'Collective Memory and Cultural Identity' [1988], *New German Critique*, 65, (Spring/Summer 1995); Jan Assmann and Tonio Hölscher (eds), *Kultur und Gedächtnis* (Frankfurt am Main: Suhrkamp, 1988), and 'Mnemohistory and the Construction of Egypt', in *Moses the Egyptian*, chapter 1.

89 This also means that memory is not simply an individual affair, but, as Maurice Halbwachs insisted, is exercised in a social framework. While in Halbwachs's view an individual is strongly dependent on society for whatever memories she can retrieve, we must also consider the reverse case, where an individual's contribution (through public symbolic acts) leads to changes in society's relations to its past.

90 Lütticken, 'An arena', 23f, cautions that re-performance may collapse into Guy Debord's 'spectacle'. Yet his conclusion is cautiously positive: 'Art can examine and try out – under laboratory conditions, as it were – forms of repetition that break open history and the historicist returns of past periods ... Operating within contemporary performative spectacle, if from a marginal position, art can stage small but significant acts of difference' (60).

91 Michel Foucault, *The Archaeology of Knowledge* [*L'Archéologie du savoir*, 1969], (New York: Pantheon Books, 1972), 7 (emphasis in the original).

92 Though Foucault does not mention Collingwood by name, his theory of history as re-enactment of past thoughts might fairly be counted as a target for his criticism. Foucault was aware of speech-act theory, as indicated by a reference to John Searle in 'What is an Author?' (1969). See Michel Foucault, *Language, Counter-Memory, Practice*, ed. Donald F. Bouchard (Ithaca: Cornell University Press, 1977), 121. The essay is under the heading 'Counter-Memory', a fascinating category that Foucault unfortunately does not explain. He defines it only negatively, in 'Nietzsche, Genealogy, History', as 'a use of history that severs its connection to memory, its metaphysical and anthropological model ...' (160).

Viennese actionism, reframed

The performance photograph, I have claimed, is a historicizing tool: neither the commodification nor the legitimation of the fugitive act, it is a window on the *past* of performance, indispensable to the contemporary practice of restaging classic events. I will show that the window has been open since the 1960s heyday of performance, when it revealed not the self-reflexive history of performance, but a performance of history, of past socio-political dimensions of its environment. This persistence of the past is explored within the peculiarly charged atmosphere of Cold War Vienna, as seen through the subtle but explosive performances of VALIE EXPORT. In her work, the document as interface between an imagined 'past present' and a later encounter might be understood as a screen used to mediate history to the future.[1] Neither simply allowing us to look at the past nor altogether mirroring our own imagination of it, there is an ambivalence in what is offered by the performance photograph that makes it politically significant; and, as EXPORT's more recent work demonstrates, these ambivalences offer extensions beyond performance and photography to architecture and monuments in public space. In the process, I will link some iconic feminist actions, among them *Touch Cinema* (*Tapp- und Tastkino*, 1968) and the chameleon-like *Body Configurations* (*Körperkonfigurationen*, 1972–82) to lesser-known performances and proposals, including EXPORT's submission to the competition for the Viennese Holocaust Memorial, won by Rachel Whiteread.

EXPORT, alias Waltraud Höllinger (née Lehner), studied textile design before entering the Viennese art scene in the mid-1960s. She adopted her artist name as a logo in capital letters in 1967, and posed for a photographic portrait with a pack of the Austrian cigarette brand Smart Export to formally 'legalize' her choice (Figure 10). In the late 1960s she developed a coherent oeuvre of film and performances collectively called 'Expanded Cinema', a concept worked out together with fellow artist Peter Weibel, reportedly upon reading an American film magazine in Sweden.[2] At this time, EXPORT adhered loosely to the Viennese Actionists, but in the 1970s, frictions with the

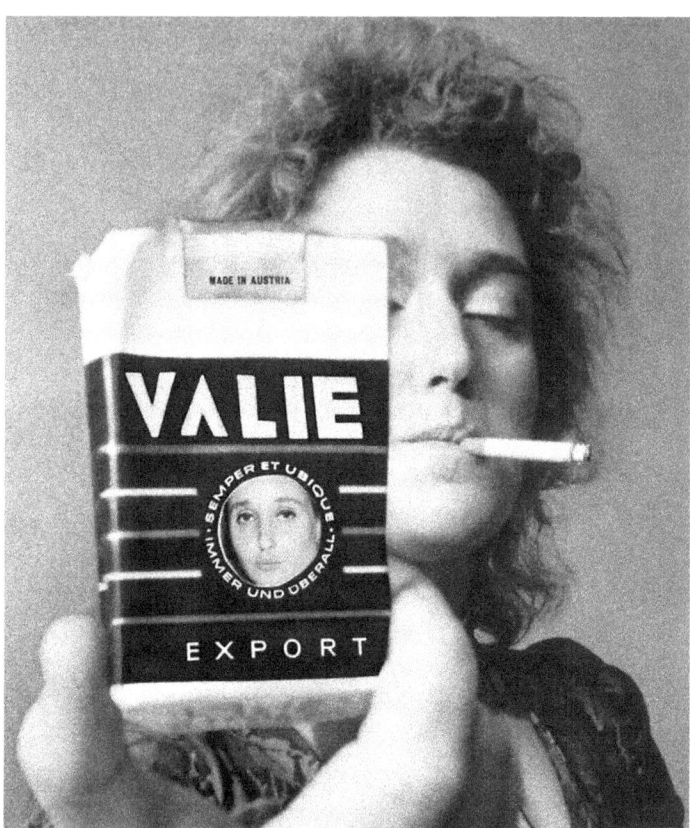

10   VALIE EXPORT, VALIE EXPORT – SMART EXPORT, 1970

group prompted EXPORT to work more or less apart in a mode she called feminist actionism (*Feministischer Aktionismus*), distinguishing herself from the machismo of the core group.[3]

There is, however, one important connection between EXPORT and the Actionists: the *Bildkompendium Wiener Aktionismus und Film* (1970), informally known as the 'Vienna Book' (*Wienbuch*), which contains the first description of *Genital Panic*. As the cover announces, Weibel edited the book 'with the collaboration' of EXPORT: then as now code for the underrated work of the female co-editor. It was the first anthology and, in a sense, the baptismal certificate of the Viennese Actionists, a term Weibel and EXPORT defined broadly to include themselves, the older concrete poets, collage-makers, and experimental cabaret performers of the Vienna Group (*Wiener Gruppe*), organicist architect Friedensreich Hundertwasser, and action painter Arnulf Rainer, alongside the four main protagonists of Actionist performance: Günter Brus, Otto Muehl, Rudolf Schwarzkogler, and Hermann

Nitsch. The *Bildkompendium* allows us to broach the difficult question of how the most radical and physically insistent of 1960s action could be conveyed in documents, a thick book in this case. The Actionists' practice involved the use of blood, excrement and other bodily fluids, self-mutilation, sex, orgiastic ritual, and the slaughter of animals – obvious challenges for any editor.[4]

Practically, the *Bildkompendium* was a scandal due to the explicitly sexual content of several images, which led to legal action against Weibel and EXPORT, but it succeeded in setting up an authoritative historical framework for Actionism, which it endowed with the canonical *-ism* of its title.[5] The text glorifies the Actionists as revolutionary outcasts rattling an ossified society, but the book's aesthetic is ambiguous: it seems to stake out a position between guerilla immediacy and cool conceptual art. More than two-thirds of the book (pages 1–239) consist of images practically without text; only a few manifestos and newspaper clippings are interspersed. The photographs themselves bear no captions, nor are authors given for the respective pieces or events. The last third of the book contains texts on individual artists, groups, and events, and image captions printed in the courier font typical of minimalism, punching out a belligerent rhetoric.[6] Thus dispensing with a running commentary, the compendium sketches social and aesthetic context mostly through juxta-positions of images, particularly with the Fluxus-oriented happenings of the Vienna Group.[7] The actions of the core members are presented with an emphasis on the sexually explicit. Genitals of both sexes are inspected or interact in various ways, dead lambs are cut open, paint is poured.

There is certainly something striking in the book's design. How could or should a reading audience encounter Actionism in this compendium? That they could and did, for better or worse, is proved by the obscenity trial. Is the shock one of documented crimes, preserving their setting in a particular time and place? Or does the furore over the book confirm Philip Auslander's dictum about the hegemony of performance photography over performance? To really answer the question, we need to consider the concrete historical audience of Actionism, and its presumed displacement, both *in* the book itself and *by* the belated readers of the book. First, the pictured audience. According to Auslander's polemical formula, 'the presence of this initial audience has no real importance to the performance as an entity whose continued life is through its documentation ...'.[8] On first sight, a big book of photos appearing less than a decade after the first actions, and just months after the latest, might seem to confirm the irrelevance of live audiences. But apart from the need for caution in advancing claims about *all* perfor-mance, the initial audience is certainly pertinent in the *Bildkompendium*. In the photographic section, detailed performance content is juxtaposed time and again with audience reactions, indeed mostly with what I would call 'uninformed' audiences. By an uninformed audience I mean persons who constitute an audience simply by being in a given location at a given time, as opposed to the invited, aesthetically sophisticated audiences of New York performance (e.g. at the Judson Memorial Church) or even Actionist studio events.

Günter Brus's *Vienna Walk* (*Wiener Spaziergang*, 1965), as presented in the book, is a case in point (Figure 11). Dressed in formal attire and soaked in white paint, with a black stripe running down the vertical axis of his body, Brus planned to walk through the city centre posing as a 'living picture'. The *Vienna Walk* was his first performance in public space, after a series of actions in private and semi-private locations, notably the 'rat-infested' cellar in Vienna's twentieth district, near the Danube canal, that served as Otto Muehl's atelier (*Perinetkeller*). It was thus Brus's first chance to address an uninformed audience.[9] Of course there were complications. As a newspaper article on the occasion of the artist's seventieth birthday retells the event: 'after a few meters, he was stopped by the police and ordered to pay a fine'.[10] The extant documentation of the event shows that Brus in fact managed to walk through the Hofburg, the imperial palace of Vienna, and down several streets before a policeman attended to his doings, but the *Bildkompendium* represents the performance through two images (Figure 12): the policeman studying Brus's papers, while an onlooker's back frames the photograph to suggest public reaction, and Brus emerging from a nearby police station. No walk through the city, just the core of the performance as it became known: Brus, the hostile police, an uncomprehending public. As we learn from the newspaper article written forty years later, the performance is exclusively thought of in these terms. The *Bildkompendium* surely deserves some of the credit. A similar design is in force for the first collaborative action by Nitsch and Mühl, the 1963 *Festival of Psycho-Physical Naturalism* (Figure 13). This took place in the more intimate Perinetkeller, but also ended with a police intervention – perhaps caused by alarmed neighbours.[11] The anthology here aligns a photograph of the action (shot by photographer Ludwig Hoffenreich) with a crowd of 'ordinary' Austrians on the street – ostensibly watching the police intervention.[12] If this claim of Weibel and EXPORT's caption is accurate, this audience does not have any access to the action, but only to its dissolution by the authorities – if that. Uninformed, for us they play the role of an eminently *informative* public, one that we readers are able to connect with the close-ups of genitals and intestines on the facing page and, by imaginative extension, elsewhere in the book. As limited as the actual audience was for many of the group's actions, taking place as they did in apartments and cellars, there was a need to plan for broader coverage that went beyond the scandalized tabloid press. Here, the function of 'original' audiences firmly situated in the past is particularly important. Far from disappearing from view or being supplanted by new audiences of the documents, they grant later viewers access to the past performance as *event*, and they act as witnesses that something has taken place. In the special case of *Genital Panic*, the imagined event may have *only* been imagined; *Bildkompendium* images, by contrast, trade on their uninformed audiences to set the stage set for future imaginative engagement with performances whose public character is not in doubt.[13]

This relationship between an event and its future, and the means by which we are granted access to the past, is one of the most interesting questions for performances scholars who do not want to get caught in an either/or position between document and action. Rebecca Schneider has posited a link between performance – especially the genre of historical re-enactment – and archival thinking, arguing that 'we are reading the archive as an act'.[14] Schneider sees the 'remains' of a performance as its relation to history. This leads her to argue that we should read performance neither as ephemeral nor as document-based:

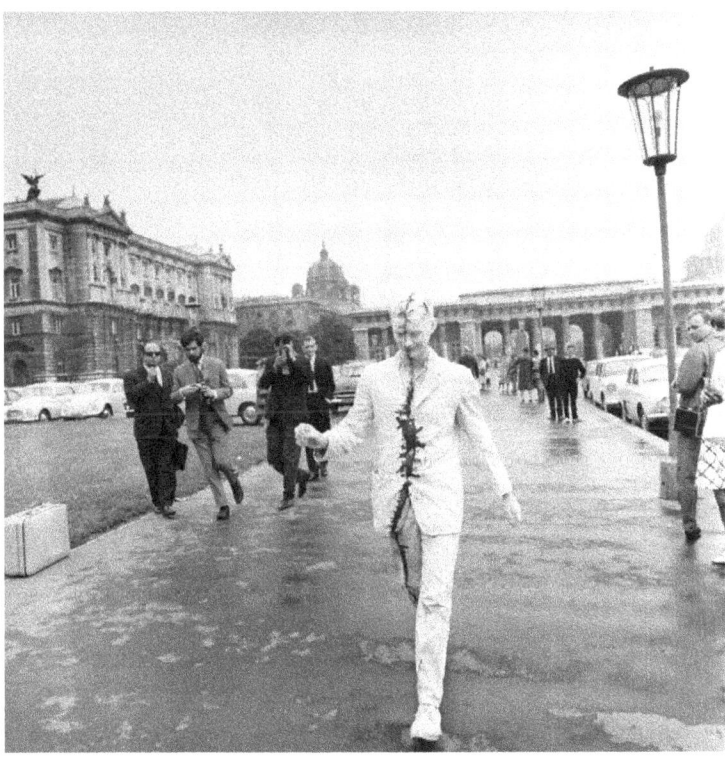

Günter Brus, *Vienna Walk*, 1965   **11**

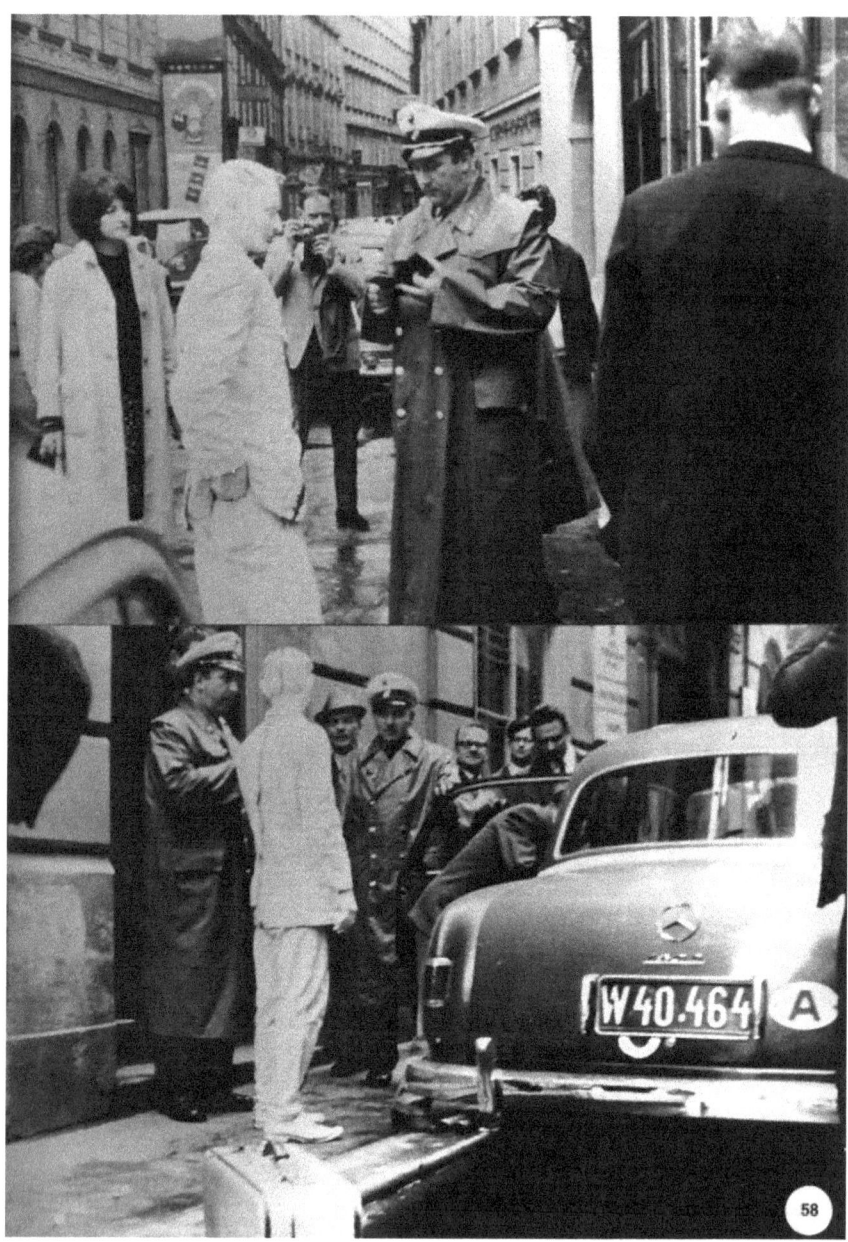

12   *Bildkompendium Wiener Aktionismus und Film*, Günter Brus, *Vienna Walk*, 1965

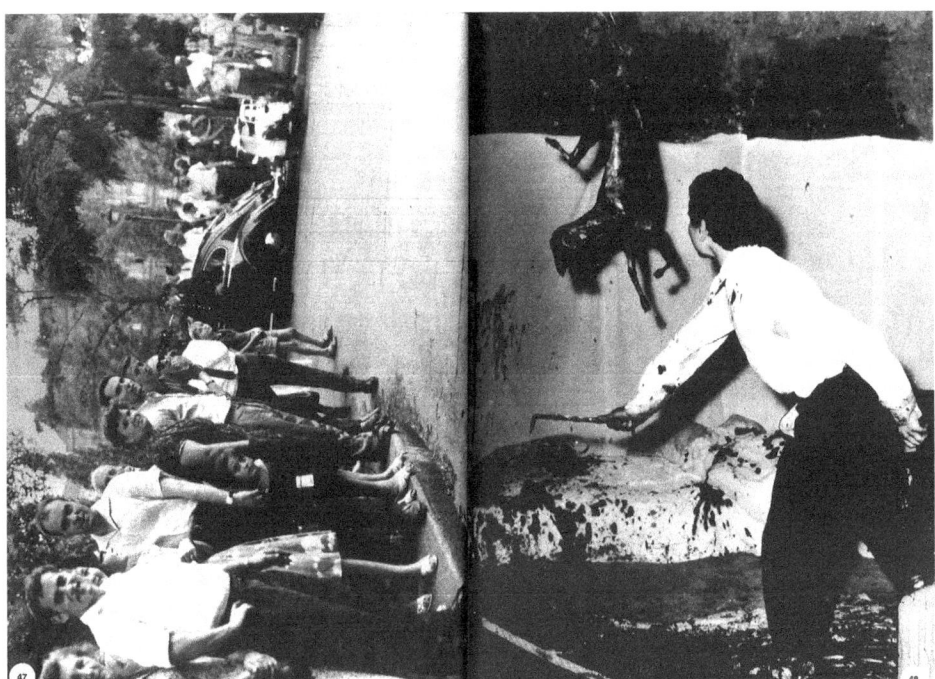

Bildkompendium Wiener Aktionismus und Film, onlookers during the *Festival of Psycho-Physical Naturalism*, 1963   **13**

not as that which disappears (as the archive expects), but as both the act of remaining and a means of re-appearance and 're-participation' (though not a metaphysics of presence) we are almost immediately forced to admit that remains do not have to be isolated to the document, to the object, to bone versus flesh.[15]

I agree that there is more to performance than photographs stored in an archive; and that flesh and bone are in no way opposed to film and celluloid. My aim here is adjacent to Schneider's: I am trying to articulate how archival objects were related to perishable acts *by artists*. To see what make these actions more than anarchic gestures of rebellion, gestures that *might* fail in a document, it is crucial to see how photography, and modes of performing for the camera, not only admit visual reportage of the event, but provoke us imaginatively to grant the images historical meaning, a meaning set to work in the present. In short, the photograph is an insight into what we interpret as the spatial, sensory, and political environment it is cut from. It is able to be this precisely because it is more than the inadequate documentation of an event without a past. The past audience is crucial in claiming an *imaginary presence* at the event – a mental act, to be sure, but in no way opposed to our sensual, corporeal, fleshly existence. Uninformed audiences are there, like the artist's later statements, not to prove but, rather, to assert reality. They cannot in most cases supply it: this is the gap in which we interact with documents.

For Weibel and EXPORT as the editors of the *Wienbuch*, the confrontation was a necessary addition to the action, and, indeed, for the history of Actionism it proved to be so. The positioning of Actionism as an art movement and as a political movement shifted focus to a larger set of circumstances. What emerged is a peculiar vision of Austro-Actionist history, with performances taken for politics, and speech-acts taken for their consequences. Images of crowds and police cordons, of actions and their punishment, reinforce above all a historical image of insurgence against a fascist police state.[16]

The mythic mediated afterlife of Actionism constructed in the *Bildkompendium* fell into place shortly after the group splintered. Nitsch relocated to Munich in 1967, Brus fled to Berlin to avoid imprisonment at the beginning of 1969, Schwarzkogler died on 20 June 1969, and Muehl, abandoning art for the sake of 'life' in 1972, went on to head two commune projects, and was convicted in 1991 and sentenced to seven years' prison for coercion and the sexual abuse of minors.[17] In light of the disintegration of the core group, the *Bildkompendium* patiently shaped the reception of Viennese Actionism as politically oppositional. While the Fluxus-oriented critic Adrian Henri, in his 1974 book on *Total Art*, wonders whether their work was 'an elaborate act of self-abasement for the sins of their fathers, or merely an echo of the hideous Nazi ethos', the 1990s bore witness to the precise opposite of such healthy scepticism.[18] At the height of the memory boom in contemporary art and public life, the Actionists could be revived as a radical yet cathartic working through of the past, a reaction not just to social conservatism but to the unwillingness of Austria's officials and population to take responsibility for their past.[19] The Actionists became rebels with a cause, a view that the *Bildkompendium* had pioneered, insofar as it concentrated on the opposition between the actions and Austrian society.[20] Certainly this redefinition was made possible by the simultaneous international success of abject art, which made the fragility of the human body once again a political cause, and the particular interest in German and Austrian post-war art as marked by the trauma of the Second World War; but it would have had no content were it not for critics and a larger audience raised on the *Bildkompendium* view of post-war Austrian (art) history.

Woman: an extension of man?

The Actionists, then, lived a second life, in some ways more eventful than their first, as documented performance, asking us to re-perform the seemingly cathartic act of commemorating historical events, even fascism. I would like to approach EXPORT and Weibel's collaborative projects, in which layers of mediation, literal and metaphorical (photography, critical commentary, and political slogans), themselves become the action, from this viewpoint. Formally, EXPORT and Weibel fused Actionism – their starting point – with a detached, conceptual approach that probed the historical formation of the self, which in EXPORT's case came to mean fundamentally a gendered body. Their experiments with reproductive media, notably film and photography, brought with them a concern with documentation, and also with the disparity between an action and its afterlife. This is obvious in a work maintaining links with Actionist shock tactics: *Aus der Mappe der Hundigkeit* (*From the Portfolio of Doggedness*) of 1969 is an act of *flânerie* comparable to the *Vienna Walk*, but orchestrates a feminist intervention in the 'order' of public space, a move not legible as pure action, but only in light of the complicated play of meaning possible in photographs.[21] The action consisted of EXPORT 'walking' Weibel through the centre of Vienna on a leash while Josef Tandl photographed them.[22] These images show EXPORT, genteel but feral in a fur coat, and Weibel, on all fours in suit and tie, first on a sidewalk and then crossing a crowded street. The title *Portfolio* emphasizes photographs over action, and in particular the critical task of selecting a sequence. In the *Bildkompendium*, the portfolio is shown as one full-size photograph and a set of contact sheets (Figure 14). The text, presumably by Weibel, reads:

> What comes so easily in a cartoon, drawing the alienation of humans in zoological forms – and then also breaks off, since it is just a drawing game – is poured into all channels of communication by this action film, which is why these threaten to go on strike, the real scene seems unreal … Portfolio of Doggedness constructs reality, it reconstructs it from the sewing kit of ideologies.[23]

Weibel and EXPORT shifted the Actionists' brooding if violent introspection to a public space threaded with convention, where it becomes an interest in the exoteric construction of the body according to norms of gender and species, enforced through bodily routines found in media channels and the 'sewing kit'. The *Portfolio* examines (by embodying) the trope of dominatrix with 'man on a leash'. Popular sadomasochism is one strand in this discourse (*Venus in Furs* and its avant-garde and pornographic reception), traditional misogyny another. EXPORT included Hans Baldung Grien's 1513 print of *Phyllis and Aristotle* (Figure 15), an exposé of overbearing wives, in a 1997 catalogue with contact sheets of *Mappe der Hundigkeit*.[24] It seems likely that EXPORT and Weibel had such images in mind, if not this print in particular, in staging their action: the legibility of the walk depends on familiarity with the schemata being challenged in a way that Actionist appropriations of Catholic ritual do not. Moreover, a blood-spattered Actionist crucifixion *looks* like shocking violence in any case, while the couple with the leash, dressed much like the

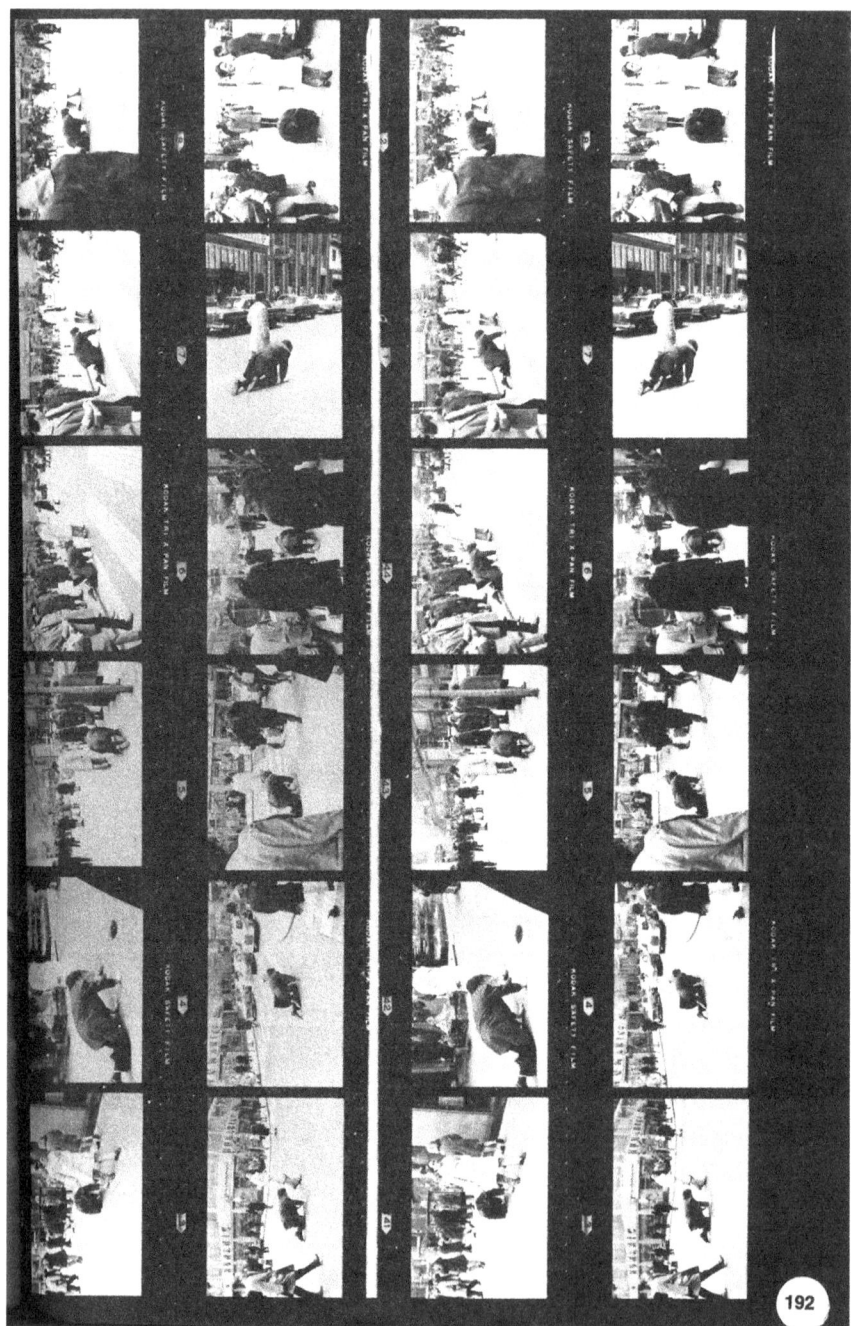

14 *Bildkompendium Wiener Aktionismus und Film*, VALIE EXPORT/Peter Weibel, *From the Portfolio of Doggedness*, 1969

bourgeois passers-by in Vienna's first district, must first establish analogies with conventional hierarchies in order to invert them.

It is this public action, and not just the real occurrence of the act, that is captured by the camera. Should this surprise us? After all, the plain act was already dense with history. What remains, after reducing the configuration of woman with man on leash to absurdity by embodying it, but to photograph it? For EXPORT and Weibel, what remains is the precise delineation of its effect on the public. The action is framed by the geography of the city, and by the uninformed Viennese audience artfully included in the prints. There are the usual signs, familiar from Brus, of curiosity, disbelief, and ridicule.

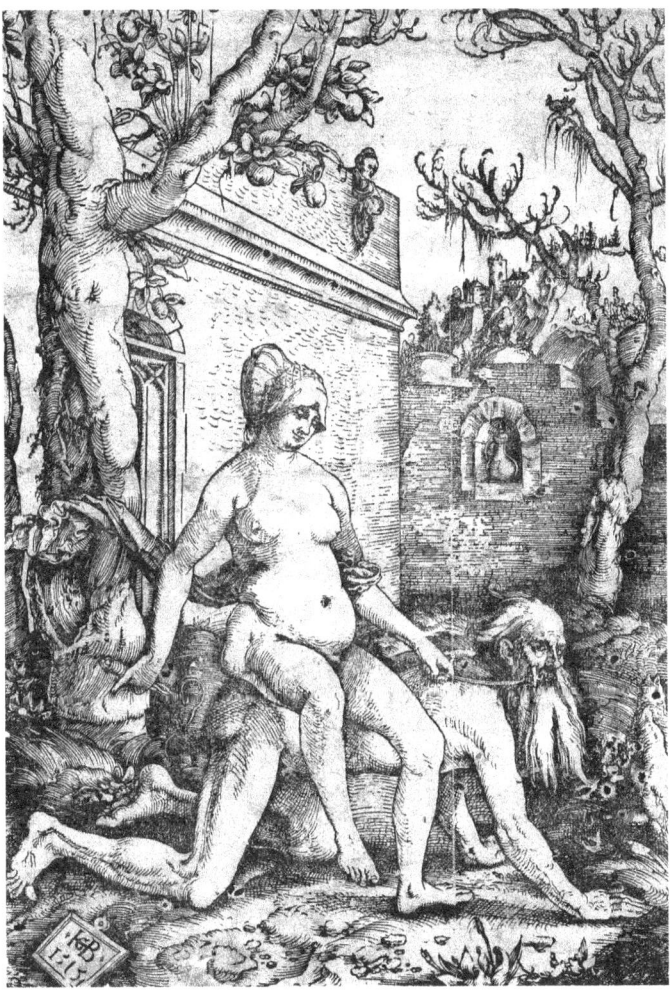

Hans Baldung Grien, *Phyllis and Aristotle*, 1513   **15**

In 1996, EXPORT chose five images for purchase by the Generali Foundation, Vienna, a real 'portfolio' which has come to be considered the 'master'
version of the piece.[25] Particularly in the fifth photograph (Figure 16), the
camera view between the backs of the bystanders invites the belated viewer to
reflect on the reaction of the live spectator – direct access to which is denied by
the same framing. The significance of live action and its documentation, and
its compatibility with imagined performance, is nowhere clearer: it *does* matter
that the walk was shot *in situ*, rather than being a studio view juxtaposed with
a crowd scene on the next page. The portfolio finds EXPORT interested in
reactions to her performances: it is also a tool for producing such reactions
retrospectively. Reproductive media not only guarantee images for contem-
plation after the fact, but in EXPORT's case, they centre on a body extended,
defined, dissected by such media, a general inquiry into the representational
dimensions of the body as *res extensa*, particularly on film. An understanding
of 'real' and 'mediated' as intertwined predicates of the represented body is a
concern that distinguishes EXPORT and Weibel from the Actionists, even as
the commitment to a political imagination of the body links them.

Most notorious among EXPORT's work of this period is *Tapp- und Tastkino*
(*Touch Cinema*), first performed in November 1968 (Figures 17 and 18).[26] The

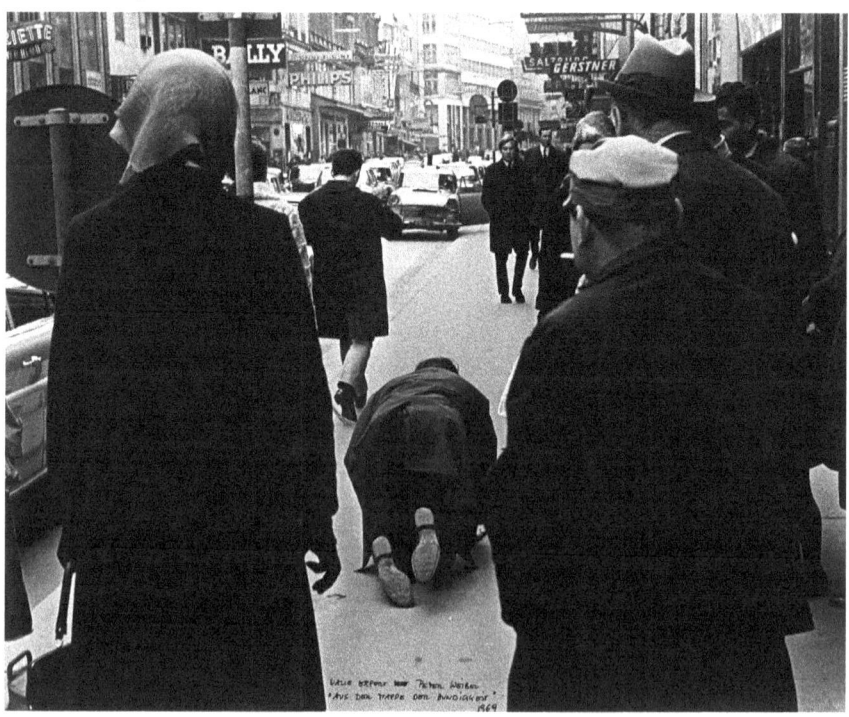

16   VALIE EXPORT/Peter Weibel, *From the Portfolio of Doggedness*

artist constructed a portable small-scale stage apparatus around her upper torso, like a puppet theatre or peepshow, with curtains concealing her naked breasts.[27] Over a megaphone, Weibel invited spectators on stage through the 'theatre curtain'. For a brief duration (one fifth of a minute, i.e. twelve seconds, in later versions expanded to thirty seconds), they were allowed to put their hands inside. A woman's skin could thus be experienced as the 'screen', a public analogue to the erotic privacy of the dark film auditorium. But the analogy went only so far: the visitor was forced to make eye contact with EXPORT, and was attended by onlookers. If the *Bildkompendium* turned the outraged reactions of Actionism's first public into a narrative to be told to a later, more sympathetic, reading public, in *Touch Cinema* (which also appeared in the *Bildkompendium*), public reception constitutes the action itself – even prior to its documentation. On the one hand, EXPORT brought up questions of male voyeurism related to those posed by *Genital Panic*.[28] On the other hand, she did not show the 'shocking' private parts, but concealed the action behind a proscenium curtain; touch disrupted the instantaneity of the film mechanism as tool of visual desire. Touch also mediated the sexual body unpredictably to the 'film voyeur', used to handling it at the remove of a pre-recorded encounter, without embarrassment or confrontation. Weaving together the perceived dichotomy of presence (the mini-theatre, 'live' action) and mediation (film, the female breasts as 'screen' or 'actors'), *Touch Cinema* was part popular spectacle, part inquiry into the body's relationship to its representation on film. Touch is made active, explicitly, whereas sight becomes not so much passive as public: as the

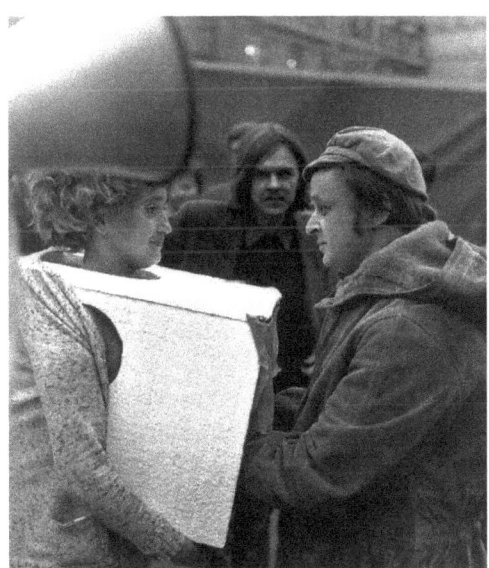
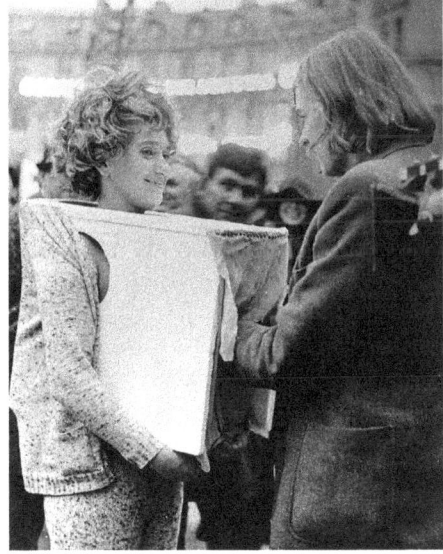

VALIE EXPORT, *Touch Cinema*, 1968   **17 & 18**

hands move around and make contact, the visible subject is held responsible in a direct way, unlike the 'wandering eyes' of the male voyeur.[29]

We can understand the significance of media as metaphor in *Touch Cinema* by briefly considering EXPORT's concrete activity as filmmaker, as well as the theoretical discourse of nascent media theory. EXPORT was a pioneer of avant-garde film in Austria, and the single female founding member of the Austria Filmmakers Cooperative (1968).[30] As experimental filmmakers interested in the relation of art film to the mass media, Weibel and EXPORT read and cited the work of Marshall McLuhan, who had become a media icon himself for his overexposed pronouncements on the new 'media society'. McLuhan was discussed in *Newsweek* and the *Partisan Review*, interviewed in *Playboy*, and played himself in films (Woody Allen's *Annie Hall*, 1977). His stardom irritated and fascinated the New Left: 'McLuhan's only move is the pop status he has inadvertently attained', as philosopher and Kaprow student Richard Meltzer complained in 1970.[31] McLuhan was equally prominent in the German-speaking world, receiving for instance the prestigious Carl Einstein Prize in 1967.[32] In the same year, Weibel showed *Der Mythos des 21. Jahrhunderts. Exkurse zu Marshall McLuhan* (*The Myth of the 21st century. Essays on Marshall McLuhan*), which he described later as 'an interactive multimedia environment, taking as the starting point of Actionism not painting but the media'.[33] Part of the work consisted of an audiotape that collaged music with a speech by Weibel on McLuhan's 'ahistorical', 'Nietzschean' approach to media. With the title, Weibel alluded to the notorious Nazi ideologist Alfred Rosenberg, whose book *Der Mythus des 20. Jahrhunderts* offers the Aryan race concept as a political myth to be put into aesthetic practice.[34] 'McLuhan's position to the future [*zum Kommenden*, literally 'that which is coming'] is comparable to Nietzsche's to German National Socialism … they are: avant-gardists of fascism.'[35] This rather strident criticism testifies to the force that Weibel and EXPORT granted McLuhan in theorizing new media. One famous slogan, 'The content of the writing is the speech', served as notation for Part Two of EXPORT's expanded cinema work *Cutting* (1967–68) (Figure 19), wherein she cut the sentence (in English) from a paper screen on which film was being projected. When finished, EXPORT was to utter the last word, 'speech', thus performing it.[36] McLuhan's actual phrase, 'the content of writing is speech', was *retranslated* from the German edition of *Understanding Media*, gaining in the process two definite articles. Unintentionally perhaps, this changed a generality into the analysis of a specific *act* relating writing with speech: EXPORT's own cutting and utterance. The point seems to be not that new media harbour a comforting old medium (speech), but that 'the "content" of any medium is always another medium'.[37]

This relay theory of media, and not any optimistic technophilia, is what haunted Weibel and EXPORT. For McLuhan, media – he regards writing,

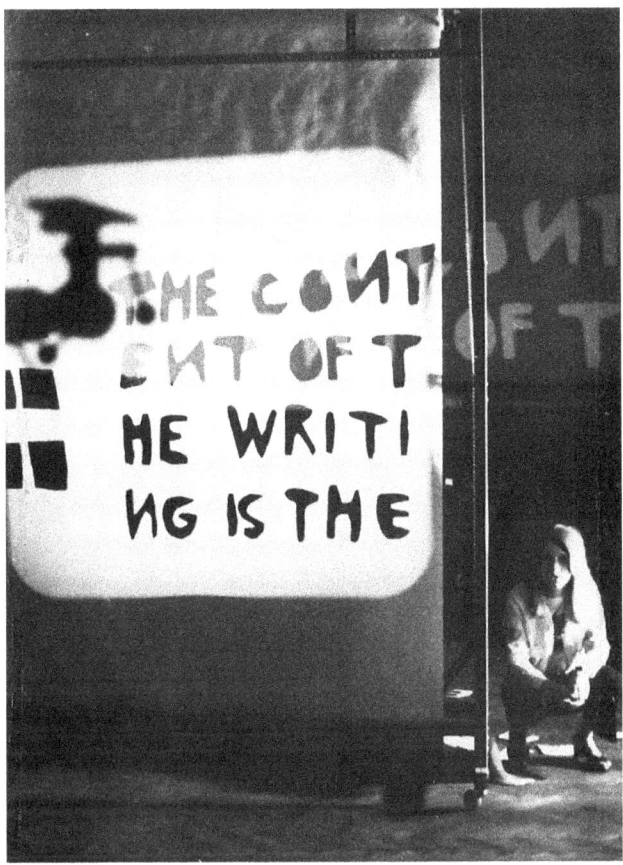

VALIE EXPORT, *Cutting*, 1967/68   **19**

language, architecture, poetry, currency, weapons, electric light, in short every technical invention and practice as a medium – are extensions of man into the environment. They do not just give better access to that environment, or power over it – they redraw boundaries between the human and the inhuman world. Thus every medium is 'new' and revolutionary at some point in history. New media refurbish the identity of the individual and of society; they change human thinking by imposing new patterns of behaviour. Print (which McLuhan as literary historian knew better than any other medium) forced Western man to think in linear terms. According to McLuhan, this made possible capitalism, modernity, and nationalism. History proceeds by displacement, as older media persist, fossilized, in the interstices of newer ones. A crude determinism – the explicit content of a medium did not matter, only its brute material character – is tempered by attention to the conventions governing media, which transcend users' intentions.[38] If the most important content of a medium is not intentions but another medium that conveys those intentions, then one may transfer the force of a stimulus from one medium to another. For McLuhan, novels are not simply replaced by film; rather, they make film possible by making its viewers:

> Typographic man took readily to film just because, like books, it offers an inward world of fantasy and dreams. The film viewer sits in psychological solitude like the silent book reader.[39]

In *Touch Cinema*, film can be interpreted as the content of the performance *and* vice versa, since the woman's breasts are the material substrate for the convention of film. *Touch Cinema*'s circular construction unsettles the conventions stabilizing each medium: in bridging the dichotomy of Actionist presence and documentation on the one hand, and of film apparatus (both camera and screen) and its erotic object on the other, it troubles the dream of the solitary viewer by turning him into intruder and collaborator at the moment of 'touching'. The shock of the performance is thus intimately related to its mediation.

With *Touch Cinema*, more than any work we have examined to this point, EXPORT moved beyond the simple '68' rhetoric of live (revolutionary) versus mediated (corrupt) representation to experiment with the concrete political effects of mediated presence. For *Touch Cinema* is not just a media metaphor; it embodies the metaphor in discrete actions and documents. The architectural construction of the box in *Touch Cinema* literalizes McLuhan's concept of medium as an 'extension of man' – woman in this case, or more precisely still, female body. This prosthetic attachment constitutes EXPORT's body as a public figure, rather than a person among others in public. And yet, a text published in the *Bildkompendium*, perhaps written by Weibel and EXPORT together, articulates an ambition to use the media to intervene *directly*, with Actionist immediacy, in the everyday. In this text, *Touch Cinema* (notably called *Touch Film*) is named a 'communication action' (in English), a term also applied to several of their early *Aktionen* which could be described as disruptions of the everyday flow of life, including *Aus der Mappe der Hundigkeit* and *Mehr Verkehrstote – Weniger Staatsbürger*, 1969 (*More Traffic Deaths – Fewer Citizens*), a thankfully failed attempt to provoke a traffic accident.[40] Communication as goal, but in a disruptive sense, is the key concept in EXPORT's text on *Touch Cinema* in the German magazine *Interfunktionen* in 1970:

> Expanded cinema is expansion of perception and communication. As expansion of perception it means experiments in new *biomedical proceedings* [in English], as expansion of communication it means exploration of a freer society.[41]

This interest in communication is contemporary with Jürgen Habermas's first formulation of his theory of *communicative action*: Habermas was to pursue the concept as a social democratic elaboration of Austin's only implicitly political theory.[42] By it he meant less the exchange of private intentions, but, rather, a systematic view of mutual autonomous actions. Calling *Touch Cinema* 'expanded communication' aiming at 'a freer society' strongly indicates that the work should be read as an intervention in the public sphere. If McLuhan ascribed to media the ability to change political systems by technical fiat (e.g. print bringing about the French Revolution), EXPORT insisted that a decisive force in society was attached to the mediated *act*. As Habermas put it in 1968, 'There appear to be meanings that can be transposed from one medium into the other. This convertibility of the meaning of sentences into actions and of actions into sentences makes possible reciprocal interpretations.'[43] According to this view, media are material communication and as such contain a performative potential analogous to 'saying as doing'. The media not only 'say and do', they get recipients to say and do *other things*, and thus distribute the performance beyond a narrow conception of presence in one location at a particular time.

This point is important, since it has consequences for the social constitution of human subjects that so interested EXPORT, particularly in its gender dimension. Just how does the transfer of speech-acts from one medium to another allow it to be effective over an expanded region of space and time? In *How to Do Things with Words*, Austin gave a familiar example: by 'appending his signature' to a contract, he can commit himself, without having to be physically present, to a certain speech-act. Commenting on this transfer of meaning, Jacques Derrida objected that the signature as speech-act does not determine its effects, since it can be faked, duplicated, and in other ways detached in time and place from the 'now' of inscription.[44] What the signature shows, says Derrida, is the opposite of extended intention. The 'one-time event', and communication in general, is not the means of transport of sense, the exchange of intentions and meanings, the discourse and 'communication of consciousness'.

> We are witnessing not an end of writing which, to follow McLuhan's ideological representation, would restore a transparency or immediacy of social relations; but indeed a more and more powerful historical unfolding of a general writing of which the system of speech, consciousness, meaning, presence, truth, etc., would only be an effect ...[45]

It is worth noting that Derrida is as much a 'determinist' as McLuhan, since for him everything from consciousness to truth and time are 'effects' of technologies of writing. Indeed, it is only the utopian dimension of McLuhan that he rejects.[46] Secondly, the claim that the persistence of intention in a printed document or other persistent medium shows it to be an illusion, alienated from momentary intention, assumes far too strong a contrast with the latter: for Derrida, it is the timeless 'self-presence' of an instant. In Derrida's account of speech-act theory, this requires perpetual re-performance: a contract, such as he ironically makes his text by having his signature printed at the end, serves the fantasy of preserving a momentary intention by turning a 'past now' into a 'future now ... a now in general'.[47] But this ignores the historical dimension of every act: the signature does not act over and over on paper: like the speech-act and the live performance, it is a historical fact, referring no longer to the present, but to the past. This can in fact be seen in the photograph of *Cutting*, where EXPORT's oral utterance of the word 'speech' is inscribed on the print in a white cartoon bubble. This is precisely analogous to Austin's signature medially 'faked' by Derrida: the inscription is needed to substitute for the absence of sound in the photograph, but it does not follow that EXPORT did not speak.[48] The legibility of this text in the photo, and of the utterance in the film, demonstrates the historical dimension of action, in particular of cross-medium performance.

In accordance with display conventions of film, rather than those of Actionism, EXPORT performed *Touch Cinema* repeatedly, in Vienna, Munich, Cologne, Zurich, Amsterdam, and London, in art institutions and at film festivals, and on the street.[49] A 1969 'screening' in Munich was the subject of a short documentary film on Austrian television, broadcast as part of a series on avant-garde art; this particular action was a re-staging exclusively for television. The film's sympathetic voiceover narration ends on a theme of feminist iconoclasm: 'The refusal of the image belongs among the emancipated art forms of a feminist aesthetic'.[50] Given such marshalling of mass media for *Touch Cinema*, one might be startled to read in a 2003 essay by novelist Marlene Streeruwitz that all documentations of the work consist of male efforts to 'win back ancestral territory'. Documentation, claims Streeruwitz, amortizes the impact of action, leaving a 'gap in history' (*Geschichtslücke*).[51] I have already argued against this position, but, for readers who identify impact with undocumented event, is there any indisputable fact that will show the document's role in turning event into monument? I think there is, if we attend to how closely EXPORT managed performers and audience as documented, and the extent to which the work's reception is itself a result of this precision.

Several widely circulated photographs of *Touch Cinema* exist apart from the film, which is shown frequently in retrospectives. Werner Schulz took the two best-known images on 14 November 1968 in Munich, on the first day of a meeting of independent filmmakers to which Weibel and EXPORT were invited.[52] They dramatize the tension between presence and mediation in the piece: in the first shot (see Figure 17), an ostensibly working-class 'visitor' is seen in profile with hands inside the box, leering at EXPORT, who seems to

one can always *act*. [68] In this sense, the manipulations of the photographs can be seen as caught up in the ambivalence of anti-humanist theory and individual agenda of the artist. EXPORT stamps her name on the corner of the document, as if she wanted to legally appropriate the document. In contrast to Brus, who in the *Vienna Walk* sought to disrupt public order directly by being a painting, or to the anarchic clouds of drawing which Arnulf Rainer and Dieter Roth applied to photographs of themselves in a dadaistic defla-tion and celebration of the conventions of action painting (Figure 23), or for that matter the visible trigger shutter hinting as self-representation in Cindy Sherman's early *Untitled Film Stills*, the *Body Configurations* serve as the visible link between applied drawing and photographed body. Only thus does the drawing gain the autonomy necessary to be plausibly taken as an analysis of real conditions afflicting the photographed body. [69] The works draw attention to a performance, while at the same time producing an analysis of its photo-graph. This might seem paradoxical, for the drawing changes what we expect a performance document to be: as objective a representation as possible of a past action. In the extreme case, of simulated or symbolic action (ranging from Klein's *Leap* to *Genital Panic*), the photograph aims to *look* objective, the asserted record of an elapsed event. The *Body Configurations* take a step not taken by Klein or EXPORT herself in *Genital Panic*: she identifies invisible forces acting on her body, forces whose reality she need not justify for, they are themselves just explanatory hypotheses for the state her body is in.

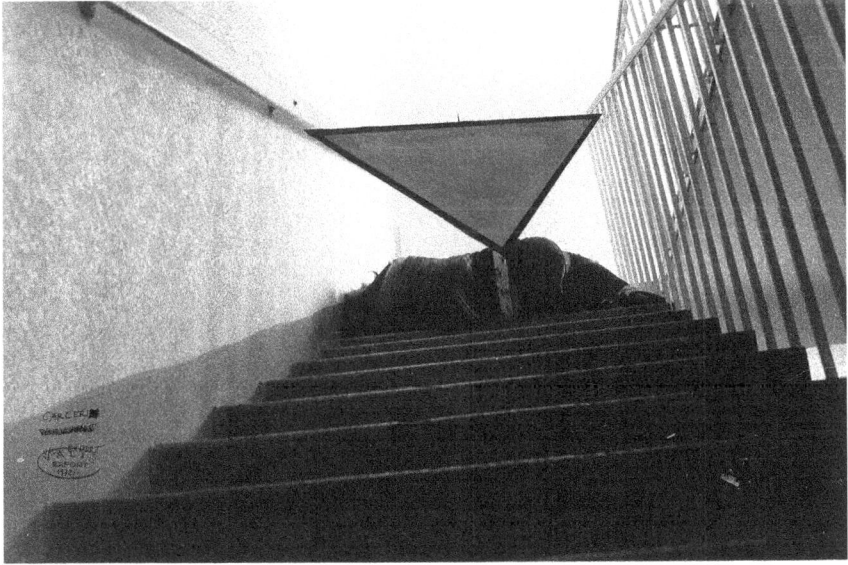

VALIE EXPORT, *Body Configuration, Carceri*, 1972 **22**

In 1976, EXPORT resumed the *Body Configurations*, this time shooting the photographs herself and taking as her subject Susanne Widl, the lead actress of her film *Unsichtbare Gegner* (*Invisible Adversaries*, 1976).[70] These photographs are set in the public architecture of the Habsburg city, presented in expansive views mostly on the *Ringstrasse* around Vienna's centre.[71] *Elongation* (Figure 24), photographed before the neo-Hellenistic façade of the Austrian parliament, is a commentary on the sexual symbolism of public power. The parliament building is suggested only through the wide staircase leading to a colonnade (the bottom of which is visible), and through the fountain in front dedicated to Pallas Athena – an opulent stage set for the confrontation between a male bearded statue astride the fountain (the personification of the river Inn) and Widl, lying on her side on one of the steps below the fountain.[72] The implied power discrepancy between the horizontal female figure and the mostly vertical architectural elements (the columns, the pyramidal pile of the fountain), is emphasized through a black diagonal line that is drawn on the photographic print from the river god's mouth to the hands of the woman. The opposition between the site of legalized male authority and displaced woman seems straightforward – authoritarian monumentality, a confrontation heightened by drawing, and the human figure reduced to the horizontality of victimhood. But things are not so simple, nor is the effect one of mournful unmasking of domination of women. Monumental architecture here speaks about the past, to be sure, but not in concrete terms. EXPORT is aware that we are products of the past as much as of the built environment, but neither is immutable, for the body in its flexibility changes, with its change of attitude, its relations to the architecture and thus the architecture itself. An act of reverence

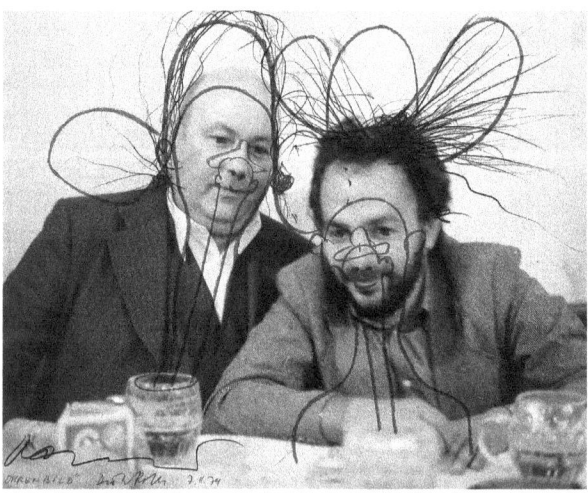

23   Arnulf Rainer and Dieter Roth, *Ohrenbild*, 1974

overdone so as to become obscene casts ridicule on its object. The body of Widl, like EXPORT's in 1972, is in fact seldom simply prostrate or supine but most often *on its side*, as if in the middle of rolling or assuming a new posture. Widl's body links up to architecture by apparently submitting to its forms, and yet, the tension is staged through theatrical poses: Widl bends, stretches, crouches, parts her legs athletically. She forcefully acts out visual analogies. She is an active victim, which makes her an agent under pressure that extant power structures make possible. This agency of the protagonist is formally accentuated by the even printing of the photographs, which makes them look more 'documentary' and less expressionistic than those of 1972. From the vague notion of a threatening public space, EXPORT gradually developed an interaction of legible bodies and authoritative public spaces. Her directorial role, and the literal detachment of autobiographical body from the protagonist on set, enables EXPORT to dissect the city symbolically through the ordering gaze of the camera, diagram, and actress.[73] The result, a confrontation of 'male' masonry and 'female' adaptability, is a performance taking place exclusively in a photographic medium. What is left out of these photographs is, however, not really out of mind but becomes a part of the enabling context of these photographic speech-acts: EXPORT and Widl walking about Vienna, engaging in a not entirely serious mode of feminist *flânerie*, mocking the important sights. Despite the rhetoric of 'invisible opponents' that EXPORT favoured at the

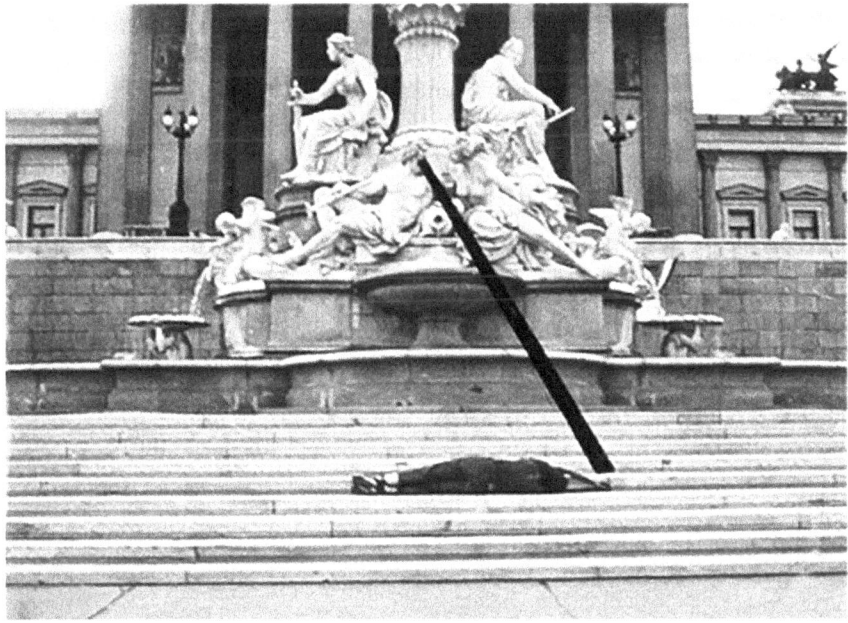

VALIE EXPORT, *Body Configuration, Elongation*, 1976   **24**

time, mechanisms of power are not hidden in the architectural fabric of the city, waiting to be unmasked, nor simply performed by Widl's body and by EXPORT's photographs and drawing, but emerge as the two (body and architecture), the three (body, architecture, drawing), or the four (body, architecture, drawing, photographer) take up an explicit relation to one another.

In 1982, EXPORT concluded the *Body Configurations* by taking up again a direct engagement with monumental architecture. This final phase of her series dealt with Vienna's most ideologically charged sites. In these works, titles no longer play on physical or psychological suggestion, but plainly denote their real settings with whatever political connotations they carry: *Justizpalast* (*Law Courts*), *Theseustempel* (a nineteenth-century replica of the *Theseum* in Athens), and most notably *Heldenplatz* (*Heroes' Square*) (Figure 25), the open space in the imperial palace complex that was the starting point of Brus's *Vienna Walk*. These are all at once sites of government, commemoration, and institutionalized aesthetics with particular relevance to post-war history, Heldenplatz being notorious as the site of Hitler's victory speech on 15 March 1938 following his march into Austria.[74] Working once more with photographer Hermann Hendrich, EXPORT posed for the photographs herself. As in 1972, the shots are closer, and linear perspective is emphasized, but in 1982 these formal strategies parse the built environment as classically monumental, oversized fragments of the past. In *Heldenplatz*, EXPORT lies on her belly on the steps leading to a war memorial that was central to Austrian fascism and is still used today.[75] Her hands are spread flat on the stones, almost as if she is 'worshipping' the heroes, but she is facing *away* from them. There is a comic element in EXPORT's upturned buttocks and the tufts of grass growing between the flagstones of the square, rather like William Pope L's much later *Great White Way* (2001–), in which the African-American artist crawls up Broadway on his stomach, dressed in a Superman costume, with a skateboard strapped to his back. Just as in Pope's biting criticism of racial imbalance in public space, there is a serious undertone to EXPORT's act. In *Heldenplatz*, EXPORT pretends to be affirming official public memory. But in overplaying her posture of obeisance, the act of commemoration becomes improper, grotesque, and ultimately combative. This over-acting is not simply insincerity, which would signify 'desecration' on EXPORT's part and touch its object only superficially. The bite of EXPORT's speech-act is its excess. People have abased themselves for nationalist ideals (and die and kill for them), so EXPORT's taking on of bodily conventions corresponding to such states of mind makes her action more than parody, and less than stage acting. It is simply a patriotic performative, taking the myth of the nation at face value, doing what it demands. EXPORT no longer needs diagrams: cropping alone conveys a similar effect.[76] Instead of making visible boundaries, she confronted monumental forms directly through scale: sometimes a posture was shot as a

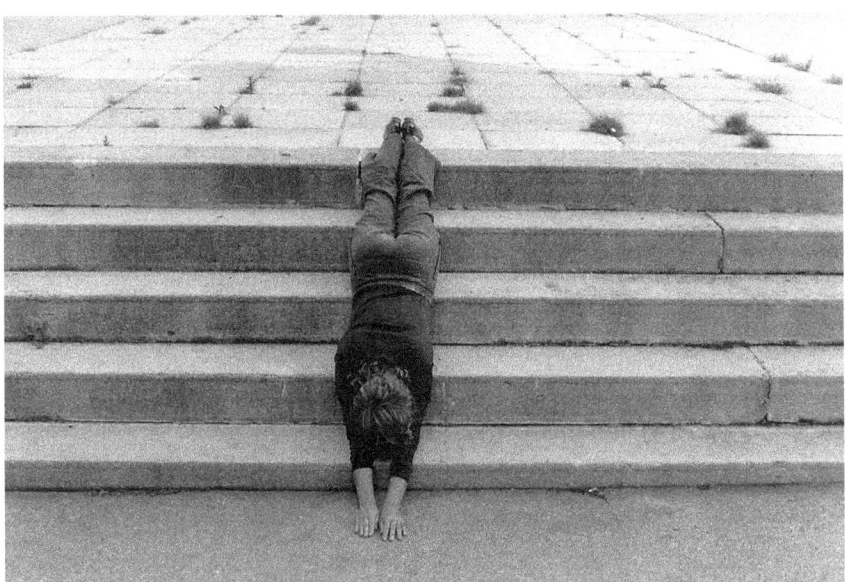

VALIE EXPORT, *Body Configuration, Heldenplatz*, 1982 **25**

close-up, and then again from a distance, often from above.[77] The new interest in framing and point of view, together with the size of the prints, brings to the surface a concern with the spectator and the limits of subjective experience implicit in the series. In *Heldenplatz*, male, female, public, and private become legible to the reader as subjective constructions through the two-edged act of the protagonist: the woman worshipping male heroes.

Comparison with a contemporary work by Peter Weibel illustrates the importance of this subjective dimension in EXPORT's project. A photographic series of 1970/71 entitled *Anschläge* [*Anschlag* is a pun: it means both 'assault', and 'wall post'] shows Weibel 'changing' the public signs of police stations, courts, and lawyers' offices by alteration of a few letters, which are scrawled on a sheet of paper held before the camera. *Polizei,* with the addition of *lügt* reads, 'the police lies' (Figure 26). The sign of the High Court (*Oberlandesgericht*), is changed to 'Oh, Shame Court' (*O Schandesgericht*) and a lawyer's sign (*Rechtsanwalt*) is made to read 'legal violence' (*Rechtsgewalt*). Weibel openly plays with the assertive function of language by using words as captions in the photograph to 'make it so', or at least to make it so that *he* thinks it to be so: there is a strange stiffness, and a very male attitude, in these confrontational works (Weibel with arms outstretched holding the letters and frowning into the camera). The relationship between individual and state here is nothing like *Heldenplatz*. In EXPORT the body acts overtly, but with ambiguous intentions: it outlines options for subjective identification within a complex and dangerous world, illuminating it partially through drawing. Weibel, on the other hand, has no doubt about the world and his role in it. He believes in the force of the gesture to bring about change: not massive political change, but changes in daily order, insofar as signs are part of the real world, and vulnerable to vandalism. In Duchampian fashion, he manipulates conventions by giving himself authority to change them. He does not ever think himself a product of these conventions, exercising authority; he is free of inhibitions, a typical avant-garde presumption declined by EXPORT.

Witnessing space as history

In 1995, EXPORT and eight other entrants were invited to submit proposals for a new competition to construct a *Monument and Memorial Site for the Jewish Victims of the Nazi Regime in Austria* (*Mahnmal*), a project suggested by Holocaust survivor and 'Nazi hunter' Simon Wiesenthal, and taken on by the city of Vienna.[78] The new site for the monument, Judenplatz, was the centre of Jewish life in the thirteenth and fourteenth centuries, but the name stems from the fifteenth century, after the Jews had been banned from the city in the wake of the Vienna Gesera (pogrom) in 1421.[79] The medieval synagogue had been demolished not long afterwards. The Judenplatz project was the first aesthetic forum in Austria for dealing with the persecution of Jews, which includes but extends beyond the Holocaust, and the first to reverse publicly

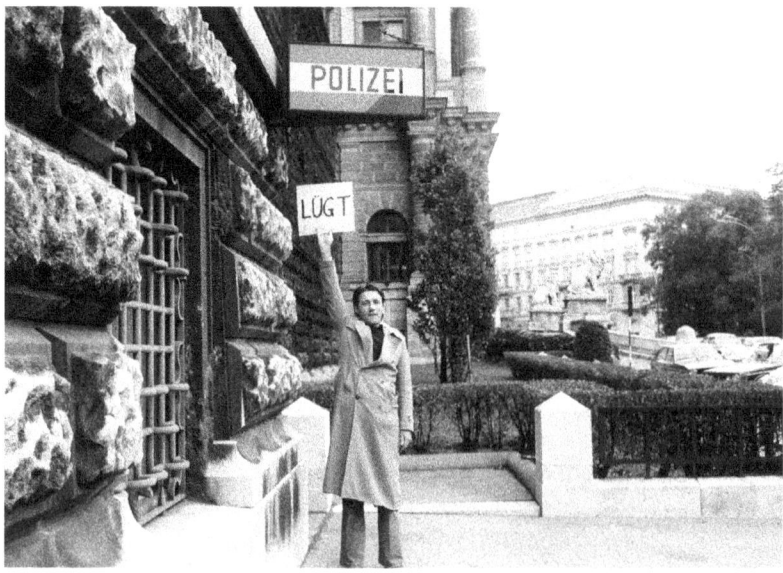

26   Peter Weibel, *Police Lies*, 1970/71

the attitude of moral amnesty that Austrians had granted themselves after the Second World War.[80]

Though presumably invited for her long-standing engagement with Viennese urban space, EXPORT was not as strange a candidate for a Holocaust memorial as one might think. She had planned a war memorial – not built, and rarely exhibited – as early as 1974. *Der Ort des Menschen* (*The Place of the Human Being*) (Figure 27) was a model for a non-commissioned monument meant to consist of a giant female hand with arched fingers, each of whose tips is pierced by metal nails. 'The monument is memory of pain and protection from pain alike', EXPORT explained in a 1980 catalogue which also contained the *Body Configurations*; the identification of a hand as site of pain and memory suggests that the body is not merely object of history but its subject as well.[81] Formally, the project sits uncomfortably between expressionism, the pop gigantism of Claes Oldenburg, Christian references (crucifixion, stigmata), and an attempt to materialize the psychic experiences of those members of the population who suffered invisibly during the war – as exemplified in the cast of a female hand. EXPORT did not represent or address either herself or any other body in particular, but a social body and its memory of pain. The fragmented female body was made to displace the authoritarian monument, putting what is oppressed in place of that which oppresses, but given the same threatening gigantism. The result is vague in its figurative symbolism and the conservative choice of material, precluding

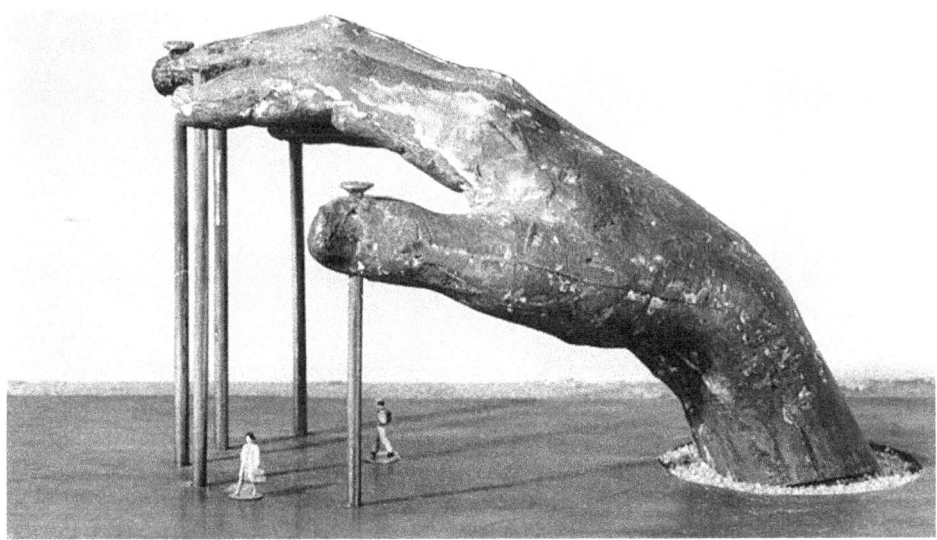

VALIE EXPORT, *The Place of the Human Being*, concept for a monument, 1974   **27**

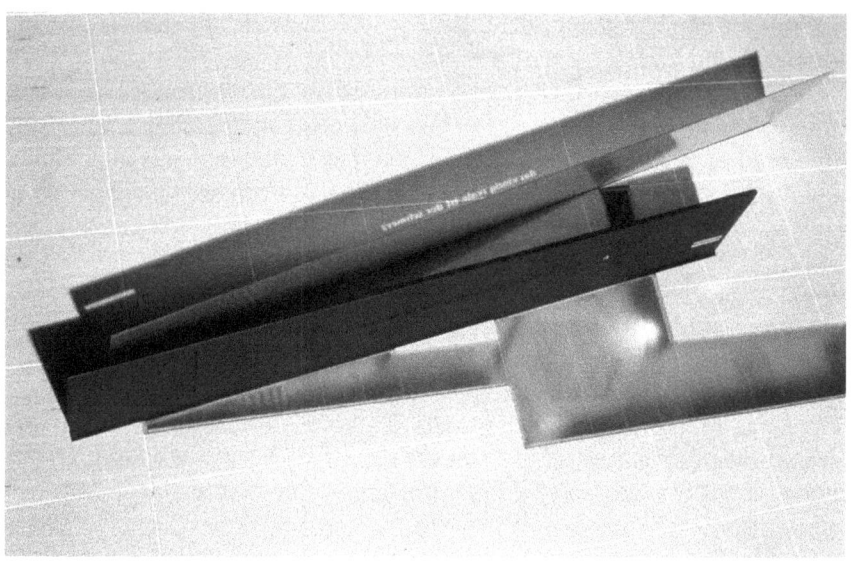

28   VALIE EXPORT, *Passage of Remembrance*, 1996

any reflection on monuments or their authoritative force. It also suggests the difficulty encountered by an avowedly anti-fascist generation in putting its experiences of wartime suffering into a historical perspective broad enough to include the Holocaust.[82]

Twenty years later, EXPORT's Judenplatz proposal *Passage of Remembrance* returned to the idea of commemoration as bodily experience, now resolutely on the part of the visitor (Figure 28). Significantly, there is also a shift in theoretical terms used: while the *Place of the Human Being* is called a monument in EXPORT's own texts, the competition at Judenplatz now asked for a Mahnmal, a term often translated as memorial, but rather different in sense. While the German word for monument, Denkmal [literally, a mark for thinking], puts emphasis on the past, Mahnmal [a mark for admonition, the word mahnen, to admonish, stemming from the Latin monere, which is in fact related to monument] is directed towards the future, coupled to a vigorous didactic component. The word gained in currency because, in contrast to Monument (also used in German) or Denkmal, it calls 'for repentance instead of emulation', as Hans Ernst Mittig put it in the 1980s.[83] This changed attitude towards commemoration plays out in the way EXPORT approaches the project in 1995. Architecturally, she contrasts the heaviness of traditional memorial architecture with the lightness of glass, designing a structure modelled both on the density of funerary architecture and the transparencies of media culture:

The *Passage of Remembrance* is a passage leading through a commemorative event. It will not unfold its meaning to the passive beholder, but requires active participation. Two walls inclined towards each other, one of dark stone, one of opaque glass, form a passage whose spatial impact is like a physical experience of the monument. When a person walks through the passage sensors activate tape texts transmitted through vertical sound-joints in the stone wall … In the wide, open part of the passage a laser integrated in the stone projects text in the opaque glass wall.[84]

Memory was to enter the installation in the guise of technology.[85] The sound sensor was planned to replay readings, music, and audio collages of Jewish oral history; the texts projected by laser onto the glass wall were to be evidence of 'human suffering' in general, whereas the stone wall was to stand specifically for 'pain suffered by the Jewish people'.[86] The plausibility of the symbolism, which still refers to pain as a common denominator, but picks out a histori-cally specific 'Jewish pain', depends on a space animated by the arrangement of digital and analogue media; the reader should no longer be surprised at their use in subjective performance. Indeed, just two years earlier, Peter Weibel employed multimedia effects for a monument he staged for the 1993 Venice Biennale. *Die Vertreibung der Vernunft. Der kulturelle Exodus aus Österreich* (*The Exodus of Reason. Austria's Cultural Depletion*; Weibel's English title is not quite equivalent to the German), consisted of more than forty monitors, on which names and brief biographies of thousands of Austrians (mostly Jewish) who were killed or exiled during National Socialism appeared in the form of end credits. A recorded voice read these names. Weibel's reference to the convention of end credits constrains the viewer's role. One can watch, without intervening or acting; the sole experience is one of the length of the list of people killed and displaced.[87] The stoically recited losses make power-lessness itself the topic of commemoration. EXPORT, in contrast, sought to individualize the experience produced by the disparate media composing her memorial through random permutation of text and sound fragments: a computer was to choose arbitrarily from a library of texts to project, exposing every visitor to a unique reading experience. The construction of individual experiences from generic, publicly available documents is consistent with EXPORT's photographic work. In entering the monument, the visitor was to enter history as an archive to be individualized. That this individualization was to be carried out by a randomizing algorithm suggests that her monument is not too distant from Weibel's after all.

At the same time, the visitor was made into an abstract figure performing remembrance for others, because the acts of walking and reading were to be visible to passing pedestrians on the Judenplatz through the semi-transparent glass surface. Being seen changes the significance of the act; for one thing, the

environment enforces a behaviour of meditative silence. Private contempla-
tion is not abolished, but brought to public attention as a visual spectacle. The
glass surface serves as a screen and frame for the spectators, its opaqueness
lending them, as performers, a certain anonymity as shadows or outlines with
subdued colour. In being thus assimilated to the memorial, the spectator is
made a silent, but eloquent, substrate of commemoration.

The use of spectators as part of the memorial in Viennese public space
might remind us of Antonio Canova's inclusion of marble mourners in his
1805 tomb of Archduchess Marie-Christine in the Augustiner Church in
Vienna, which so disturbed sculptor and psychologist Adolf Hildebrand
(Figure 29).[88] Canova's is a masterstroke of decorous suggestion. A funerary
cortège with some bearing on the original ceremony is perpetually on display
for the spectator, indicating the funerary respects due to an enlightened
noblewoman. Whether the quiet acts of perception of visitors to the *Passage
of Remembrance* could have had any appreciable effect on an outside spectator
is not so clear. For the task has grown in complexity: to make history and not
just grief visible through the body. The glass highlights this theatrical effort,
while sheltering the experience of the visitor inside.[89] I can only speculate
to what extent this calibration would have resulted in a legible – or usable –
interface between history and experience, or in an unwelcome display of the
visitors to an indifferent public outside the memorial. EXPORT's proposal was
not included in the final round of the competition.[90]

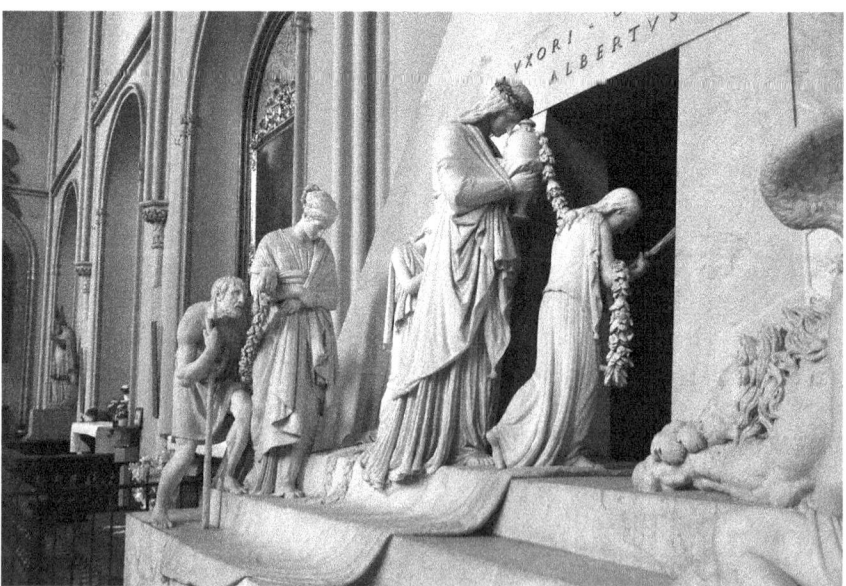

29   Antonio Canova, *Cenotaph of Marie Christine of Austria*, Vienna, 1805

British sculptor Rachel Whiteread's winning design could not have been more different: a reinforced concrete cube accented by a texture resembling the rustication on the base a Renaissance palazzo, which on closer look resolves itself into rows of books on library shelves, substantiates the victory of the document as self-sufficient monument (Figures 30 and 31). On a closer look, one notices that the books' pages, not their spines, face the visitor. The 'nameless library', as it is commonly called, is inaccessible, not only physically but narratively as well, since the books' legible bindings either constitute the interior of the wall or are available only on the sealed interior. Whiteread has resisted politicians' demands to provide access through the memorial, if not literal then at least visual or symbolic, to the remains of the medieval synagogue the foundation of which was unearthed during the construction work.[91] By bracketing out the historical content of the site, Whiteread hoped to secure attention to (failure of) the historical as a discipline of remembering. One might contrast this usefully with EXPORT, who offered to make the dig underneath visible through a glass panel in the floor, but mediated this by having water flow through the hollow glass panel.[92] One might say that Whiteread froze the document, rendering it illegible in concrete; EXPORT, on the other hand, is confident in the ability of new media to activate texts and persons. Ironically, it is Whiteread's monolith that makes the striking photograph, whether in a close-up of the book forms or as a neoclassical crypt in the midst of a public square still subtly reminiscent of medieval city planning. EXPORT's high-tech memorial, with its translucencies and reflections, would probably not have translated so well to snapshots and press photos: all its technology is aimed at the experience of a spectator on the ground. Perhaps this is why her proposal failed: she exposed the visitor to both history and a general public, but this public, which her own performances since the 1960s had addressed, is discontinuous in time and space.

Just as Whiteread's monument was nearing completion, EXPORT explored the performative dimension of transparency in her first executed architectural project, the *Transparente Raum* (*Transparent Cube*) of 1999–2001 (Figure 32). The cube can be seen as a condensation of her feminist performances in public space, particularly *Touch Cinema*, and her investigation of the relations between public architecture and female experience. In many ways, the concept of the glass cube in the urban environment is another attempt to make visible the connection between social environment and history, and in this case also possibly to change it. The cube is both contemporary social (behavioural) architecture, and a monument to gendered urban experience. It consists of glass panels in a steel frame, built under the tracks of Otto Wagner's Wiener Stadtbahn (1894–1901).[93] It was initiated as part of a project for urban development on the 'belt' of Vienna (Gürtel), a ring road around the inner districts of Vienna (not to be confused with the smaller 'ring' which runs around the

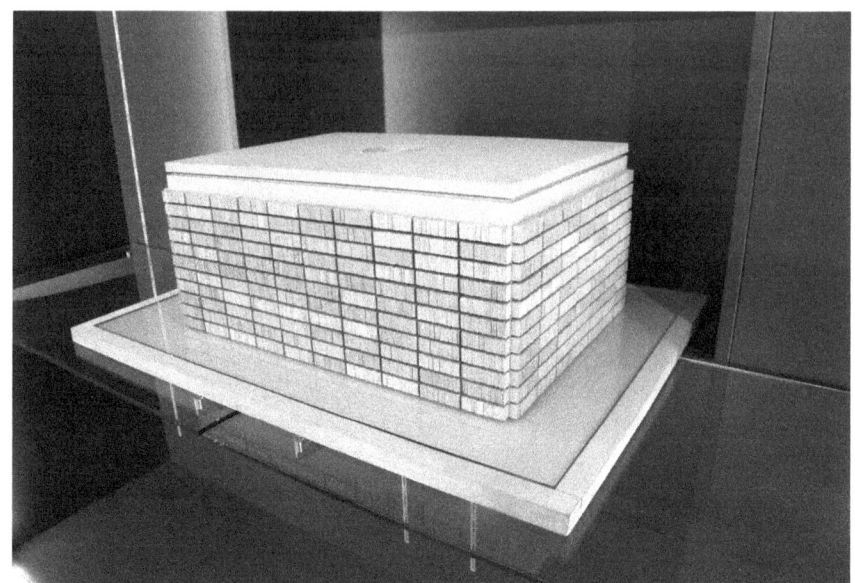

30 Rachel Whiteread, model submitted for the competition of the *Monument and Memorial Site for the Jewish Victims of the Nazi Regime in Austria*, 1995

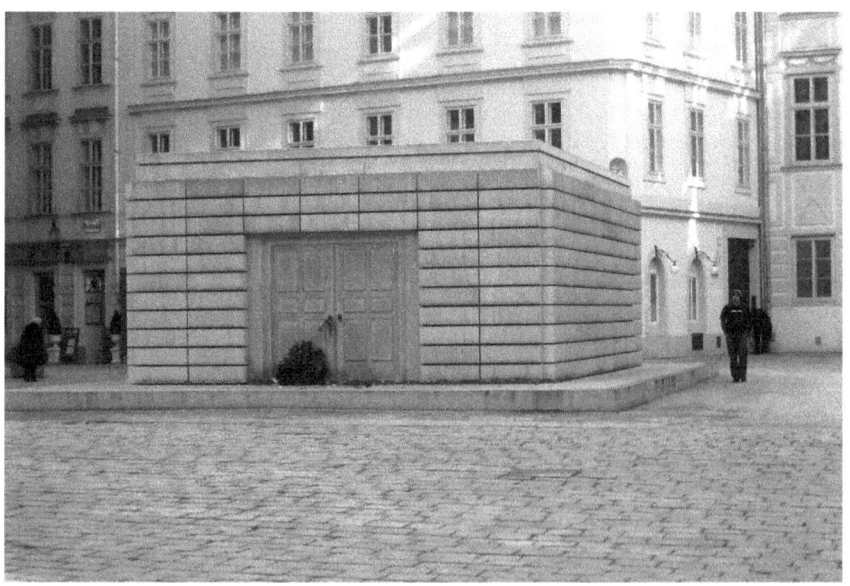

31 Rachel Whiteread, *Monument and Memorial Site for the Jewish Victims of the Nazi Regime in Austria*, 1995

first district), funded by the European Union.[94] The neighbourhood was (and to a certain extent remains) marked by problems due to heavy traffic, low property values, and, in particular, brothels. EXPORT's aim was to offset the dynamic of the active male selecting subservient female companions with this project. Women should be visible in her cube as autonomous and self-determined participants in art and, by extension, in the urban environment. Transparent Cube thus retains EXPORT's concern with the transitivity of subjects into objects that has characterized her public art since *Touch Cinema*. Yet, in the wake of subtler investigations ranging from *Body Configurations* to the Judenplatz proposal, EXPORT seems no longer interested in violently upsetting the force of a male gaze directed at the objectified female, and more interested by the literal consequences of making women radically visible in public space.

The choice of glass as material makes these motives clear, but it also raises questions: first, if glass architecture, with its rhetoric of wares on display, makes possible an extension of female autonomy into the supposedly male-dominated space outside. The 'making seen' immediately brings up problems, for the glass cube can easily be read as a showcase, with all its objectifying qualities. On the other side, as theorists of transparency in architecture have

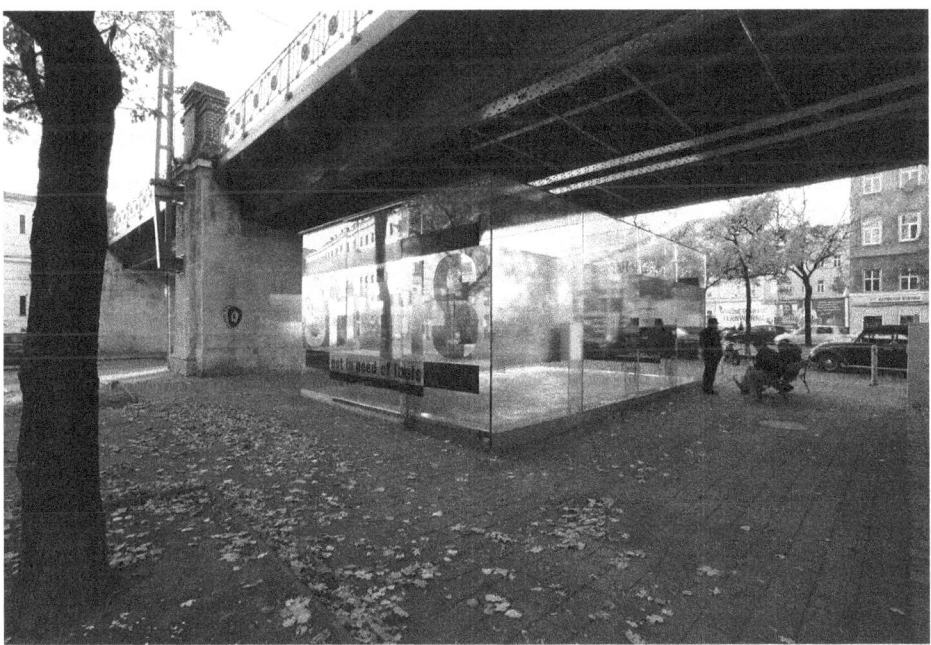

VALIE EXPORT, with Silja Tillner, *Transparent Cube (Kubus EXPORT)*, 1999–2001, with **32** installation by Victoria Hindley (2010)

pointed out since the 1980s, glass is also often a mirror, visually disconnecting inside and outside, and making for unsettling effects of glare and reflectance that change with the outside conditions (day/night, bright light/clouds).[95] Is this instability of the glass enclosure a deliberate effect that connects to, say, Dan Graham's complex investigations of the public and private life in his *Alteration to a Suburban House* (1978), where a mirror should have reflected parts of the living room into the suburban neighbourhood? Who is supposed to present herself in EXPORT's cube, and for what purpose? The cube is fitted into the industrial architecture of the train tracks above, melding the motive of abidance with that of movement: two sides of the cube can be opened to 'make […] the glass-body into a passage'.[96] All interaction in and around the cube is supposed to become a public act, both in the present – where, as the site of art exhibitions, it is to serve as affirmation of powerful female action, or at least fair interaction of the sexes – and as intrusion into the past, the social conditions that influenced the present, and thus literally into the fabric of the city. But there are issues with this approach. The position is exposed and potentially uncomfortable, resembling a public stage even in the intimate dimensions of a small art space.[97] EXPORT delegates the performance of public gendered conditions; in some way, the visitors are made to play a pantomime, much as Manfredo Tafuri has described the condition of inhabiting Mies van der Rohe's houses and offices.[98]

That the architecture would – filled with people – become a speech-act for those outside of it, an affirmation of female visibility, is a principle analogous to the function of the witness in *Passage of Remembrance*, and to the role of the photographed body in *Body Configurations*. Indeed, EXPORT's development as an architect in many ways mirrors the development of her performances: from the confrontational experience of the *Place of the Human Being*, through the complex relay of presence and mediation in the *Passage of Remembrance*, to the sublime legibility and simplicity of the *Transparent Cube*, of which the photographic analogue might be the 1982 *Heldenplatz*. Why, then, is the built object inconclusive in a way in which the photographic performances are not?

I think the indeterminacy of the audience, which is in a strong sense the *subject* addressed, makes this form of monument ambiguous. Let us remember the text *Corpus More Geometrico*, and in particular its claim that EXPORT's 'bodywriting is always also sociography and cultural history'. The body as part of cultural history becomes 'writing', a document that can bring to a reading audience an *image* of the 'environment body', not the *actual* environment body, socio*graphy* rather than society with all its visible bodies and invisible valuations. This environment is actively mirrored and thus made legible *in* the body as 'living', according to EXPORT, and not as a passive reflection. EXPORT's phrase 'Environment body' ('The body-pictures deliver pictures of the cultural environment-body') is a term used in the plural (environmental bodies) by Edmund Husserl to describe those things that the self-aware subject finds in space.[99] It is telling that for EXPORT the term is singular, suggesting a monolithic block of a body, almost like a hostile entity comprised of cultural forces, from which individual 'bodypictures' (*Körperbilder*) must be extracted. Husserl insisted that while the empirical self is part of the world, experiences are always directed, intentional acts (*intentionale Erlebnisse*) of a transcendental subject. Experience is always 'experience of *something*' but also always experience *for me*.[100] This 'me' is the 'transcendental me', for whom the feelings, thoughts, and historical facticity of the body and person (including gender) are just objects to be considered. This is bound to sound 'not only one of the most timidly conservative, but also one of the most dogmatic of philosophical standpoints'.[101] But its suggestiveness for EXPORT's use of media cannot be denied. Much of her work depends on the possibility of critically regarding not just her body, but her empirical self in its entirety, as an object. What would this mean to EXPORT? By directing our attention to some part of consciousness, and neglecting others, we can 'put out of action' (*außer Aktion setzen*) phenomena and thus reflect on our relation to them.[102] Setting parts of our experience 'out of action' and pointing to the possibility of constructing experience out of disparate data is important to EXPORT. This applies not only to the *Body Configurations*, where we see an alienated but informative exchange with the built environment, but also in *Touch Cinema* and the Juden-platz proposal, where the glass is an interface with history and at the same time an obstacle between participant and spectator. EXPORT's *documents* are the transcendental subject, in which the empirical EXPORT is analysed: a state dramatized in the modified prints of the *Body Configurations* and in films like *Adjunct Dislocations*, wherein two first-person cameras (one mounted on the breast, one on the back) are combined with a third-person, side-on view of EXPORT's body.[103]

The documentary nature of EXPORT's transcendental ego, which is to say, her attempt to analyse her own experience, poses a challenge to her shift to architecture. In the *Transparent Cube* there cannot be a transcendental subject, of course, only real subjects in the city. The *Cube* marks an important shift from body in architectural space to architecture, as it shows EXPORT moving from critique to construction. By the means of the architecture, EXPORT tries to delegate the performance to spectators, a move that *looks* effortless but may prove to be the hardest step to take.

Notes

1 The screen as Lacanian 'locus of mediation' between subject and object is of less interest here than the role played by the literal film screen in carrying the past (the film) into the future (the cinema), and its ambivalent material character, apparently translucent (like a window), but in fact reflective (like a mirror). For a related

usage, see Pamela M. Lee, 'Bare Lives', in Matthias Michalka (ed.), *X-Screen: Film Installations and Actions in the 1960s and 1970s* (Cologne: Walther König, 2004), 70–86.

2 'In Schweden, da haben wir diese Zeitschrift entdeckt, film culture, ist draufgestanden, expanded arts. Das war für uns eine unglaubliche Bestärkung. Und da habe ich gesagt, nennen wir unsere Sache "expanded cinema." Denn dieser Begriff war ja in Amerika schon früher da, nur haben wir ihn nicht gekannt. Wir haben '67 schon diese Projekte gemacht, sind in Wien aufgetreten, nur haben wir nicht gewusst, wie wir das nennen sollen.' Hilde Schmölzer, 'Weibel und Export', in *Das böse Wien. Gespräche mit österreichischen Künstlern* (Munich: Nymphenburger Verlagsanstalt, 1973), 181. Weibel must be referring to George Maciunas, 'Expanded Arts Diagram', in *Film Culture*, 'Expanded Arts Special Issue', 43 (Winter 1966), 7, reprinted in Hanns Sohm (ed.), *Happening und Fluxus. Materialien* (Cologne: Kölnischer Kunstverein, 1970), n.p. American scholars cite Gene Youngblood's book *Expanded Cinema* (New York: Dutton, 1970), which equates the term with 'expanded consciousness' (41). The influence is unlikely, given Weibel and EXPORT's debt to Fluxus. EXPORT recalls first encountering Youngblood's book much later. VALIE EXPORT, interview with the author, audio file, New York, 19 February 2007. Besides *Tapp- und Tastkino*, other works of 'Expanded Cinema' are *auf + ab + an + zu*, *Adjungierte Dislokationen* (1973), *Ping Pong* (1968), *Cutting* (1967/68), and *abstract film no. 1* (1967/68).

3 VALIE EXPORT, 'Aspects of Feminist Actionism', *New German Critique*, 47 (Spring–Summer 1989), 69–92. The 1977 German original was published in Gislind Nabakowski, Helke Sander, and Peter Gorsen (eds), *Frauen in der Kunst* (Frankfurt am Main: Suhrkamp, 1980). EXPORT never performed with the Actionists, apart from operating the lights at the *Art and Revolution* event that was organized by the Socialist Student Association (SÖS) and took place at Vienna University in June 1968. In Maren Lübbke, 'Künstlerische Passagen zum Strukturwandel der Öffentlichkeit. Interview mit VALIE EXPORT', *Noema Art Journal*, 44 (Vienna, 1997), 77, EXPORT credits mainly American happenings and Body Art, while in Vienna the 'sense of elation' ('Aufbruchsstimmung') was of importance to her. Roswitha Mueller, *VALIE EXPORT: Fragments of the Imagination* (Bloomington: Indiana University Press, 1994), xix, argues that the Actionists and EXPORT are alike in 'breaking social, sexual and cultural taboos', but that the 'use of technology' sets her apart. On the Actionists as 'boys' club', see Hildegard Fraueneder, 'Körperrituale: Die Entmachtung des Repräsentativen in der Kunst VALIE EXPORTs und Friederike Pezolds' (Doctoral dissertation, University of Salzburg, 1988), 69.

4 On the aesthetics of Actionism, see my essay 'The Ugliness of the Avant-garde', in Andrei Pop and Mechtild Widrich (eds), *Ugliness. The Non-Beautiful in Art and Theory* (London: I.B. Tauris, 2013).

5 The legal action against Weibel and EXPORT was discussed in the Austrian daily newspapers: See for instance *Kurier* (21 April 1971). The group, which carried out *Aktionen*, may well have taken the name Wiener Aktionisten (Viennese Actionists) from the book (in English, *Image Compendium Viennese Actionism and Film*). Weibel refers to the term as his invention; more decisively, in an interview, Brus refers to 'Viennese Actionism, as Peter Weibel called it'. 'Günter Brus', in Danièle

Roussel, *Der Wiener Aktionismus und die Österreicher. Gespräche* (Klagenfurt: Ritter, 1995), 131, 23.

6 Pages 241–67 contain captions, followed by a 'synopsis' (biographies, description of groups and events on pages 269–94), and a chronology. It is striking how this has determined not just the content but the style of later scholarship: a voluminous recent exhibition catalogue has over three hundred pages of images, followed by captions, biographies, and manifestos. See Pilar Parcerisas, Hubert Klocker, and Danièle Roussel, *Viennese Actionism*, Exh. Cat. Centro Andaluz de Arte Contemporáneo [Sevilla] (Barcelona: Actar, 2008).

7 On the Wiener Gruppe (Friedrich Achleitner, Konrad Bayer, Gerhard Rühm, Oswald Wiener), see especially Gerhard Rühm (ed.), *Die Wiener Gruppe* (Hamburg: Rowohlt, 1985), the expanded version of an anthology originally published in 1967. It is likely that Rühm's precise, unobtrusively edited anthology may have inspired Weibel and EXPORT's own work, and perhaps Sohm's 1970 Fluxus collection.

8 Auslander, 'The Performativity of Performance Documentation', 6. This crucial sentence concludes, rather obscurely, by insisting that viewers are interested in 'the artist's work, not the total interaction'. On the question of 'totality' in performance, see below.

9 The action was scheduled for the evening before an opening of Brus's work in a Viennese gallery. Brus voiced discontent with the exhibition; he had intended to show only photographic documentation of his actions, but, according to Dieter Schwarz, was talked into including paintings. He considered his action as a counter-pole to the 'art' exhibition. See Dieter Schwarz (ed.), *Aktionsmalerei – Aktionismus. Wien 1960–1965. Eine Chronologie von Dieter Schwarz* (Zurich: Seedorn, 1988), 69. See also Peter Weibel, 'Zur Aktionskunst von Günter Brus', in Hildegund Amanshauer (ed.), *Der Überblick/Günter Brus*, Exh. Cat. Museum Moderner Kunst (Vienna and Salzburg: Residenz, 1986), 33. The newest publication on Actionism, edited by curator Eva Badura-Triska and Hubert Klocker, marks a significant turn in explaining Actionism out of painting. See *Vienna Actionism. Art and Upheaval in 1960s Vienna* (Cologne: Walther König 2012), and my review, 'Lights! Camera! Action!' *Art Journal*, 71, 4 (2012), 122–4.

10 'Völlig weiß bemalt und nur durch einen schwarzen Strich quasi zweigeteilt, so wollte er, einem lebenden Bild gleich, vom Heldenplatz zum Stephansplatz gehen, wurde allerdings nach wenigen Metern von einem Polizisten wegen Störung der öffentlichen Ordnung zu einer Geldbuße verdonnert', Andrea Schurian, 'Wilde Striche und Streiche: Günter Brus', *Der Standard* (28 September 2008).

11 See Hubert Klocker, 'Viennese Waltzes: Viennese Actionism and the Law', in Daniel McClean (ed.), *The Trials of Art* (London: Ridinghouse, 2007), 273–86.

12 According to the image credits in Weibel and EXPORT, *Bildkompendium*, these photographs are also taken by Hoffenreich.

13 See my article, 'The Informative Public of Performance: A Study of Viennese Actionism, 1965–1970', *TDR. The Drama Review*, 57:1 (217) (Spring 2013), 137–51.

14 Rebecca Schneider, 'Performance Remains Again', in *Archaelogies of Presence*, 64–81, this quote 74.

15 Schneider, *Performing Remains*, 101, and 'Performance Remains Again', 71. Schneider regards versions of her own text, which first appeared in 2001, as 're-dos': see

'Performance Remains Again', 78.

16 See Peter Weibel, *Das offene Werk. 1964–79* (Ostfildern: Hatje Cantz, 2006), 429, for the text of a 1968 newspaper article wherein Weibel defends an Actionist event by comparison with the persecuted Jews.

17 Muehl's commune, prison term, and his commune in Portugal are discussed in an interview with Peter Roos and Christof Siemes, 'Ich bin Drunten der Dreckige', *Die Zeit* (26 February 2004). He died in May 2013

18 Adrian Henri, *Total Art. Environments, Happenings, and Perfomance* (New York and Toronto: Oxford University Press, 1974), 169.

19 Hubert Klocker interprets the work as response to National Socialism and wartime destruction in his English-language publications, notably 'Gesture as Object: Liberation as Aktion: A European Component of Performance Art', in Paul Schimmel (ed.), *Out of Actions: Between Performance and the Object, 1949–1979* (The Museum of Contemporary Art, Los Angeles. London/New York: Thames and Hudson, 1998), 159–95. Peter Gorsen finds in Actionist destruction a 'cathartic, healing, and even therapeutic effect', meant to assuage a longing caused by direct (in Muehl's case) or indirect war experience. 'Viennese Actionism and the Celebration of Psychophysical Naturalism', in Julius Hummel (ed.), *Wiener Aktionismus. Sammlung Hummel* (Milan: Mazzotta, 2005), 92. Danièle Roussel takes up the therapeutic theme in her 1995 book of interviews, *Der Wiener Aktionismus und die Österreicher. Gespräche* (Klagenfurt: Ritter, 1995).

20 Philip Ursprung is an exception to this trend in 'Catholic Tastes: Hurting and Healing the Body in Viennese Actionism in the 1960s', in Amelia Jones and Andrew Stephenson (eds), *Performing the Body, Performing the Text* (London/New York: Routledge, 1999), 138–52, where he argues that the Actionists *staged* themselves in this manner, with the police as their 'ideal audience'. See also his 'More than the Art World Can Tolerate: Otto Muehl's Manopsychotic Ballet', *Tate Etc.*, 15 (2009), 56–61.

21 The Generali Foundation, Vienna, translates the title as *Portfolio of Doggedness*. Hundigkeit is not a word, but would mean literally 'doglikeness', with no suggestion of tenacity. In Weibel and EXPORT, *Bildkompendium*, the title is given as *Aus der Mappe der Hundlichkeit* (*From the Portfolio of Dog-likeness*), 290. The authorship of this work is disputed. The explicitly feminist actions in which Weibel took part, such as *Touch Cinema* and *Portfolio of Doggedness*, are usually considered EXPORT's, but Weibel claims co-authorship for these works in his oeuvre catalogue *Das offene Werk*. I attribute *Touch Cinema* entirely to EXPORT, as no evidence apart from Weibel's claim in *Das offene Werk* suggests his co-authorship. It is listed as EXPORT's in the *Bildkompendium*, 297. The speeches that Weibel gave at performances of *Touch Cinema* were certainly his own. In a recent interview, he protests: 'there is documentary proof now that *Touch Cinema* was worked out collaboratively. Back then, feminism turned it into a work by VALIE EXPORT alone. I see in regard to my own example, how history is being manipulated', Herwig Höller and Thomas Wolkinger, 'Knallhart', *Falter*, 05/2007 (31 January 2007), online: www.falter.at/web/print/detail.php?id=421. Weibel also lists EXPORT's *Genital Panic, Adjunct Dislocations*, the monument *Der Ort des Menschen*, and several others as collaboration projects. Weibel, *Das offene Werk*, 590.

22 They were filmed by Ernst Schmidt and Hans Scheugl, who can be seen in the first image of the *Mappe*.

23 Weibel and EXPORT, *Bildkompendium*, 260. '… was im zeichentrickfilm so leicht fällt, die verdinglichung und entfremdung des menschen in formen der zoologie zu zeichnen, und dort dann auch abfällt, eben weil es nur zeichnenspiel ist, schüttet dieser aktionsfilm in alle kanäle unserer kommunikation, weswegen dann auch diese zu streiken drohen, unwirklich erscheint die reale szene … Aus der Mappe der Hundigkeit stellt Wirklichkeit her, stellt sie wieder her aus dem Flickzeug der Ideologien'. The word I rendered as 'sewing kit', *Flickzeug*, can also mean 'repair kit' (as for a bicycle), but the feminine connotation is central here.

24 *Split: Reality VALIE EXPORT* (Vienna: Museum Moderner Kunst Stiftung Ludwig, 1997), 65.

25 The head of the collection and research at the Generali Foundation, Doris Leutgeb, confirmed that 'the selection and particular compilation' was done by EXPORT on this occasion, possibly with Sabine Breitwieser (then director of the Generali). The portfolio is considered a 'unique copy'. Email from Doris Leutgeb to the author, 13 March 2012. EXPORT's dealer, Galerie Charim, Vienna, has an edition for sale.

26 *Tapp- und Tastkino* means literally 'Tap- and Touch/Grope Cinema'. *Touch Cinema* is the standard English name. Pam Lee notes that the title 'stresses the haptic implications or physical consequences of the filmic medium, however much pornography is claimed as the realm of fantasy'. Lee, 'Bare Lives', 81.

27 The first box, constructed from Styrofoam, did not survive the first two actions. EXPORT had another box made out of aluminium, which was not returned to her after the exhibition *Film als Film* in Germany in 1977–78, according to archival files at the Generali Foundation. EXPORT had a reconstruction of the aluminium box made for the exhibition *Out of Actions*, Museum of Contemporary Art, Los Angeles (1998). Finally, a reconstruction of the first version in Styrofoam was made by EXPORT in 1999 and purchased by the Generali Foundation. Archive of the Generali Foundation, Vienna: file GF0002080.01.0-1999.

28 Lee, 'Bare Lives', 81, sees both works as making public of the private, and subject of the object.

29 One should mention the unavailability in 1968 of feminist psychoanalytic film theory à la Laura Mulvey.

30 With Kurt Kren, Hans Scheugl, Gottfried Schlemmer, Ernst Schmidt, and Peter Weibel. EXPORT's early films, such as *Menstruationsfilm* and *Orgasmus* (both from 1967), can be read as feminist manifestos.

31 Richard Meltzer, *The Aesthetics of Rock* (New York: Something Else Press, 1970), 274, note 6. See also Lewis P. Lapham, 'Introduction to the MIT Press Edition', in McLuhan, *Understanding Media: The Extensions of Man* [1964], (Cambridge, Mass.: MIT Press, 1994), ix. McLuhan had a long-running debate with Raymond Williams, on which see the latter's *Television: Technology and Cultural Form* (London: Fontana, 1974), and McLuhan's review in *Technology and Culture*, 19:2 (April 1978), 259–61.

32 For his German reception, see 'München leuchtet', *Die Zeit* (13 October 1967); 'Zurück ins Dorf', *Der Spiegel* (11 November 1968). 'Das Jahr des Schweins', *Der Spiegel* (9 June 1969), reports on the youth movement and culture, mentioning Frank Zappa, Janis Joplin, Yayoi Kusama, VALIE EXPORT, and marijuana parties.

McLuhan is described in 'Das Jahr des Schweins' as 'Underground Prophet' (146).

33 Weibel, *Das offene Werk*, 366.

34 Alfred Rosenberg, *Der Mythus des 20. Jahrunderts* (Munich: Hoheneichen, 1930).

35 '… mcluhans position zum kommenden ist der von nietzsche zum deutschen nationalsozialismus vergleichbar … sie sind: avantgardisten des faschismus'. *Das offene Werk*, 368–73, this quote 371–2. A re-evaluation of the left critique of McLuhan is Paul Grosswiler, *Method is the Message. Rethinking McLuhan through Critical Theory* (Montreal: Black Rose Books, 1998).

36 Part II of *Cutting* is subtitled 'hommage à marshall mcluhan'. The sentence is said to be 'zitiert nach mcluhan', and both German and (false) English are given in Weibel and EXPORT, *Bildkompendium*, 260. This suggests use of the German edition of *Understanding Media. Die magischen Kanäle* (Düsseldorf/Vienna: Econ-Verlag, 1968).

37 McLuhan, *Understanding Media*, 8. In continuation: 'The content of writing is speech, just as the written word is the content of print, and print is the content of the telegraph.' Weibel's notes on *Cutting* indicate the resonance of this line of reasoning of McLuhan's: 'die substitution führt direkt zum menschen …', Weibel and EXPORT, *Bildkompendium*, 261.

38 There is a justly famous passage: 'Suppose we were to say, "Apple pie is in itself neither good nor bad; it is the way it is used that determines its value". Or, "The smallpox virus is in itself neither good nor bad, it is the way it is used that determines its value". Again, "Firearms are in themselves neither good nor bad; it is the way they are used that determines their value". That is, if the slugs reach the right people the firearms are good. If the TV tube fires the right ammunition at the right people it is good'. McLuhan, *Understanding Media*, 11.

39 McLuhan *Understanding Media*, 293.

40 Weibel and EXPORT, *Bildkompendium* lists the following 'communication actions': Weibel, *Action Lecture*, 1968 (on the political uses of media); *Exit*, 1968 (part of EXPORT and Weibel's *W.A.R. – Kriegskunstfeldzug* project in Germany); EXPORT, *Ping Pong*, 1968; Weibel/EXPORT, *Das Magische Auge*, 1969 (part of *W.A.R.*); and *Publikumssprenger*, 1969 (part of *W.A.R.*; EXPORT whips the audience in a movie theatre).

41 '… expanded cinema ist expansion der perzeption und der kommunikation. Als expansion der perzeption experimente in neuen biomedical proceedings, als expansion der kommunikation exploration einer freieren gesellschaft'. *Interfunktionen*, 4, (March 1970), 169.

42 'Communicative action' first appears in Jürgen Habermas, *Technik und Wissenschaft als 'Ideologie'* (1968), *Erkentniss und Interesse* (1968), and *Protestbewegung und Hochschulreform* (1969) [all published in Frankfurt am Main by Suhrkamp]. The link with speech-act theory is fully worked out in *Theorie des Kommunikatives Handeln*, 2 vols (1981), but Habermas's turn to linguistic philosophy came earlier: his 1969/70 Frankfurt University seminar 'Über Sprachtheorie. Einführende Bemerkungen zu einer Theorie der Kommunikativen Kompetenz' was printed in Vienna as a pirate edition (Hundsblume Edition 4, 1970).

43 Further: 'What was true of linguistic communication is also true of communicative action. In neither can the context of an individuated life history structured

by ego identity be directly expressed.' Habermas, *Knowledge and Human Interests*, translated by Jeremy J. Shapiro (Boston: Beacon Press, 1971), 165.

44 Austin, *How to Do Things with Words*, 60. Derrida, 'Signature, Event, Context', 328–30.

45 Derrida, 'Signature, Event, Context', 329. Derrida's text was first delivered at the Congrès international des Sociétes de philosophie de langue française in Montreal in 1971 (the theme was 'communication').

46 This is also true of McLuhan's other French critic, Jean Baudrillard. See Andreas Huyssen, 'In the Shadow of McLuhan: Jean Baudrillard's *Theory of Simulation*', *Assemblage* 10 (December 1987), 7–17.

47 Derrida, 'Signature, Event, Context', 328. John Searle, 'Reiterating the Differences: A Reply to Derrida', *Glyph*, 1:1 (1977), 200, argues that Derrida confuses 'relative permanence' of a speech-act with repeatability: in the passage this is obvious, as Derrida turns a written 'now' (*maintenant*) into a 'now in general' (*maintenance*).

48 Lee, 'Bare Lives', 76, describes this act as 'realizing the meaning of the sentence in performance'.

49 I refer to archival material in the Generali Foundation for the chronology. The first performance took place on 11 November 1968 at the award ceremony of a film festival in Vienna, where another work of 'Expanded Cinema' by EXPORT, *Ping Pong*, had won the award for the festival's Most Political Film. Instead of 'screening' that work (an invitation to shoot ping pong balls at the screen), EXPORT performed *Touch Cinema*, supposedly under protest from the audience (Weibel and EXPORT, *Bildkompendium*, 261). Three days later, EXPORT performed on Stacchus Square in Munich. For another chronology, see Sylvia Szely (ed.), *Export Lexikon. Chronologie der bewegten Bilder bei VALIE EXPORT* (Vienna: Sonderzahl, 2007), 138–9.

50 The documentary *Wiener Underground* was made by Peter Hajek and Helmut Dimko for the series *Apropos Film* (ORF) and was broadcast on 12 September 1969. The series included a visit to Andy Warhol's Factory (1970), but the focus was on Austrian artists. The series premiered on 5 January 1968.

51 Marlene Streeruwitz, 'Wer sieht. Wer sagt. Was. Wie. Kann das'. In *VALIE EXPORT: Mediale Anagramme*, Cat. Neue Gesellschaft für bildende Kunst (Berlin: Akademie der Künste, 2003), 186.

52 Treffen unabhängiger Filmmacher, at the Künstlerhaus in Munich. See the review in the *AZ* Feuilleton, Axel Görg, 'Fuchshorn und Striptease' (15 November 1968). Photographer Werner Schulz was one of the managers of the *undependent film center* in Munich, which organized the event. Weibel and EXPORT, *Bildkompendium*, 261.

53 Régis Michel finds that EXPORT's impassivity turns her into a statue, even as the box reifies the body. *VALIE EXPORT*. Cat. Centre national de la photographie, Paris (Montreuil: L'Oeil, 2003), 24, 27.

54 Ed Sommer (b. 1932) is a filmmaker, sculptor, photographer, and in 1966–69 was German correspondent of *Art International*; Werner Nekes (b. 1944) is a filmmaker and owner of an extensive collection of visual media. Archive of the Generali Foundation, Vienna, folder on *Touch Cinema*, no index number. Werner Nekes has a homepage: www.wernernekes.de.

55 Weibel and EXPORT, *Bildkompendium* affords the best impression of the action, though it lacks the drama of the framed photograph. There is a large panoramic shot by Peter Kochenrath with Sommer and a fair-sized crowd. On another page are ten photographs, apparently contact sheets from square two-inch negatives, showing EXPORT walking, smiling at Weibel, being touched by Nekes, etc. The crucial shot with Sommer, being square, reveals more of the urban fabric and Weibel's megaphone than does the better-known cropped version.

56 The first photo was published in most EXPORT catalogues and many newspapers, in the German tabloid *Quick* ('Das erste Tastkino der Welt', 14 November 1968); in *VALIE EXPORT*, Exh. Cat. (Linz: Oberösterreichische Landesgalerie, 1992), 259; *Ob/De Construction*, figure 1 (inside of cover); Saxenhuber, *VALIE EXPORT*, 26, 27 (plus panorama view); *Valie Export. Kritisches Lexikon der Gegenwart*, 47/18 (Munich: Weltkunst und Bruckmann, 1999) 4; *Valie Export. Gabriele Münter Preis* (Frauen Museum Bonn, 1997), n.p.; *VALIE EXPORT. Eine Werkschau. Exhibition Folder* (Vienna: Edition Sammlung Essl, 2005), figure 6; Schimmel, *Out of Actions*, 169. The second photo was published in Görg, 'Fuchshorn und Striptease', as well as in 'Der erste Tapp- und Tastfilm', and Norbert Thomas, 'Im Tastkino bis an die Brust', both in *Stern*, 1968.

57 'Exhibitionisten an die Front', in the German journal *Der Spiegel* (21 April 1969), 194; Wolfgang Kudrnofsky, 'Dem Publikum die Peitsche', *action. Filmzeitschrift*, 5 (May–June 1969), 21; 'Nun ist es genug! Skandal auf der Strasse', *Film*, 46/47 (November 1969); Fred Viehbahn, 'Neues Trommelfeuer auf alte Konsumenten. Underground explosion wurde fast zur Nummernrevue', *Kölner Stadtanzeiger* (5 May 1969); Peter Hajek, 'Tapp, tapp, ein film. Austria Filmmakers Cooperative in München beliebt und zu Gast', *Kurier* (12 November 1968), 11; 'Zum Angreifen', *Süddeutsche Zeitung* (15 November 1968); the *Kölner Stadtanzeiger* (10 May 1969); *Stern Österreichausgabe*, 18 (1970); *Quick* (11 December 1968).

58 See 'Das erste Tastkino der Welt'; Karl Stankiewitz, 'Sogar das Kopierwerk streikte', *AZ*, 265; Görg, 'Fuchshorn und Striptease'; 'Der Kasperl kommt', *Stern* (10 December 1968), among others.

59 See Margarete Lamb-Faffelberger, *Valie Export und Elfriede Jelinek im Spiegel der Presse. Zur Rezeption der feministischen Avantgarde Österreichs* (Frankfurt am Main: Peter Lang, 1992).

60 The poster, used for the Spring Arts Festival of the University of Cincinnati in April 1968 (an event attended by Nitsch, who also had a poster by Sontag and Tina Dutton), is reproduced in Sohm, *Happening und Fluxus*, n.p.

61 On the importance of performance for a new experience of the audience, see, for example, Gavin Butt, 'Happenings in History, or, The Epistemology of Memory', *Oxford Art Journal*, special issue 'On Installation', 24:2 (2001), 113–26.

62 The text was first printed in 1987 in the catalogues *Self. Neue Selbstbildnisse von Frauen* (Bonn: Frauenmuseum Bonn, 1987) and *ConText* (Vienna: Secession, 1987) and has been reprinted several times.

63 'Als plastische Posen, als lebende Bilder und Skulpturen signifizieren meine fotografischen Körperkonfigurationen nicht nur die Doppelbilder der (geometrischen und menschlichen) Körper, sondern die Körperschrift ist auch immer Soziografie und Kulturgeschichte. Die Körperbilder liefern Bilder vom kulturellen Umgebungs-

körper'. EXPORT, 'Corpus More Geometrico'. It is a striking feature of EXPORT's prose, which I shall interpret in due time, that the environment does not consist of other bodies, but of a single body opposed to the subject.

64 The series consists of the subsets *Body Configurations in Nature* (1972/74) and *Body Configurations in Architecture* (1972/76/82). I will concentrate on the latter. Photos taken in Belgium by Eric Timmermann in 1974 are omitted in most catalogues. *VALIE EXPORT. Körpersplitter* (Linz: Edition Neue Texte, 1980), 39, 43. Another catalogue, *Körperkonfigurationen 1972–76* (Innsbruck: Krinzinger Gallery, 1977) adds to *Body Configurations* a series called *Körperstellungen: Nachstellungen* (*Body Positions: Persecutions*), photographs by EXPORT of Monika Hubman posing as Madonna (after Michelangelo's *Pietà*) with a washing machine and a sewing machine alternately, as well as drawings by EXPORT on similar themes such as *Madonna on the Stove* (*Die Madonna auf dem Kochherd*). In the text EXPORT wrote for the catalogue, she describes the *Body Configurations in Nature and in Architecture* as the first step in her investigations, and the *Körperstellungen* as the second step, from actual locations into the territory of cultural imagery: 'In the paintings of the past, an archive of postures has condensed without being noticed.' ('In den Gemälden der Vergangenheit hat sich unbemerkt ein Archiv der Körper-haltungen niedergeschlagen.') Preface, n.p. The text is dated October 1976. The 1980 catalogue *Körpersplitter* includes additional drawings, photographic varia-tions on the Madonna theme, and the wax model for a monument called *Der Ort des Menschen* (1974). Roswitha Mueller discusses the *Body Configurations* in her 1994 book *VALIE EXPORT. Fragments of The Imagination*, particularly 96–102, and 109–13.

65 Thomas de Quincey, *The Confessions of an English Opium-Eater* [published in the *London Magazine*, September and October 1821], *Works of Thomas de Quincey* (Edinburgh: Adam and Charles Black, 1862), I: 263–4: 'Creeping along the sides of the walls you perceived a staircase; and upon it, groping his way upwards, was Piranesi himself … Again elevate your eye, and a still more aerial flight of stairs is beheld, and again is poor Piranesi busy on his aspiring labours …'. De Quincey had not seen any of Piranesi's *Carceri*: 'I describe only from memory of Mr. Coleridge's account.'

66 This reading is confirmed by the artist's name, stamped in the form of her logo on the lower right. In addition, the title 'CARCERI' is written on the document. This is typical of the series, in particular in 1972.

67 Gilles Deleuze, 'Ecrivain non: Un noveau cartographe', *Critique*, 343 (December 1975), 1207–27, reprinted in Gilles Deleuze, *Foucault* (Paris: Minuit, 1986), 31–51.

68 Deleuze, 'Ecrivain non'.

69 This explains my difference from the interpretation in Jill Christina Dawsey, *The Uses of Sidewalks: Women, Art, and Urban Space, 1966–1980* (Doctoral disserta-tion, Stanford University, 2008), chapter 2. Dawsey reads the *Body Configurations* as subversive acts of feminist mimicry of the kind adapted from Roger Caillois by Luce Irigaray and applied by Craig Owens to the *Pictures* artist.

70 *Unsichtbare Gegner* might be described as a feminist variation on the *Invasion of the Body Snatchers* (1956). The credit line reads: 'Director: VALIE EXPORT in co-operation with Peter Weibel, script: Peter Weibel in co-operation with VALIE

EXPORT, based on an idea of VALIE EXPORT.'

71 The Ringstrasse was built in place of the older city fortification wall, which was demolished in 1857. As part of a vast urban development plan, a new university building, the parliament, city hall, art university, several ministries, and private palaces were erected along this circular street in the late nineteenth century.

72 Theophil von Hansen built the Parliament in 1873–84. Carl Kundmann added the fountain in 1893–1902. Four figures (three female, one male) stand for the principal rivers of the Empire: the Danube, Elbe, Vlatava, and Inn. The gender of the personifications is presumably due to that of the names.

73 For Fraueneder, the shift to Widl posing in the architecture takes away the tensions (and to some extent the political potential) conveyed in the earlier *Body Configurations*: Widl's body 'poses', and 'the discourse between architecture and body happens … not as contrast, but as similarity'. Fraueneder, 'Körperrituale', 121.

74 Austrian writer Thomas Bernhard called his reckoning with fascist tendencies *Heldenplatz* (Frankfurt am Main: Suhrkamp, 1988). The play met with outraged reactions, notably the pouring of liquid manure in front of the Burgtheater during the premiere on 4 November 1988 to show that Bernhard was 'fouling his own nest'. Given Brus's chosen backdrop of the imperial palace, his figure also serves as the counter-image to a hero on Heldenplatz, an absurd living statue, ephemeral, defaced by the black stripe, and persecuted.

75 This particular space in the Äussere Burgtor, the 'Outer Fortress Gate', was supposed to serve as a monument to the soldiers who died in the Napoleonic Wars. It became a First World War memorial at the end of the 1910s, and was rebuilt in 1933/34 as a Hero Monument by architect Rudolf Wondracek. Hitler and Göring visited the site on various occasions. Next to the monument, a room was designated to the victims of the 'Struggle for Austrian Freedom' (meaning resistance against National Socialism) in 1965.

76 The 1982 photographs are much larger than before. According to EXPORT's gallery, the size of these vintage prints is 56–79cm, while the 1982 photographs are 148×210cm for the *Law Courts*, 120×181cm for *Theseustempel* (Stufen), compared to the more intimately sized 42×60cm of the *Carceri*, for example. Email from Kurt Kladler, Galerie Charim, 6 February 2008. The 1982 photographs are singular prints, while those before exist as print editions of three pieces each. The exact date of production of these prints is unclear. It is generally difficult to pin down dates and variants of the *Body Configurations*. According to Hermann Hendrich, many of the early prints were exhibited without drawing. Interview with the author, 29 January 2008. Audio file. Kladler confirmed that early prints without drawing are in circulation.

77 Hendrich recalls photographing from a ladder. Interview with the author. Audio file.

78 There were probably several reasons for this competition: apart from the world event of the collapse of the Eastern Bloc, for Austria the so-called Waldheim affair, over the election of Kurt Waldheim, a former Wehrmacht soldier, as president of Austria, was significant: during the campaign for the presidential elections of 1986 candidate Kurt Waldheim's Wehrmacht membership during the Second World War and his possible involvement in the deportation of 40,000 Jews from Greece to

Auschwitz were made public, and raised broad questions about individual responsibility under Fascism. Nevertheless, Waldheim won the election by a landslide. An international commission was appointed, which found that Waldheim was not personally involved in war crimes, but that he most likely knew about the deportations. See International Commission of Historians, Hans Rudolf Kurz (ed.), *The Waldheim Report* (Copenhagen: University of Copenhagen Press, 1993). The on-going debate about the Berlin *Monument for the Murdered Jews of Europe* of course also played into the decision. The other participants were Clegg & Guttmann, Peter Eisenman, Zvi Hecker, Ilja Kabakov, Karl Prantl/Peter Waldbauer, Zbynek Sekal/Eduard Ebner, Rachel Whiteread, Heimo Zobernig. On the jury were the mayor of Vienna, architect Hans Hollein, curators Harald Szeemann and Robert Storr, Simon Wiesenthal, and members of the Jewish Community Vienna. See Lucas Gehrman (ed.), *Judenplatz Wien 1996. Competition Monument and Memorial Site dedicated to the Jewish victims of the Nazi Regime in Austria 1938–1945* (Bolzano/Vienna: Folio, 1996); Simon Wiesenthal (ed.), *Projekt: Judenplatz Wien* (Vienna: Zsolnay, 2000); special issues of the *Wiener Journal*, 205 (1997) and *Wiener Jahrbuch für Jüdische Geschichte, Kultur & Museumswesen*, vol. 3 (1998), and Holger Thünemann, *Holocaust-Rezeption und Geschichtskultur. Zentrale Holocaust-Denkmäler in der Kontroverse. Ein deutsch-österreichischer Vergleich* (Idstein: Schulz-Kirchner 2005).

79 On the Wiener Gesera, see Eveline Brugger, Martha Keil, Albert Lichtblau, Christoph Lind, and Barbara Staudinger (eds), Österreichische Geschichte. Supplementary volume: *Geschichte der Juden in Österreich* (Vienna: Ueberreuter, 2006), vol. 15. That the history of Jews is a supplementary volume is telling.

80 The question whether Austria was annexed by Germany or joined voluntarily is complex: Hitler forestalled a referendum by marching into Austria on 12 March 1938; he met no military resistance, and a manipulated plebiscite held on 10 April overwhelmingly 'ratified' Austria's union with Germany. See Hermann Hagspiel, *Die Ostmark. Österreich im Grossdeutschen Reich 1938–1945* (Vienna: Braumüller/Universitätsverlag, 1995), and Alexander Potyka (ed.), *Betrifft Anschluss. Ein Almanach* (Vienna: Arbeitsgemeinschaft Österreichischer Privatverlage, 1988). Alfred Hrdlicka's *Mahnmal gegen Krieg und Faschismus* (*Memorial against War and Fascism*), erected on the Albertinaplatz in the centre of Vienna in 1988, had been the only catalyst for a long-overdue debate about National Socialism. The public controversy about its commission by the city of Vienna led to calls for a different kind of memorial, one specifically dedicated to the Jewish victims of Fascism. See Thünemann, *Holocaust-Rezeption*, 180ff. The issue of remembering Jewish victims in Austria centred on Hrdlicka's problematic visualization: a bronze statue of a Jew kneeling on the pavement, scrubbing it with a brush (a humiliation forced on Viennese Jews). On the scandal of these 'paperweights', see *Die Zeit* (10 February 1989), 62.

81 'Das Monument ist Erinnerung an Schmerz wie Schutz vor Schmerz gleicherweise'. *Körpersplitter*, 96. The model is owned by the Austrian Gallery Belvedere, Vienna. The project is in part autobiographical: EXPORT's father died in the war, and her mother raised her and her two sisters in Linz.

82 On the use of the terms 'Holocaust' versus 'Auschwitz' and 'Shoah' see Chapter 4.

83 Hans Ernst Mittig, 'Das Denkmal', in Werner Busch (ed.), *Funkkolleg Kunst. Eine Geschichte der Kunst im Wandel ihrer Funktionen* (Munich: Piper, 1987), 556. The term Mittig uses for repentance is *Umkehr*.

84 'Proposal by VALIE EXPORT', Gehrman, *Judenplatz Wien*, 52–4 (bilingual text).

85 Paul Virilio had argued in 'The Overexposed City' ('La ville surexposée', first published in *L'espace critique*, Paris: Christian Bourgeois, 1984) that new technologies have brought with them the impossibility to perceive history in the city. Instead of collective memory, technology (which, according to Virilio, has transformed cities at their core) brought about the establishment of 'permanent presence'. It is perhaps no coincidence that the first German translation of the text was commissioned for the catalogue Peter Weibel edited for the Ars Electronica festival in Linz, Austria, in 1994.

86 Gehrmann, *Judenplatz Wien*, 54.

87 A handwritten letter by Weibel states that the installation 'is variable in dimension and number [of monitors] … also, the sound can be used or not, depending on the conditions'. Archive of the Museum of Modern Art, Vienna.

88 Adolf von Hildebrand, *The Problem of Form* [1896], trans. Max Meyer and Robert M. Ogden (New York: Stechert, 1907), 113.

89 The most important text on transparency in architecture is probably Colin Rowe and Robert Slutzky, 'Transparency. Literal and Phenomenal', *Perspecta*, 8 (1963), 45–54.

90 The two projects considered in the last round of discussion were a concrete sculpture 'inspired by gothic flying buttresses and the roof timbering of Polish synagogues' by Zvi Hecker, and the project by Rachel Whiteread. Gehrman, *Judenplatz Wien*, 33, 58. On the complicated execution, see Daniela Koweindl, 'Ein Mahnmal für die Ermordeten Österreichischen Juden' (Master's thesis, Institute of Art History, University of Vienna, 2003).

91 'Verfahrensregeln und Aufgabenstellung zum Wettbewerb (gekürzte Fassung)'. In Gehrmann, *Judenplatz Wien*, 31. As the jury put it: 'Ms. Whiteread considers it incompatible with her concept to add any openings to the building, according to the protocol of the debriefing after the decision of the Jury.' Ibid. Tellingly for contemporary memorial culture, the idea of using only the remains of the synagogue as a memorial was voiced by various parties. Cf. Françoise Choay, *The Invention of the Historic Monument* (Cambridge: Cambridge University Press, 2001) [*Allégorie du patrimoine*, 1992]. The Jewish Museum Vienna, which oversees the archaeological site, outlined the synagogue on the pavement of the square around Whiteread's memorial in 2010 in order to give visitors a sense of the historical layer underneath the visible architecture.

92 On this suggestion, the jury had obvious practical concerns about flowing water in an architectural site.

93 See Magistrat der Stadt Wien (ed.), Der transparente Raum (Vienna: MA 57 – Frauenförderung und Koordinierung von Frauenangelegenheiten, 2000). EXPORT's Allentsteig memorial (1998) to the population deported by the National Socialists to make room for a military base is also made of glass. See Rudi Palla (ed.), Erinnerungsstätte Allentsteig – eine Dokumentation (Vienna: Triton, 1999).

94 The European Union project Gürtel Plus was soon merged with the initiative URBAN. The architect overseeing the entire operation was Silja Tilner. She

approached EXPORT for realization of the cube. Madeleine Petrovic, *Der Wiener Gürtel. Wiederentdeckung einer Prachtstraße* (Vienna: Brandstätter 2009), 89–103.

95 See Anthony Vidler, 'Transparency', in *The Architectural Uncanny. Essays in the Modern Unhomely* (Cambridge, Mass.: MIT Press, 1992), 216–25; Jeff Wall, 'Dan Graham's Kammerspiel', [1985] in *Real life Magazine: Selected Writings and Projects, 1979–1994*, ed. Miriam Katzeff, Thomas Lawson, and Susan Morgan (New York: Primary Information, 2006), 194–217; Beatriz Colomina, 'Double Exposure: Alteration to a Suburban House' [2001] in *Dan Graham*, ed. Alex Kitnick (Cambridge, Mass.: MIT Press/October Files, 2011), 163–71.

96 VALIE EXPORT, 'Der Transparente Raum', in Magistrat der Stadt Wien (ed.), *Der Transparente Raum* (Vienna: MA 57 – Frauenförderung und Koordinierung von Frauenangelegenheiten, 2000), 138.

97 Richard Sennett discusses the 'isolation in the midst of visibility' in the glass architecture of the international style in *The Fall of Public Man* (Cambridge: Cambridge University Press, 1977), 13.

98 Manfredo Tafuri, 'Il teatro come città virtuale. Da Appia al Totaltheater', *Lotus*, 17 (December 1977), 30–53.

99 Edmund Husserl 'Systematische Raumkonstitution', *Ding und Raum. Vorlesungen 1907*, Husserliana, vol.16, ed. Ulrich Claesges (Den Haag: M. Nijhoff, 1973), 301. *Die Umgebungskörper* is plural, *der Umgebungskörper* singular. In *Corpus More Geometrico*, EXPORT cites Maurice Merleau-Ponty, whose *Phénoménologie de la perception* (Paris: Gallimard, 1945) [German ed. 1966] extends Husserl's project. A connecting link may be philosopher and art critic Peter Gorsen, who published EXPORT's 'Feministischer Aktionismus'. Gorsen wrote a dissertation on phenomenology, supervised by Theodor Adorno and Jürgen Habermas; it was published as *Zur Phänomenologie des Bewusstseinsstroms* (Bonn: Bouvier, 1966).

100 Edmund Husserl, *Ideen zu einer reinen Phänomenologie und phänomenologischen Philosophie*, vol. I: *Allgemeine Einführung in die reine Phänomenologie* [first pub. 1913] (Tübingen: Niemeyer, 1980), 64–5.

101 David Bell, *Husserl* (London: Routledge, 1990), 197. It should be said that Bell, who feels this way about only one phase of Husserl's work (his 'transcendental idealism'), does not think Husserl really believed in a 'transcendental ego', but merely used this rhetoric for his practical analysis of mental acts (204–5).

102 Husserl, *Ideen*, I: 53–6, on the varieties of bracketing, among them außer Aktion setzen. Austin called his enterprise 'linguistic phenomenology' in 'A Plea for Excuses', *Philosophical Papers*, 182.

103 I am referring to *Adjungierte Dislokationen I* (1973). With one super-8 camera mounted on her back and one on her chest, EXPORT walked from an apartment in Vienna through parts of the inner city and then on to the suburbs. Hermann Hendrich filmed her in turn with a 16mm camera. The installation consists of the three films projected together, with Hendrich's view at left and the two 'first-person' camera views at right.

3 Sites

On 23 December 1974, the International Committee of Concern for Academic Freedom in Yugoslavia drafted an open letter to Marshal Tito. Signed by Noam Chomsky, A.J. Ayer, Paul Ricoeur, Jürgen Habermas, Jaakko Hintikka, and other public intellectuals, the letter was printed in the *New York Review of Books* in February 1975. As 'friends of the country, who admire Marshal Tito's achievements for the liberation of the Yugoslav peoples', the signatories expressed concern about the recent 'infringements on academic freedom', in particular the repression of intellectuals and laws endangering the autonomy of universities.[1] The philosophers' protest was aroused by Tito's attempts of the preceding few years to expel professors at Belgrade University who were members of Praxis, a philosophical circle active since 1964. Praxis, devoted to the adaptation of Marxism to the Yugoslav idea of self-management, was decidedly anti-Stalinist, and had been in open conflict with the official party line on many occasions. Its orientation was cosmopolitan, with Ernst Bloch, Erich Fromm, Jürgen Habermas, Ágnes Heller, Herbert Marcuse, and Henri Lefebvre on the editorial board of its multilingual journal, *Praxis International*.[2] The open letter captures the disorienting Yugoslav situation of the time from a Western perspective. On one hand, for left intellectuals, Yugoslavia, a non-aligned country with fewer restrictions (citizens could travel abroad, for example) and its autonomy from Russia, was an island of hope amidst Cold War oppositions. Nevertheless, within what Bojana Pejić retrospectively calls 'laissez-faire-Socialism', freedom of speech and the press was infringed by severe censorship.[3]

When Tito visited Zagreb four years later in 1979, Sanja Iveković sat on a balcony overlooking the official parade. What resulted was her most famous work, *Trokut (Triangle)* (Figure 33). The work, as seen in her retrospective at the Museum of Modern Art (MoMA) New York in 2012 or at *documenta 12* in Kassel, consists of four photographs and a text. We see: 1) The upper part of a high-rise building, photographed from below, with a person standing on its roof; 2) A dark convertible, accompanied by police motorcycles; 3) The artist, lounging on the balcony, feet up, in shorts and a T-shirt with '... ash of

America' legible around the picture of a flexed arm holding a gun. She reads a book – in another version, she holds the book and a cigarette, and a whiskey bottle is visible below; 4) a view of the street from above with crowds and policemen milling around a Yugoslav flag. In galleries, the images are often placed to correspond with a viewing position on the balcony: Iveković at right, building above left, car middle left, crowd below left. The written text aligns images with actors:

> The action takes place on the day of the President's visit to the city, and it develops as intercommunication between three persons:
>
> 1. a person on the roof of a tall building across the street from my apartment;
> 2. myself, on the balcony;
> 3. a policeman in the street in front of the house.
>
> Due to the cement construction of the balcony, only the person on the roof can actually see me and follow the action. My assumption is that this person has binoculars and a walkie-talkie apparatus. I notice that the policeman in the street also has a walkie-talkie. The action begins when I walk out onto the balcony and sit on a chair, I sip whiskey, read a book, and make gestures as if I perform masturbation. After a period of time, the policeman rings my doorbell and orders that 'persons and objects are to be removed from the balcony.'[4]

Photographs and text seem to cohere into a narrative, yet leave enough space, and loose ends, for us to have some discomfort in entering an imagined Yugoslavia of the late 1970s: flags, a motorcade, surveillance political and behavioural, a small, modernist balcony in what one presumes is a small, modernist flat.[5] As work of art, *Triangle* has been revived for its aptitude to show a politicized (from our 'Western' perspective), somewhat exotic version of high-quality international post-war avant-garde art, in particular at the intersection of feminist performance and conceptual photography. And yet: did the act of defiance really take place? And at the time claimed, almost exactly a year before Tito's death? Iveković inducts the policemen and the security staff (there is no way to know their identity) into her performance about the infiltration of the private sphere (house and body) by the State. The photographs are suggestive in contrasting the private sphere with military representation, but it is the stipulation of a narrative by the artist and the subsequent relationship between photographs and text that allows us to enter the story: I would almost say, it *makes* the confrontation, since there is neither pretended masturbation nor police intervention in any of the images. The site of this confrontation, however, is by no means a photograph, or a collection of them. It is Zagreb at the end of the golden age; a fiction, perhaps, but no more so than the troubled but virtuous Yugoslavia of the *New York Review*. The open letter itself is equally interesting for its performative self-consciousness: the way the signatories, become a political committee in the act of publishing their missive, try to aid their Yugoslav colleagues by praising the regime. And by printing the letter in a prominent American paper, they made sure that Tito, who was unlikely to be impressed, was *not* the only addressee. The document also reveals, as Austin found in his later thinking on the subject, that performance and representation are inseparable.[6] Paying attention to this inseparability of performance and representation and to the tension between them is important to Iveković's act: from what really happened on her balcony, to the discussion about private and public life that its documentation sparked in its own time (the end of Tito's reign) and which continues to mutate into nostalgic longing for a lost Yugoslav past.

This chapter, then, deals with the question of site: real, fantasized, remembered, or implicit, but always understood as a specific context, a place in the

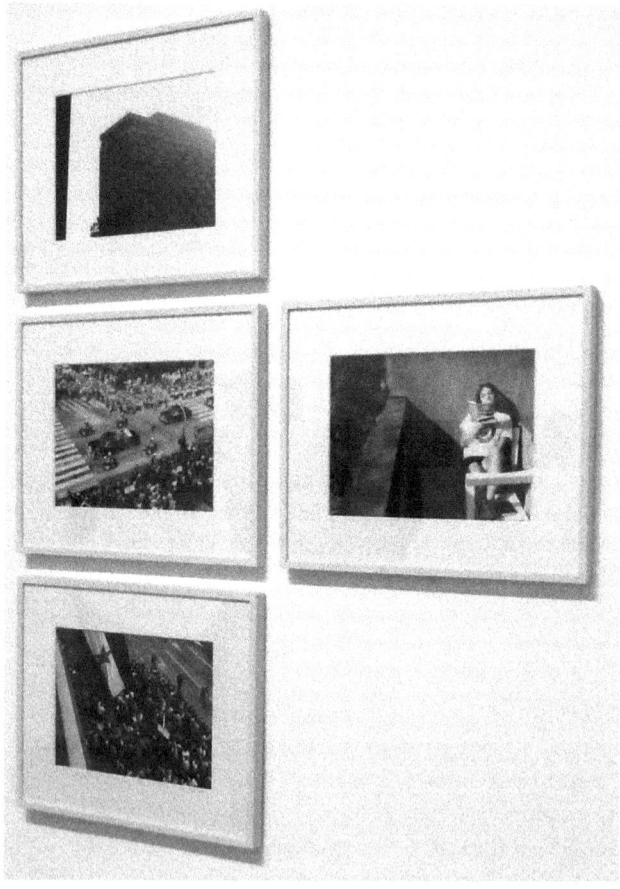

33   Sanja Iveković, *Triangle*, 1979, installation shot at Museum of Modern Art, New York, 2011

past where a documented performance joins the real world. The site thus temporalized is crucial to performance, and to the monument. I examine it through the lens of Tito-era Yugoslavia, a context that provides *me* with a maximal cultural distance: I am here in particular on the outside, unsure of where I stand and with little implicit orientation. How to enter the picture thus becomes an explicit problem. The site returns us to the complexity of the act: as documented, can it be read as an agreement between artist and audience? How does site differ, due to changing context and a deepening historical reference, every time it is re-instantiated through display of performance documents? Does site, in turn, determine commemoration?

Current theories of site and site-specificity, developed out of dissatisfaction with the practice and theory of minimalism, and tied to an emerging interest in institutional critique, are my starting point here.[7] Scholars, critics, and artists have discussed 'site' not simply as a particular geographical location, but as a larger theoretical construct which embraces history, politics, and economics. Indeed, they have gone further, addressing colonial legacies, urban gentrification, and the institutional and non-institutional fate of art.[8] Yet, what binds these concerns together? Is there a clear sense in the discourse as it comes down to us that a site-specific work must *occupy the site* it is 'specific to'? Is Martha Rosler's photographic and textual series, *The Bowery in Two Inadequate Descriptive Systems* (1974–75), site-specific? As a photographic installation it occupies a gallery, but that need have nothing to do with the neighbourhood it analyses. The answer to such questions, in the discourse as it stands, must appear arbitrary. For my concern in particular, the constitutive role of site, freed from a questionable claim to priority through specificity, encompasses audience, space, and the conditions that make performances work in the Austinian sense – not necessarily *in* their site, but also retrospectively in documents re-contextualized in various display contexts. This notion of site depends on time, because the performative moment can be rendered historical through the production of documents. Later audiences re-imagine original sites, fractions of which they encounter in documents; imagination is infused with its own particular circumstances, past and present. Site as time, then, will determine my investigation.

To develop my argument, it is necessary to confront the orthodox notion of site specificity as a property specific to monumental sculpture. Take Richard Serra's *Tilted Arc*, commissioned by the government-run Arts in Architecture Program and erected on Federal Plaza in 1981 (Figure 34). The artist famously defined the site-specificity of the 12-meter-high steel sculpture with the motto 'to move the work is to destroy the work'. This utterance, not compatible with all of Serra's practice prior to *Tilted Arc*, emerged in a public controversy (usually called a 'trial', due to the hearings held to decide the matter) that led to the removal and thus, in Serra's terms, the 'destruction' of *Tilted Arc* in

1989.[9] The trial attracted much attention at the time, drawing leading critics and historians to testify in favour of Serra, and has generated much art-critical and historical work since, concerning the possible conflicts between public art and its audience. I do not wish to rehearse the debate here but, rather, to ask what we would, from today's point of view, consider the specificity of the work. Is it really Federal Plaza, with its nondescript government buildings, carrying their own particular histories and constructing a space for pedestrians, that is the site of our passionate debates about public art? Is not the site we mean when we talk about *Tilted Arc* just as much the hearing room, the arguments and publications of the prominent historians, politicians, and journalists, the conviction that today there would be no opposition to a Serra sculpture? It is not that reception is more important than inception, but that the *work itself*, as powerfully contextualized in the publications related to the dispute, *became* as much about public art, government sponsorship, and freedom of expression as about 'what it's like to be on Federal Plaza'.[10] This could all be subsumed under the idea of the site's 'historicity', which of course would apply more or less implicitly to all places, but there is more. On an understanding of site-specificity that links an object's identity with its site, as in Serra, *Tilted Art* is now siteless, but so is Rosler's *Bowery* and *all* ephemeral art. That seems to me too narrow an account of site, in performance, photography, and conceptual art surely, but in monumental sculpture as well. It would be far more apt, it seems to me, to index a work's site-specificity to time, as in fact has been the intent in the last decades of many artists who favour interventions over objects. Serra's work *was* exclusively about the Federal Plaza when it was installed (he had no brief about free expression in 1981), but it became about much more. The 'site' becomes a spatio-temporal continuum that occupies not just one place at one moment, but shifts with the character of the work and of the place it occupies: it can be carried into the court-room, newspapers, or some classroom, in which I restaged the trial with my students. This is not to say that all of these are equally or indifferently sites of *Tilted Arc*: its built site has a conceptual priority, since the arguments were about its right to be *there*, and not in my classroom. But it is to say that, as the significance of the work shifts from a steel monolith to a matter of principle, its site shifts as well. And this is true even of the Federal Plaza: what interests us as art historians is not this particular square in New York today, but as it was inhabited and argued about in 1985. Site, then, even at its most literal, involves a factual and imaginative reconstruction of past sites. This is especially true of ephemeral art, which is often incomprehensible without a context accessible only through photographs and textual accounts of sites that are no more. I shall show this through several works of the Yugoslav 1970s, concentrating on a 1973 slide installation by Marina Abramović, *Freeing the Horizon*, which was restaged with surprising formal and discursive effects in her 2010 retrospective *The Artist*

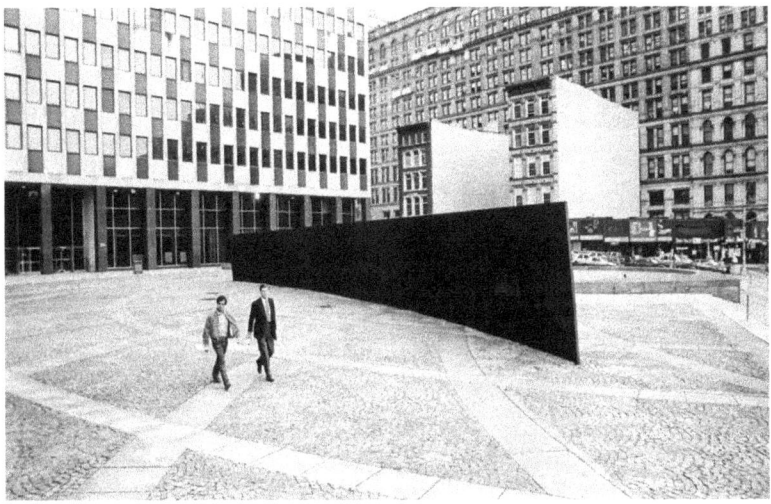

Richard Serra, *Tilted Arc*, 1981   **34**

is Present at the Museum of Modern Art, New York. I end with Abramović's wildly ambitious theatrical autobiography, *The Life and Death of Marina Abramović* (2011–12), which in a sense generalizes *and* ends the theoretical concern with site found in the performative monument by absorbing it into the artist's construction of her own context.

Liberalism and constraint

Before 'site' can be a theory of how objects or performance link to the past, it must fulfil a humbler function: how does it situate art in Yugoslavia under the rule of Josip Broz Tito? How do audience, politics, and space play together? Urban experience, political action, and viewer experience are linked here through the process of document-making. In Belgrade, I enter an explicitly politicized context, one that operated on state-sponsored public gestures that allowed sufficient intellectual freedom for a vigorous (and public), sometimes oppositional, culture to develop. What do these tensions tell us about the connection between performance and place?

One might characterize Tito's domestic politics schematically by saying that they rested on a charismatic personality cult and a strong creation myth for Yugoslavia as having been founded by Partisans who freed the country from fascist occupation.[11] Within this framework, artists interested in the relations between individual agency and the public sphere had to more or less explicitly work through related issues of propaganda, censorship, and the symbols of a glorious past extending into the present in the person of Tito.

Iveković's *Triangle* serves as a warning that we cannot interpret such work as either didactic or idiosyncratic, for the spilling over of public life into private life is the theme of the work. Indeed, taking Iveković's ostensible provocation into account, the spilling over of private life into public life is itself foregrounded. The complexity of the situation, not just in Belgrade but equally in Iveković's Zagreb and urban Yugoslavia generally, placed resistance to Tito's paternalism side by side with sincere admiration for the president. There is a refusal in *Triangle* to pay attention to the cult in favour of private pleasures, both physical and intellectual, and this refusal to join in with the crowd might be a real breaking of the rules, but there is also obvious enjoyment in mocking the spectacle on the street, and in presenting Iveković's own supposedly erotic excitement in political terms. The ambivalence of political art in Yugoslavia, at least art concerned with censorship and propaganda, is a product of performance: in 'propagating' or 'censuring', artists act in ways consistent with the policies in question. They both represent and reproduce constraint. In this overlapping of action and description, official and oppositional culture, and artist and audience, the site is manifestly political, official even, but shot through with ironic practices of criticism. The most obvious symbol of this system, the communist star, can help us enter this complex cycle.

Let us take a classic example. Abramović's *Rhythm 5* (*Ritam 5*), also called *Star of Fire* in contemporary catalogues and newspapers, was performed in the course of the Third April Meeting in 1974 in the courtyard of the Student Cultural Centre (Studentski Kulturni Centar, SKC) in Belgrade (Figure 35). The artist constructed a five-pointed star in brushwood, which served as both stage and perimeter for her performance; at the centre of the star was bare pavement. A Croatian critic, Zrinka Jurčić, praised the action as a 'salvation from useless discussions about art' accomplished by a 'female priest of art'.[12] How was this accomplished?

> Outside the SKC, in front of the building, she made a skeleton of a star, the edges filled with sawdust and oiled. The action started with the lighting of the star, she walked around it, cut the hair on a wig she was wearing and then she cut her own hair almost down to the bare skin, then her nails from both hands and feet. She then lay inside the star waiting for the fire to burn down.[13]

Abramović reportedly fell unconscious, due to lack of oxygen, and had to be carried out of the star by an audience member.[14] Although this intervention was unplanned, the open planning and eventual rescue shifted agency from Abramović to the audience, in spite of the latter's slowness to act, noted by contemporary critic Milanka Lečić:

> The audience did not participate, they stood as passive observers, without doing anything, which you could see at the end of the ritual, when Marina Abramović remained supine inside the burning star, and everybody stood still,

observing the situation. No one with the exception of one man realised the ritual had ended.¹⁵

Despite the audience-critical tone, the issue is not the supposed complacency of an audience unwilling to commit itself ethically. Lečić faults the audience cognitively rather than morally: what it failed to do was to notice that the *ritual had ended*. This reading opens a perspective on the political stakes of ritual central to Iveković's *Triangle* as well. The viewers, on a conventional reading, finally took responsibility for the physical process embodying the symbol; they ended Abramović's probing of her strength by removing her body from the harmful stage she had identified with the symbol of the republic.

For the contemporary Yugoslav audience, the association of the star with the Tito government must have been manifest, though Abramović took care to choose a symbol with broad connotations, ranging from the Christian tradi-

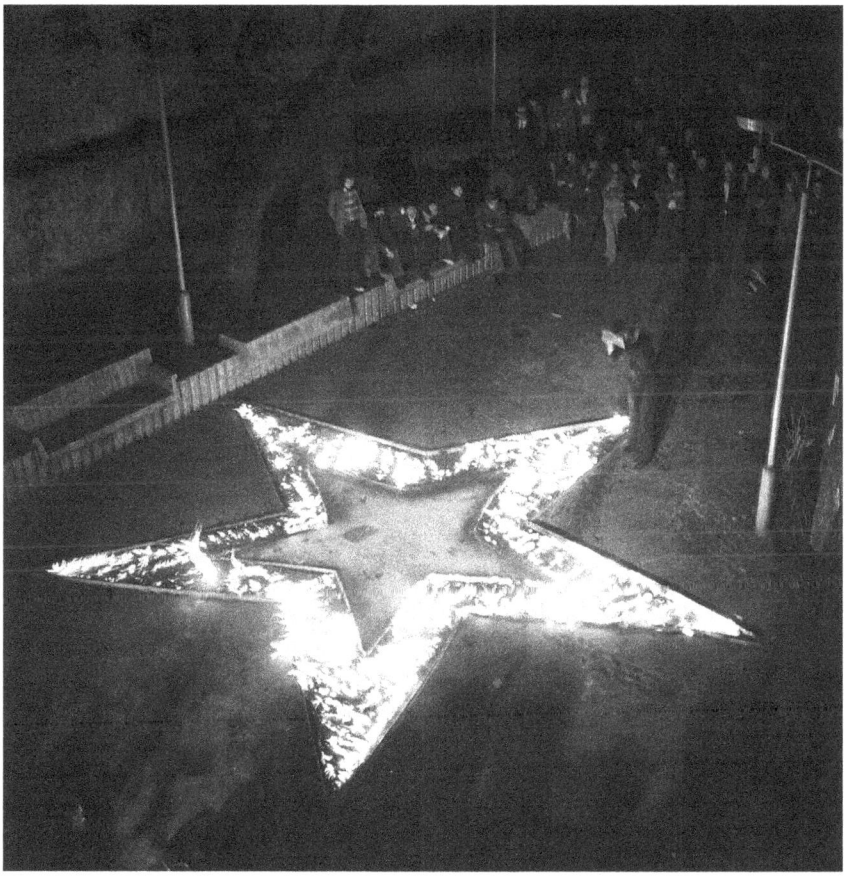

Marina Abramović, *Rhythm 5*, 1974   **35**

tion (where the symbol stood for the five senses, or for the five wounds of Jesus) to mathematical perfection in the tradition of the Pythagoreans, the symbol of the microcosms of various secret societies and mysticisms, from whence it had, of course, been widely mobilized as a symbol for international socialism, featuring centrally in the flag of the Socialist Federal Republic of Yugoslavia, the sign under which she 'was born', as the artist stated herself.[16]

It is plausible that Abramović wished to bind the political symbol that shaped her childhood to her body in a ritual of her own devising, but institutional context is important.[17] The SKCs (operating in Belgrade, Zagreb, and Ljubljana) were a concession to the students from Tito after protests in June 1968, a way of 'pacifying the young generation's growing discontent with any form of authority'.[18] In the capital, the SKC was administered through Belgrade University, and it became the focal point of the cultural avant-garde after its foundation in 1971.[19] The 'officialdom' of the star requires rethinking in such a context. Abramović's forced passivity within the ostentatious symbolic space of the burning star, *within* the student preserve, can also be read as an aggressive, performed passivity, urging the audience to step in and interrupt the performance; it was also a comment on institutional constraint as such. A relay of responsibility, the documents lend themselves to political re-interpretation. In a 2006 text, filmmaker and curator Lutz Becker, who attended the Third April Meeting, sees the work as outright protest:

> This performance in which the artist staged a specific cleansing ritual seemed to me a kind of exorcism. There was an element of self-sacrifice, which echoed the sacrifice of the generation that had founded Yugoslavia during the war of liberation and the Revolution (1941–45). But the star of the revolution, the guiding star of the parents' generation was, so it seemed to me, devouring the children of this revolution. This performance provided an insight into the psyche of a generation that had been kept in a state of 'permanent adolescence', politically overruled by the old establishment.[20]

This reading is of course informed by the passage of some years after the dissolution of Yugoslavia into Serbia, Croatia, Bosnia-Herzegovina, Slovenia, Montenegro, Macedonia, and Kosovo.[21] Becker, the sympathetic foreigner, evokes the melancholy image of a post-war generation made passive, even infantilized, by the realization of its parents' ideals.[22] Abramović's use of the star accommodates such political moralizing, as well as the more subtle interpretations that the artist and her critics volunteered in 1974, only because it externalized inarticulate relations to it (feelings, habits, intentions) through a ritual that others could join in principle to the extent that its symbol was publicly available, but only joined in practice due to the manifest danger to the performer. The 'least active' moment of *Rhythm 5*, Abramović's unconsciousness, transfers action to the public. I would go further and say that it *produces* a public of fellow performers. At the core of this performance is authority: resting in the symbols used, but especially in the transfer of activity from Abramović to the public.

In arguing that *Rhythm 5* is about authority, I return to a thesis about the historicity of performance designed to overcome the opposition of presence and mediation so hotly debated in relation to Abramović's late work. In this context, Becker stands for mediation, reading the star allegorically; on the other side stand theatre theorists, who see in Abramović a final dismantling of representation in favour of bodily entry into social mechanisms.[23] According to this view, the star is a turning point, wherein experience is seen to outweigh conventional meaning. Thus, writing of Abramović's self-mutilation in the form of the star in *Thomas Lips* (Innsbruck 1975), Erika Fischer-Lichte insists: 'When Abramović cut the star into her skin, the spectators did not hold their breath or feel nauseous because they interpreted this as the inscription of state violence onto the body but because they saw blood flowing and imagined the pain on their own bodies.'[24] Such a reading of *Thomas Lips* could be turned to *Rhythm 5*: the audience rescued Abramović from fire and smoke, not state violence, one could say. But to oppose politics and experience thus is to miss the point of performatives in the public sphere, as the star is also, in virtue of Yugoslav political context, the national symbol.

Abramović has on various occasions renounced the interpretation of her work as political, or of herself as 'political artist.'[25] These denials reflect a view of her art as neither official art nor a heroic dissidence but, what may be more interesting, an investigation of the relations between the two. Every public act, however introspective, has as complement a receiving public, just as every document implies a reader. In 1974, Abramović lived and worked in a political context wherein the contemporary hero cult had taken on explicit continuity with old monuments – from the May Day Parade to the State celebrations of Tito's birthday on 25 May – one in which the 'political body' had become a synonym for 'the people.'[26] This political body is of course to a certain extend abstracted, removed from its naturally shifting physical state, as it is from the lived experience of her Belgrade spectators. Abramović bridges the two by letting the body function as a document in her performances. In a context where politics was saturated with personality, the investigation of political symbols took on biographical, deeply sensuous dimensions: shortly after Tito's death, Iveković produced *Tito's Dress* (1981–82), a sheet of paper with the five outlines of what looks like the same naked woman, into whose silhouette Tito's portrait is photomontaged. Tito becomes a dress, a skirt, a bathing suit, a backpack, a sun umbrella (Figure 36). The work plays on a notion of the body politic, now merged with the desire for the leader, who protects the body while touching the woman's skin – merging sexual desire with the authoritarian infiltration of the political into the intimate.

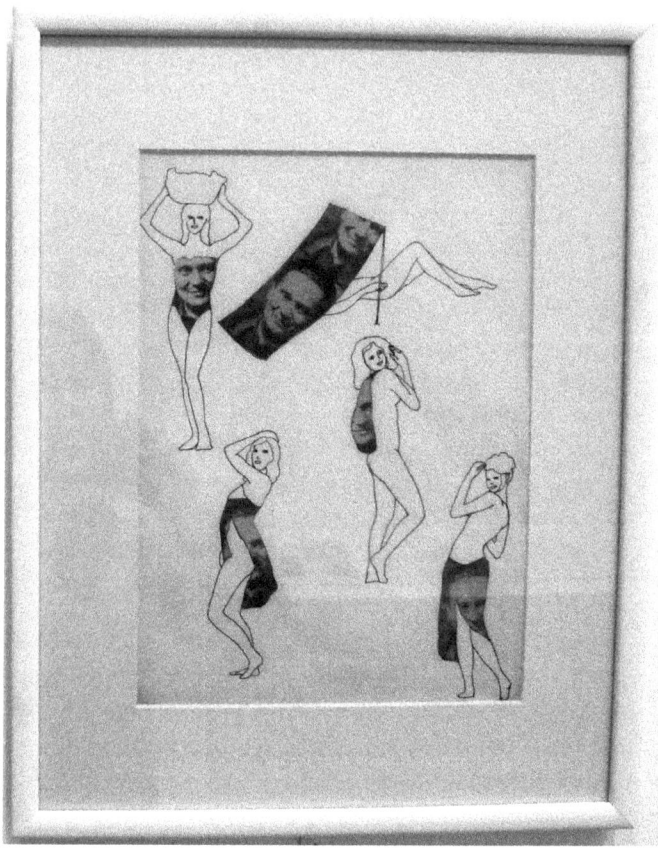

36   Sanja Iveković, *Tito's Dress*, 1981/82

On various later occasions, notably in the late 1980s and since, when political tension in Yugoslavia turned into civil war, Abramović projected herself into the role of the charismatic leader, the narrator or protagonist of a historical myth. This identity formation gave political shape to *Rhythm 5*; on the other hand, there remains the question of how international audiences, whose political formation differed considerably from Abramović's, read her documents. To grasp this, we first need to see how explicitly Yugoslav circumstances were conserved in documents, whether mechanical or bodily, and how these could be interpreted 'off site'. The shift in performance and its interpretation will allow us to see how Abramović's practice locates its site and its public, but also how it packages the 'total speech-act' (display, context, reception) to account for change and the passage of time, that is, for performance becoming a monument.

The visible and the invisible Belgrade: Abramović's *Freeing the Horizon*

In June 1973, Abramović presented a slide installation at the SKC in Belgrade entitled *Freeing the Horizon* (Figures 37 and 38).[27] It consists of modified colour photographs screened on eight projectors set up in the rotunda of the SKC building.[28] Abramović had shot the images herself in late spring 1973 on a stroll along the main axis of Belgrade's historic centre, Prince Michael Street (Ulica Knez Mihailova), leading to what was then Marshall Tito Street (Ulica Maršala Tita).[29] After developing the negatives, she covered portions of the prints with white and blue acrylic paint, reshot them on colour slide film, and projected the results.[30] An archival photograph in the SKC Archive shows Abramović in a preparatory stage before the projection begins (Figure 39). In the photograph she sits in the centre of the oval gallery space, hand-operating a slide projector. The installation reinforced the experience of architecture as lived space. Each projector showed one slide for the duration of the evening, turning the hall into a photographic panorama. The fact that the slides did not change is important: Abramović was not pursuing the contemporaneous practice of a sequential slide lecture in the sense of Robert Morris or Dan Graham.[31] An immersive experience of presence and absence constituted itself statically around the visitor.

Due to the long-standing absence of the slides, scholars have tended to assume that the piece was projected in black and white, although black-and-white slide film is a rarity, even in Eastern Europe.[32] This assumption evidently

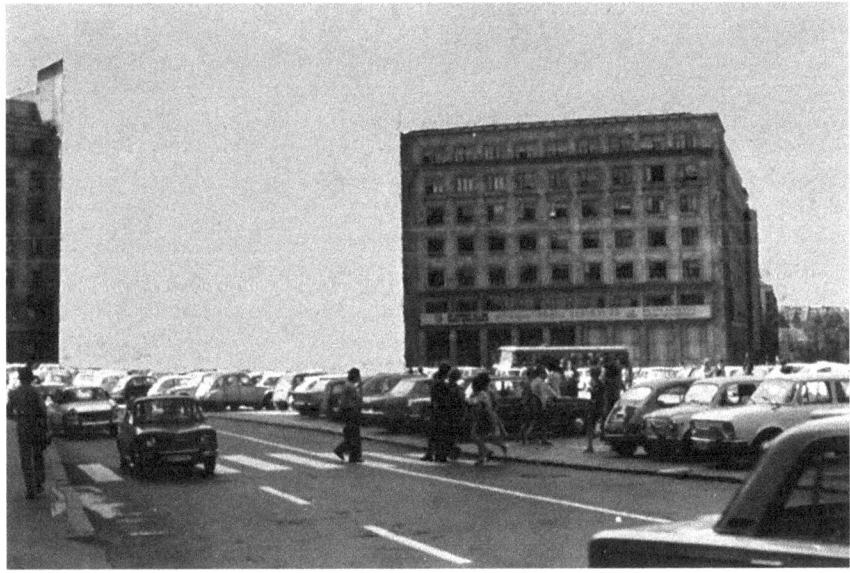

Marina Abramović, *Freeing the Horizon*, 1973   **37**

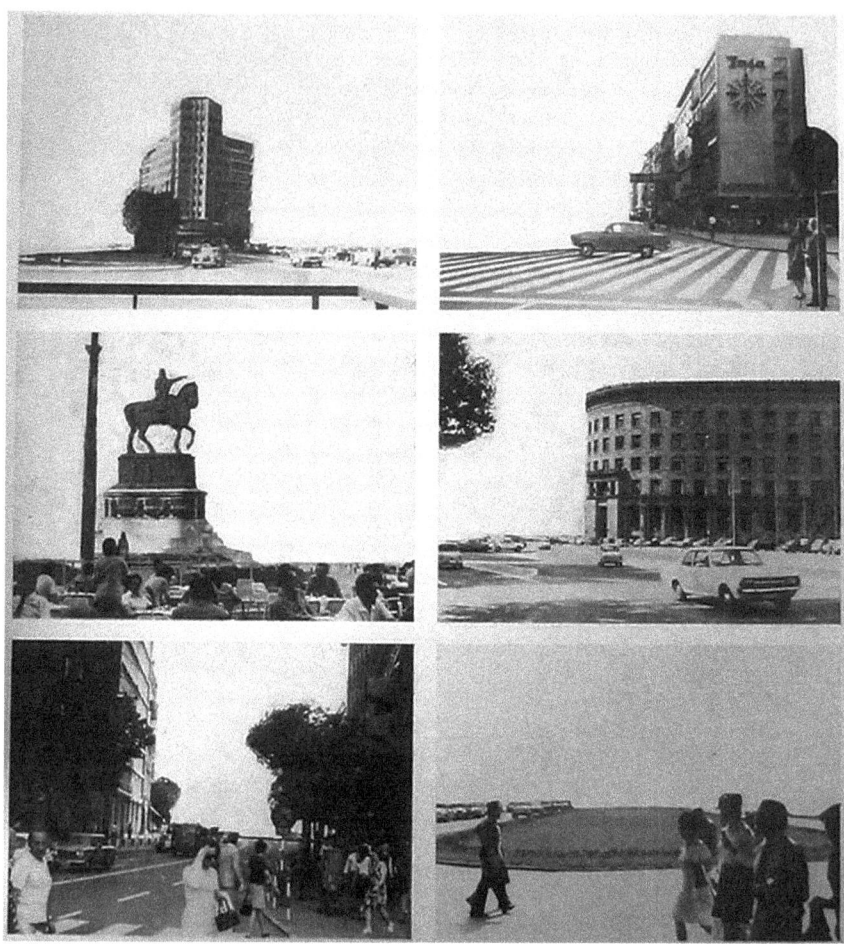

38   Marina Abramović, Hand-out *Freeing the Horizon*, 1973

resulted from the black-and-white photocopy Abramović had distributed to her audience. The hand-out, which the artist has described as an 'invitation card', has done duty for the absent slides in catalogues and art historical texts.[33] This documentary remainder of the event (but not of the projection) has determined the work's reception in a very particular way, informing critical reception of both medium and live experience circa 1973. This reception history took a turn with the 2010 retrospective *The Artist is Present* at the Museum of Modern Art. In the wake of the war and bombardment of Belgrade in the late 1990s, the historical resonance of the slides' subject had shifted. Abramović responded with a change in presentation: in a room dedicated to the artist's biography, the work was screened on a sole projector, among exhibition posters, snapshots, and mementoes like Abramović's art diploma

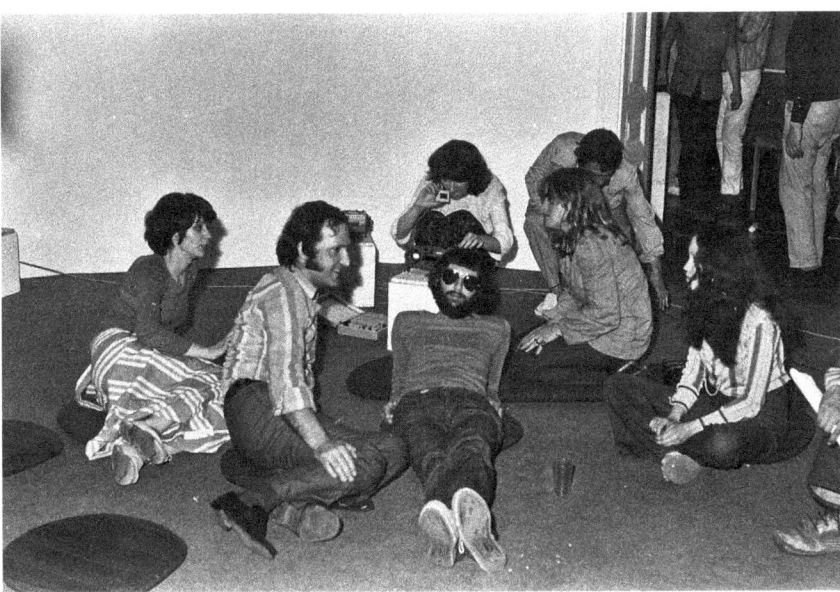

Marina Abramović preparing *Freeing the Horizon* at the Student Cultural Center,   **39**
June 1973

and her parents' war medals (Figure 40).[34] The projector lit up the wall above the display cases, with one slide steadily replacing another in the manner of a long-lost family album, revealing unfamiliar statuary, a cut-up cityscape, and people in bright summer dress. In New York, the projection seemed nostalgic, the evocation of a lost Eastern Europe, the context personal. 'Looking at this piece', Abramović notes in the MoMA catalogue, 'I was struck by the realisation that some of the buildings from this project had been bombed and destroyed during the war in 1999.'[35] The MoMA projection became just what the original was not: a slide lecture on war and nostalgia. With site, form, and context now linked to a sepia-tinted vision of Yugoslavia, the piece made possible retrospection at the price of the complex political involvement of the 1973 event.

To start describing the work from documents accessible today, the most immediate quality of *Freeing the Horizon* is that it used photographic means on a panoramic scale.[36] It also made visible the discontinuity of illusion: the perspective of the 35mm prints must have been distorted by the sloping walls of the SKC, with gaps and overlapping edges that could only have amplified the internal discontinuity due to painterly erasure within the slides. As panoramist, Abramović created a disillusioned illusion, its truth-value disconnected from the collection of 'reality effects' on display, comprised of Belgrade streets and residents, starkly outlined against a white or blue

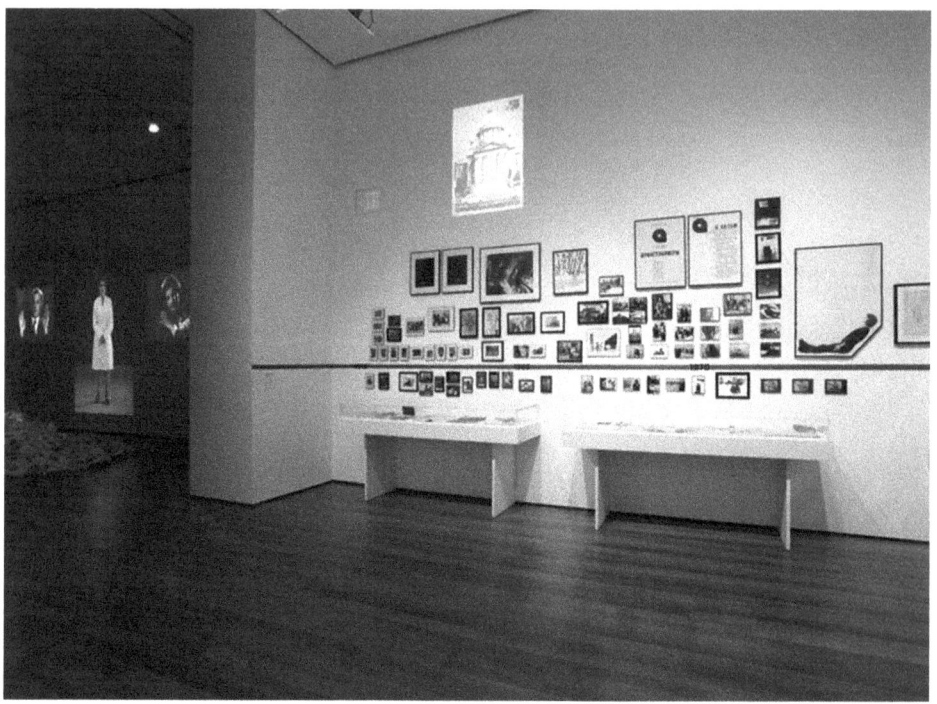

40   Installation view of Abramović's retrospective at Museum of Modern Art, 2010

sky.[37] The panoramas of the nineteenth century are often seen as attempts to produce unhindered views through a controlled and controlling environment, granting illusions of omnipresence and control while in reality fixing the subject in a windowless room, often in a clearly defined position in its middle.[38] *Freeing the Horizon* operated with this manipulation of the field of vision, but its technical inconsistency and, especially, its juxtaposition with what must have been far more coherent experiences of walking in Belgrade assured that it would fall short of subjective effects of omniscience. For instead of exotic destinations, the illusion Abramović offered was only the familiar city – deprived of important landmarks, to be sure, but in a provisional and laborious manner, not miraculously freed of them. The panoramic mode of illusion-formation is thus replaced by documentation of illusion-formation. The act of erasure in white and sky-blue acrylic paint, a material symbolic of post-war abstraction and monochromes, seems to bring about an aesthetically utopian city devoid of government buildings. This simulated reality of a walk through the city, and the critical practice of walking familiar from Situationists and related theorists, is flattened onto an elliptical wall space.[39] The paint does not, as in a real panorama, cement an urban illusion, but it does contribute to the illusion that Abramović wants to bring about, a practice of 'free' looking.

And yet freedom and constraint are put in a challenging tension. If a classical panorama sought to create an illusion in which the spectator collaborated by believing it, thankful for the sheer novelty of its experiences, Abramović uncouples compelling experience from truth-claims. But on what does she thus cast doubt? On the seamless image of socialist well-being, which she fragmented, or on the fragmenting activity of the oppositional artist herself? This is at least an initial ambiguity.

It seems necessary to sketch more fully the institutional context wherein Abramović staged her gesture. The SKCs were run fairly independently by the universities, mostly by students of art and art history, and became meeting places for a loose group of younger artists.[40] Of them, the SKC in Belgrade became the most important base for exchange between Yugoslav and international artists. The yearly April Meeting – Expanded Media Festival, held at the SKC and consisting of exhibitions, actions, lectures, and conferences, was the most influential caucus of new art in Eastern Europe, beginning with its first year in 1972, when Italian artist Gina Pane participated with her performance *LIFE–DEATH–DREAM*. Video screenings that year included works by Allan Kaprow and Dennis Oppenheim. Two years later, Joseph Beuys took part in the April Meeting (the same year that Abramović performed *Rhythm 5*).[41] Yugoslav and international artists performed side by side, though the tension between paternal authority and freedom under Tito that brought about the SKC and its unhindered activities must have provoked rather different attitudes.[42] Most importantly, Yugoslav artists did not believe themselves to have effected an ideological break with the public order which sponsored them – and which they may have hoped to improve. How to translate this state of dependency into art? One way that I have already discussed is to present the mechanisms of power in performance as blandly and neutrally as possible. *Freeing the Horizon* works through the rhetoric not of state symbols, but of truth-claims ascribed to photography. These are shown quite literally in its symmetrical acts of photographing and re-photographing.

In playing the censor and recording herself in the process, Abramović not only makes documentation of a mode of image manipulation, but appropriates it in order to 'free' herself and others – whether they want to be freed or not. This interpretation of *Freeing the Horizon* gains in force when we take into account a related earlier work called *Project – Empty Space* from 1971 (Figure 41). Produced for the international theatre festival Art BITEF, in some sense the forerunner of the April Meetings, *Project – Empty Space* pursued a similar ambivalent evacuation of the city through photography.[43] Abramović had planned to install the work in public, showing two photographs both indoors at the SKC and outdoors on Republic Square in the centre of Belgrade. Ultimately, the project was realized only at the gallery. A text of Abramović's of this period describes the action as follows:

> Two gigantic photos on Republic Square in Belgrade B.C. The same two photos in the Gallery of SKC (both photographs are taken from the same angle). One represents the theatre Atelje 212 between two neighbouring houses and the other the empty space between the same houses.[44]

Abramović's account of the photographs mentions the theatre and then simply 'the empty space between the same houses', as if this space existed just as firmly.[45] In the photograph, the theatre is occluded with paint. There is a parallel here between pictorial manipulation and action: the photographs no more existed in public space than did the empty space where the theatre in fact is. This is a doubly imaginary action. And yet we puzzle over it and wonder whether it did, somehow, elusively take place. As a work of conceptual art, it did: it is preserved in the catalogue. The original photographs, if they still exist, have not resurfaced in any of Abramović's retrospectives. But there is no way to make that out in the grainy reproductions of the catalogue, within the 'empty space'. Abramović left the black writing on the sign mounted on

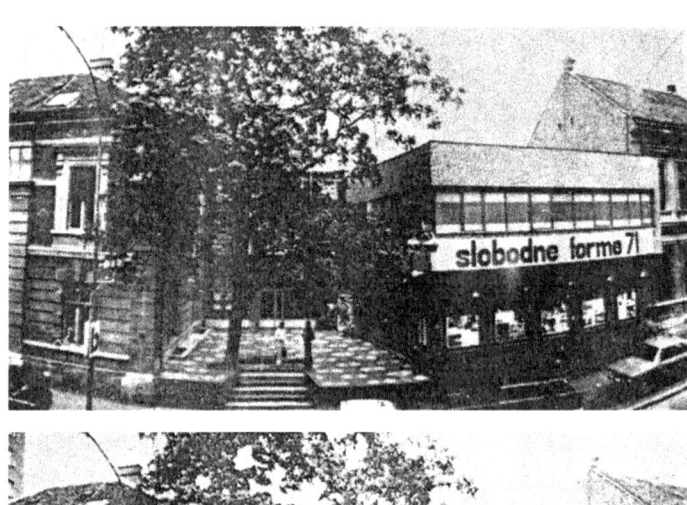

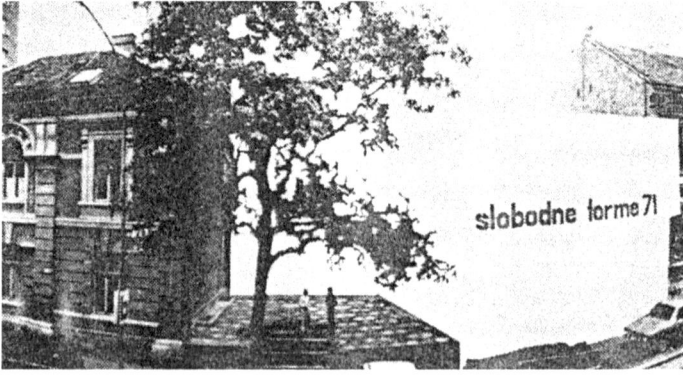

41a & b   Marina Abramović, *Project – Empty Space*, 1971

the theatre façade: *slobodne forme 71* ('free forms 71'). Abramović ironically partakes of this freedom in erasing the venue, the site of the event advertised. The assertion of the existence of an 'empty space between the houses', as the result of her manipulation, cements the analogy to censorship: it manipulates reality simply by claiming that the erasure has already taken place. The irritating ambivalence of making visible the process while declaring it to be the 'reality' in deadpan manner constitutes the political life of this piece – for an official act to be effective, it must be serious. Site here is very much a real corner of Belgrade, but one vulnerable to political fiat. The wall text makes manifest Abramović's awareness that authority operates through the ambiguity between stating (the already real) and decreeing (making something the case politically):

> State – you are standing
> instruction – go!
> result – empty space[46]

These instructions pair an assertion about the viewer's condition ('stating' that 'you' are standing) with an imperative from the artist (['you'] 'go!') to produce the desired result, empty space. This result is not quite objectively real, but no mere figment of subjective imagination either, being backed by authoritative commands and the modified photograph.

It would be convenient to say that Abramović's family connection to the political ruling class is the cardinal issue here, whether or not the young artist was aware of it. But such a claim would be too easy, for at issue are not the artist's intentions, but the way she obliges spectators to take a position in the process of manipulation. Whatever they may have thought of the artist and her biographical stake in the work before them, the work, like the instructions to *Project – Empty Space*, made them collaborators. Italo Calvino, writing a few years later, describes a similar urban intervention in a particularly dystopian chapter of *If on a Winter's Night a Traveler* (1979). The resemblance is stunning:

> Walking along the great Prospects of our city, I mentally erase the elements I have decided not to take into consideration. I pass a ministry building, whose façade is laden with caryatids, columns, balustrades, plinths, brackets, metopes; and I feel the need to reduce it to a smooth vertical surface, a slab of opaque glass, a partition that defines the space without imposing itself on one's sight. But even simplified like this, the building still oppresses me: I decide to do away with it completely; in its place a milky sky rises over the bare ground.[47]

Calvino's character soon proceeds to erase 'all people in uniform' and eventually all passers-by except his love interest. But when he hurries toward her, he is intercepted by the secret police: he could not erase them. On the contrary, 'section D', as they are styled, see him as a collaborator in the task of remaking the world. 'But', asks the protagonist surprised, 'weren't you the ones who were always talking … of expansion …?' They reply with bureaucratic cool: 'Tendentially, something that might seem negative in the short run, in the long run can prove an incentive …'.[48] Calvino's morality tale might seem to warn against subjective freedom won at the cost of severing oneself from political reality. But the peculiar interest of his story lies in how much power he grants the subjective intervention. It really works, people and places stay erased, the protagonist gets a bit closer to the woman he loves, and to the secret police who want to harness his destructive potential. Now, consider for a moment the image of the neo-classical Yugoslav Federal Assembly as projected by Abramović, with blue sky glaring between its columns as if there were no one home to legislate, as if no one could be home (Figure 42). Such an evacuation

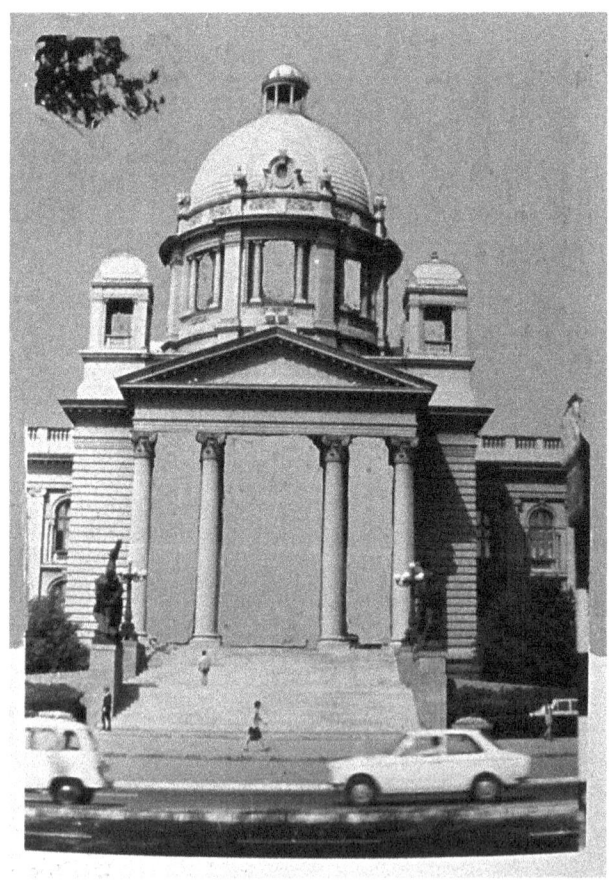

42   Marina Abramović, Federal Assembly (*Freeing the Horizon*), 1973

may well have answered to strong feelings in a SKC audience, but the power to put it into practice belonged only to the authority it faced. As with Calvino's dreamer, Abramović's act of liberation is authoritative in itself.

It remains to ask what kind of audience Abramović was trying to conjure out of her SKC spectators. I turn once more to the photocopy that Abramović produced for the event (Figure 38). In contrast to the use of colour slides, redolent of the anti-aesthetic, family snapshots, and vacations abroad, the black-and-white of the photocopy recalls journalism, minimizes the signs of painterly erasure, and brings what is left into emphatic focus. Remaining buildings stand almost like cut-outs against the white paper. The audience, as we can see in archival photographs, carried the sheet into the installation (Figure 43). Starting in standard reading direction, from left to right and top to bottom, in the first image at upper left everything but the Palace Albania

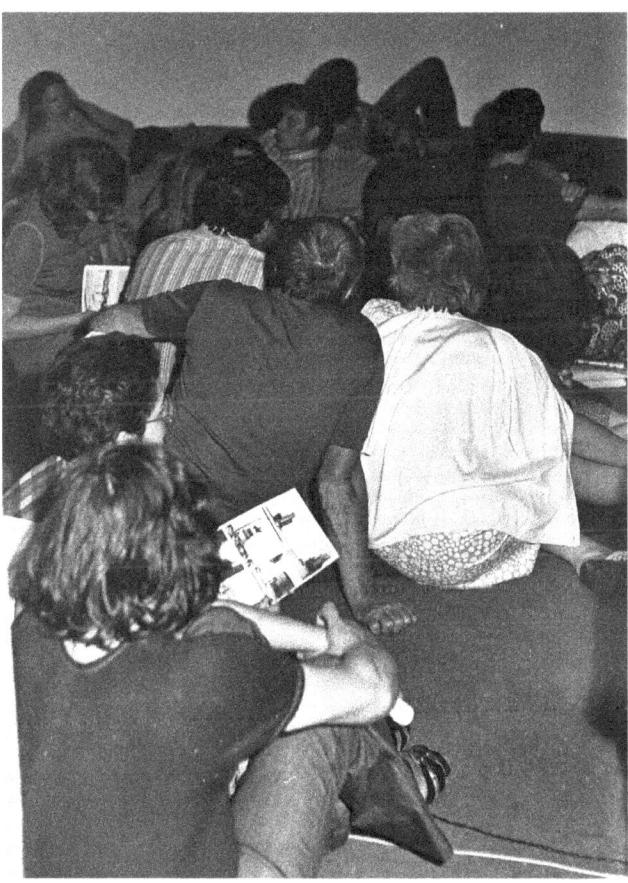

Audience during *Freeing the Horizon*, 1973   **43**

in Terazije Square is removed. This high-rise building, built in 1938–40, is historically significant: it was the edifice where the planting of the red flag by the Red Army and Yugoslav partisans announced the liberation from German occupation in 1944. In the second image, a department store shares Ulica Knez Mihailova with one car and some pedestrians. The National Theatre on Republic Square is missing from the third image, putting into stark isolation the nineteenth-century equestrian statue of Prince Mihailo (1823–68), the first ruler of an independent Serbia. In the fourth image, the union headquarters is removed, leaving a space adjacent to the Museum of Revolution, directed by Abramović's mother; the museum had been the Communist Party headquarters for two decades after the war.[49] In the last two images, passers-by dominate. At left, we are on Kolarčeva Street, with the view of Terazije Square removed; the final image shows pedestrians walking past the lawn in front of City Hall, which has been painted over.

Are the formal qualities and sequencing of the hand-out at all important? After all, the audience saw both copies and colour slides. I would argue that *Freeing the Horizon* achieved its full specificity, a political specificity crucially tied to site in both physical and temporal senses, through the coexistence of these documents. A social bond in particular is the work of the hand-outs: they make the audience accomplices in the imaginary action. Possession of the hand-outs, which resemble anonymous leaflets, is concrete evidence of a shared experience, one that may incriminate the carriers, or identify them among themselves as participants in a common cause. This implicit collaboration is characteristic of the SKC in 1973 as *temporally indexed site*: it cannot be recovered in any MoMA retrospective, however thoughtfully done.

The aesthetics of power, with its overwhelming experience, remains something on the walls of the SKC, which can be recreated only imaginatively; but the gallery audience had at least two other versions of reality at its disposal: its own experiences and the photocopy in its hands. This reading audience is formed through the making and distribution of the hand-outs, as much as through the act of projection and the pragmatic task of inviting an audience to an event at SKC. That the audience was itself photographed examining its sheets of paper, which makes it into collaborators, is eloquent testimony to the performative status of Abramović's copies, which begin with her snaps of Belgrade and end, fittingly, with snaps of the SKC and of her public imagining her snaps of Belgrade.

Site specificity here is not in particular experiences or memories, which we could set out to imagine, but in dated conditions that are not necessarily lived through, but which condition experiences of the event. This is no privileging of the live event on a 'site' pretext. The gallery projection was not a uniquely rich experience, but a specifically meaningful one. That this had to do with distribution of the document (the hand-out), resulting in the formation of an acting (reading) public, is supported by an announcement for *Freeing the Horizon* that appeared in a Serbian newspaper in 1973. Abramović is quoted as follows:

> My ideal has been expanded media for a long time, and my experiments tonight are a continuation of earlier ones. I wish to remind the people of everyday experience, of that which they lost the power to perceive and the possibility to enjoy.[50]

Through expanded media, which I have coupled with self-conscious use of the document, Abramović invites her audience to complicity in an act of monument-making and erasure, involving others in her (imaginary) urban planning and its real distribution in the gallery screening and hand-out. Again, we should be careful not to interpret this distribution as 'in itself' a revolutionary act or protest gesture. In taking the leaflet, the public did take responsibility, but in an act that is fundamentally ambiguous: an act that could be contextualized in two divergent ways, as civil disobedience or as the spontaneous demonstration of solidarity for which communism was famous. The imaginative performance of every audience member, and transmitted through verbal and written histories of the piece, ultimately determines – though of course, only in individual cases – which context is stronger. That in the afterlife of the event an urban-revolutionary interpretation came to dominate, supplemented by Abramović's post-civil-war interpretation, shows how a site-specific work shifts in meaning, as the knowing Belgrade inhabitant is superseded by a non-Yugoslav reader anxious to place Abramović historically.[51]

Anonymous authority

Having seen how subtly Abramović introduced political gestures in *Freeing the Horizon* and *Project – Empty Space* through the medium of photography and a strategy of removal, and how much this depended on the implicit knowledge of a public I have called temporally site specific, it is worth seeing how far such a model can extend. When she left Yugoslavia in 1975, Abramović came to work before international publics extending beyond Belgrade. Her body became an interface between individual and global issues, mediated by both myth and desire. We may gain insight into the generic mobilization of site specificity by considering it as a generic complement of 'being public', a tendency not absent in Abramović or Iveković, but most clearly explored by Abramović's male contemporary and colleague Braco Dimitrijević, an artist who dealt extensively with heroic and monumental markers in public space.[52]

  In 1971, he began a series called *Passers-by* that he would continue in various geographical and political contexts and media over the next decades (Figure 44). For the exhibition Zagreb Salon 1971, he produced large (two by

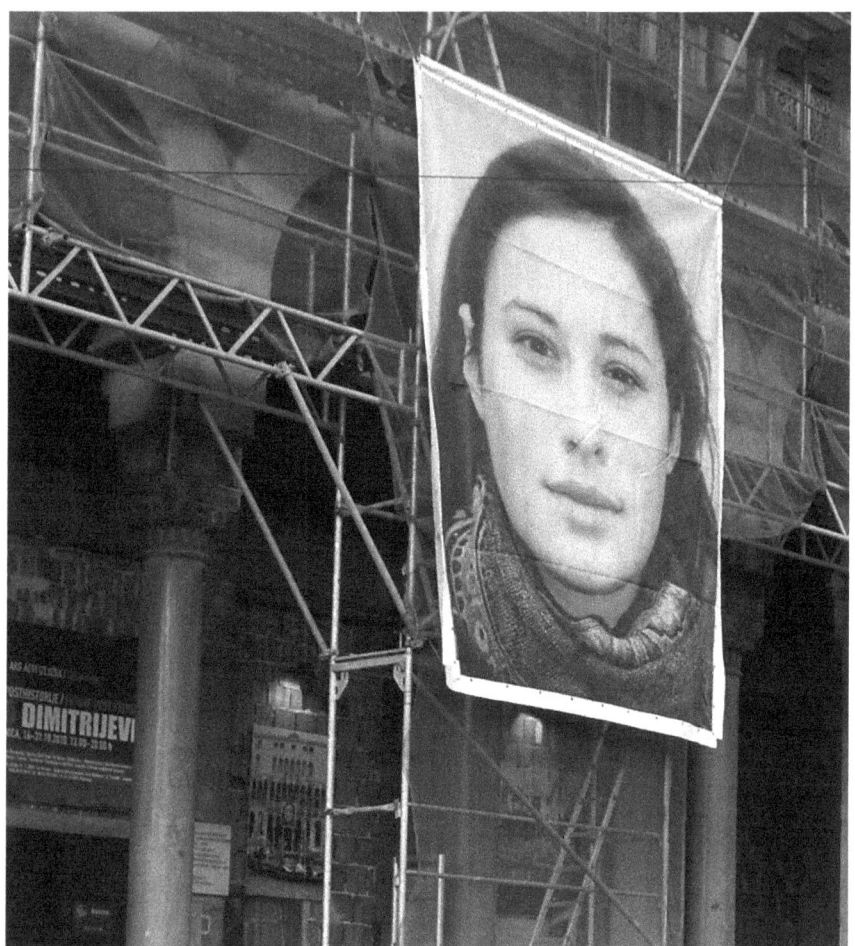

44   Braco Dimitrijević, *Poster for exhibition in Sarajevo*

three metres) portrait photographs of three persons he had supposedly met on the street (a young woman, and elderly woman, and a middle-aged man), and mounted these images on an imposing façade on Republic Square (today Ben-Jelacić-Square) in Zagreb.[53] The full title of the piece, *Passers-by whom I met by chance at 1:15pm, 4:23pm, and 6:11pm in Zagreb*, gives the exact times of day but not the actual date of the encounters.[54] Dimitrijević emphasizes as the object of his critique not official monuments as such but the 'acceptance' of public faces as belonging to politically important individuals. It is the inference as to the identity of public figures that Dimitrijević challenges. He addresses the complicity of ideology and public art through a nondescript 'questioning process' that he wishes the spectator to apply to the 'next' monument.

By monumentalizing private persons, Dimitrijević called into question the binding character of monuments to public figures and historical events. His strategy in this on-going series is one of mimesis, both of forms and of their public venues: depending on the rhetoric used in the particular public spaces he worked in, he chose various media, from the academic bust sculpture to the photographic bust, associated in Yugoslavia above all with the ubiquitous portraits of Tito found in both private and public space.[55]

And yet, in order for the piece to really work, both the uninformed and the informed audience are needed: the latter to reconstruct the possibility of a speech-act that worked on the uninformed audience. The unknown 'heroes' become, for the viewer in the know, anti-heroes or decoys. Tension arises at the point where the two audiences meet: where the informed public imagines (however justifiably) a contentious public sphere in which the uninformed audience participates and is changed by the encounter with the 'heroes'. The implicit split between a 'naïve public' that simply acts on political conventions installed in public space, and an informed public who reflects on these conventional performances and contributes to their reform, becomes explicit in another of Dimitrijević's works. Upon entering St Martins School of Art in London, Dimitrijević began producing marble plaques with names of people from the neighbourhood, and soon started working on a bust to an unknown passer-by, allegedly a 'heretic piece in the context of the prevailing St. Martins' idiom of abstract welded metal sculpture'.[56] What interested Dimitrijević, of course, was not formal invention but self-consciousness in the presentation of public art. When the bust was unveiled in a park in London, Guy Brett wrote in the London Times:

> For one day last week, a new piece of public statuary appeared in the garden of Berkeley Square. The craggy bust on top of a massive plinth, the nameplate in heavily incised gold letters, looked remarkably like a hundred others of London's public monuments. In fact the whole thing was made of fibre-glass and was put there by a young Yugoslavian artist, Braco Dimitrijević, a post-graduate sculpture student at St. Martins School of Arts. Its subject was a 'public figure', but not in the usual sense. Dimitrijević had sculpted 'A Casual Passer-by I Met at 1:10pm'.[57]

The article reveals Dimitrijević's address to a reading public while still (crucially) positing the unsuspecting stroller to whom the work looks like one of 'a hundred other' monuments. It is this anonymity that initially gives the work its bite. A different kind of reading experience follows, informing the reader that the bust depicts a person still alive: 'David Harper, born 1924', reads the inscription. The sole interest of this identity, besides the trivial one that he was a chance acquaintance of Dimitrijević's, is in allowing spectators to reflect on the function of monumental publicity. In doing so, an uninformed public and an informed one coalesce.

The legacy of Dimitrijević, with its dry citation of political power, is more persistent in performance art of the former Yugoslavia than it might appear. In 2007, three Slovenian artists legally changed their name to Janez Janša, a name belonging to a popular conservative politician in Slovenia who, in 2011–13, was Prime Minister of that state.[58] The three artists, born between 1964 and 1973, exhibit their notarized name-change documents and organize lectures and re-performances; above all, they organize monumental installations spelling the name JANEZ JANŠA, whether on a mountain in the Slovene Alps, in a star on the Hollywood walk of fame, in light at the Ars Electronica Festival in Linz, or in parasols on Copacabana Beach in Rio de Janeiro.[59] The results are provocative and should lead to substantial discussion on the ground about Slovene politics; the calculated use of media in the spelling of the politician's name is as pertinent to mass politics today as are Dimitrijević's plaques and posters. If one could object to the work on politico-aesthetic grounds, it is perhaps by saying that the art theory (readymade, signature, series) combined with nothing but the ideologue's name, a site-specific context rigidly indexed to the performers and not responsive to the sites of its re-appearance, exhausts itself as content: the political point, like a blown-up passer-by, is a foregone conclusion leaving no room for the transformation of more intractable experience.

In Dimitrijević's work, publicity as a generic limit of private experience is used to generate historical meaning. The deceptively neutral act of conveying information changes the viewer's context, not making a passer-by politically important so much as throwing into doubt the inference to the political importance of public figures. This is where Abramović fits in: by conjoining private experience and public symbolism, she brings into contact the two elements held apart by Dimitrijević, the rehearsal and the critique of power. Her half-informed spectators struggle with their own reactions to places and symbols. Her own action in *Rhythm 5* or the slide show is neither fully public nor fully private: Abramović constructs herself as 'private' subject through public discourse. Abramović carried on this project so consistently that the site and its temporalized audience come to appear central not just in the work of Iveković or Dimitrijević or the Janšas, but in much post-war political art.

The construction of co-presence

In Yugoslavia, given Abramović's very public experience of growing up in a celebrated Partisan family, the issue of political identity was most concrete, her body itself serving as a document of historical struggle, of pre-determined and self-determined facts. In this sense, her role was neither counter-revolutionary nor an authoritarian confirmation of charismatic leadership. Abramović would continue to test authority (her own) in relation to ideology and ritual, and ultimately to her audience, in much of her later work.

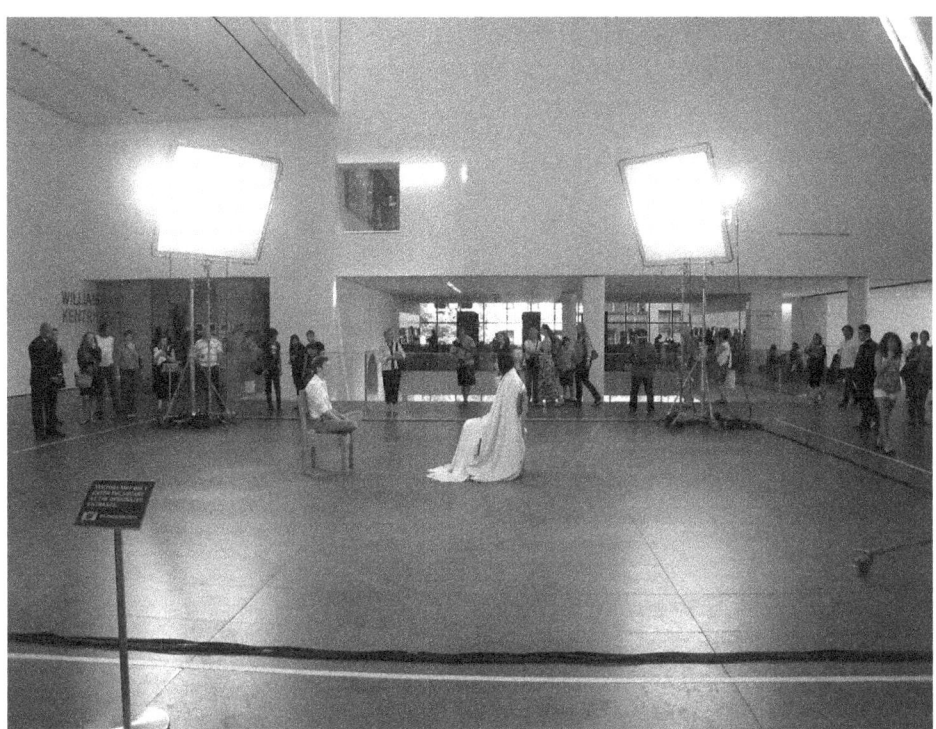

Marina Abramović, *The Artist is Present*, 2010   **45**

Since the 1990s, Abramović's increasingly theatrical yet static staging of herself and her circumstances creates events intrinsically hospitable to the document, or, better, live acts which carry the truth-claims normally residing in the mediated retrospect of the document. In her performance on occasion of her 2010 MoMA retrospective, *The Artist is Present*, she was literally 'present', as the title put it, for the duration of the exhibition, sitting on a chair in the foyer of the museum, with a second chair for visitors (Figure 45).[60] Abramović had sat before for long stretches without eating or drinking, from collaborations with Ulay of the 1980s to a famous gallery show in New York that captured the attention of the media, being immortalized among other places in the television serial *Sex and the City*, whose protagonist opines that Abramović stuffs herself with burgers at night when the gallery is closed. A secret visit is arranged, and Abramović's stoical perseverance proves genuine. To this public persona of the committed artist, cemented by the arduous interpretations of *Seven Easy Pieces*, *The Artist is Present* adds only the role of the spectator, as generic as any in Dimitrijević.

Indeed, not much happened, even though audience members sitting across from her often seemed, or tried to seem, moved: Abramović was there, but

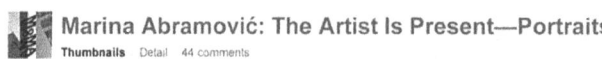

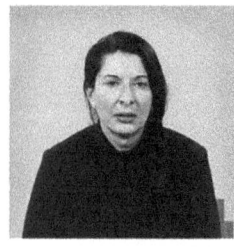

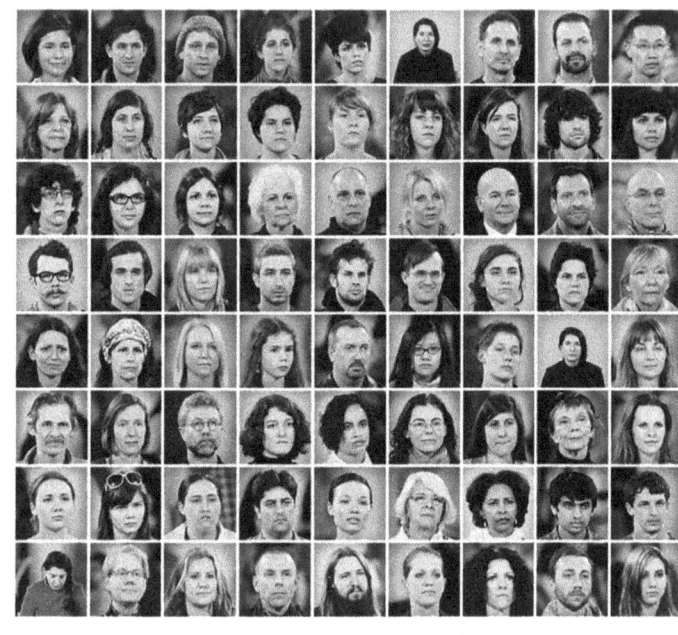

46   Marco Anelli, photographs from *The Artist is Present* on flickr.com

nothing else.[61] For all the monotonous simplicity of their experience, the performance was complex, particularly in its publication: sitters were filmed and photographed by Marco Anelli, and the images put online on flickr.com and the MoMA web page (Figure 46). In order for this to be possible, one had to sign a copyright release before sitting, though later in the exhibition, a sign told visitors that on entering they agreed on being photographed and distributed. The bright lighting made the staged situation tangible, and the colour portraits show similarities to Thomas Ruff's series of evenly lit portraits of his friends, which the artist himself has discussed within the framework of surveillance and police observations during the 1970s in Germany.[62]

The empty chair that Abramović had put in front of her own (at first, with a table between them) is a development in her practice of assembling a commemorative audience. This might seem a strange way to put it. After all, the official focus was co-presence: of artist and visitors below, while historical Abramović performances were perpetually being carried out by others on the sixth floor of the MoMA. I think the (mostly hostile) critical reactions to this authoritative approach were justified; but I see these reactions as in turn valid from the point of view of the artist. It might have been that the critics expected too much: the performance was, and was meant to be, a generic probing of artist–audience relationship inside the context of the MoMA, and the presence on offer was just as much that of the art institution, one of the most influential sites of canonization, the adjacent art market, curatorial and artistic ambition, particularly when the exhibition is a retrospective. Given this conspicuous and even aggressive contextualization, the seeming lack of historical context in the photographic portraits as placed on the internet made it possible for them to be taken as the events themselves, plentiful and self-explanatory. They became thoroughly identified with the piece. Though taken on different days, and even though the experiences photographed are distinct, one after the other, and connected only through the possible waiting time together at the entrance to the confined part of the atrium, the photographs became part of individual experience even before one entered (if one did). In a way, the photographs are the proof that the piece took place, but also, that there was real 'encounter' – some started crying, which was much made of by the press. And as the performance recedes into the past, the photos will, I think, become more closely incorporated into the work, as relays between co-performers and witnesses, stabilized by our knowledge of them and what they leave out (the static live encounter and the brilliantly lit atrium arena) and, foremost, by our acceptance of the way in which they communicate this performance.

This coming to the fore of the photographs was no coincidence. During a semi-public workshop I attended at MoMA just after the exhibition closed in summer 2010, which consisted of dialogue and short lectures by Abramović, curator Klaus Biesenbach, Caroline Jones, Nancy Spector, and Coco Fusco, Anelli's images were presented on a giant monitor. While Abramović explained her reasons for the work and the preparations for it, and recapitulated her own experiences and the claim that a community had established itself between the visitors, it was the images that were offered as proof.[63] Abramović postulated communal acts of recollection after the performance, but the work was being recollected as it ran, not least in photographs that left out precisely the 'co-presence', that is, the simultaneity of artist and spectator, that it so emphasized in the literature on Abramović. It was not necessary, indeed it was a bold move to leave this out, for the fragmentary state of the portraits better allows reconstruction: our own necessarily partial experience is set alongside documents of such experiences, until a fairly 'solid' object of performance is constructed.[64] This constructed state only appears to be more fragile than a 'documented presence' in the usual sense: its flexibility might make for more intelligibility as the work ages. In ten years, a new audience might read the photographs wistfully: hair, dress, and make-up will be dated, and the context as conspicuous, if not as remote, as Belgrade under Tito.

However one might judge Abramović's recent endeavour, it remains enlightening in terms of merging performance into the sphere of the monument. The 'sites' of these mass-media monuments are carefully considered and often time sensitive. Most often she evokes the context of (ex-)Yugoslavia, as in *Balkan Baroque* (Venice Biennale, 1997), widely and rightly understood as an allegory of the civil war in Yugoslavia.[65] Elsewhere, she examines historical myth through her own biography and bare body, as in *The Hero* (2001) (Figure 47), a video dedicated to her father in which Abramović sits on a white horse in a landscape with a white flag in her hand, as if enacting a kind of historical epic in which nothing happens. *Portrait with Tito* (2004) (Figure 48) seems a retrospective response to Iveković's *Tito's Dress*: Abramović poses in tights and high heels, holding a portrait of Tito in front of her bare torso, not without irony, for Tito's dark tie in front of Abramović's pubic area comes to resemble female genitals.[66] She swerved back from the personal to the interpersonal and even intercultural with *Balkan Erotic Epic* (2005), a multi-channel video installation wherein Abramović set in motion myths and fables from the 'Greater Balkan' region. In all this, there is less the ego of the 'international star artist' wishing to identify a region and epoch with her person, than the displaced performer attempting with ever more laborious means to bring as much temporal and cultural context of her performance 'with her' into a less specific and perhaps indifferent future. The generic notion of the New York

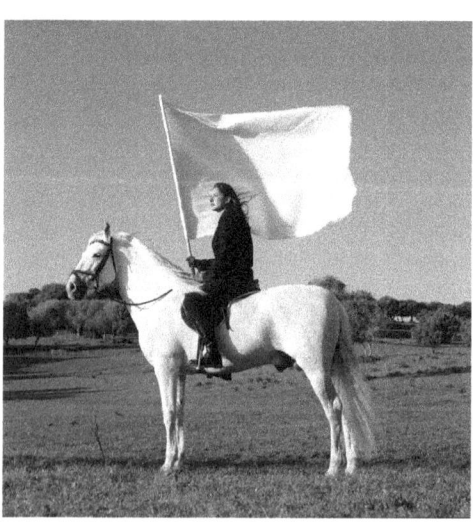
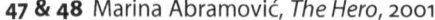
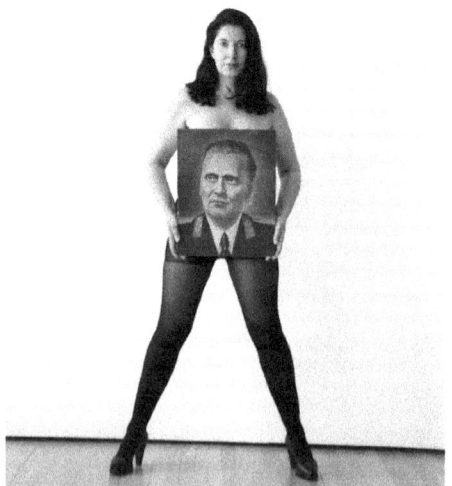

47 & 48 Marina Abramović, *The Hero*, 2001   Marina Abramović, *Portrait with Tito*, 2004

museum, whether MoMA or the Guggenheim, is as much part of Abramović's performances as is Federal Plaza for Serra. But this specificity does not consist simply in the fact that the museum canonizes Abramović, nor that Abramović is pointing this out: just as in Serra's case it does not simply consist in the Plaza with or without Serra. Site and artwork merge in our regard to sites imagined, yet imbued with the significance of their temporal reality, which, as time passes, becomes less literally accessible to us. What results is a temporal layering of fact and fiction in need of documentation and historical discourse so as to come into being.

Self-monuments

Having sketched the way Abramović builds performance on site-specific documents, and their gradual adaptation for an international public, I would like to conclude with some of her most recent work, executed just months before the final version of this text. This is not out of an attachment to strict chronology, or 'newness' as such, but because this work combines in monumental form her prior ways of approaching the specific and the generic. *The Life and Death of Marina Abramović*, first performed at the Manchester International Festival (MIF10) on 9–16 July 2011, and encored for Art Basel on 13–15 June 2012 (Figure 49), is directed by Robert Wilson, and stars, beside Abramović, Willem Dafoe and singer Antony of Antony and the Johnsons. The work is theatre through and through, with Dafoe as hyper-talkative narrator reprising his work with the Wooster Group, intricate set pieces bathed in intense colour and light with tableau-vivant effects set to music, rather than a narration that unfolds in interaction and dialogue. It would be easy to dismiss the work as an application of high production values to the artist's fascination with herself, and indeed it is the sixth of her 'biography' works, which commenced in 1989.[67] But, as with reductive explanations in terms of family life, such criticism says little about the form and content of the work as staged. This is particularly

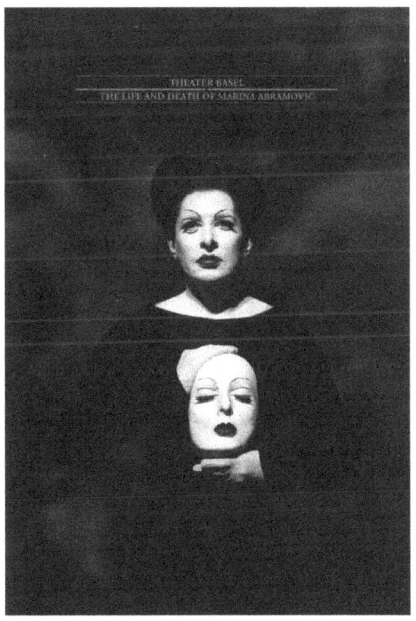

Marina Abramović, *The Life and Death of Marina Abramović*, 2012   **49**

relevant to *Life and Death*, where the key biographical event is (for the time being) fictional: Abramović's death. The piece starts tellingly enough with a funeral scene, wherein the three masked actresses in three coffins stand for the artist. There are similarities to earlier attempts to stage her life and work as biography, which saw Abramović, for example, descending on stage in the form of a Cretan snake goddess. What is new in *Life and Death* is the focus on private life rather than artistic curriculum vitae, in particular on the emotional bonds to parents and lovers. Emotions are not reconstructed: masks and heavy make-up allow only for generic *commedia dell'arte*-like expressions. What is important for the continuing engagement with site and context is the shifts between actors and real persons, most prominent in the decision to have Abramović play not herself but her mother.[68] This is in part conventional film and theatre practice, especially in 'epic' plays that involve different stages of a protagonist's life: we see little girl Abramović, student Abramović, Abramović with Ulay, etc. But her own appearance in the role of her mother, dressed in an imperious black dress and saying nothing – only clicking her metal heels – breaks the realist mould without, in Wilson's usual manner, breaking the contextual bonds of self-location that connect Abramović to the role.

This implicit grounding allows Abramović, in a way, to play not just her birth, life, and death, but the entire microcosm that housed her and her performances. She is not just her mother, she is Tito: in the mother's elegant evening gown one cannot help recalling her and Iveković's 'Tito-dresses'. The rupture with Abramović's 'authentic presence' in the taking of a theatrical role permits the 'relative presence' of a whole gallery of historical figures, above all her father as she recounts him and the mother she impersonates. This may be routine for actors, but not for Abramović, who poured scorn on theatrical illusion as recently as 2010.[69] There were anticipations of this in the 2005 restaging of her own *Thomas Lips* as *Lips of Thomas*, to which she added herself wearing the cap of a partisan, thus 'becoming' her mother. This shift has implications for all her performance, above all her interest in restaging her work and that of others, or, as at MoMA, in letting others restage her performances. I do not wish to make a psychological argument, but one based on the construction of temporally unavailable sites by the audience on the basis of performance. *Life and Death* points up the ambiguities of the body as historically determined, as a document, subsisting between fact and fiction, variable as well through the expectations we bring to it. Abramović-as-Abramović's-mother, or Abramović's-mother-as-Abramović, is a singular performance. It is, however, in a sense, a hopeless gesture, because no work can envelop all its own context. An effort to screen post-war Yugoslavia in Manchester or Basel is just that: it cannot become the act of authority it represents, as *Rhythm 5* or *Freeing the Horizon* did, however provisionally.

This limitation can be clearly felt in the only public monument in a traditional sense that Abramović has designed. The *Spirit of Mozart* was built in 2004 in Mozart's native city of Salzburg by the private Salzburg Foundation (Figure 50).[70] It consists of a fifteen-meter-high steel chair and eight steel chairs of normal dimensions, which can be sat upon but not moved, placed facing the very tall chair. The work is officially described as 'interactive', the audience being invited to take part in the performance – to take a seat, as it were. There is a formal resemblance to *The Artist is Present*, and to Abramović's *Transitory Objects* of the late 1980s. These were sculptures made of massive materials such as amethyst and iron, shaped into shoes, chairs, and other usable objects. Sounding cognate with the psychoanalytic term 'transitional objects' (supposed to aid a shift from maternal to worldly objects of desire), Abramović's transitory objects are themselves the subjects of change: they are to 'trigger physical or mental experiences among the public through direct interaction. When the experience is achieved the objects can be removed.'[71] That this is done in durable materials suggests that, for Abramović, ephemerality is more a matter of use and experience than of physical essence. In Salzburg, the work is meant to last (though it was moved), but the interaction promised is ambiguous if not impossible.[72] There is nothing to interact with

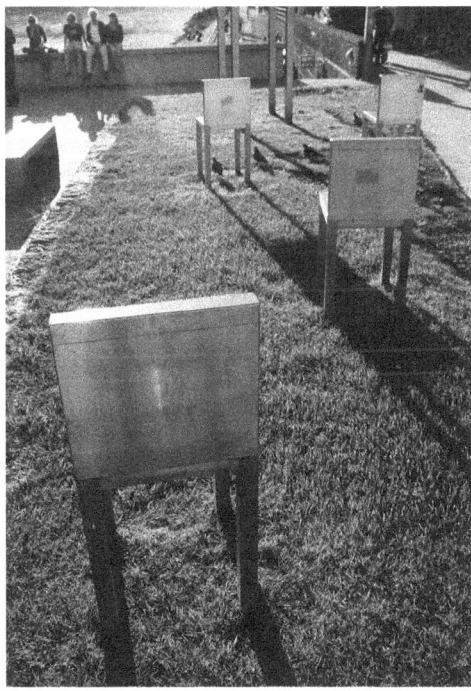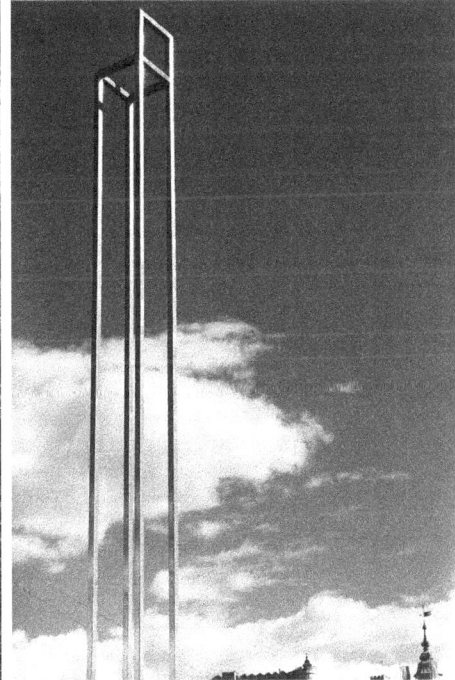

Marina Abramović, *Spirit of Mozart*, 2004   **50a & b**

but the inaccessible 'chair of Mozart', which only a giant could mount.[73] That and the city. This double strategy of distancing and myth formation is pertinent to all of Abramović's work, so I should like to end with a question raised at the start: how do art and context intertwine as site? The hierarchy in the Mozart monument is obvious. Through it, Abramović reveals a problem with democratic commemoration as much as with co-presence in a performance. In both cases, spectators have to act: at the least, to take responsibility for subjective acts. The Salzburg audience cannot perform anything but its lack of access. This constraint is as firm as Mozart's chair is unreachable. One can look to the sky and concede his genius – and the explanatory text assures us that Abramović is in awe of Mozart's music. Sincerity is of course a precondition of 'making it so', and, I would add, for making history plausible. Abramović gives the visitor to the *Spirit of Mozart* the following advice: 'Sit down on the chair Close your eyes Look inwards Lose track of time.'[74] The hint of irony is the only reminder that a monument's function is to reflect on history, not to take its place.

Notes

1 'Letter to Tito', *New York Review of Books*, 22:1 (6 February 1975). The letter has been reprinted frequently. It was a successor to an open letter sent by the Eastern Division of the American Philosophical Association in early 1973 (approved on 29 December 1972), and printed in Charles H. Kahn and Robert S. Cohen, 'Crackdown in Yugoslavia', *New York Review of Books*, 20:3 (8 March 1973).

2 A famous summer school on the island of Korçula took place from 1964 to 1974. Praxis influenced and was influenced by the Yugoslav student movement: many of its members taught at the universities in Zagreb and Belgrade. Its issues were devoted to subjects as diverse as contemporary interpretations of Hegel and the problem of censorship in Eastern Europe, and a long-standing discussion of the 'stagnation' of the Marxist movement. Articles concerning Yugoslav cultural politics included Svetozar Stojanović, 'The June Student Movement and Social Revolution in Yugoslavia', *Praxis*, 3–4 (1970); Stefan Morawski, 'Censorship versus Art', *Praxis*, 1–2 (1974); and Antun Žvan, 'Ecstasy and Hangover of a Revolution', *Praxis*, 3–4 (1974).

3 Bojana Pejić borrows the term from Denis Rusinov to describe the years in Yugoslavia after 1965. Bojana Pejić, 'Sozialistischer Modernismus und die Nachwehen', in Lóránd Hegy (ed.), *50 Jahre Kunst aus Mitteleuropa* (Vienna: Museum Moderner Kunst, 1999), 118.

4 Museum of Contemporary Art, Zagreb (ed.), *Sanja Iveković* (Zagreb, 1998), 27.

5 See also Bojana Pejić, 'Metonymical Moves', in Silvia Eiblmayr (ed.), *Sanja Iveković. Personal Cuts* (Vienna: triton, 2001); Roxana Marcoci (ed.), *Sanja Iveković: Sweet Violence*. Cat. Museum of Modern Art (New York, 2011); and Ruth Noack, *Sanja Iveković. Triangle* (Cambridge, Mass.: MIT Press, 2013). Noack discusses the performance versus the performance documents, and also issues of curating and

display (10). Noack describes the photographs carefully: according to her, the book is T.B. Bottomore's Elites and Society (5). I would like to thank Ruth and Verso publishers for allowing me to see the proofs of the book.

6 See Austin, *How to Do Things with Words*, chapters 4 and 11, and especially 'Performative-Constative'. Several signatories of the letter to Tito – Habermas, Ayer and Hintikka especially – were very familiar with Austin's work.

7 On site-specificity see Lucy Lippard, 'Art Outdoors, In and Out of the Public Domain', *Studio International* (March–April 1977); Rosalind Krauss, 'Sculpture in the Expanded Field', *October*, 8 (Spring 1979); Miwon Kwon, *One Place After Another. Site-Specific Art and Locational Identity* (Cambridge, Mass.: MIT Press, 2004); and James Meyer, 'The Functional Site; or, The Transformation of Site Specificity', in Erika Suderberg (ed.), *Space Site Intervention. Situating Installation Art* (Minneapolis: University of Minnesota Press, 2000). Harriet Senie and Sally Webster provide a definition that probably captures the consensus around 1990: 'Site specificity might be established through formal aesthetic links or through historical and cultural references. It implies no single style.' 'Editor's Statement. Critical Issues in Public Art', *Art Journal* 48:4 (Winter 1989), 288.

8 See Thomas Crow, 'Site-Specific Art: The Strong and the Weak', in Crow, *Modern Art in the Common Culture* (New Haven: Yale University Press, 1996); Rosalyn Deutsche, *Evictions. Art and Spatial Politics* (Cambridge, Mass.: MIT Press, 1996); and Douglas Crimp, *On the Museum's Ruins* (Cambridge, Mass.: The MIT Press, 1993), for the broader political stakes of site specificity, particularly in the 1980s.

9 See Martha Buskirk and Clara Weyergraf-Serra (eds), *The Destruction of Tilted Arc* (Cambridge, Mass.: MIT Press, 1991); Harriet F. Senie and Sally Webster (eds), *Critical Issues in Public Art* (Washington, D.C.: Smithsonian Institution Press, 1992); Benjamin Buchloh, 'Vandalismus von Oben', in Walter Grasskamp (ed.), *Unerwünsche Monumente. Moderne Kunst im Stadtraum* (München: Verlag Silke Schreiber, 1989), 103–19.

10 One could say that the key event in this transformation is Buskirk and Weyergraf-Serra's book of documents from the controversy.

11 Tito himself had been the leader of the partisans fighting the Nazi occupation during the Second World War, before becoming Prime Minister of Yugoslavia in 1945. See Richard West, *Tito: And the Rise and Fall of Yugoslavia* (New York: Carroll & Graf, 1995). In 2010, thirty years after Tito's death, the archival material of his office was made accessible. There are a number of new publications about Tito's life and political career. A good collection of essays is Manojlović Olga Pintar, Mile Bjelajac, and Radmila Radić (eds), *Tito – Vidjenja i tumačenja* (Belgrade: Institut za noviju istoriju Srbije; Arhiv Jugoslavije, 2011). In Yugoslav social science of the 1970s there is a heated debate, followed in *Praxis*, on the desirability of what was already being called the 'partisan myth'. Partisan myths were of course common throughout Eastern Europe (cf. Andrzej Wajda's 1958 film *Popiol i Diament*), as indeed in France and other formerly occupied countries.

12 Zrinka Jurčić, 'Život u Umjetnosti' (The life in art), *Oko* (Zagreb, 8 May 1974), n.p.

13 Jurčić, 'Život u Umjetnosti'. Several newspapers and journals reported on *Rhythm 5*; a satirical review of Abramović's *Rhythm 5* and *Rhythm 10* together was published by Radivoje Bojičić in *Jez* (May 1975).

14 That the rescuer was Joseph Beuys is a persistent rumour, helped perhaps by a suggestively blurry photograph of the rescue. Beuys held a lecture on 19 April 1974 at the SKC during the Third April Meeting, and took part in a discussion of 'Expanded Media or New Art' on 20 April (other prominent participants were Tom Marioni, Achile Bonito Oliva, and Francesco Clemente). In an interview for *Oko*, Abramović recalls being carried out by her colleague Radomir Damnjanović. Jurčić, 'Život u Umjetnosti'. Later she described the event thus: 'When flame touches my leg and I still don't react, two persons from the public enter the star and carry me out.' Toni Stooss (ed.), *Marina Abramović. Artist Body. Performances 1969–1997* (Milan: Charta, 1998), 72.

15 Milanka Lečić, 'Treci Aprilski Susret. Lutanja Umesto Susreta'. Press clip collection, folders 1974 and 1975, SKC Archive, Belgrade.

16 The flag of the Socialist Federal Republic of Yugoslavia consisted of blue, white, and red bands (the pan-Slavic colours), with a red star outlined in yellow in the centre as the symbol of international communism (the USSR had just the yellow outline, with the hammer and sickle, on a red flag). The Yugoslav partisans had a similar flag, with a solid red star on a white band. The new flag of Serbia and Montenegro omits the star. Newspaper reports were circumspect concerning the political reference of the burning star, however. When a contemporary viewer asked directly how the star should be interpreted, Abramović cited, in deadpan manner, the pentagram's ambiguous richness of meaning: 'The star is what it is. I just put it in another relation. I myself was born under the sign of the five-pointed-star in 1946 in a partisan family, so it was present from my childhood till today, and [I used it] also because it is similar to man, because both have five limbs.' Jurčić, 'Život u Umjetnosti'.

17 Bojana Pejić argues that Abramović introduced ritual into Yugoslav post-war art, which she defines (after E.M. Meletinski) as 'the "effective" or "practical" aspect of myth'. Bojana Pejić, 'Being-In-The-Body. On the Spiritual in Marina Abramović's Art', in Friedrich Meschede (ed.), *Marina Abramović* (Ostfildern-Ruit: Cantz, 1993; on the occasion of the exhibition *Wartesaal* at the Neue Nationalgalerie Berlin), 33.

18 Branislav Dimitrijević, 'A Brief Narrative of Art Events in Serbia after 1948', in IRWIN (ed.), *East Art Map. Contemporary Art and Eastern Europe* (London: Afterall, 2006), 291.

19 On the organization and history of the SKC, see Friedemann Malsch, 'Das Studentski Kulturni Centar, Belgrad', *Kunstforum International*, 117 (1992), 194–9. Art activities in 1970s Belgrade are put in political perspective by Lutz Becker, 'Art for an Avant-Garde Society', in IRWIN (ed.), *East Art Map. Contemporary Art and Eastern Europe* (London: Afterall, 2006), 390–400. See also Dunja Blažević, 'Wer Singt da Drüben? – Kunst in Yugoslawien und danach 1949–89 …', in Lóránd Hegy (ed.), *50 Jahre Kunst aus Mitteleuropa* (Vienna: Museum Moderner Kunst, 1999) 81–96.

20 Becker, 'Art for an Avant-Garde Society', 396. In retrospect, Becker emphasizes the independence of the various Yugoslavian Student Cultural Centres. Zoran Erić, curator at the Museum of Modern Art in Belgrade, vouches for this. Interview with the author, June 2007.

21 Kosovo's independence was disputed by Serbia as late as 2011.

22 Abramović noted in an interview with a Sarajevo paper that 'the star ... always followed me, drawn on my birth certificate, on my flag. I asked myself what it meant: control and restriction. To put it on my stomach was like liberating myself from it.' Marija Gajicki, 'Intervju Marina Abramović', *Nezavisni* (30 October 1998).

23 Thus Herbert Blau, *The Audience* (London/Baltimore: Johns Hopkins University Press, 1990), 166: 'One of the unsettling issues in such an event is its own exercise of social control over the spectator, and in some disturbing ethical sense, the complicity of the spectators with the clear and present danger – as when, indeed, in that subsequent warp of the participation mystique, some participants did pick up razors and, on Marina Abramović's passive body, began to make incisions.' Blau is referring to 1974's *Rhythm 0*.

24 Fischer-Lichte, *Transformative Power of Performance*, 18. Abramović performed *Thomas Lips* on 24 October 1975 at Galerie Krinzinger in Innsbruck, Austria, and at the Guggenheim in 2005 as *Lips of Thomas*. Of this routinely mistitled work, Abramović writes: 'This performance in the beginning was originally to a real person with the name Thomas Lips. But later on I re-performed the piece for the Guggenheim and I changed the name to Lips of Thomas.' Email to the author from Marina Abramović, 9 June 2009. The change of title may be a deliberate distantiation on Abramović's part from personal to broadly Christian connotations (e.g., doubting Thomas). A poster announcing *Thomas Lips* at Galerie Krinzinger actually shows the cutting of the star. Whether the poster is printed after the fact or the piece had been performed earlier remains unclear. Abramović writes that she cut the star 'more than once'. In some catalogues the work bears a third, perhaps transitional, title, *Thomas' Lips*. See, e.g., Friedrich Meschede, *Marina Abramović* (Stuttgart: Edition Cantz, 1993), 304.

25 Abramović also does not consider herself a feminist artist. See Klaus Biesenbach, 'Interview with Marina Abramović', in Kristine Stiles, Klaus Biesenbach, and Chrissie Iles, *Marina Abramović* (London: Phaidon, 2008), 20: 'Second question – did you or do you consider yourself a political artist? Abramović: No. Biesenbach: Third question – did you or do you consider yourself a feminist artist? Abramović: Absolutely not, never.'

26 Bojana Pejić draws attention to the biologistic terminology of the Yugoslav Communist Party (League of Communists), from 'state organs', to 'the hand of justice'. She sums up the conflict between party and person by recounting an anecdote told by her mother: after the war, a woman rumoured to have had sexual relations with German soldiers was discussed publicly. The woman stood up and said: 'Comrades, my cunt is not political.' Pejić, 'Being-In-The-Body', 31. This saying is suggestive both for EXPORT's *Genital Panic* and Iveković's *Triangle*.

27 An early translation from the 1970s calls the piece *Releasing of the horizon*. The original title is *Oslobadjanje vidokruga*. Verso of handout of artist, Archive of the SKC, Belgrade. Abramović also began her performance work proper in 1973. There is an interesting analogy in this title to her trilogy *Freeing the Body* (Berlin: she moves to drum beats until she cannot move any more), *Freeing the Voice* (Belgrade: she screams until the voice is lost), and *Freeing the Memory* (Tübingen: she utters words until she cannot think of any more) of 1975. These works are usually seen as pursuing states of meditative emptiness. See Stooss (ed.), *Artist Body*, 122–31.

28 According to Abramović, she 'demonstrated the process in the form of a slide installation in an oval room with eight slide projectors, showing a 360 degree perspective'. 'Freeing the Horizon', in Germano Celant (ed.), *Marina Abramović. Public Body. Installations and Objects 1965–80* (Milan: Charta, 2001), 50.

29 The name of the street was changed in 1992 to Ulica srpskih vladara (Street of the Serbian Rulers), and subsequently to Ulica Kralja Milana (King Milan Street), which it remains.

30 '*Freeing the Horizon* was made very simply. I photographed the streets and buildings myself and developed the photographs and covered parts of the photographs with simple acrylic white paint. Then I re-photographed them again and made slides out of them.' Email from Marina Abramović to the author, 26 February 2009.

31 Particularly, Graham's project *Homes for America* (1966/67), first shown in Robert Smithson's and Nancy Holt's loft space. See Rhea Anastas's entry on Graham in Darsie M. Alexander (ed.), *Slideshow* (Baltimore: Baltimore Museum of Art; and University Park, Pa.: Pennsylvania State University Press, 2005), 111–13.

32 Of course Abramović could have used colour slide film to shoot black and white paper prints, resulting in black and white projected images. Neither this option, nor that of colour slides, is explored in the literature.

33 'In a small room, a circle of slide projectors projected a panoramic sequence of large black and white images of Belgrade round the walls. As the sequence progressed, more of the city was removed, until the final image showed people in an open space.' Chrissie Iles, 'Cleaning the Mirror', in Chrissie Iles (ed.), *Marina Abramović. Objects Performance Video Sound* (Oxford: Museum of Modern Art Oxford, 1995), 22. Iles refers to the work as *Project – Empty Space*, the name of a related piece by Abramović, which I shall discuss. The recent MoMA catalogue adds to the confusion. An illustration caption describes the photocopy as 'slide installation (black and white, silent)', while a catalogue entry shows colour images and describes them as 'retouched colour photos'. Klaus Biesenbach (ed.), *Marina Abramović, The Artist Is Present* (New York: Museum of Modern Art, 2010), 24, 54. In conversation with me on several occasions Abramović has called the copy an 'invitation card'.

34 The fact that Abramović's parents were partisan heroes, and her grandfather a politically important patriarch of the Serbian Orthodox Church, has long become part of the artist's self-presentation and public mythology.

35 Biesenbach (ed.), *The Artist is Present*, 54.

36 Jonathan Crary calls panoramas 'distinctly non-photographic forms' in 'Géricault, the Panorama, and Sites of Reality in the Early Nineteenth Century', *Grey Room*, 9 (Autumn 2002), 18. See also his *Techniques of the Observer. On Vision and Modernity in the Nineteenth Century* (Cambridge, Mass.: MIT Press, 1992), 112–13. For Crary, the panorama is a transitional technology between the stable fixing of the spectator's place in perspective painting and the distributed, physiologically invasive viewing apparatuses of the late nineteenth century. Crary does not mention photographic panoramas, a 1880 specimen of which is published in Nigel Westbrook, Kenneth Rainsbury Dark, and Rene van Meeuwen, 'Constructing Melchior Lorichs's Panorama of Constantinople', *Journal of the Society of Architectural Historians*, 69:1 (March 2010), 63, figure.2.

37 'Reality effect' is Roland Barthes' term for a new mode of seeking assent to the reality of a representation on the basis of contingent detail, manifesting itself in realist novels (e.g. Flaubert's *Madame Bovary*). Crary emphasizes that Barthes applied the term not only to texts, but also to objects, exhibitions, and so on; the visual force of the term lies in its picking out the detail as 'model of the "real"'. Crary, 'Géricault', 11–12.

38 Stephan Oettermann, *Das Panorama. Die Geschichte eines Massenmediums* (Frankfurt: Syndikat, 1980), 18–19, and 33ff. Zone Books, co-founded by Crary, published an English edition, *The Panorama: History of a Mass Medium*, translated by Deborah Lucas Schneider (New York: Zone Books, 1997).

39 Henri Lefebvre's *Le Droit à la ville* comes to mind, a text asserting the 'need to creative activity, for the oeuvre (not only of products and consumable material goods), of the need for information, symbolism, the imaginary and play'. Henri Lefebvre, *Le Droit à la ville* (Paris: Éditions Anthropos, 1968), quoted from English excerpt 'The Right to the City', in Gary Bridge and Sophie Watson (eds), *The Blackwell City Reader* (Oxford: Blackwell, 2005), 367–73, 373. Lefebvre discusses mainly West European cities. Abramović probably knew of the Situationists and Lefebvre's writings: Lefebvre's books were available in Serbo-Croat starting in the 1950s; in addition, he served on the editorial board of *Praxis*. In 1986, five years before his death, he submitted a text and proposal (together with architects Serge Renaudie and Pierre Guilbaud) for the New Belgrade Urban Structure Improvement by the Yugoslav State, in which he connects the 'self-management' of Yugoslav socialism to urban practices. See Lukasz Stanek, *Henri Lefebvre on Space. Architecture, Urban Research and the Production of Theory* (Minneapolis: University of Minnesota Press, 2011), 233–44, and Ljiljana Blagosević, 'New Belgrade: The Capital of No-City's Land', in Zoran Erić (ed.), *Differentiated Neighborhoods* (Belgrade: Museum of Contemporary Art, 2009), 22–33.

40 In Belgrade, an informal group was established, comprising Marina Abramović, Nesa Paripović, Raša Todosijević, Zoran Popović, Gergely Urkom, and Era Milivojević participated.

41 Beuys and Abramović both also participated in the Edinburgh Festival in 1973. Abramović, who participated together with Todosijević and Urkom, performed *Rhythm 10* on 19 August at the Richard Demarco Gallery, and Beuys held his *12 Hour Lecture*. On the early years of the April Meetings, an SKC publication is indispensable: Studentski Kulturni Centar (ed.), *Prosireni Mediji* (Belgrade, 1974, partly in English). The meetings were suspended 1992–2001, and resumed in 2002. See the website of the SKC, www.skc.org.rs. An excellent tabular overview of art activities in Serbia during the 1970s can be found in *Nova Umetnost U Srbiji. Pojedinci Grupe Pojave. 1970–1980* (Belgrade: Cat. Muzej Savremene umetnosti, 1983). Just in 1971, Joseph Kosuth and Yves Klein exhibitions both took place in February. 'American Film' at the Filmski Centar in August and September 1969 showed Andy Warhol, and 'At the Moment' (April 1971, curated by Nena and Braco Dimitrijević) included Daniel Buren, Victor Burgin, Giovanni Anselmo, and others. The cultural climate in Serbia is well discussed in Branislav Dimitrijević, 'A Brief narrative of Art Events in Serbia after 1948', in IRWIN (ed.), *East Art Map. Contemporary Art and Eastern Europe* (London: Afterall, 2006), 287–96.

42 Political censorship concentrated on film, while artistic practices of performance, conceptual art, and land art were considered marginal, even as art in public space started to play a greater role. Interview with the curator at the Museum of Contemporary Art Belgrade, Zoran Erić, by the author, Belgrade, July 2007.

43 BITEF (Beogradski Internacionalni Teatarski Festival/Belgrade International Theatre Festival) began in 1967, and presented works by John Cage, Merce Cunningham, The Living Theatre, La Mama Troupe, and others. Art BITEF (1968–73) was launched by Biljana Tomić in co-operation with Germano Celant, Harald Szeemann, Joseph Beuys, etc., to concentrate on art. See Biljana Tomić, 'Art – Life – Utopia', in Kröller-Müller Museum, *Living Art on the Edge of Europe* (Bielefeld: Kerber, 2006), 63. In 1971, Abramović showed concurrently with Oliva's show, which included Alighiero Boetti, Jannis Kounellis, Mario Merz, and Giovanni Paolini.

44 *Drangularijum*, Cat. *Student Cultural Centre*, 1972, n.p. [bilingual text]. Abramović confirmed in an email to me that the project took place only at the gallery; it was shown there in September 1971. Atelje 212 opened in 1956 and became the most important theatre in Belgrade and, since 1967, the location of BITEF. In the catalogue of the 1995 Abramović exhibition in Oxford, *Project – Empty Space* is said to have taken place in Republic Square during the 1971 BITEF Festival. See also Celant (ed.), *Marina Abramović. Public Body*, Appendix, 485. The theatre moved into a new, larger building in the 1990s.

45 The definite article in English translation ('*the* empty space') implies an object, rather than a concept that may or may not be instantiated. Serbo-Croat has no explicit articles, but the strict parallelism between the two clauses, and the phrase 'а … је празан простор' do suggest 'the empty space'.

46 *Drangularijum*, n.p. Oddly, this portion of the text is not reproduced in the parallel Serbian description of the work. The English text concludes: 'Text exhibited in the Gallery', which at least suggests that Abramović's instructions for 'producing' empty space were available to spectators of the photographs in the SKC.

47 Italo Calvino, 'What Story Down There Awaits Its End?' *If on a Winter's Night a Traveler*, translated by William Weaver (San Diego/New York/London: Harcourt Brace Jovanovich, 1981), 244. A kind of urban subtraction is also described at the end of Vladimir Nabokov's *Invitation to a Beheading* (New York: Putnam, 1959), first published in Paris in Russian in 1938.

48 Calvino, *If on a Winter's Night a Traveler*, 249.

49 Today, it is the Museum of Yugoslav History (Muzej Istorije Jugoslavije).

50 Press clip collection 1973, Archive of the SKC, Belgrade.

51 Ai Weiwei's *Study of Perspective* series, 1995–2010, in which the artist 'gives the finger' to famous tourist monuments (by 'putting them into perspective'), might be an apt contrast. Ai Weiwei's ironic 'framing' of the sites relies on the idea of a quick, touristic intervention; on a visit to Egypt, I was cajoled by tour guides to hold my finger over the distant image of a pyramid for the purpose of a novelty souvenir in just the same manner.

52 Dimitrijević was born in Sarajevo in 1948, the son of a prominent artist, and was educated at the art academy in Zagreb (1968–71) as well as the Saint Martins School of Art in London (1971–73). Like Abramović, Dimitrijević became inter-

nationally known in the 1970s – he participated in the 1976 Venice Biennale, and had numerous solo exhibitions in Western Europe starting in the early 1970s, i.e. at the Museum Ludwig Cologne and Kunsthalle Bern, 1984; Tate London, 1985; Museum Moderner Kunst Vienna, 1994; Hessisches Landesmuseum Darmstadt, 1995; he also participated in documenta 6, 1977, and documenta 9, 1992.

53 According to Dunja Blazević, the building was reserved for party representatives, Blazević, 'Wer singt da drüben? Kunst in Jugoslawien und danach ... 1949–1989', *Aspekte/Positionen. 50 Jahre Kunst aus Mitteleuropa 1949–1999* (Wien: Museum Moderner Kunst Stiftung Ludwig Wien 1999), 90.

54 The original title is *Prolaznici koji sam slucajno sreo u 13:15, 16:23 i 18:11 sati u Zagrebu 1971.*

55 The 'unknown hero' as a satirical trope on propaganda is at least as old as George Orwell's *1984*, with its fictitious helicopter pilot; the myth of the Yugoslav common-man hero, and his touchy relation to partisanship and collaboration in the Second World War, is finely dissected in Dušan Makavejev's film *Nevinost bez Zastite* ['Innocence Unprotected'], released internationally in 1968. Makavejev used the footage of a 1941 Yugoslav movie about the love between an acrobat (Dragoljub Aleksić, a famous acrobat in real life) and a young woman (threatened with marriage to a rich, old, evil man), spliced with archival footage of the German occupation of Yugoslavia, as well as with newly filmed interviews with the elderly cast of the original, suggesting that resistance and collaboration were far more a grey area in the 1940s than the partisan myth allowed for.

56 Adrian Morris, 'Biography', in *Braco Dimitrijević. Culturescapes 1976–1984. Gemälde. Skulpturen. Fotografien* (Cologne: Museum Ludwig, 1984), 127.

57 Guy Brett, 'Private Faces in Public Places', *The Times* (18 April 1972), 10.

58 The three 'Janšas' are originally Emil Hrvatin, Davide Grassi, and Žiga Kariž. Their activities are kept up to date on www.janezjansa.si, as well as Aksioma – Institute for Contemporary Art, Ljubljana, www.aksioma.org.

59 The first of these performances, 2007's *Horse Saddle* (Konjsko sedlo), took place on Mount Triglav, a three-peaked mountain in the Julian Alps with rich connotations for Slovenian nationalism, and which appears on the post-Communist Slovenian flag in lieu of the communist star. It is the site of a 1968 performance by the OHO group, re-staged by the Janšas as *Mount Triglav on Mount Triglav* on 5 July 2007. See www.reakt.org/triglav (accessed 29 December 2012).

60 Klaus Biesenbach (ed.), *Marina Abramović. The Artist is Present* (New York: Museum of Modern Art 2010).

61 See Aaron Rutkoff, 'The Artist Who Makes People Cry', *Wall Street Journal* (29 April 2010), online edition, blogs.wsj.com/metropolis/2010/04/29/the-artist-who-makes-people-cry/ (accessed 3 May 2011).

62 Thomas Ruff in conversation with Philip Pocock (*Journal for Contemporary Art*, 1993) www.jca-online.com/ruff.html. Most critics did not like the aggressive mediation. See Carrie Lambert-Beatty, 'Against Performance Art', *Artforum*, 48:9 (May 2010), 208–12; Caroline Jones, 'Staged Presence', *Artforum*, 48:9 (May 2010), 214–19. Amelia Jones wrote a highly critical (and disappointed) article on the impossibility of presence in recent performance art: '"The Artist is Present"'. See also my article, 'Ge-Schichtete Präsenz und zeitgenössische Performance. Marina

Abramovićs *The Artist is Present*', in Uta Daur (ed.), *Authentizität und Wiederholung* (Bielefeld: Transcript, 2013), 147–67. Anelli published a book entitled *Portraits in the Presence of Marina Abramović* (Bologna: Damiani, 2010; with texts by Klaus Biesenbach and Chrissie Iles).

63 The idea for the slide projection was Biesenbach's, as I was told during the workshop. Judging from the comments online, we can say that some kind of community formed on the internet, which included lengthy comments by the people portrayed in their photographs, replies to comments, and so on.

64 In my 'Ge-Schichtete Präsenz', I revive a view of Bertrand Russell's that public objects can be constructed out of correlations of private experience. See Bertrand Russell, *Our Knowledge of the External World* (Chicago/London: Open Court, 1914), chapters 3–4. On the context of these ideas, see Omar W. Nasim, *Bertrand Russell and the Edwardian Philosophers: Constructing the World* (New York/Basingstoke: Palgrave Macmillan, 2008).

65 A description of *Balkan Baroque* goes as follows: 'The installation. Images are projected onto the three walls of the space. My mother, my father, and myself. One the floor are two copper sinks and one copper bath filled with water. Performance: In the middle of the space I wash 1,500 fresh beef bones, continuously singing folksongs from my childhood.' Kristine Stiles considers *Balkan Baroque* as forming a trilogy with *Cleaning the Mirror I* (1995), wherein Abramović cleaned a human skeleton, and *Cleaning the House* (1996), in which she scrubbed beef bones. Kristine Stiles, 'Cloud with Its Shadow', in Kristine Stiles, Klaus Biesenbach, and Chrissie Iles, *Marina Abramović* (London: Phaidon, 2008), 45. Stiles sees the connection between Abramović's upbringing and use of her body thus: 'An understanding of her work depends in part upon learning that although she internalized the necessity for adherence to severe disciplinary measures at home and to communist principles in the public sphere, Abramović also externalized their psychosomatic effects in body actions for others to witness' (34).

66 In a recent interview, Abramović recalls 1968 and her role as student secretary of the Communist Party: '[After the student protests] we were asking Tito for thirteen points, like more freedom, a multi-party-system, freedom of expression so that people could write what they wanted and criticize the system.' Later, 'Tito had given a talk, and out of the thirteen points he had accepted only four totally uninteresting things, like better food, but not the major things. One of the things given to us was the Student Cultural Centre … That evening there really was a party, like everything was fine. I was so disgusted by the whole thing that I burned my communist membership … But that Student Cultural Centre became the main focus, a place where I really knew art was happening.' Interview with Biesenbach, in Kristine Stiles, Klaus Biesenbach, and Chrissie Iles, *Marina Abramović* (London: Phaidon, 2008), 10.

67 Marina Abramović, 'Biografie als Material', in Theater Basel, *The Life and Death of Marina Abramović* (brochure for The Life and Death of Marina Abramović, Basel, 2012), 5. Claire Bishop, 'Unhappy Days in the Art World? De-skilling Theater, Re-skilling Performance', *The Brooklyn Rail* (December 2011–January 2012), finds a new competence in tension with avant-garde strategies, and which she attributes to a large extent to choreography, which plays a large role in *Life and Death*.

See www.brooklynrail.org/2011/12/art/unhappy-days-in-the-art-worldde-skilling-theater-re-skilling-performance (accessed 30 December 2012).

68 At various ages, she is in turn played by others, including male actors. She does come to play herself in the later scenes; the decision to impersonate her mother is presumably her own in concert with Wilson.

69 'This is what I think: to be a performance artist, you have to hate theatre. Theatre is fake: there is a black box, you pay for a ticket, and you sit in the dark and see somebody playing somebody else's life. The knife is not real, the blood is not real, and the emotions are not real. Performance is just the opposite: the knife is real, the blood is real, and the emotions are real. It's a very different concept. It's about true reality.' Interview with Robert Ayers, 10 March 2010, stored in Ayers' digital archive of interviews, *A Sky Filled with Shooting Stars*, www.askyfilledwithshootingstars.com/wordpress/?p=1197 (accessed 30 December 2012). This polemic is cited in Sean O'Hagan's interview in the *Observer* (3 October 2010), where *The Life and Death* is already announced.

70 See Salzburg Foundation, *Kunstprojekt Salzburg. Moderne Kunst auf alten Plätzen* (Vienna: Brandstäter, 2008), 18ff. Abramović's earlier work, *Chair for Man and his Spirit* (1993, 1996, 1997), or *Chair for Animal Spirit* (1998), involving site-specific arrangements of chairs, may be seen as precursors to *Spirit of Mozart*. An iconography of the chair in contemporary monuments is given in a lecture by Pietro Conte, 'Du Monument invisible au monument impossible. Chaises monumentalisées de Leipzig à Salzbourg', at the conference 'The Monument in Question', Deutsches Forum für Kunstgeschichte, Paris, June 2012. A publication, edited by Céline Trautmann-Waller, is in progress.

71 D.W. Winnicott, 'Transitional Objects and Transitional Phenomena. A Study of the First Not-Me Possession', *International Journal of Psycho-Analysis*, 34 (1953), 89–97. The Abramović quote, and the description of the objects as interactive, is from Celant (ed.), *Marina Abramović. Public Body*, 84.

72 For fourteen months it stood on a traffic island at the side of the old city ('Ferdinand-Hanusch-Platz'), before being moved to the other side of the river in October 2005. Wilfried Schaber, Magistrate for Spatial Planning, City of Salzburg, claims that Abramović prefers this location. Email to the author, 20 August 2012.

73 'Mozart's chair' has no bottom – a decision no doubt designed to enhance visibility, but also inaccessibility.

74 www.salzburgfoundation.at/content/blogcategory/60/42/lang,en/ (accessed 27 July 2012).

4 Monuments

In the three preceding chapters, we saw: 1) that performance has a history, to which both documents and re-performances refer (Abramović at the Guggenheim); 2) that the relation between ephemeral bodily acts and their documentation engages with the urban fabric in monumental fashion (EXPORT in Vienna); 3) that the resulting documented performance is site specific in the sense of preserving into an uncertain future particularities of place and time (Abramović in Belgrade). What remains to be discussed is the direct political connection of the individual to history that can take place through performance. Of particular interest is how artists since the 1970s worked through issues of political identity and the sense of belonging to a nation, and, in response, the search for a commemorative practice addressed both to the individualization of history and the demand to bring it about by communal agency. The question may be posed of post-war Austria, Yugoslavia, and even today's global art practice, but there is no better place to ask it than Germany during the Cold War, when there were two Germanies competing for identification as Germany under circumstances in which the term 'nation' had become taboo. The discussion circled around the broader, abstract notion of the public sphere, but the real geographic and political state, with its catastrophic history, can be read as the subtext of the debate. I investigate key moments in the artistic practice and the concepts of agency in public space that inform them, showing how the monument, seen as an authoritarian obstacle to action, turns into the performative monument, an object or site that contractually binds its audience in self-aware acts of commemoration. In the process, nation is sometimes only rhetorically displaced by community, but, with the fall of the Berlin Wall and the unification of Germany in 1990, it resurfaces in contexts where neither community nor individual action seem equal to the task of representing a political relation to the past.

After introducing the debate on how political identity could be formed through public objects around 1970, my first key case study is the German pavilion of the 1976 Venice Biennale, whose contributions revolve around nation and nationality, addressed not directly but through the rather abstract options of conceptual site-specificity. Two of the three artists working in that pavilion, Jochen Gerz and Joseph Beuys, became prominently engaged in public art – Beuys coined the now-global practice of 'social sculpture' (*soziale Plastik*), while Gerz became the leading designer of performative monuments in Germany and elsewhere. I look at his landmark work in a suburb of Hamburg, the *Monument against Fascism*, in the second part of this chapter, reading Gerz as an aesthetic test case of then-contemporary political development of speech-act theory, the theory of communicative action of Jürgen Habermas. That such a theory can be embodied in a monument says something about its qualities, but also about its historical limits. For both a theory focused on process and a commemorative practice based on public discourse can lose sight of historical content in the heat of debate.

In the decades since the Hamburg memorial, performative monuments have entered the mainstream. In fact, the 1980s and 1990s can retrospectively be characterized as obsessed with memory and memorials. In Europe and the United States, calls for remembrance of victims of the State and its inhabitants' wrongdoings, from the colonial period to the Vietnam War, led to a reconsideration of monument practice. Whether the settlement on a formal language and a particular mode of interaction turns commemoration into an ahistorical spectacle of mere bodily submission to history, or of touristic consumption thereof, will be considered at the end of this chapter. The competition for the *Monument to the Murdered Jews of Europe* in Berlin allows me to think through the problematic illusion that an audience, the Germans specifically, could 'perform' history in order to successfully 'overcome' it, in contrast to performatively taking stock of history as a personal share of responsibility for the future.[1] The concept that needs to be critically examined as art-historical bearer of this problematic national ideology of self-overcoming is the 'countermonument', a term introduced in the late 1980s and since then used in inflationary manner both as description and as value judgement of memorial projects. I am in this final chapter entering an established discourse, namely the memory debate in Germany and the new monument emerging from it, and I hope that a re-reading of this debate and of the practice it brought about will help to arrive at a constructive critique of memory culture.

A monument to German public spheres

Is Germany allowed a national identity? In 1996 the most prominent theorist of the consensual, cultural nature of memory, Aleida Assmann, turned the question provocatively on its head: 'Can Germans afford not to have it?'[2] It is not that Assmann thinks national self-esteem the main goal of politics, like the conservatives who exclaim that 'Germany is abolishing itself' by not imposing stricter demands on the integration of immigrants.[3] Rather, Assmann draws attention to the fact that precisely by refusing to formulate a notion of nation the Left has ceded the field to conservative identity-mongers.

This reluctance to consider national identity on the Left has not always been the case in the post-war era, although the Left has, understandably, had difficulty articulating a national or political identity free of authoritarian implications. Let us start with how such identity was tied to the monument in the theoretical discussion concerning the public sphere in 1970s Germany. In 1972, sociologist Oskar Negt and filmmaker Alexander Kluge published *Public Sphere and Experience*.[4] Often read as an answer, ten years on, to Jürgen Habermas's *Structural Transformation of the Public Sphere*, Negt and Kluge split the conception of homogenous public spheres on the bourgeois model, shared by Habermas and his teachers Adorno and Horkheimer, to claim crucial differences in the public spheres of different social classes (gender is not discussed).[5] Though of the same generation (Habermas was born in 1929, Kluge in 1932, Negt in 1934), Negt and Kluge addressed a generation of Germans born during or after the war, who questioned the allegiance of the individual to a fatalistic notion of political authority which had been their parents' understanding of the past (and their alibi).[6] They embraced the counter-cultural discourse of the 1960s. In the search for less hierarchical aesthetic structures to express the emerging 'counter-public spheres', Negt and Kluge saw the public monument mostly as the negative marker of an 'old' authoritative system that should be dismantled. This is unsurprising, given fascist obsession with monumentality and the cynical instrumentalization of monument commissions in the East–West conflict.[7] It might then come as a surprise that Negt and Kluge devote a whole appendix to the monument, entitled, programmatically, 'The public sphere of monuments. Public sphere and historical consciousness.' The subtitle indicates quite a demand for the monument, and a crucial one on a model of non-state public spheres, that of maintaining historical consciousness. Alas, the means are not up to these ends:

> Essentially, the monuments we find in the Federal Republic are meant as tribute for the dead, for heroic acts, but most of all, they are depictions of authoritarian personalities. [...] If this were history, no present would be able to gain experience from it.[8]

Despite wartime efforts of architects to re-establish monumentality within a functioning communal life – in contrast to the monumentality of fascism and Stalinism – notably those of Sigfried Giedion, for decades after the war the monument haunted public discourse as the symbol of authoritarian politics.[9] Why was Giedion's tradition of rethinking the monument in the sense of a new form of monumentality, one that should aid in the formation of community and allow free social interaction, unavailable to Negt and Kluge? In part, the answer is disciplinary – the debate took place primarily around architects, planners, and architectural historians – and in part aesthetic and ideological. In a 1944 lecture on the 'new monumentality' Giedion mentions Picasso's *Monument en Bois* (1930) (Figure 51), an oil painting showing an expressionist head (never executed as a public monument) as adequate to representing the suffering of war.[10] Giedion thought Picasso's expressionist phase, embodied in *Guernica* (1937), captured 'our attitude towards war' and that it could serve as a 'memorial to the horrors of this period'.[11] To establish a practical monumental language for the victims of war, freed of triumphal rhetoric, proved more difficult. The problems surfaced prominently in two international competitions, both of which failed: neither the competition for a monument in Auschwitz, headed by the sculptor Henry Moore in the late 1950s, nor the British-run search for a 'Monument to the Unknown Political Prisoner' of 1953 attracted submissions appropriate to the challenge, at least according to the juries, both of which called off the contests with no winners.[12]

Why then did Negt and Kluge evoke this 'failed' practice, the monument, at all? Was there a particular role for commemoration in their outline of a

THE NEED FOR A NEW MONUMENTALITY

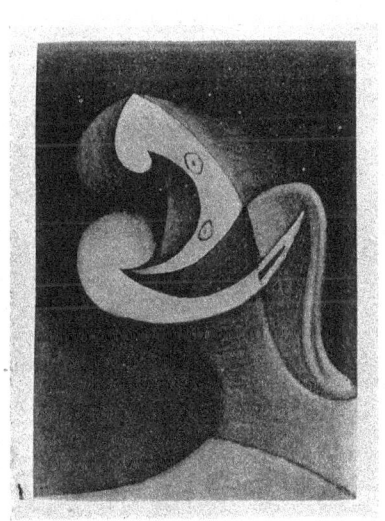

567

Pablo Picasso, *Monument en Bois*, 1930   **51**

proletarian public sphere? The motive for their interest in spaces of commemoration lies in their investment in experience as a category that encompasses history non-institutionally, and in the form of their project, less as a sociological study than a kind of manifesto for the formation and technological advancement of a new public sphere. In the 1940s, Giedion had identified a need for communal life that monuments could help to meet; this remained a largely utopian, organic notion of society, as it was with Frank Lloyd Wright. In 1972, 'experience' was a politically partisan term: Negt and Kluge equated class structure with the experience that forms social groups and their spaces of action.[13] To understand Negt and Kluge's interest in the monument, we can begin from their assertion that experience binds the individual to the social matrix and in turn to a historical structure of such matrices. The experience that Negt and Kluge have in mind is a historical function allowing them to see proletariat and bourgeoisie as lived positions rather than fixed class memberships. This appealed to a New Left unsatisfied with the Stalinist idealization of the proletariat, but also to an Old Left baffled by the often playful class identities of student revolutionaries.[14]

Negt and Kluge merged utopian Marxism with a belief in the revolutionary force of mass media – Kluge was a filmmaker committed to changing film and television production in the Federal Republic. Monuments were synonymous with coercive and class-divided space, argued Kluge in one of his first films – a documentary on National Socialist architecture entitled *Brutality in Stone*.[15] Significantly, in formulating their alternative, no contemporary example came to hand, so Negt and Kluge reached back to the golden age of Russian Constructivism to make their point. Their ideal, *proletarische Denkmalsöffentlichkeit* [the proletarian public sphere of the monument], is represented in the appendix on monuments by a photograph of Vladimir Tatlin's 1919 model for the unbuilt *Monument to the Third International*.[16] Tatlin's project, as Negt and Kluge saw it, embodied 'an important perspective of the sensual implementation of historical consciousness'.[17] The tower should have housed the legislative and the propaganda ministry inside a swivelling metal structure vaguely resembling a torqued Eiffel Tower. Negt and Kluge saw in mass media potentially democratic institutions – and in Tatlin's tower a mass media monument.

And yet, a monument with the ministry of propaganda above the 'people' hardly lets go of the 'authoritative claim to be remembered'. In the spirit of 1968, Negt and Kluge insisted that a monument be anchored in the present and engage its audience sensually. 'Experience' as master category of commemoration was not all that new, and in particular revolutions, both the French and the Russian, had meticulously staged feasts, re-enactments, processions, and other experiential forms of commemoration.[18] Negt and Kluge differ only in stressing the importance of media as part of the contemporary public sphere, available for the shaping of the public opinion in the form of durable monuments.

In this sense, they had travelled far from Habermas's influential historical account of the development of a liberal bourgeois public realm in his *Structural Transformation*, which in Adornian fashion presents the mass media at the end as a dangerous 'polarization' of public opinion. Habermas did not discuss architecture or the monument explicitly in his book, but it enters the analysis through a significant detail. Habermas emphasizes the role of eighteenth-century London coffee-houses, where news were read and vigorously debated. In order to enable discussion through anonymous contributions, one particular coffee-house mounted 'a lion's head … through whose jaws the reader threw his letter'. Excerpts were then published under the title 'Roaring of the Lion'.[19] Habermas points out the dialogue form and 'proximity to the spoken word' in this process – to which I would add that the speech-acts take on the colouring of the architectural monument that harbours them, so they can be taken comically as the irate pronouncements of the 'roaring lion'. In this discussion between equal – male, of course, as access to coffee-houses was restricted (most of all socially, sometimes officially) to men – because anonymous partners, enabled by an architectural element (a decorative and traditional one at that), the performative monument or public object permitting acts of shaping the public sphere surfaces *avant la lettre*. But of course, in 1962, when Habermas wrote, the roaring lion was not *avant la lettre* so much as *devant la lettre*, a historical, nostalgic, foreign vision of free political speech.

It is just this nostalgia that moves Negt and Kluge to complain that, should the Federal Republic have anything like Tatlin's tower, it would be turned into a beer hall. The link between experience as a category binding individuals to history and action persists in Habermas's and Negt/Kluge's accounts of the public sphere as nostalgic exemplars of past public spheres. From this no positive suggestion for new monuments emerges. When Negt and Kluge make such an effort, the result is retrospective: less a plan for the future than the mourning of a future that never came to be. It was the Biennale in Venice that forced artists to confront the present, and thus, the nation.

The crisis of representing the nation

In November 1975, Joseph Beuys and his younger colleagues Jochen Gerz and Reiner Ruthenbeck made a joint visit to Venice. They were invited on this planning trip by the German commissioner of the Biennale, Klaus Gallwitz, an unprecedented move on the part of the curator, indicating institutional desire to have artists respond specifically to the site.[20] In the early 1970s the Biennale had suffered a political crisis, culminating in the cancellation of the 1974 exhibition. The causes were several. Protest against the pavilions' restrictive monographic orientation and the neglect of women artists led to a general crisis of the Biennale; the restructuring of the administration led to problems during preparations, and ultimately to the cancellation of the national exhibitions at the Giardini. In its place, small exhibitions, film series, and plays took place in October and November of 1974. Carlo Ripa di Meana, the president of the Biennale, declared Pinochet's military coup in Chile the focus of these events: the Italian Pavilion in the Giardini showed Chilean political posters and broadside manifestos, Chilean movies were screened, and the pointed title of the catalogue-manifesto that the Biennale published on the occasion was *Per una cultura democratica e antifascista – For a democratic and antifascist culture.*[21] The press was therefore anxious to see the 1976 selection not just as a return to normal, but as paradigmatic for a Biennale newly attuned to problems of authority and nationalism. These discussions must have resonated strongly for German participants due to the split into the Federal Republic in the West and the German Democratic Republic (GDR) in the East. Since 1895 the Biennale had maintained a system of national pavilions and commissioners, which meant that artists represented not just themselves but their nation-states. The problem of nation thus surfaced concretely for German artists *outside* of Germany. The pavilion belonged to the Federal Republic; East Germany did not exhibit in Venice until the early 1980s, and then not in the German pavilion. How did post-war German artists approach this problem? The 1976 contributions show the constructive frictions, even failures, in merging identity and politics through forms of social sculpture. German artists of a generation that 'transcended national boundaries in their commitment to their art and ideas', in the words of German art dealer Konrad Fischer – or at least tried to do so – were thus put in the unenviable position of self-presentation as Germans.[22]

The architecture of the pavilion added to this historical burden: its neo-classical façade, built in 1909, was adjusted to National Socialist taste in 1938, with heavy piers fronting the entrance and the addition of a massive inscription, 'Germania', which is Italian and Latin for Germany, but also the name that Hitler intended for the city of Berlin after the Second World War.[23] National Socialism used the Biennale as a means to show its official artists internationally, and the focus after 1945 only reversed course. German expressionism was given pride of place, serving both as rehabilitation and as a clinging to a lost national specificity – after all, as late as 1938, 'degenerate' expressionist Emil Nolde was convinced of the superiority of 'Germanic art'.[24] Only in the late 1960s did contemporary artists receive commissions. Notably, Gerhard Richter's *Forty-Eight Portraits* in 1972, an international pantheon of great men supposedly chosen at random from a dictionary, pointedly contained famous German-speaking Jews like Einstein and Kafka. This work has become canonical of the post-war art and public image of Germany: importantly, it opened the discussion of German identity in the Biennale context.[25]

The three contributions to the 1976 exhibition, four years but only one Biennale after Richter's, could not help but be a response to it. They were Joseph Beuys's *Tram Stop*, a tall, composite column (Figures 52 and 53), Jochen Gerz's *The Centaur's Difficulty when Dismounting the Horse*, a hollow wooden horse (Figure 54), and Reiner Ruthenbeck's *Doorway*, a holding pen made of rubber ropes (Figure 55). Venice 1976 is a moment of crisis: the difficulties in overcoming the monument witnessed here are a first attempt not to express but to generate historical consciousness, to invent forms of commemoration as a social practice equal to the task of addressing the fascist past. In Venice, the tools are still being developed.

Beuys's *Straßenbahnhaltestelle*, or *Tram Stop*, placed in the main hall of the pavilion, was subtitled *Monument for the Future*, an odd but significant phrase, if we reflect that every monument qua memorial refers to the past, with a particular present agenda of course. But Beuys's monument is not *to* the future but *for* the future: not the monument's subject matter but its use is being rethought. *Tram Stop* took as its point of departure a war monument –

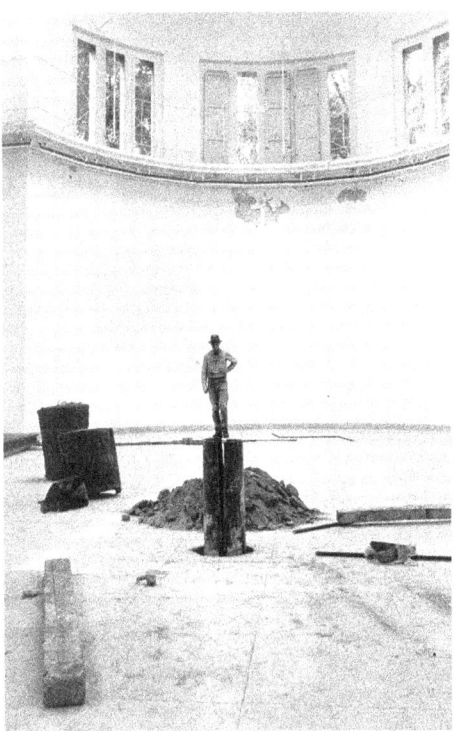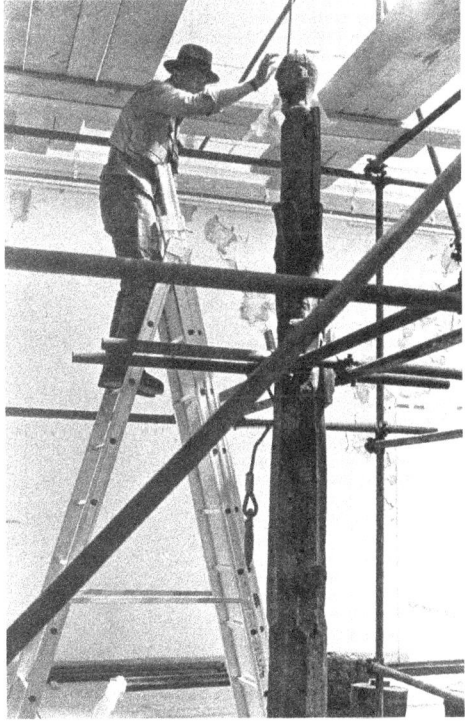

Joseph Beuys, *Tram Stop* at the German Pavilion, Venice Biennale 1976 **52 & 53**

sometimes called a monument to peace – in the German city of Kleve, where Beuys grew up. It was built in the seventeenth century and ended up after many vicissitudes near a tram stop frequented by the young Beuys on his way to school. 'This object probably brought me to sculpture', Beuys announced in an interview at the pavilion's opening, underlining the original's place in his biography and career.[26] The Kleve monument had consisted of a culverin, a small dragon-headed cannon, posed upright with military mortars around it serving as buttresses, and a cupid on top representing the victory of Venus over Mars. It has been in a fragmentary state, sans Cupid, since the nineteenth century. Beuys cast what was left of the original, with considerable additions: he welded an expressionist open-mouthed head to the cannon's muzzle, cast without permission, as it later turned out, from a model by his former student Beatrix Sassen, who had left it in the art academy in Düsseldorf.[27] Beuys also positioned a tramway track on the floor of the pavilion, along with a crank used to move tracks. In addition, he drilled into the floor and foundations of the pavilion, excavating rubble allegedly left over from the old Venice Campanile,

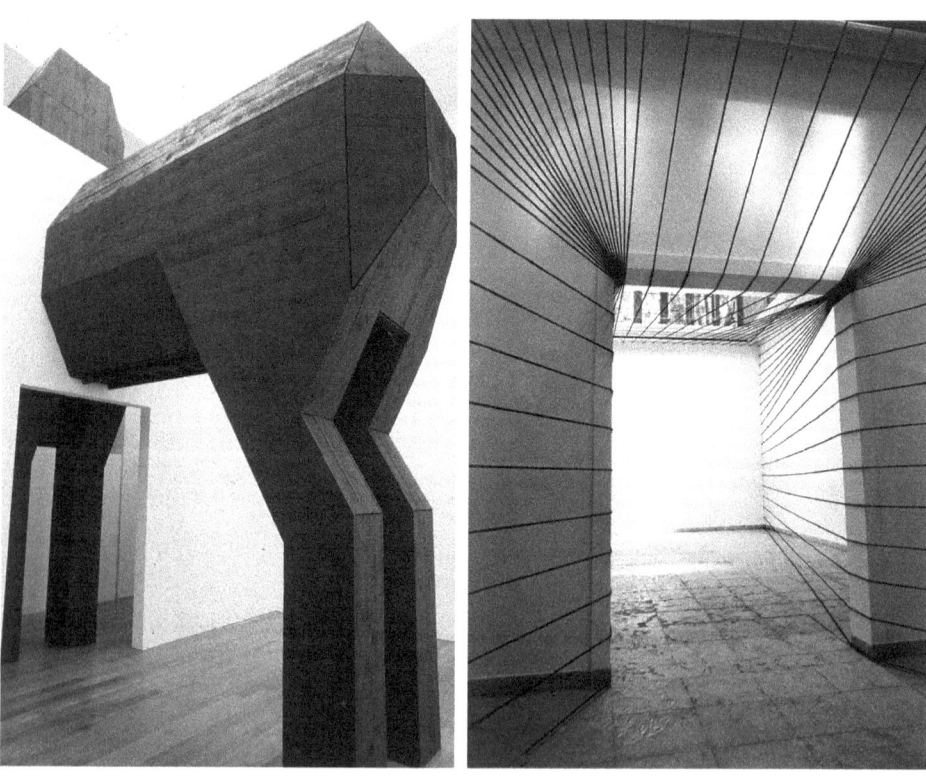

54 & 55 Jochen Gerz, *The Centaur's Difficulty when Dismounting the Horse*, 1976   Reiner Ruthenbeck, *Doorway*, 1976

which had collapsed in 1902. Given the German tradition of seeing the Campanile as a monument to Italian antiquity, it is tempting to read the claim of the 'authenticity' of the rubble as a reversal of myths on Beuys' part: in excavating the past, he erects the future in Venice, in a specifically German key.[28]

These heterogeneous geographical and chronological origins made the work difficult to read: German newspaper critics lamented the need for a 'manual' – the pavilion guide – to make sense of the symbolism.[29] *Tram Stop* connected baroque Kleve (the canon and mortars), the Kleve of Beuys's childhood (the tram tracks), and the history of Venice (the Campanile, or at least the myth thereof). But what historical narrative could reconcile these disparate layers? Or is the unavoidable mixture and lack of narrative continuity in one's own memory what Beuys intended 'the future' to grasp? Or the optimistic postmodern claim that a contemporary monument, in its anachronism, suspends time and national boundaries? The act of reproducing and altering a monument may be a comment on the ever-changing nature of monuments, a modernist theme first made explicit by Alois Riegl at the turn of the twentieth century.[30] How do we pare down this swarm of competing interpretations, so typical of Beuys's projects?

By the time he came to Venice, Beuys had operated at the intersection of performance and sculpture for over a decade – theorizing his endeavour as *soziale Plastik*, social plastic art, a term he preferred over sculpture for its implication of a malleable material to be shaped.[31] *Soziale Plastik* spanned human activities from breathing, thinking, and political action, to traditional art production and the hyperactive emission of ephemera in the manner of Fluxus, all seen as means of shaping the environment to social ends. At the same time he paid meticulous attention to the material qualities of his preferred media, notably fat, felt, wax, and bronze. This allowed Beuys to present objects and performances as part of the same stream of activity, which he insisted on portraying as political agitation. In the Biennale catalogue, Gallwitz thus claimed *Tram Stop* as an action, 'since the aim was to re-establish and to restore history'.[32] The use of rubble hints that the monument is ephemeral; both ontologically, as an object that can be destroyed, and epistemologically, for without spectators it falls into oblivion.

If *Tram Stop* is a meditation on the extrahuman limits on historical consciousness, how is the massive assembly of bronze and stone rubble legible as an action? The key is Beuys's use of photographs of the installation process. These foreground the bodies of Beuys and the labourers: working, resting, conversing, 'baptizing' the monument. We can read them through the tradition of performance photography and film such as Hans Namuth's *Pollock '51* and Henri-Georges Clouzot's *Mystère Picasso*, with their heroic male artists at work. In the Venice photos, the impressive and characteristic figure of Beuys orchestrates the event. He is shown heading a performance encompassing students, friends, and Venetian workers. The disjecta membra of the monument serve as props, much like the felt, fat, and other talismans used by Beuys in actions. Most striking are the photos by Buby Durini, an Italian baron, biologist, oenologist, and friend of Beuys, who switched from scientific microphotography to documenting the art world and, in the 1980s, collaborated with Beuys on an ambitious project to plant endangered trees on the Durini estate in Bolognano under the title *La difesa della natura* (*The defence of nature*).[33]

Beuys' monument may be unstable metaphorically, but his photographic identification is full of authority. It turns the past into an action that it then celebrates. The event character that Beuys wanted was emphasized when *Tram Stop* was purchased by the Kroller-Muller Museum in Otterlo shortly before the Biennale opened. Beuys sold it under the condition of a new display regime: the cannon was to be shown only horizontally after the Biennale ended. 'I wanted the erection only once… I wanted to do the thing once, but considering the whole thing in the context of an action, and not like a sculpture that can be rebuilt here and there afterwards,' Beuys explained.[34] This provoked art critic Werner Spies to ask whether Beuys had in mind Gustave Courbet's demolition of the Vendôme column during the Paris Commune.[35] The analogy, if justified, indicates in the trope of artist as destroyer of obsolete monuments a disjunction in *Tram Stop* between the past, vulnerable and heterogeneous, and the present, wherein the past is forcefully conjured. In laying the column flat, Beuys stressed that the future is not in the object, which was demoted to a relic of past performance, but in those acting on it. In Otterlo, that is, the future, the only action that counts is Beuys's decision to lay the monument flat. Interaction is arrogated to the artist. Beuys replaces the authority of the past with the authority of authorial stipulation, turning monument into a performance document.[36] The context of the museum in fact fossilizes the social sculpture into a relic.

The museum as less than innocent site of memory plays a major role in Beuys's dealing with history. Most interesting for our problem are two early works that openly dealt with the Holocaust, Beuys's entry to the competition for a monument in Auschwitz, and his more private *Auschwitz Demonstration*. The proposal that a young Beuys submitted to the Auschwitz committee two decades before his Venice pavilion consisted of three gates made of concrete – asymmetrical quadrangles on stilts – that were to be placed on the train tracks leading to the crematorium (Figure 56). Their heights were to be five, nine, and twenty-five metres, and they were to be spaced 375 metres apart, with the largest gate closest to the camp gate. The gates were to lead the visitor to a sculpture resembling a polished silver bowl at the centre of the camp.[37] In the 1979 exhibition catalogue introducing Beuys to an American audience, Caroline Tisdall wrote that in this proposal Beuys underlined the 'way the victims were brought to Auschwitz on the railway line which entered the gates', describing the gates as '"signal" sculptures', with no mention of a silver bowl, which Beuys himself explained as 'chandelier, plate, crystal, flower, monstrance'.[38] One might well say that Tisdall's omission makes for a better monument. The symbolism of the bowl plays uneasily with Christian, specifically Catholic, connotations: a monstrance is the container of the Eucharistic bread, i.e. Christ's body, which the priest holds aloft at Mass. The religious theme, taken not historically but mystically, is obviously problematic.[39] In addition, it melts the question of nationality, and of national guilt, into one of universal suffering and redemption. Not that an interest in redemption is incompatible with critical reckoning. At the war's end, Karl Jaspers had raised the issue of personal responsibility precisely through the insistence that without personal introspection and conversion, democracy would not take hold in Germany. His 1946 book, *Die Schuldfrage* (literally, 'The guilt question', understandably translated as *The Question of German Guilt*), distinguished between criminal, political, moral, and metaphysical guilt, all of which he attributed to Germans, arguing for individual taking of responsibility beyond the legal proceedings addressing 'criminal' guilt and designed to absolve the nation as a whole.[40]

The problem in Beuys's attempted gesture at Auschwitz crops up, in a way, for any attempt to carry out Jaspers's program. If, as Jaspers argued, accusations of collective guilt are as questionable as attempts at collective absolution (resembling in both cases the superstitious burning in effigy or scapegoating of individuals), if the only valid approach to commemoration is individual, how can one prevent it from derailing into the mere venting of feelings about

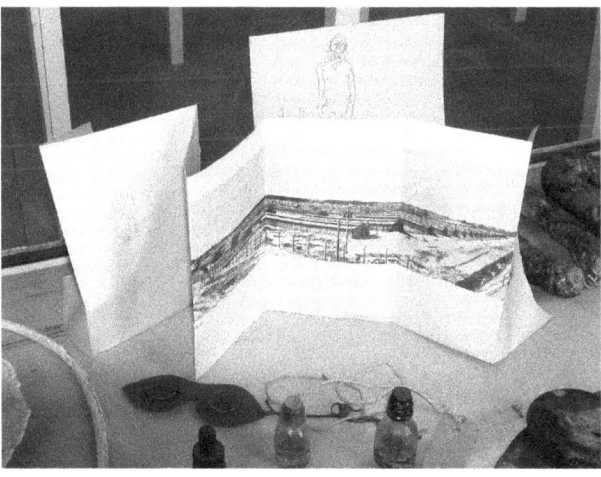

Joseph Beuys, *Auschwitz*, 1957   **56**

the past? In the Auschwitz project, this manifests itself as an ambiguity of public address: there are elements of a performance of history delegated to the visitors, manifested in the gate-like structures meeting the visitor head on, but also an abstraction of the facts of Auschwitz in a ritual drama reminiscent of the Stations of the Cross. The serenity of Beuys's proposal turns Auschwitz into a cathedral, paradoxically if inadvertently pointing to Catholic complicity.[41] This is premature transcendence, as if problems were solved that had not even been posed.

But perhaps Beuys felt, with some justification, that the means he had developed were compelling after all. Beuys reused some of the entry materials together with objects produced between 1956 and 1964 in his 1968 *Auschwitz Demonstration*, a museum showcase filled with references to religion and extermination, like a crucifix and a hotplate. The possibility and the difficulty of the *Auschwitz Demonstration* are encapsulated in the title. Does the work stand for an act of demonstrating performed by Beuys or his audience, or is the very presentation in a glass case, originating from a museum in Munich, a disembodied, even automatic mode of self-examination? The display case in *Auschwitz Demonstration* recalls both the museum, with its distancing of history, and the display of goods in a store, resembling Claes Oldenburg's pop showcases with inedible cakes or burgers. Putting Beuys's achievement in positive terms, we might say that he points to the lack of any shared institutional means of commemoration in the art of Germany and other European nations at this time.[42] Returning to Venice, one way to understand Beuys's contribution and its problems is to say that here he assembled a historically specific set of wreckage in the institutional enclosure of the pavilion. The concept of the museum could stand for all of Beuys's dealings with history: he envisioned his art working ritually, but the absence of conventions for political ritual, together with the aesthetic ritual of passive gallery spectatorship, results in a fantasy of the monument-maker *cum* shamanistic auteur, performing a funeral rite for the audience.[43] The museum as deterrent to action is Beuys's problem: it makes his memorials melancholy and nostalgic, where he wants them to be future-oriented and pragmatic. The memorial in action reveals a closed ritual, which leaves behind only relics (photographic and sculptural) for museum audiences to admire.[44]

In the absence of political common ground, Beuys's Venice monument replaced the political authority of the nation with a kind of charismatic authority of the individual who belongs to it. Indeed, it may seem that the only public resource for political ritual available to West Germans after the war was the taboo language of Nazi monumentality. Jochen Gerz's first comments after the visit to the Giardini in November 1975 show how quickly he identified the question of nation and political persuasion with the history of the pavilion:

The pavilion is not a half way thing. Architectonic Blitzkrieg. You get the feeling the whole thing has been lying on an oak desk in Berlin and was sent down wham bang by phone. Only even measurements. Door 2:3. No details: Bunker.[45]

Gerz's view of art as a weapon, and of the somehow permanent performance of aggression in the pavilion architecture, becomes the subject of his installation, *The Centaur's Difficulty when Dismounting the Horse*. The *Centaur*, resembling in fact a hollow wooden horse, was installed in two adjacent rooms in the left wing of the building, with most of the abdomen and rear of the horse in one room, and the upper body in the other. The ceiling of the building cut off the sculpture at the neck, or so it appeared; in fact there was no head. Its belly was accessible by a ladder between the rear legs, which can be seen tucked under the belly in photographs taken during the Biennale. Apart from the wooden horse divided by the pavilion wall, Gerz displayed twenty-four manuscript pages from a journal written in preparation for the piece (written, like Leonardo's notebooks, in reverse), and ten monochrome paintings in brown covering colour (Figure 57). The horse was a threatening but fragmentary object of perception, as there was no way to grasp the whole from one position. The name was of course a purposeful jumble, since the visual reference is to the Trojan Horse, with the intruder – the 'man' part of the centaur – played by Gerz himself, who claims in his journal to have lived inside the sculpture for 'a couple of days'.[46] The allusions in this historically dense work are literary but threatening. German fascination with Greek art, anchored in nineteenth-century philhellenism, was the official aesthetic of National Socialism, driven by the Nazi belief in a mythic connection between the German and Greek 'races'.[47] Gerz may have been poking fun at the monumental sculptures of the two most prominent occupants of the German pavilion under Hitler, Arno Breker and Josef Thorak.[48] In the installation in Venice, the symbolism of the Trojan Horse extended beyond the horse to represent the pavilion, and

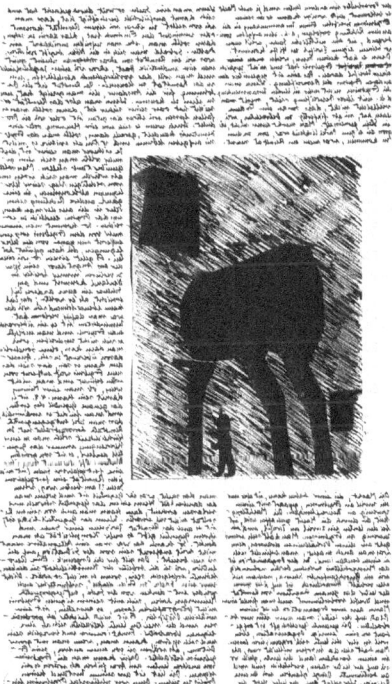

Jochen Gerz, *The Centaur's Difficulty when Dismounting the Horse*, 1976

57

perhaps Venice itself, as Troy. In seeming to celebrate the ploy that ended the Trojan War, Gerz positioned the horse as a destructive, even self-destructive, element inside the architecture. The *Aeneid* tells how the Trojans dismantled their own city wall to get the horse inside, suggesting that they were partly responsible for their fate. Is the *Centaur* an imaginative invitation to dismantle the pavilion, the real monument? Or a threat of architectonic blitzkrieg from the official German artist? It is hard to decide. Gerz's hostility to both the pavilion and his role as public artist is summed up in the metaphor of the trap meant to destroy the city and its inhabitants. This ambiguity implicates the viewer in the functioning of the monument.[49] In parsing Gerz's metaphors, we must take our places imaginatively as the authors or the victims of violence.

Given this directness of address, it should not come as a surprise that Gerz came to sculpture out of performance in public space. In the 1968 work *Attenzione l'arte corrompe*, he affixed labels with the slogan 'attention, art corrupts', on Italian landmarks, including the copy of Michelangelo's David in the Piazza della Signoria in Florence (Figure 58). This action, preserved wholly in photographs, is sceptical of the monument and its reception in tourism, but it also pokes fun at fears of corruption informing anti-monument discourse. In this case we should be careful not to see this work prematurely as a subver-

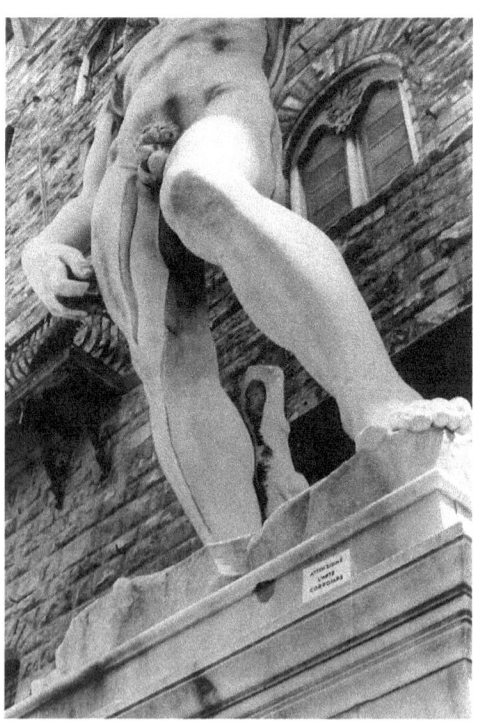

sive urban practice opposed to authoritarian monumentality. Rather, Gerz takes up a historical lineage of monuments like Habermas's lion which were used in public ways clashing with or subverting their official purpose. Gerz may even have had a particular Renaissance practice in mind: the Pasquino, a fragment of ancient sculpture unearthed and displayed publicly in Rome in the sixteenth century (Figure 59). Roman citizens attached anonymous poems to it satirizing papal politics. These were collected, printed, and disseminated, much to the annoyance of the authorities; the Pasquino remains in use today, and was presumably not forgotten during the politicized 1960s in Rome.[50] *Attenzione,*

58 Jochen Gerz, *Attenzione, l'arte corrompe*, 1968

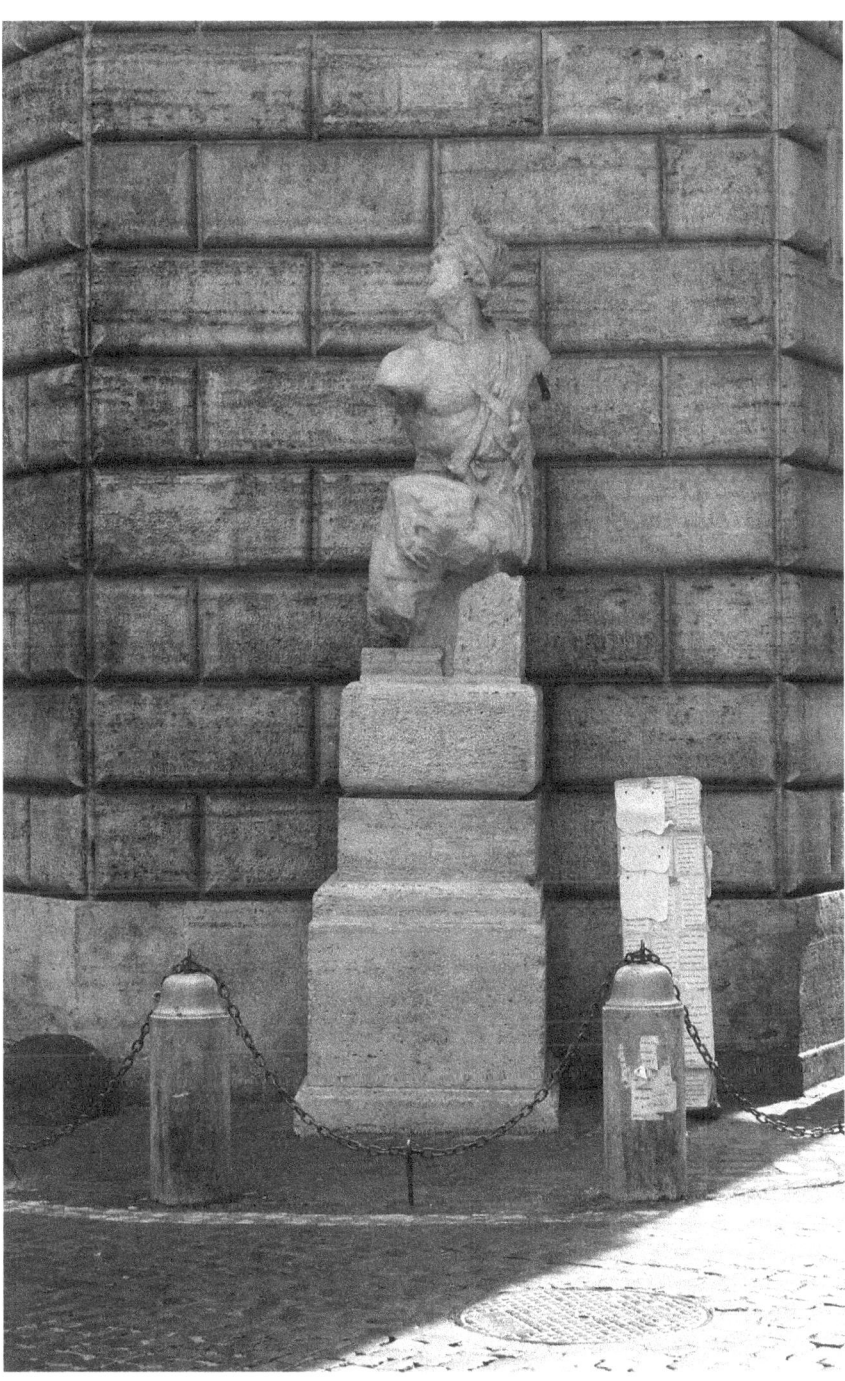

Pasquino, Rome

l'arte corrompe operates at this intersection of language, anonymous performance, and monument; what is new is the fixing and monumentalizing of
performance through a photograph, which perpetuates Gerz's interventions in
public space much in the way that Beuys would commemorate his own 'action'
at Venice. What is missing in Beuys and in *Attenzione*, in comparison with
the Pasquino tradition, is any way for the audience to take part in the performance. Gerz's mature work can be seen as a long-term effort to restore a shared
practice of dispute to the public monument. His projects use written language
not because of its presumed anti-aesthetic properties as in conceptual art, but
because of its extra-aesthetic appeal as a shared medium of communication.[51]

Gerz's early work clarifies the affinity of his and Beuys's Venice projects. In
both, performance destabilizes the monument, which is re-established at the
intersection of action and history: Beuys by shaping the reception through
photographs, interviews, and the change in display, Gerz by threatening,
ambivalent allusions, an indeterminacy of content aided by the rumour of
unknown actions performed inside the horse, and the display of illegible diary
entries and monochrome images that look like they had been painted over. Both
artists combine myth, history, and biography in an attempt to engage spectators individually, in ways radically unlike the institutionalized performance
of history in French Revolutionary and fascist mass rallies. Neither artist has
found a new convention suited to the goal of individualized commemoration.

It is interesting to compare the two to Reiner Ruthenbeck's *Doorway*. It
consisted of black rubber ropes stretched through the door connecting the
two side rooms at his disposal. The ropes barred access to the rest of the space,
corralling spectators in two triangular enclosures. The tension between the
elegant construction and its restrictive function emphasized the authority of
the sculptural intervention, and, indirectly, of the space itself. Like Gerz's, it is
an ironic act of violence.[52] In its concrete physical effect, that of a brute force
blocking traffic, it is literally social sculpture. It boils down the monument,
however interactive and physically dispersed, to a mechanism of visitor
manipulation.

The countermonument in action

The question of German self-representation in Venice, though unanswered,
brought forward new combinations of bodies and monuments. These are
seen, for the first time, not as opposed but as complementary forces in social
space. The pavilion of the mid-1970s was an ideal site for this struggle, for
it represented not simply art institutions, but a phantom Germany: split by
the Cold War, and perpetually revolving around an unresolved past. The key
step not taken in Venice, but carried out later by Gerz and other artists in
Europe and the United States, notably Maya Lin, in the 1980s, is the delegation

of the performance to the audience. As we may learn by reflection on the Pasquino, and processional architecture, audiences have always acted around, in response to, and with monuments, which have sometimes been ephemeral. The innovation of 1980s countermonuments was to recognize and codify this audience reaction as part of what the monument itself sought to achieve. The most prominent case is Jochen Gerz and Esther Shalev-Gerz's *Monument against Fascism* in Harburg, a suburb of the city of Hamburg.[53] The monument was erected in 1986 as a simple square column, twelve metres high, surfaced in lead (Figures 60 and 61).[54] Jochen Gerz won a closed competition launched by the Social Democratic Party of Harburg, a working-class district of Hamburg on the southern outskirts of the city, in 1983. Several other proposals touched on performance art: *documenta 6* participant and self-proclaimed 'living artwork' Timm Ulrichs submitted multiple proposals, and reached the final round with an offer to research significant buildings of the Nazi past, remove single steps from their stairwells, and finally mount these together in a large staircase on the square in front of the city hall. The stairs were to have borne plaques identifying their former locations. Abstract sculptor H.D. Schrader proposed a bowl made of basalt, one half of which was supposed to be shot (possibly by the Federal Armed Forces) before the inauguration, making visible the horror of war – an inventive use of performance in sculpture, but also, as in Ulrichs's case, a whimsical citation of National Socialism.[55] In contrast, Gerz won with a monument that presupposed its eventual disappearance. 'The concept is simple', begins Gerz's first letter to the city.[56] A text – presented in seven languages and placed on a plaque next to the column – was to address visitors and passers-by to scratch their names into the surface with a steel bolt:

> We invite the citizens of Harburg, and visitors to the town, to add their names here to ours. In doing so we *commit* ourselves to remain vigilant. As more and more names cover this 12 metre tall lead column, it will gradually be lowered into the ground. One day, it will have disappeared completely, and the site of the Harburg monument against fascism will be empty. In the end it is only we ourselves who can rise up against injustice.[57] [my emphasis]

Vandalism occurred against the column only weeks after the inauguration, and pro-fascist sentiments, racist comments, and swastikas appeared among the accumulating signatures. Some of the signatures were even scratched out.[58] Nevertheless, the column was lowered into the ground as planned, in eight instalments, over the course of seven years.[59]

In the Anglophone monument discourse, the Hamburg column became a paradigm case of the *countermonument*, a term coined by American scholar James Young for this distinct species of memorial art. Young sees here a decisive break in the form and politics of the monument:

A monument against fascism, therefore, would have to be a monument against itself: against the traditionally didactic function of monuments, against their tendency to displace the past they would have us contemplate – and finally, against the authoritarian propensity in monumental spaces that reduces viewers to passive spectators.[60]

The crucial first claim is that a monument against 'fascism' is a monument 'against itself'. By extension, we get the orthodox post-war view of the monument as 'fascism' itself. Though Young does not cite Negt and Kluge, the claims made on behalf of Gerz's work are resonant to the German theoretical debate since 1970: the countermonument offers to combat just those features which Negt and Kluge despised in public art. The model certainly serves a need in memorial culture, but it ought not to be taken, as it too often is, as an endpoint of discussion. The 1998 *Encyclopedia of Aesthetics*, for instance, prefaces the entry 'monument' as follows: 'to appreciate the relevance of monuments as subjects of aesthetic inquiry, this entry comprises two essays: Historical Overview, Twentieth Century countermonuments'.[61]

The term's success has overshadowed the complexity of the practice

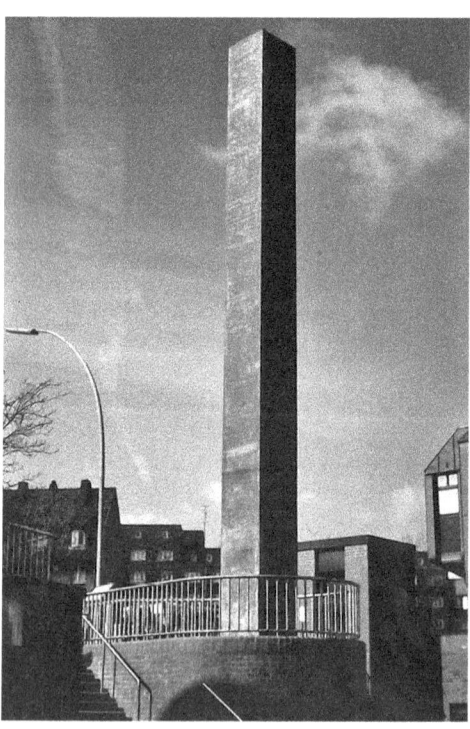
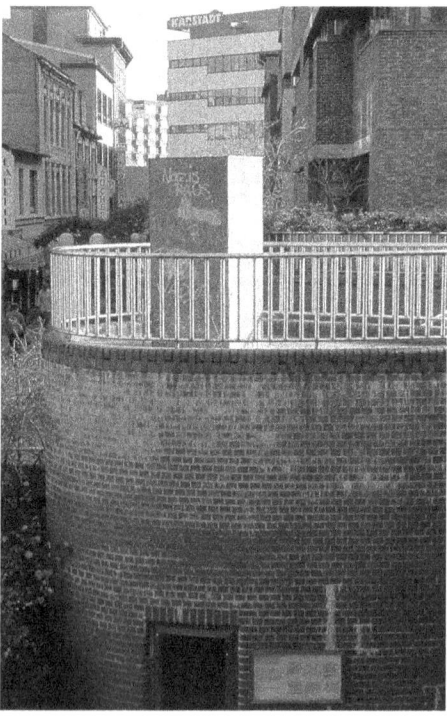

60 & 61 Jochen Gerz and Esther Shalev-Gerz,   Vandalism against *Monument*
Monument against Fascism, 1986   *against Fascism*, 1988

it identifies. In particular, the target of the 'counter-' is misunderstood. 'Counter'-monument implies that the problem in question is the genre of the monument, rather than a changed social context, and in Germany, a past that can be confronted only critically. These challenges required not new objects freed of old attributes, but a change in the practice of commemoration, in particular its purpose. In focusing attention on objects, the term also shuts out the manifold contributions of performance and conceptual art in producing these monuments. One also wonders what is left of the monument's force, with didacticism and authority gone. If countermonuments are a critique of nationalist commemoration, what gives them the authority to mount such a critique? And how do they relate to the past, if not in the old ways?

To answer these questions, I would like to reconsider the *Monument against Fascism* as social practice rather than as countermonument. Young in fact stresses the 'dialogical quality of every memorial space' in a methodological preamble.[62] But he concludes from this that individual presence before the monument is necessary in order to directly experience and even write about the monuments in question. My discussion of the mediation and delegation of presence in documents like contracts and performance photographs stands against such a claim. The speech-act model proves helpful in seeing how Gerz's monument binds its spectators politically. I draw particular attention to the affinity between speech-acts and 'communicative action', a concept through which Jürgen Habermas hoped to criticize modern Western democracy within a constitutional, not a revolutionary or authoritarian, framework.

How can a monument act socially? I start with the monument-critical aspect emphasized by Young. Gerz himself subtitled the Harburg memorial *Gegendenkmal* (usually rendered 'anti-monument', in fact the German cognate of Young's 'countermonument'), in order to mark his detachment from traditional celebratory memorials. Yet the very call for and the selection of candidates for the Harburg commission had excluded as unfit traditional monuments: this was to be a monument *against* something, and those allowed to compete for it were mainly former sculptors turned performers or 'consistent art-refusers', as Jochen Hiltmann called himself.[63]

How to interpret the vandalism, then? Every signature, as well as every swastika that appeared on the column, served as a transcript of performances enacted on or against the column. The vandalism was neither welcome nor unexpected. In his first proposal, Gerz already anticipated uninvited reactions:

> Of course it can happen that citizens and visitors write other things on the column than their names, for example pro-fascist slogans. This does not bother me, the monument is a *Relevator* [Gerz's coinage, presumably from Latin *relevare*, to show], not a false piety, a photograph of the city as it really is, not how it imagines itself or in its Sunday best. Contemporary sculptures often provoke only graffiti, why not turn the tables and make use of the writing as testimony.[64]

The column, imagined as a 'photograph' of its social surroundings, points to the intersection of the monument and the document that has proven so important in the history of post-war performance and public art. Indeed, the Harburg Memorial can be regarded as a document written and read by the public: whether as photograph revealing the city we have stopped seeing, or as modernist monolith defaced by local youth, the monument is no longer a tool of propaganda but a political lightning rod making inarticulate tensions visible.[65] It is, despite the rhetoric of objectivity, not a neutral recording of public opinion but a critical survey: one that, declaring its own stance, takes stock of the agreement and disagreement that it provokes.

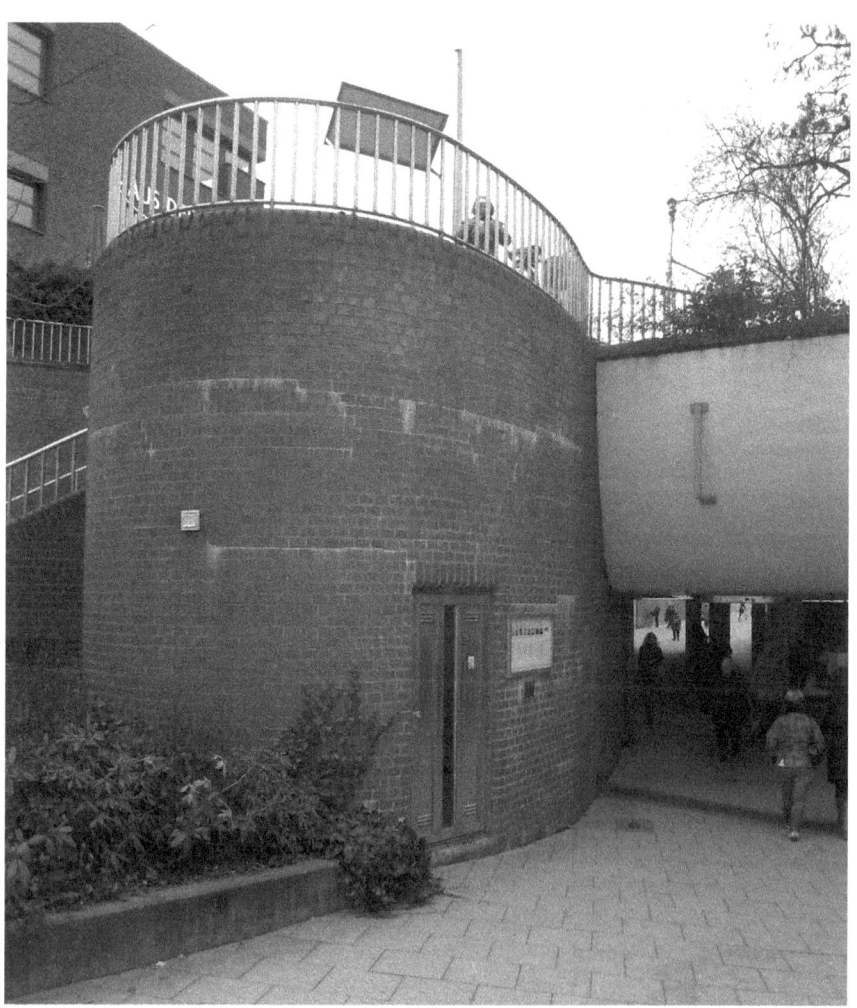

62   Site of *Monument against Fascism*, with window and underpass

The documentary function explains why part of the submerged column remains visible through a small, sealed glass window in the hollowed-out base of the monument, resembling the exhibition of a geologically interesting stratum of the earth's past (Figure 62). In addition to this 'peep-hole', documentation panels were installed near the window and on the platform, with photographs of the successive lowerings to supplement the text of the invitation.

The 'invitation to desecration' is thus by no means a refusal of authority but, rather, a form of 'vigilance', a monument to the hostility that it documents. It accounts for the sensitive lead surface. What about the imposing columnar form, the monument's strongest continuity with traditional monuments? Given Gerz's experience in Venice a decade earlier, may we see Beuys's *Monument for the Future* as the forerunner of the *Monument against Fascism*? The formal and functional analogy of a temporary upright column makes this plausible; Gerz might have been impressed by Beuys's combination of monument and performance. But there is a decisive difference between a column that is lowered once at the artist's will, and one that is lowered in increments depending on audience action: a difference in the relation of monument and performance, which is here that of spectators. Yet the monument remains an official commission. We have seen Gerz struggling with this difficulty in Venice: how did he manage to solve it in the harder context of an anti-fascist monument in suburban Hamburg? The question remains mysterious as long as we regard the countermonument as self-defeating by definition. In signing or defacing, 'citizens', as Gerz calls them, choose for the duration of the performance to enter or reject a contract offered by the artists. The artists extending this invitation had themselves been invited to execute it by officials on the city council. The monument thus still possessed authority, which it delegated to the public. How does delegated performance cope with a swastika scratched in lead?

I would see these utterances as performative contradiction (*performativer Widerspruch*), a term used by Habermas to highlight the ethical implications of the socially binding nature of language. 'Using lies, I finally convinced H that p' is a typical example.[66] The statement is valid as information, but as an act of a real speaker, the claim is self-defeating: one has deceived rather than convinced someone by telling lies. Habermas generalizes this semantic argument into a set of social and moral presuppositions under which all communication takes place. The end result for Habermas is a minimal ethics that starts with the basics of conversation and draws from it political conclusions: in particular, one can criticize a variety of self-serving political utterances for contradicting the very assumptions of free speech under which they are phrased.[67] This abstract political theory can be made concrete in the case of Holocaust commemoration. The call for a conciliatory memory on the part of Germans is likely to run into a performative contradiction with the stubborn contents of memory, of German aggression and genocide, or even the idea of remembering: to remember the Holocaust in a conciliatory manner may mean to forget it.[68]

This shift in the means of commemoration from aesthetic to social convention, more than any opposition to monumentality, is what constitutes the originality of the Harburg monument. We can see this most sharply in contrasting it to a prominent engagement with fascism through performance of a decade earlier. Anselm Kiefer's 1968 project *Besetzungen* (*Occupations*), published in 1975 in the German art journal *Interfunktionen*, caused widespread indignation.[69] The photographs showed Kiefer in Roman ruins, public squares, his own studio, and romantic seascapes, his hand lifted in a Nazi salute, wearing knee-breeches and boots vaguely resembling a Nazi uniform. There is no pictured audience: only the reading audience witnesses the forbidden gesture, with the photograph as proof of its occurrence. But the difficulty begins just then. Because the audience is not represented in Kiefer's photos, the witness function of the audience is not explicitly anchored in a narrative. Is Kiefer saluting a *Führer* somewhere out of view? Or does he play the *Führer* himself? Is the camera lens, and thus the audience, the receiver of Kiefer's greeting?

It is we, the viewers of the photograph, who make the gesture function.[70] To see this, we must reconsider the relevance of pro-fascist slogans in a broader context. Consider the exhibition *Mirroring Evil: Nazi Imagery/Recent Art*, held by New York's Jewish Museum in March–June 2002.[71] Featuring conceptual- and pop-based investigations of fascist aesthetics, the exhibition was a mix of the trivial (Lego concentration camps) and the narcissistic: an artist inserting himself, holding a Diet Coke can, into a photograph of Buchenwald.[72] Such manoeuvres, like Kiefer's Hitler salute, might have been meant to 'involve the artist' in the supposedly seductive evil being worked through: as Buchloh said in defence of Kiefer, with German history 'you have to inhabit it to overcome it'.[73] Take perhaps the most suggestive work in *Mirroring Evil*, Boaz Arad's montage of Hitler speeches, cut to get the *Führer* to utter the words 'Hello, Jerusalem, I am sorry' in Hebrew (*Shalom, Yerushalayim, ani mitnatzel*). Peter Schjeldahl, sceptical of the show, singled out Arad for praise, comparing his work to Bruce Nauman's reply to the authorities of Hanover, who had asked him for a Holocaust monument: 'The work would feature a sign that said, "We are sorry for what we did, and we promise not to do it again".'[74] Nauman had second thoughts, and it is understandable why: even if it were true, as Schjeldahl claims, that the quoted sentiment is 'what the world has wanted to hear from Germany and, really, *all* that the world has wanted to hear', the speech-act is problematic attributed to a corporate 'we' (we Germans), and particularly coming from Bruce Nauman. By the same token, it is effective and funny in Arad precisely because of its implausibility in the mouth of its utterer: the work is not an alternative-universe fantasy about Hitler apologizing, but a concise statement by Arad of the gap between such a world and ours.[75] The effect, as in Kiefer, may be liberating: it cannot leave room for the response of an audience willing to take responsibility for its own actions. In contrast to this provocative play with evil, the Harburg monument demands public response through its very design. The public's actions are not just complementary to but a physical component of the monument. The taking on of German identity by visitors (certainly not all German citizens) is carried out by the act of signature, without collapse into redemptive myth.

In the performative monument, the 'doing by saying something' that is the essence of the performative is made to refer to the past in present actions. Commemoration is always a public act, not a private call to remembrance, a gesture that may be performed alone, but is in principle accessible to others, not a feeling or an internal representation. Commemoration is not memory in the sense of personal remembering, however powerful and necessary this may be. For it is this public nature of commemoration that makes it politically relevant. The commemorator shows others that she commemorates. This does not make it a celebration of presence, or of direct revolutionary action: for commemorative action, consisting of speech-acts, is symbolic, conveying commitment to act rather than changing reality in one go. And since it is no simple eruption of the body, it can be preserved, and remain legible, and binding, through the documents that come into being around the new monuments, and which the monuments, as in Harburg, sometimes dramatically embody.

The content of commemoration

In the decades after the Second World War, the distinction between commemoration as I have defined it and personal catharsis and subjective taking of responsibility in the sense of Jaspers was often vague. Such complex and contradictory performances as those of Venice 1976 were needed for a politically effective language of social commitment to develop. Seen in this context, the Harburg monument is by no means unique.

> The 1980s in Germany were the years of urgent struggle about history: while domestic and foreign politics remained calm, apart from short gusts and a stagnant and worsening Cold War policy, the German pasts resurged from its self-induced sleep. Hardly a self-respecting city existed that did not establish a historical museum or extend or reorganise the existing one during these years.[76]

This note in the *Frankfurter Allgemeine Zeitung* by historian Michael Jeismann describes the boom in commemoration, starting in the 1980s, in orthodox terms as an awakening of historical consciousness. History features prominently in the rhetoric of the era: most importantly, the *Historikerstreit* or

Historians' Dispute brought the question of personal and collective responsibility into political focus. Newly defined restitution laws and resulting claims from the descendants of Holocaust victims brought a new public interest in the question whether 'all' Germans should be held responsible for National Socialism, and just to what extent responsibility had to be taken by generations born shortly before, during, and after the war. Conservative historians took the offensive, arguing that Nazi crimes were a response in kind to Soviet atrocities (Ernst Nolte), or that German civilian suffering under the Red Army was conceptually on a par with the extermination of the Jews (Andreas Hillgruber).[77] Yet this conservative academic offensive is only one half of the story. Amidst this debate concerning history, there was a shift away from the concept of history and its concomitant, nation, towards a postmodern conception of individual involvement with a history considered fragmentary. The umbrella term that came to stand for these various approaches, sometimes set up as a reformed history, sometimes as a direct critique of official history and its national commitments, was memory.[78]

Habermas actively entered the Historians' Dispute. In 'Concerning the Public Use of History', an essay published in the weekly *Die Zeit* in 1986, he argued against letting young Germans off the hook for their national past. Pointing to the 'historical milieu on which following generations build', he argued that 'our own life is linked inwardly, and not just by accidental circumstances, with that context of life in which Auschwitz was possible'.[79] In disclaiming responsibility, Germans denied their heritage altogether. National identity, for Habermas, could not be achieved with the Holocaust subtracted from it.[80] Germans had a 'co-responsibility' that persisted and would outlive participants in the war:

> There is the obligation we in Germany have – even if no one else is prepared to take it upon themselves any longer – to keep alive the memory of the suffering of those murdered at the hand of Germans, and we must keep this memory alive *quite openly* not just in our own mind. These dead have above all a claim to the weak anamnestic power of a solidarity which those born later can now only practise through the medium of the memory, which is always being renewed, which may often be desperate, but which is, at any rate, active and circulating.[81] [my italics]

As Habermas makes clear, from his title on down, history has to be kept alive publicly: this requires a boom in projects concerning public memory. But the idea of solidarity with the victims raises difficulties: how this solidarity with the dead can be achieved, and whether, as Habermas rather mysteriously puts it, this is some claim that the dead make on living Germans. Habermas indeed struggles to explain how solidarity through memory might redeem the past:

> The anamnestic redemption of an injustice, which cannot of course be undone but can at least be virtually reconciled through remembering, ties up the present with the communicative context of a universal historical solidarity.[82]

Can Auschwitz be reconciled, even virtually, through public memory? Habermas, for all his effort to counteract the conservatives' levelling approach (arguing that all dead are the same), falls victim to his own wish for historical solidarity. The term cannot do the work Habermas asks it to do, for solidarity is also claimed with soldiers, families, indeed all Germans who suffered in the war. Habermas shared with his conservative opponents the idea that memory can be made public because it is shared.[83] Of course he differed in emphasizing the memory of Auschwitz for a generation of Germans who were born after the war, but theoretically and practically, his demand does not seem able to exclude the memory and solidarity claims advanced by German nationalists.

There is a way out for the liberal conception of public memory as a social relation to the past, but it requires shifting ground from the inextricably subjective concept of memory to that of acts of commemoration. Habermas, surprisingly perhaps for a philosopher with a reputation as a rationalist, argues that memory needs emotional involvement that leaves the 'third person' of academic debate and switches to the 'first person'. In 'The Public Use of History', he approvingly cites Claude Lanzmann's documentary *Shoah*, screened on public television in Germany in 1985, and based entirely on the oral accounts of Holocaust survivors and camp personnel. Dispensing with historical footage, *Shoah* asks us to share in an 'almost physical process of the work of remembering'.[84] This process differs subtly from Beuys's cathartic performances or Kiefer's wry complicity, but a shared problem surfaces: the purpose of an individual appeal. Does memory, speaking through human witnesses, cause sympathy in us? What if we sympathize with the wardens? Such misunderstandings of the postmodern turn away from master narratives and towards individualized experiences of history, as bodily affect and narrated memory lead to politically ambiguous results in the most ambitious commemorative project in post-war Germany, the *Monument to the Murdered Jews of Europe* in Berlin. Two decades might be an imperfect distance from which to appraise the issue, but it must be revisited: for the appeal to individual memory signals less a way out of 'history from above' than a means to evade precisely the hard questions that critics like Habermas and Assmann associate with memory.

Beyond mourning?

The Historians' Debate not only brought up and left unsettled issues of responsibility; it left unanswered the question of how the Holocaust should be remembered by a generation born after the war. With the reunification of

Germany in 1990, the issue changed suddenly from obstacle to a necessary means for national identity. For, however else they may have differed, East and West Germans have the Holocaust in common. In the quote that introduces this chapter, Aleida Assmann called for historians to think through this identity, taboo in left circles, or else, Assmann warned, 'the vacancy would be occupied by others'.[85] A protagonist of German memory studies, Assmann used the term 'group memory' (*Gruppengedächtnis*), which she distinguishes both from 'individual remembrance of history' and historical research. Group memory is for Assmann a means of preserving history by appealing to a trans-generational, often oral or unofficial narration of the past.[86] This sought-after group memory would make remembrance consist of conscious acts bridging the caesura of the war and forgetfulness by integrating older witnesses and participants with ones born after the war. The discussion sounds much like Habermas a decade earlier, but the tone has grown more urgent: why did memory appear particularly significant in the mid-1990s? Could it be that Germans, working to reintegrate two states that had been separate for nearly half a century, desperately need a shared memory? Some five years after the reunification, when Assmann wrote her text, the issue was again at the forefront of conservative politics, and liberal public intellectuals like Assmann responded. National identity had, as we have seen, been a touchy subject since the 1950s. In the 1980s, before the fall of the Berlin Wall, and one might say in its stead, the conservatives used a nostalgic rhetoric, calling for a reunification in terms of regaining the 'German centre of Europe'.[87] This distinctively West German discourse gained political currency in the attempt to build a national monument for all dead of the Second World War under the motto of 'not dividing the dead into victims and perpetrators'.[88] A conservative government tried to install this national monument in Bonn, capital of the Federal Republic. Criticized among others by Habermas for this symbolic levelling, the national monument was ultimately established at the *Neue Wache* (New Guard House), a building designed by Friedrich Schinkel in the early nineteenth century in the centre of Berlin (that is, East German Berlin). This former royal guard house, which had served as a memorial since 1931, opened as the *Central Memorial of the Federal Republic of Germany for the Victims of War and Tyranny* in 1993.[89] In the striking fact that a liberal like Assmann came to advocate the use of memory to build national identity, we feel the sea change in political facts: with the hurried integration of the GDR, one seemingly could not evade the national question without falling into nationalism. Assmann demands an identity based on 'conscious acts of remembrance', not reassuring myths. This comes with a specific subject matter: 'Collective remembrance as nation means in this sense: a trans-generational knowledge about the crimes committed by Germans.'[90] Of course, a collective memory devoted exclusively to national crimes is as hard to institute as to maintain in its negative function. Just such a project was undertaken with great determination in Berlin in the last decade of the twentieth century. All the problems internal to German post-war identity surfaced in the debate and execution of the Berlin *Denkmal für die ermordeten Juden Europas* (*Monument to the Murdered Jews of Europe*). After fifteen years, several rounds of competitions, changing juries, political interventions and debate, the monument for the Jewish victims of National Socialism was inaugurated in 2005 (Figure 63).

At first, the initiative had been private: in August 1988, journalist Lea Rosh called for a memorial for the murdered Jews as a 'visible signal of confession'.[91] The religious term is Jaspersian, but the emphasis on visibility is consistent with the commemorative turn. After hearings, debates, and political lobbying, a development association was founded on 7 November 1989, two days before the fall of the Berlin Wall.[92] With the unification of the Federal Republic and the Democratic Republic less than a year later, in October 1990, the project took on new urgency: Berlin was to be the capital, and the monument was to be the first project of a unified Germany dealing with the Holocaust. In 1994, a competition for the *Denkmal* was launched 'nation-wide', open to artists and 'related professions … as long as they have lived or worked in the Federal Republic for at least six months', while twelve additional participants, not all Germans or residents, were personally invited to contribute.[93]

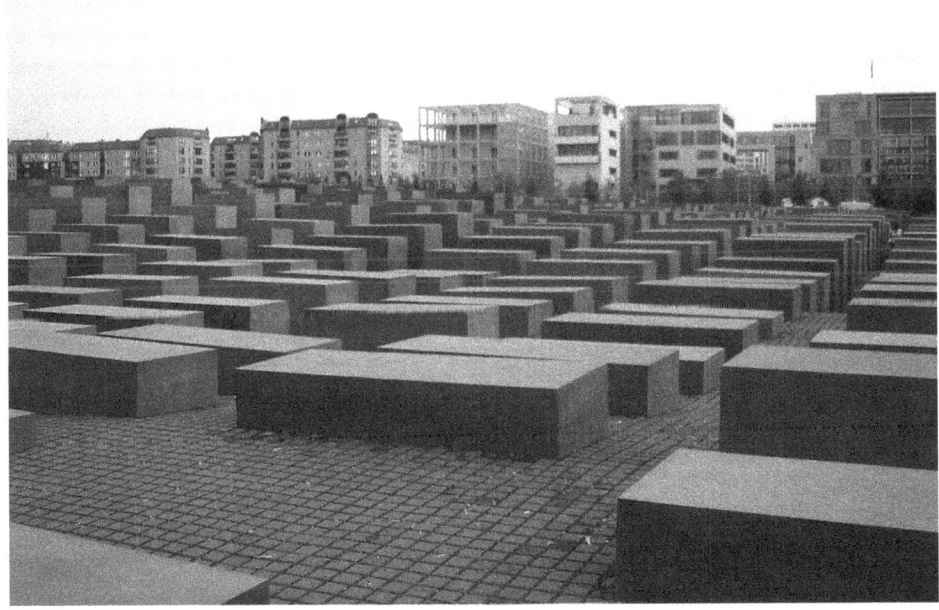

Peter Eisenman, *Monument to the Murdered Jews of Europe* (inaugurated 2005)   **63**

Characteristically, two winners were proclaimed, but ultimately, only one project was considered: a group headed by Christine Jackob-Marks proposed to engrave the names of all Jewish victims on an enormous concrete plate. Formally there is a certain rapport between this proposal and Maya Lin's *Vietnam Veterans Memorial* in Washington D.C., with its list of American casualties in Vietnam, although the naming of the Jewish victims in a German context would have been a starkly different gesture. On the one hand, the successor of Hitler's Reich would be visibly acknowledging these deaths. On the other hand, with the iconographic approximation of a funerary stone, history would be made to 'rest in peace'. A false identification between the German commemorators and 'our dead' lingers in the symbolism. Jackob-Marks probably envisioned an involvement of the audience with the engraved names similar to the one that made Lin's memorial a success. But the horizontal monumentality of Jackob-Marks's slab and the implausibility of discovering the names of all victims were criticized. Ultimately, Chancellor Helmut Kohl vetoed the proposal in 1995, and a scholarly colloquium was launched at the beginning of 1997 to reconsider the proposed site, political context, iconography, and meaningfulness of a monument. The result was a new, closed competition in July 1997.[94]

What surfaced was a demand for representative but not conspicuously monumental design. After the hearing of the eight short-listed competitors in mid-November 1997, the work of four teams was presented in detail to a wider public, even though the jury had favoured only two, according to official transcripts: a proposal by German architect Gesine Weinmiller, and one by American architect Peter Eisenman and American sculptor Richard Serra.[95] Despite differences in symbolism and scale, both projects fragmented the monolith into a multiplicity of stone steles that suggested a space somewhere between a cemetery and a labyrinth. Meanwhile, the initiator of the project, Lea Rosh, favoured a proposal by Jochen Gerz, who was therefore included in the final round, while Daniel Libeskind, the architect of the Jewish Museum Berlin, was nominated by political authorities.[96] Finally, in January 1998, the Serra/Eisenman project was declared the winner.[97]

I conclude this chapter by comparing the monument as built with Gerz's proposal, which stands, as we might expect, for interaction, a language-based approach, and – this came to play a role in the development of the winning project itself – a combination of personal experience and historical research (Figure 64). To some extent, Gerz's proposal is an ideal candidate for Assmann's version of 'group memory', with its vision of national identity through intergenerational dialogue. The pitfalls of this particular project thus have much to tell us about the German national project today and its relation to memory.

According to Gerz's plan, thirty-nine steel light poles, sixteen metres high, were to be erected in a grid pattern. In glowing filaments, the question

'Why' was to be illuminated at the top of these poles in many languages. The answers submitted by visitors were to be engraved into the pavement of the square. This process was to continue for several years, and after the space on the ground was exhausted, answers should continue to be collected but no longer inscribed. The performance was intended never to end. What seems like a practical limitation (the running out of space) was presented by Gerz as a theoretical duality:

> The space exists in two conditions, the modifiable and the irrevocable. The irrevocable condition is reached once the space is filled with answers. Paradoxically though, the modifiable condition of the Monument-Memorial [*Denk-und Mahnmal*] is the permanent one, because the answers of the visitors are still collected after the inscriptions have ended. This on-going process makes the temporal dimension of the monument-memorial nearly as inconceivable as the number of six million murders.[98]

Gerz's distinction between modifiable and irrevocable, and his emphasis on the former, is a refinement of the thinking about time and action already visible in Harburg. But in insisting that the 'irrevocable' form is paradoxically the changing one, Gerz cannot help pointing to an asymmetry between the first and the second phases: the first set of answers is inscribed, the second set is only collected and stored (or are they thrown away?). True, the Harburg column disappeared when full, but there was no invitation there to continue signing in the absence of a place to sign. By contrast, in the Berlin proposal, acts of answering, in remaining possible, are more public in function in the first phase than in the second. Gerz must have felt the discrepancy, for he awkwardly compares the open-ended process of collecting answers with the number of Jewish victims commemorated. A poetic transformation of the spectator was still expected, despite the focus on survey answers. The visitor was to become part of the memorial, Gerz explained, for 'remembrance is the awakening from mourning, as well as a revolt against its cause and the powerlessness of suffering … nothing can represent this in substitution, not art and not politics'.[99]

In the jury protocols, concern was voiced that Gerz's proposal was didacti-

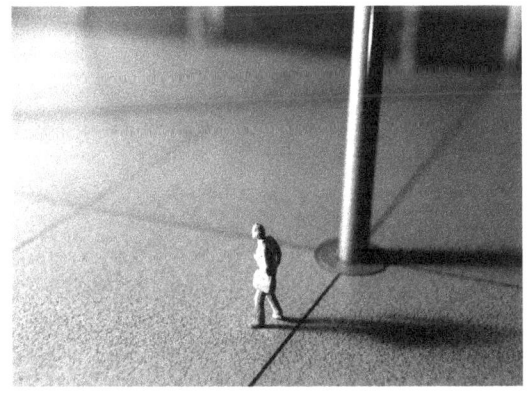

Jochen Gerz, *Why Did It Happen?* Proposal for the *Monument to the Murdered Jews of Europe*, 1997   **64**

cally strong but formally deficient, and the question vulnerable to misinterpretation.[100] I suspect that part of the issue was that the interaction Gerz intended (the 'answers') was too liable to give rise to 'performative contradictions', non-answers that no one wanted to see engraved in stone. The openness of Gerz's question also lessened its binding character: there are no such questions on legal documents. Surely Gerz did not here intend a concise articulation of commitment as in Harburg, but a more introspective articulation of responsibility.[101] Would a reply from a Neo-Nazi have been self-defeating? Or just an unpleasant dilemma for the authorities responsible for the inscriptions? 'Why?' seems to legitimize all answers, in contrast to the clear call for public commitment in Harburg. Gerz must have known the difficulties. The confrontational staging of the question on tall, overwhelmingly bright poles and the publication of answers seem desperate bids for appropriate response rather than narcissism and exhibitionism. But the indeterminacy of the intended result also reveals the difficulty of trying to perform 'group memory' on a national scale.

The winning project, with its brooding physical presence, appealed both to partisans of traditional monumentality and to proponents of cathartic memorial experience.[102] Indeed, it combined the two in an architecture intended to subject visitors to physical discomfort. Initially, the project consisted of approximately 4,000 concrete piers, with heights ranging from zero to nine meters, arranged on uneven ground in an randomized order simulating the entry of chaos into a disciplined grid. The piers were to be separated by passages so narrow (92cm) that only one person could pass through at a time. There was 'no goal, no end, no path directing one in or out', Eisenman and Serra explain in the first proposal, insisting that the focus was not on the weighty material, or education but, rather on the disorienting experience of walking through the forest of steles.[103] Communication between persons walking near each other was to be disrupted; the idea was to single out the visitors without affording them privacy, or as jury member James E. Young described it, to 'depredate us from orientation'. Such a feeling, according to Young, is both visceral and political: 'part of what Eisenman calls the "uncanny" derives precisely from the feeling of danger … from the demand that we have to find our own path to and through remembrance'.[104] Young conveys the project's intention of physically humbling the visitor. But the final identification of physical and political unease is questionable, for 'finding our way' in a space and in memory are not the same thing. Just how far apart they can be is shown by a controversial project of the Slovenian collective Janez Janša, which I discussed in the previous chapter. *Signature, Event, Context* consisted of the three artists walking around the Eisenman monument, tracing a pattern with GPS devices that, on an aerial photograph of the monument, spells out 'Janez Janša', the name it took from the conservative Slovenian politician. The work was a *succès de scandale* in the 2008 Transmediale exhibition (aptly titled CONSPIRE), being thrown out at the last minute by curator Nataša Petrešin-Bachelez, re-admitted with Bachelez disclaiming responsibility, and documented in the House of World Cultures. The group defends the exercise in its press releases, citing Young on the lack of 'intrinsic meaning' in memorials: 'each visitor makes their own experience of memory at a memorial'.[105]

I do not know how Young himself would respond to the hermetic political theatre of Janez Janša, but the expanded concept of memory that they both rely on has a distinguished lineage, stretching beyond the memory debate. It was shaped by Maurice Halbwachs's sociological study of memory at the beginning of the twentieth century, which released memory from a defini-tion in strictly biological terms and transferred it into the cultural realm.[106] Halbwachs recounts one story that is particularly suggestive for our theme. A displaced Inuit girl in the eighteenth century had to be shown images of her original surrounding (seals, boats, huts) in order to recall her homeland. Memory is thus dependent on social interaction and mediation:

> It is in society that people normally acquire their memories. It is also in society that they recall, recognize, and localize their memories … most frequently, we appeal to our memory only in order to answer questions which others have asked us, or that we suppose they could have asked us.[107]

Halbwachs was most interested in the mechanisms of recall and their depend-ency on outside groups such as family, church, class, or any sort of commu-nity. The distinction between individual memory ('experience') and collective memory ('culture') remains slippery today, as does the question of how memory is involved in a social act of constructing the specific history of a group. In Halbwachs's analysis, memory is open socially at both ends: we *make* memories in public and we *speak* (recall) them in public. We might interpret Halbwachs in two ways: first, we could argue relativistically that memory is always a myth designed to fit a social occasion of remembering. The trouble with this view is that it turns memory into a tool for social control. In the worst case, it would serve much the same purpose as Greek and German myth did in fascism. But this view neglects both the personal and the objective dimension of memory. The Inuit girl's memory was provoked, not determined, by the documents she saw in Europe. In turn, the reception of her memory by witnesses is a social event, which binds that memory to subjects who did not themselves experience it. It is suggestive to think that, had she lived a century later, the images used to jog her memory would have been photographs. It seems better to conclude that memory depends on society to become public knowledge, but this does not necessarily determine its contents.[108] Individual memory, in concert with documents, can oppose as well as meet collective demands. The making public of memory may well be an instigation to commemoration: it is not its goal.

The idea that discomfort could constitute remembrance points to unwarranted assumptions that unmediated experience lies at the centre of commemoration, and probably of art and politics as well. Experience has been central to the German monument debate at least since Beuys and Negt/Kluge, and its problems have never been resolved. Eisenman and Serra made experience central even as they fractured the monolithic threat of the old national monument into feelings of unease located in individual spectators. These were no longer thought to be capable of visual mastery of the intact monolith, but had to interact with its fragments. In the course of the on-going debate about the symbolism and feasibility of the project, and demanded revisions, Richard Serra left the collaboration in 1998.[109] Eisenman, working alone, reduced the number of piers, adjusted their measurements and integrated a free area beyond the actual monument with trees flanking the site. An image suggested by the press was now explicitly incorporated into the project description: the monument was to be a 'labyrinth'.[110] The lowering of the piers in turn toned down the 'feeling of physical danger', while keeping the impression of uncanny instability.[111] Considering Serra's inclined steel sculptures, sometimes intermingled to construct the impression of a labyrinth, disorienting the visitor and inducing feelings of possible collapse, one suspects that the artist was disappointed with the diminution of this confrontational element.

These changes aside, the monument always worked with the expectation of a visitor contribution – not contractual but affective. In this it succeeded, if not quite as predicted. Typical of the public's search for an affective interaction with the monument, and of its surprises, is the daily stream of visitors, young and old, who pose for smiling photographs amidst the stelae, many of which end up as profile pictures online. Contrast this with the 'experience' of an academic who felt 'actively confronted with a realistic experience of the gradual loss of embodiment, with the experience of disembodiment and death … asked by Eisenman to live through the emotional experience of Holocaust victims symbolically'.[112] Experience cannot be argued with, but exclusive reliance on it reveals a dangerous identification between self and history. The idea of assimilating oneself to the victims via bodily discomfort is complacent, and for a German spectator hoping to establish a political relation to the monument, deeply problematic.

In Berlin, the narcissistic implications of the project were balanced by a documentary centre, the idea for which seems to have originated with Gerz's proposal. The centre came into discussion after the many revisions of the Eisenman project and was initially advocated by Social Democratic politician Michael Naumann.[113] 'I am writing to you in regard to your meeting with Mr. Michael Naumann', Jürgen Habermas wrote Eisenman in December 1998, 'and would like to ask you not to give in to any alternative that might be offered to you.'[114] Habermas had not been an advocate of Eisenman's design, but he opposed the idea of scuttling the monument in favour of a (politically flexible) information centre. He may have seen the switch to the 'third person' unfit for keeping the memory of the Holocaust alive. But he also distrusted the political ambiguity of 'some sort of institution for historical instruction: such a place can be tacitly turned into something else, once the climate shifts'. His own ideal was the monument as 'index finger' pointing rigidly to the past.[115]

Ultimately, despite the voices raised against the proposal, a compromise was reached, pronounced an 'improvement' by Eisenman, who again reduced the number of piers (to circa 1,500), and added a building to house a documentation and education centre.[116] The final structure opened in 2005, with 2,711 piers, a subterranean information site (architecture by Eisenman, exhibition concept and design by Dagmar von Wilcken), lecture halls, a room with the exemplary vitae of fifteen Holocaust victims, a room with audio recordings of the names of all known victims, based on research from the central memorial site Yad Vashem in Jerusalem, a screening room for historical footage, and rooms for events such as book presentations. The project absorbed all prominent strategies proposed in the decade-long competition. Experience and learning are kept separate but adjacent, with no claim to the taking of responsibility. Perhaps none is possible in Berlin, not just because national responsibility is too heavy a burden for any individual to bear, but also because no individual can, alone, enact the nation. There is no clearer sign of this than

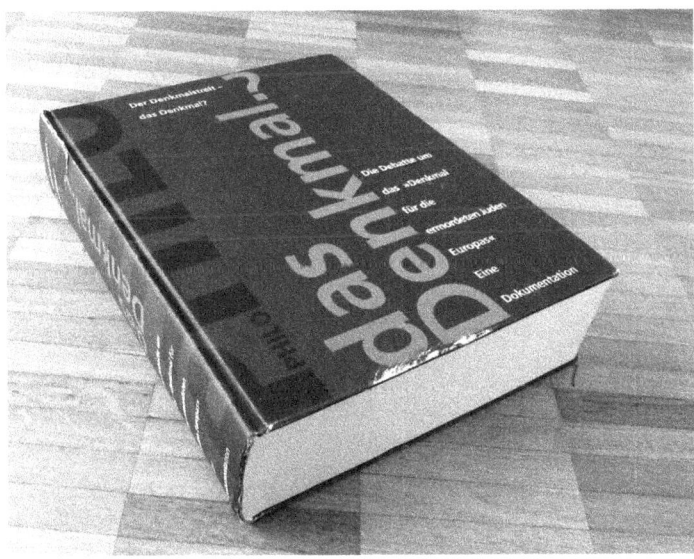

Book, *Der Denkmalstreit – das Denkmal?*   **65**

the monumental *Der Denkmalstreit – das Denkmal? (The Monument Debate – the Monument?)*, a 1250-page compilation of proposals and articles concerning the Berlin monument (Figure 65). On its back cover, a simple motto reads 'a cross-section through the soul of the nation' (*Ein Querschnitt durch die Seele der Nation*), a questionable pronouncement at least.

There are limits to doing by saying or in saying so. The reality created in such cases is not historical but social. This explains the value of the performative in commemoration: acts of commemoration can compel us to take responsibility for the past, and thus hold significance for the future. They ought not to be taken as mirrors of the soul, even the abstract soul of a nation. The attempt to shatter the authoritarian claim of monumental architecture has at times derailed into utopian calls for experience and the mass subject, but also brought about efforts to make authority legitimate through public participation. The new monuments sought to be democratic by being non-authoritarian. And yet they could never dispense with authority, for else how could they oppose fascism? The kind of authority they represent, at its best, approaches self-coercion – what Habermas calls the 'unforced force' of reason. In these two words we have the problem of the performative monument. Its problem of whom to obey, and with what right, eloquently mirrors post-war German politics.

Notes

1 *Vergangenheitsbewältigung*, 'coping with', or rather, 'overcoming' the past, is a persistent term in German and Austrian memory debates; the physical-sounding word *bewältigen* ('tackling' is an English cognate) suggests that once the past is sufficiently overcome, no obstacle remains.

2 Aleida Assmann, 'Zwischen Pflicht und Alibi', *Die Tageszeitung* (20 March 1996), reprinted in Ute Heimrod, Günter Schlusche, and Horst Seferens (eds), *Der Denkmalstreit – Das Denkmal? Die Debatte um das Denkmal für die Ermordeten Juden Europas. Eine Dokumentation* (Berlin: Philo, 1999), 504–6.

3 The reference is to a book by Social Democrat and former board member of the Deutsche Bank, Thilo Sarrazin, *Deutschland schafft sich ab: wie wir unser Land aufs Spiel setzen* (Munich: Deutsche Verlags-Anstalt, 2010), a bestseller full of racist fantasies about immigrants making Germany 'stupider'.

4 Oskar Negt and Alexander Kluge, *Öffentlichkeit und Erfahrung. Zur Organisationsanalyse von bürgerlicher und proletarischer Öffentlichkeit* (Frankfurt am Main: Suhrkamp, 1972). Kluge and Negt, who was Habermas's former research assistant in Frankfurt, do not claim to criticize Habermas, but stress the different experience of proletarians, leading, they argue, to a proletarian public sphere not modeled, as Habermas argued, on the bourgeois version. Uwe Hohendahl, in an article concerned with the public sphere after 1989, points out that the German post-war debate was not really between Habermas and Negt/Kluge, but between these positions on the left and a considerably more pessimistic, conservative position

articulated by Reinhart Koselleck in *Kritik und Krise* (Freiburg: Alber, 1959), to which Habermas explicitly responded. See Uwe Hohendahl, 'Recasting the Public Sphere', *October*, 73 (Summer 1995), 27–54.

5 Jürgen Habermas, *Strukturwandel der Öffentlichkeit. Untersuchungen zu einer Kategorie der bürgerlichen Gesellschaft* (Nuewied am Rhein: Luchterhand, 1962), explores the emergence of a critical bourgeois public sphere parallel to the free market, and its coming under threat due to the mass media. Jürgen Habermas, *The Structural Transformation of the Public Sphere. An Inquiry into a Category of Bourgeois Society*, translated by Thomas Burger (Cambridge, Mass.: MIT Press, 1991).

6 This fatalism is diagnosed by Habermas in Martin Heidegger's 1927 *Sein und Zeit*. See Jürgen Habermas, 'Work and *Weltanschauung*: The Heidegger Controversy from a German Perspective', *Critical Inquiry*, 15:2 (Winter 1989), 431–56.

7 In West Germany, the commemoration of the victims of National Socialism served as warning against communism. What surfaces already, perhaps subconsciously, is the core argument of the German *Historikerstreit* (Historian's Dispute) in the 1980s, when historian Ernst Nolte denied the Holocaust's particularity in comparison to the Gulag. In the *Bundesrepublik* (West Germany) in general, anti-communist policies mingled with the view on the recent past: with the Second World War as the political and historical caesura, 'Auschwitz' (until the 1980s the synonym for the Holocaust) did not feature as a concrete historical event but, rather, was mythified as the end of civilization. Even Theodor Adorno's essay 'Was bedeutet Aufarbeitung der Vergangenheit?' (1959), in *Erziehung zur Mündigkeit* (Frankfurt am Main: Suhrkamp, 1970), quickly shifts attention from 'Auschwitz' to the 'system' responsible for it, 'state capitalism'. On the terminology, see Norbert Frei, 'Auschwitz und Holocaust. Begriff und Historiographie', in Hanno Loewy (ed.), *Holocaust: Die Grenzen des Verstehens. Eine Debatte über die Besetzung der Geschichte* (Reinbek bei Hamburg: Rowohlt, 1992), 101–9. In East Germany, communist opposition to National Socialism became a state creation myth, culminating in the cynical naming of the Berlin Wall as 'antifascist barrier' by the East German government.

8 Negt and Kluge, *Öffentlichkeit und Erfahrung*, 448. There is an English version, *Public Sphere and Experience* (Minneapolis: University of Minnesota Press, 1993) by Peter Labanyi, Jamie Owen Daniel, and Assenka Oksiloff. Excerpts were published in *October*, 46 (Autumn 1988), 60–82, though unfortunately this aesthetically pertinent appendix on monuments was not included.

9 The 'Nine Points on Monumentality' (1943) argued for the importance of monumentality to a functioning community and, in particular, for a thoroughgoing collaboration between architects, painters, and sculptors.

10 Sigfried Giedion, 'The Need for a New Monumentality', in *New Architecture and City Planning. A Symposium*. Edited by Paul Zucker (New York: Philosophical Library, 1944). Giedion mentions fireworks and light architecture as possible forms of a contemporary monumentality. He also elaborates on the distinction between 'pseudo-monumentality', a legacy of the nineteenth century ('take some curtains of columns and put them in front of any building, whatever its purpose', 555), and real monumentality.

11 Giedion, 'The Need for a New Monumentality', 566.

12 See International Auschwitz Committee, *The Auschwitz Monument* (Comité international d'Auschwitz, 1958); Jonathan Huener, *Auschwitz, Poland, and the Politics of Commemoration* (Athens, Oh.: Ohio University Press, 2003), 150–69; and Robert Burstow, 'The Limits of Modernist Art as a "Weapon for the Cold War": Reassessing the Unknown Patron of the Monument to the Unknown Political Prisoner', *Oxford Art Journal*, 20:1 (1997), 68–80.

13 The German word for 'experience' used by Negt and Kluge, 'Erfahrung', has a philosophical lineage in Kant, Hegel, and Heidegger. But in understanding its resonance around the 1970s, another tradition should be stressed: the notion of lived experience coming out of British empiricism, picked up around the turn of the century by Ernst Mach, William James, and Henri Bergson, and revived in authors like Norman O'Brown, John Dewey (in *Art As Experience* (New York: Putnam, 1934)) and countercultural art terms like 'expanded consciousness' and 'expanded media'.

14 For this purpose, one must place Habermas, however inadequately, among the 'Old Left' with his teacher Adorno, a tireless critic of the tactics of student protesters. A marker of this is the volume edited by Oskar Negt rather comically called *Die Linke antwortet Jürgen Habermas* (Frankfurt am Main: Europäische Verlagsanstalt, 1968) ('The Left answers Jürgen Habermas'), with replies to Habermas's criticism of student tactics, which it reprints.

15 *Brutalität in Stein* (1959), with Peter Schamoni. In 1987, Kluge founded the DCTP (Development Company for Television Programming), which produces news programmes for German commercial television.

16 The Third International or Communist International was founded in Moscow in 1919 with the goal of overthrowing all bourgeois regimes. Negt and Kluge quote mainly from René Fülöp-Miller, *Geist und Gesicht des Bolschewismus* (Vienna, 1926), which was republished under the title *Fantasie und Alltag in Sowjet-Russland. Ein Augenzeugenbericht* (Berlin: Elephanten Press, 1978). Tatlin's project was prominent during that time. Architect and art historian Adolf Behne, member of the German Werkbund, used it as the illustration at the end of his influential text *Der moderne Zweckbau* (Munich/Vienna/Berlin: Drei Masken Verlag, 1925), 72–3, quoted in Moravánsky, 'Monumentalität', in Ákos Moravánszky (ed.), *Architekturtheorie im 20. Jahrhundert. Eine kritische Anthologie* (Vienna: Springer, 2003), 376. New considerations can be found in the exhibition catalogue of the Tinguely Museum Basel, *Tatlin. Neue Kunst für eine neue Welt* (Ostfildern: Hatje-Cantz, 2012).

17 'Er zeigt aber eine wichtige Perspektive der sinnlichen Umsetzung von geschichtlichen Bewusstsein.' Negt and Kluge, Öffentlichkeit und Erfahrung, 452.

18 The classic texts are Mona Ozouf, *La fête révolutionnaire, 1789–1799* (Paris: Gallimard, 1976), translated as *Festivals and the French Revolution* (Cambridge, Mass.: Harvard University Press, 1988), and George Mosse, *The Nationalization of the Masses. Political Symbolism and Mass Movements in Germany from the Napoleonic Wars through the Third Reich* (Ithaca/London: Cornell University Press, 1975). See also Wendy C. Nielsen, 'Staging Rousseau's Republic: French Revolutionary festivals and Olympe de Gouges', *The Eighteenth Century*, 43:3 (Autumn 2002),

268–85. A view of citizenship as performance practice from ancient Greece to Washington, D.C. is David Wiles, *Theatre and Citizenship: The History of a Practice* (Cambridge: Cambridge University Press, 2011).

19 Habermas, *The Structural Transformation*, 42.

20 See Klaus Gallwitz, 'Journal', in Klaus Gallwitz (ed.), *Biennale 76 Venedig. Deutscher Pavillon. Beuys. Gerz. Ruthenbeck* (Stuttgart: Cantz, 1976), 4.

21 *La Biennale di Venezia: Per Una Cultura Democratica Antifascista* (Venice: La Biennale, 1974). The catalogue in fact consists of a small slipcase with 29 leaflets. It was the first year of Carlo Ripa di Meana's presidency of the Biennale. There were several movie series, dedicated to Vertov, Buñuel, and also, more concretely, to a 'Chronicle of Fascism', and documentaries on Chilean activism (among them an evening entitled 'Hommage to Allende' and several documentaries on the 1973 putsch); the Teatro La Fenice staged Popular Chilean Music. See also Annette Lagler, 'Der Deutsche Pavillon', in Christoph Becker and Annette Lagler (eds), *Biennale Venedig. Der Deutsche Beitrag* (Ostfildern: Cantz, 1995), 58. The Biennale Archive holds an exchange of letters between Gallwitz and the Biennale concerning complications due to lack of formal administration. Archive of the Biennale di Venezia, Arti Visive, 'Germania', box 253.

22 Quoted in Stefan Germer, 'Intersecting Visions, Shifting Perspectives: An Overview of German–American Artistic Relation', in *The Froehlich Foundation: German and American Art from Beuys and Warhol* (London: Tate Publications, 1996), 23.

23 See Annette Lagler, 'Der Deutsche Pavillon'. Germania is, of course, also the name of Roman historian Tacitus' eulogistic book on the German tribes, which had inspired German nationalist sentiment since the fifteenth century and had a particularly prominent place in National Socialist education and propaganda.

24 Nolde protested his inclusion in the 'Degenerate Art' Exhibition in 1937 in a letter to Joseph Goebbels, which said: 'my art is German, strong, sincere'. See Russell Berman, 'German Primitivism/Primitive German. The Case of Emil Nolde', chapter 6 in his *Cultural Studies of Modern Germany: History, Representation and Nationhood* (Madison: University of Wisconsin Press, 1993), 113.

25 Benjamin Buchloh calls *Forty-Eight Portraits* the first work 'to confront the status of the traditional tools of commemoration' in 'Gerhard Richter's Work of Mourning', *October*, 75 (Winter, 1996), 69.

26 Guido de Werd, 'Strassenbahnhaltestelle – Tramstop – Fermate del Tram', in *Joseph Beuys. Strassenbahnhaltestelle. Ein Monument für die Zukunft* (Kleve: Freundeskreis des Kurhauses und Koekkoek-Haus Kleve, 2000), 9.

27 Beuys changed the mouth and several details in recasting. See Simone Scholten, '"Ausgehen muss man ja von dem, was Gegenwärtig ist"', in *Strassenbahnhaltestelle*, 26–67; on the reuse of the head, 47. Another version of *Tram Stop*, cast around the same time, is now part of the Collection Marx, Berlin. See Heiner Bastian (ed.), *Joseph Beuys – Skulpturen und Objekte*, vol. 1. Exh. Martin Gropius Bau Berlin (Munich: Schirmer/Mosel, 1988), 286.

28 The Campanile fell without warning, without harming anyone, and was rebuilt from its own rubble, or, as the Venetian slogan goes, 'dov'era com'era' (where it was, as it was). For contemporary accounts, see Gregorio Gattinono, *Il campanile*

di San Marco: monografia storica (Venezia: Fabbris, 1910) and Antonio Fradeletto, *Il Campanile di San Marco Riedificato: studi – ricerche – relazioni* (Venezia: Ferrari, 1912). Fradeletto was one of the founders of the Biennale, whose administration he oversaw until 1919. The peculiarly German history of seeing the Campanile as a monument to Italy's past is evident in a book published the year of the collapse by art historian Paul Schubring, *Unter dem Campanile von San Marco: ein Nachruf zur Erinnerung an Venedigs stolze Tage* (Halle a. S.: Gebauer-Schwetschke, 1902).

29 *Frankfurter Allgemeine Zeitung* (31 July 1976), reprinted in *Strassenbahnhaltestelle*, 212.

30 Alois Riegl, *Der Moderne Denkmalkultus, sein Wesen und seine Entstehung* (Vienna: W. Braumüller, 1903), translated as 'The Modern Cult of Monuments: Its Character and Origin', *Oppositions*, 25 (1982), 21–50. Riegl distinguishes several 'values' of monuments, from intention to 'historical' and 'age' value. He is perhaps the first historian to think through the relative stance of a monument as time passes. His own intent was to promote the importance of the *Alterswert* (age value) as a brake to historicist practices of excessive restoration. The importance of Riegl for contemporary monument debates is discussed in my article 'The Willed and the Unwilled Monument. Judenplatz Vienna and Riegl's *Denkmalpflege*', *Journal of the Society of Architectural Historians (JSAH)*, (September 2013).

31 See Mark Rosenthal, 'Joseph Beuys. Staging Sculpture', in *Joseph Beuys. Actions, Vitrines, Environments* (Houston: Menil Collection, 2004), 24. The German word *Plastik* is less unusual than 'plastic art' is in English: it is a standard word for sculpture, like *Skulptur*, and figures in Johann Gottfried Herder's classic treatise on sculpture and its beholder, *Plastik: Einige Wahrnehmungen über Form und Gestalt aus Pygmalions bildendem Traume* (Riga: J.F. Hartknoch, 1778).

32 'The work on the "Tram Stop" was not only the preparation of an environment, it was also an action. In any case, Beuys interpreted it thus, since the aim was to re-establish and to restore history. "The hard work of remembrance" had to be performed on a project with widely ramified roots and which had to prove its actuality in this predestinated place at Venice.' Gallwitz, 'Journal', 16.

33 The collection of Durini was donated to the Kunsthaus Zurich in 2011, on the occasion of the exhibition *Beuys Voice*, co-curated by Buby Durini's widow, Lucrezia De Domizio Durini. The extensive catalogue exists also in an English edition, Lucrezia De Domizio Durini, *Beuys Voice* (Milano: Electa, 2011). According to the biography, written by Domizio Durini, Buby Durini also helped with the installation itself, in particular with the water issues that the artist encountered while drilling. 'Beuys. Leben und Werk', 142–3, and 'Remember Buby Durini', 960 (both in Durini, *Beuys Voice*, German edition. One particularly striking image shows the cannon-column with Beuys behind it, only his arms visible. Beuys visually merges with his piece, at once Pygmalion and Galatea, male creator and precarious monument-action. As if underlining the force of this image, Beuys silk-screened it for a poster shown in Bologna in 1977, with his signature above the welded head, and used it for a silk-screened numbered edition of 150 published by Durini's wife, the gallerist Lucrezia di Domizio Durini. The close connection between Beuys and the Durinis for other projects is well documented in the catalogue.

34 Scholten, *Strassenbahnhaltestelle*, 74.

35 Werner Spies, 'Die Schwierigkeiten des Zentauren. Ruthenbeck, Gerz und Beuys auf der Biennale in Venedig', *Frankfurter Allgemeine Zeitung* (31 July 1976), 19.

36 Benjamin Buchloh, probably the most vocal critic of Beuys, attacked his privatization of avant-garde conventions, and self-promotion as a healer of a catastrophic German history. See Benjamin H.D. Buchloh, 'Beuys: The Twilight of the Idol', *Artforum*, 5:18 (January 1980), 35–43, reprinted frequently. Buchloh's apt criticisms coexist with glaring errors: e.g. confusing Crimea with Siberia. The 1970s were full of 'individual mythologies', as the *documenta 5* of 1972 was entitled, and the strategy cannot be dismissed out of hand. See also Dirk Luckow, 'The Reception of Joseph Beuys in the USA, and Some of its Cultural/Political and Artistic Assumptions', in Claudia Mesch and Viola Michely (eds), *Joseph Beuys. The Reader* (Cambridge, Mass.: MIT Press, 2007), 287–303.

37 See Mario Kramer, 'Joseph Beuys: "Auschwitz Demonstration" 1956–1964', in Eckhart Gillen (ed.), *Deutschlandbilder. Kunst aus einem geteilten Land* (Cologne: DuMont, 1997), 293–307, and Franz Joseph van der Grinten, 'Beuys' Beitrag zum Wettbewerb für das Auschwitzmonument', 199–203. Kramer mentions sketches, wood models, and reworked photographs as preparatory work. Van der Grinten describes the bowl as circa 6.5 meters wide and 2.3 meters high, placed on the floor without base.

38 Caroline Tisdall, *Joseph Beuys* (Cat. Solomon R. Guggenheim Museum, New York, 1979), 21, and for the Beuys quote, Kramer 'Joseph Beuys', 294. Kramer points out that the various sketches and objects related to the Auschwitz memorial reappear in different contexts in Beuys's oeuvre. Ibid., 295.

39 The problematic concept of 'rebirth' in Beuys's oeuvre is discussed in a roundtable discussion with Benjamin Buchloh, Rosalind Krauss, and Annette Michelson undertaken on the occasion of Beuys's Guggenheim exhibition, 'Joseph Beuys at the Guggenheim', *October*, 12 (Spring 1980), 11.

40 Jaspers referred to God as the ultimate institution judging this individual effort. He distinguished between accusation from outside (for crimes committed) and the inner accusation of non-resistance to the rise of fascism. This guilt was to be overcome through 'purification' [*Reinigung*] of the individual. While crimes were to be punished and states held liable, moral guilt required penitence. Karl Jaspers, *Die Schuldfrage: Ein Beitrag zur deutschen Frage* (Zürich: Artemis Verlag, 1946), 15.

41 Beuys was brought up a Catholic, and attended a Catholic primary school from 1927 to 1932. On Beuys's memorials and their appeal to transcendence, see Gene Ray, 'Joseph Beuys and the After-Auschwitz Sublime', in Gene Ray (ed.), *Joseph Beuys. Mapping the Legacy* (New York: D.A.P., 2001), 54–73.

42 Beuys in fact fits the thesis of Alexander and Margarete Mitscherlich's influential book, *Die Unfähigkeit zu trauern. Grundlagen kollektiven Verhaltens* (Munich: Piper, 1967).

43 Dieter Mersch is typical of German authors in finding Beuys 'an exception, a shaman, a seer'. *Ereignis und Aura. Untersuchungen zu einer Ästhetik des Performativen* (Frankfurt am Main: Suhrkamp, 2002), 276. See also Rolf Famulla, *Joseph Beuys: Künstler, Krieger und Schamane* (Giessen: Imago, 2008).

44 Claudia Mesch's dissertation 'Problems of Remembrance in Postwar German Performance Art' (Ann Arbor: Michigan, UMI, 1997) deals at length with Beuys' museum reception: for an excerpt, see Mesch, 'Institutionalizing Social Sculpture', in Mesch and Michely (eds), *Beuys Reader*, 198–217.

45 Jochen Gerz, *The Centaur's Difficulty when Dismounting the Horse* (Munich: Kunstraum Munich, 1976), 123. See also *Jochen Gerz, Griechische Stücke. Kulchur Pieces*, Wilhem Hack Museum (Heidelberger Kunstverein, 1985), 62–75.

46 Volker Rattemeyer and Renate Petzinger (eds), *Jochen Gerz. Performances, Installationen und Arbeiten im öffentlichen Raum. Oeuvre catalogue*, vol. 1 (Nuremberg: Verlag für Moderne Kunst, 1999), 10. The catalogue is bilingual; I have cited its English text.

47 Hitler's fascination with Greek classicism is discussed by Gunnar Brands, 'Zwischen Island und Athen. Griechische Kunst im Spiegel des Nationalsozialismus', in Bazon Brock, Achim Preiß (eds), *Kunst auf Befehl? Dreiunddreißig bis Fünfundvierzig* (Munich: Klinkhardt und Biermann, 1990), 103–36. See also Erwin Panofsky, *Hercules am Scheideweg – und andere antike Bildstoffe in der neueren Kunst* (Leipzig: Teubner, 1930), on the cultural tradition of German appropriation of Greek origins.

48 Neither artist faced any consequences for their work under fascism: Thorak, an Austrian, exhibited in his home town of Salzburg in 1950 and died in 1952; Breker settled in Düsseldorf after the war, where he died in 1991 after an astonishingly long career.

49 Hans Haacke would win the Biennale prize in 1993 with his destruction of the marble floor of the pavilion, at a time when commemoration had become one of the most important issues in German art. Since then, the pavilion has been a popular site of political criticism. See Klaus Bussmann (ed.), *Hans Haacke. Bodenlos* (Stuttgart: Cantz, 1993). Bussmann starts his preface with a 'disclaimer': 'Nobody familiar with Hans Haacke's work would think of calling him an official artist [the German word used is *Staatskünstler*, state artist]. In this respect, the German pavilion at the Venice Biennale is the wrong place for him.' (5); Lagler, 'Der Deutsche Pavillon', 71–2; Petra Kipphof, 'Bodenlos in den Gärten der Kunst', *Die Zeit* (18 June 1993).

50 I would like to thank Peter Parshall from the National Gallery of Art, Washington, D.C., for this important reference. See Bernhard Schweitzer and Franz Hackenbeil, *Das Original der sogenannten Pasquino-Gruppe* (Leipzig: Hitzl, 1936), and more recently Laurie Nussdorfer, 'Ritual and Protest in Early Modern Rome', *The Sixteenth Century Journal*, 18:2 (Summer 1987), 173–89.

51 'Practice' as social activity founded in language is a theme of post-war social theory. See John Rawls, 'Two Concepts of Rules', *Philosophical Review*, 64:1 (January 1955), 3–32; Jürgen Habermas, *Erkenntnis und Interesse* (Frankfurt am Main: Suhrkamp, 1968); Pierre Bourdieu, *Esquisse d'une théorie de la pratique* (Gèneve: Droz, 1972); and Michel de Certeau, *The Practice of Everyday Life* (Berkeley and Los Angeles: University of California Press, 1984), originally *L'Invention du quotidien* (Paris: Gallimard, 1980).

52 One is reminded of Claes Oldenburg's ironic drawing of a monument blocking traffic in New York. On these, see Jo Applin, '"Strange Encounters": Claes

Oldenburg's "Proposed Colossal Monuments" for New York and London', *Art History*, 34:4 (September 2011), 839–57.

53 The work is often attributed to Jochen Gerz alone. However, Esther is officially co-author. The first proposal was submitted by Jochen Gerz in February 1984. Esther is first mentioned as co-author in a May 1985 letter from Gerz to the cultural office of Hamburg-Harburg: 'Meine Frau Esther Shalev, Bildhauerin aus Jerusalem, die einen Teil ihrer Familie in Litauen in Kzs verlor, hat mir nach dieser Sitzung gesagt, dass sie die Arbeit mit mir zusammen machen will, falls es zu einer Ausführung kommen würde.' Letter from Gerz, 7 May 1985. Office of Cultural Affairs, Hamburg (Kulturbehörde Stadt Hamburg), records on art in public space, 'Bezirk Harburg – Mahnmal gegen Faschismus Rathausmarkt Harburg.' File number 30-075.85/14, document number K 42. The monument was supposed to be situated in front of the city hall; however, due to technical difficulties, and supposedly because of the artists' preferences, it was moved. File number 32-075.85/14.1, document number VA 11/63.23-10. The distinction between *Denkmal* and *Mahnmal* has no literal equivalent in English. *Denkmal* is the usual word for monument, while a *Mahnmal* admonishes. The official English for the Harburg project is 'monument'.

54 Formal influence of American minimalism is obvious in the Hamburg monument. Minimalism was much shown in Germany since the late 1960s; its presence is discussed in Christine Mehring, *Blinky Palermo: Abstraction of an Era* (New Haven: Yale University Press, 2008), chapter 4, and in Germer, 'Intersecting Visions'. A closer affinity might be land artist Walter De Maria, who was less interested in anthropomorphism than in monumentality as such. In 1977, Gerz showed at *documenta 6*; for the same exhibition, De Maria inserted his *Vertical Earth Kilometer*, a one-inch thick brass rod, into the earth in front of the Museum Fredericianum, where it is still visible. See 'Löcher. In Kassel soll ein tiefes Loch gebohrt werden. Unfug oder Kunst?' *Der Spiegel*, 19 (1977), 89–90.

55 All the proposals can be found in the Office of Cultural Affairs, Hamburg, file 'Materialband zu 32-075.85/14.2'. The proposals were exhibited in Harburg City Hall in January 1985. See the review signed (wi), 'Die Modelle hatten nur sehr wenig mit dem Antifaschismus zu tun. Fünf Vorschläge für Mahnmal vorgestellt', *Harburger Anzeiger und Nachrichten* (31 January 1985). Press clip collection, Office of Cultural Affairs, Hamburg.

56 'Es handelt sich um ein einfaches Konzept: ein an allen Kanten abgerundetes Rechteck (Höhe 7m, Breite 4.5m, Tiefe 1.12m) mit einer überall gleichen Oberflächen Schicht aus Blei – so präsentiert sich das Mahnmal am Tag der Einweihung. Es befindet sich keine Schrift oder sonstige Bezeichnung drauf ... In einer unbekannten Anzahl von Jahren wird das Mahnmal unter dem Erdboden verschwunden sein, nur ihr oberer Teil, wird als Aufsicht etwas über Bodenniveau herausstehen. Auf der Oberseite, die vorher unsichtbar war, steht die Inschrift, die allen, die nachher an dieser Stelle vorbeikommen, mitteilt, dass die Stadt Harburg hier ein Mahnmal gegen den Faschismus errichtete, das in ... Jahren mit ... Unterschriften bedeckt wurde, und sich jetzt hier in der Erde versenkt befindet. "Möge es nie mehr nötig sein."' Project file: 'Bezirk Harburg – Mahnmal gegen Faschismus Rathausmarkt Harburg', file number 32-075.85/14.1. This proposal was received 1 February 1984.

57 The board text is printed in Jochen Gerz and Esther Shalev-Gerz, *The Harburg Monument against Fascism*, ed. Achim Könneke (Ostfildern, Ruit: Hatje, 1994), 9.

58 See an article signed (rav), 'Harburgs Mahnmal schon beschmiert', *Harburger Rundschau* (13 October 1986); 'Mahnmal geschändet', *Morgenpost* (16 October 1986); and Uwe Spriestersbach, 'Etwas anderes erwartet?' *Harburger Rundschau* (23 October 1986). The District administration of Harburg sent a statement to the press expressing its hope that after a while the vandalism would abate. It did not, but the press did. Bezirksamt Harburg, Press Release, 15 October 1986, file number 32-075.85/14 – Presse.

59 The column was lowered by 140cm whenever a segment was more or less full. See Andreas Hapkemeyer (ed.), *Jochen Gerz. Res Publica. The Public Works* (Ostfildern, Ruit: Hatje: Cantz, 2000), 52.

60 James E. Young, 'Memory, Countermemory, and the End of the Monument', *At Memory's Edge. After-Images of the Holocaust in Contemporary Art and Architecture* (New Haven: Yale University Press, 2000), 96. Young traces the emergence of the countermonument to Germany in the early 1980s. He has engaged with Gerz's project for quite some time: see 'The Counter-Monument. Memory against Itself in Germany Today', *Critical Inquiry*, 18:2 (Winter 1992), 267–96, reprinted in James Young, *The Texture of Memory: Holocaust Memorials and Meaning* (New Haven and London: Yale University Press), 27–48.

61 *Encyclopedia of Aesthetics*, ed. Michael Kelly, vol. 3 (Oxford: Oxford University Press, 1998), 272; the entry 'countermonument' is authored by James E. Young.

62 Young, *Texture of Memory*, xii–xiii.

63 *Consequente Kunstverweigerung* was Hiltmann's motto for not producing art; Ulrichs engaged in it too.

64 'Natürlich kann es sein, dass die Bürger und Besucher, anderes auf die Skulptur schreiben als ihren Namen, z.B. pro-faschistische Parolen. Das stört mich nicht, das Mal ist ein Relevator, keine Frömmelei, ein Foto der Stadt, wie sie wirklich ist, nicht wie sie sich vorstellt oder sonntäglich putzt. Zeitgenössische Skulpturen provozieren oft als einziges Bekritzelungen, warum nicht den Spies umdrehen, die Beschriftung als Zeugnis dienlich machen.' Project file: 'Bezirk Harburg – Mahnmal gegen Faschismus Rathausmarkt Harburg', file number 32-075.85/14.1, received 1 February 1984. The idea that the tensions between state and the public as well as the tensions between different publics are constitutive of a functioning dialogue were very actual in scholarship around 1990: see Rosalyn Deutsche, 'Art and Public Space: Questions of Democracy', *Social Text*, 33 (1992), 34–53, and Pamela Lee's review of the Skulptur Projekte Münster, 'Public Art and the Spaces of Democracy', *Assemblage*, 35 (April 1998), 80–6.

65 The prominence of the documentary function, treated as provocation, connects this project to Gerz's *EXIT – The Dachau Project*, ten years earlier. There, Gerz used the bureaucratic language of the museum of the Dachau concentration camp to argue that the language shows a continuation of authoritative ideology. The one remarkable difference lies in the 'making' of the document by the audience. In *EXIT*, Gerz had presented the visitors with *his* documents pointing towards an assumed continuation of 'fascist' language. In Harburg, the inscribed column

becomes a document of *enactments* by the audience. Jochen Gerz and Francis Lévy, *EXIT. Das Dachau Projekt* (Frankfurt am Main: Roter Stern, 1978); Jochen Gerz, *EXIT* (Zurich: Howeg, 1998). An interesting commentary is Armin Zweite, 'Jochen Gerz "Exit" – Materialien zum Dachau Projekt (1972/74)', in E. Gillen (ed.), *Deutschlandbilder. Kunst aus einem geteilten Land*. Cologne: DuMont, 1997), 442–4. For Young, *EXIT* is significant for the shift in the attitude towards commemoration in Germany. James E. Young, 'Memory against Itself in Germany Today. Jochen Gerz's Countermonuments', in *At Memory's Edge*, 124.

66 Jürgen Habermas, 'Diskursethik', *Moralbewußtsein und kommunikatives Handeln* (Frankfurt am Main: Suhrkamp, 1983), 105; translated by Christian Lenhardt and S.W. Nicholsen as 'Discourse Ethics', *Moral Consciousness and Communicative Action* (Cambridge, Mass.: MIT Press, 1990), 90. Habermas takes the term from Karl-Otto Apel, 'Das Problem der philosophischen Letztbegründung im Lichte einer transzendentalen Sprachpragmatik', in Bernulf Kanitschneider (ed.), *Sprache und Erkenntnis* (Innsbruck: Inst. für Sprachenwissenschaft d. Univ. Innsbruck, 1976), 55ff. Apel borrows from Jaakko Hintikka, 'Cogito, Ergo Sum: Inference or Performance?' *Philosophical Review*, 71:1 (January 1962), 3–32, where the utterance 'I do not exist' is found to be self-defeating. The effect was discussed by Austin for cases of Moore's Paradox, statements like 'the cat is on the mat but I don't believe it is', which Austin explained by sincerity and other conditions on speech-acts. Austin, *Philosophical Papers*, 248–50.

67 'Demonstrating the existence of performative contradictions helps to identify the rules necessary for any argumentation game to work; if one is to argue at all, there are no substitutes.' Habermas, 'Discourse Ethics', 95.

68 In calling an inscribed swastika a performative contradiction, I distinguish such acts from 'simple' vandalism: the column itself was shot, the glass of the viewing window broken (and also shot once), and so on. This vandalism concerns only the 'Relevator' function of the column, the legibility of its inscribed surface, not its political content. On the inscriptions, see the chronology in Gerz and Shalev Gerz, *The Harburg Monument against Fascism*, 34–5.

69 See Sabine Schütz, *Anselm Kiefer – Geschichte als Material. Arbeiten 1969–1983* (Cologne: Dumont, 1999), 122f, and Götz Adriani (ed.), *Anselm Kiefer. Bücher 1969–1990* (Stuttgart: Cantz, 1990), 13. Reportedly many professors were outraged over a work they considered pro-fascist. See also Matthew Biro, *Anselm Kiefer and the Philosophy of Martin Heidegger* (Cambridge: Cambridge University Press, 1998), 25–31, and Anselm Kiefer, *Heroische Sinnbilder* (Munich: Schirmer/Mosel, 2008). Another, genuinely affirmative project of Kiefer's at the time, *Für Genet*, makes obvious reference to Genet's *Funeral Rights* (1953), a study in mourning and the erotic appeal of the fascist male. On Genet's book, see Susan Sontag, 'Fascinating Fascism', *Under the Sign of Saturn* (New York: Farrar, Strauss, Giroux, 1972), 73–105; Pascale Gaitet, 'Sleeping with the Enemy: Jean Genet's Erotic Reconfiguration of the Occupation', *SubStance*, 87, Special Issue on the Occupation, 27:3 (1998), 73–84; and Lionel Abel, *Important Nonsense* (New York: Prometheus Books, 1987), 171–8. See also Christine Mehring, 'Continental Schrift: the Story of Interfunktionen', *Artforum*, 42:9 (May 2004), 178–83. According to Mehring, the source of

her information is an interview with Benjamin Buchloh, former editor of *Inter-funktionen*, in New York City, 24 February 2004, and a telephone interview with founding editor Friedrich Heubach on 29 February 2004. Email from Christine Mehring to the author, 13 December 2007. On the divergent reception given to Kiefer's work in Germany and the United States, see Frank Trommler, 'Germany's Past as an Artifact', *Journal of Modern History*, 61:4 (December 1989), 724–35, and Andreas Huyssen, 'Anselm Kiefer: The Terror of History, the Temptation of Myth', *October*, 48 (Spring 1989), 25–45. See also Lisa Saltzman, *Anselm Kiefer and Art after Auschwitz* (Cambridge: Cambridge University Press, 1999), 54–6.

70 Andreas Huyssen phrased it the following way: 'What if Kiefer, here too, intended to confront us with our own repressions of the fascist image-sphere? Perhaps his project was precisely to counter the by now often hollow litany about the fascist aesthetization of politics, to counter the merely rational explanations of fascist terror by recreating the aesthetic lure of fascism for the present and thus forcing us to confront the possibility that we ourselves are not immune to what we so rationally condemn and dismiss.' Huyssen, 'Terror of History', 38–9. Buchloh confirmed that Marcel Broodthaers, visited by Buchloh in the hospital, withdrew his offer to help the magazine with an edition of his work, exclaiming 'Who is this fascist claiming to be an anti-fascist?' *Interfunktionen* was discontinued soon after, in part as a result. Interview with the author, 30 October 2008. Mehring renders Broodthaers' question thus: 'Who is this fascist who thinks he's an antifascist?' 'Continental Schrift', 178.

71 The timing was good, given Bush's talk of an 'Axis of Evil' in his 2002 State of the Union Address.

72 Lisa Saltzman, 'Readymade Redux: Once More the Jewish Museum', *Grey Room*, 39 (Autumn 2002), 90–104, discusses the problematic status of the readymade in this political context. She begins with Art Spiegelman's reply to the exhibition, a cartoon entitled 'Duchamp is Our Misfortune' in the 24 March 2002 *New Yorker*: a swastika on a wall reappears at the Jewish Museum, where its Neonazi author explains it, champagne in hand.

73 Mehring, 'Continental Schrift', 178.

74 Peter Schjeldahl, 'The Hitler Show: The Jewish Museum Revisits the Nazis', *The New Yorker*, 78:6 (1 April 2002), 87.

75 An analogue is George Steiner's *Portage to San Cristobal of A.H.*, a novel which first appeared in *The Kenyon Review*, 1:2 (Spring 1979), 1–120, about the fictitious capture of Hitler in Brazil by Nazi-hunters.

76 Michael Jeismann, 'Zeichenlehre. Vom nationalen Kriegsgedenken zum kulturellen Gedächtnis', in Michael Jeismann (ed.), *Mahnmal Mitte: eine Kontroverse* (Cologne: DuMont, 1999), 21. See also Rudolf Augstein, *'Historikerstreit.' Die Dokumentation der Kontroverse um die Einzigartigkeit der nationalsozialistischen Judenvernichtung* (Munich: Piper, 1987).

77 Andreas Hillgruber, *Zweierlei Untergang: Die Zerschlagung des Deutschen Reiches und das Ende des europäischen Judentum* (Berlin: Siedler, 1986). Nolte leaned in this direction since his 1960s comparative work on international fascism, but his article 'Die Vergangenheit, die nicht vergehen will', in *Frankfurter Allgemeine*

Zeitung (6 June 1986), ignited the debate.

78 Kerwin Lee Klein has shown that memory played a small role in sociology and cultural studies before the 1980s: 'On the Emergence of Memory in Historical Discourse', *Representations*, 69 (Winter 2000), 127–50. See also Klein's *From History to Theory* (Berkeley/Los Angeles: University of California Press, 2012).

79 Jürgen Habermas, 'Vom öffentlichen Gebrauch der Historie', *Die Zeit* (7 November 1986), reprinted with additions in Habermas, *Eine Art Schadensabwicklung* (Frankfurt am Main: Suhrkamp, 1987). Published in English as 'Concerning the Public Use of History', *New German Critique*, 44 (Spring/Summer 1988), special issue on the *Historikerstreit*, 40–50, this quote 43. The article contains a lengthy dissection of Hillgruber's book in particular. See Augstein, '*Historikerstreit*.'

80 Habermas writes: 'The Nazi period will be much less of an obstacle to us, the more calmly we are able to consider it as the filter through which the substance of our culture must be passed, insofar as this substance is adopted voluntarily and consciously…'. 'Public Use of History', 45.

81 Habermas, 'Public Use of History', 44. The term 'weak anamnestic power', seems to adapt to memory the 'weak messianic power' attributed by Walter Benjamin to past generations in his *Theses on History*. See the discussion of Benjamin in Jürgen Habermas, *The Philosophical Discourse of Modernity* [1984], translated by Frederick G. Lawrence (Cambridge, Mass.: MIT Press, 1990), 11–16.

82 Habermas, *Philosophical Discourse of Modernity*, 15.

83 The importance of this fact is pointed out by Habermas, 'Public Use of History', 49. We should keep in mind that the *Historikerstreit* evolved as a series of essays in German newspapers, not in academic venues.

84 Habermas, 'Public Use of History', 41.

85 Aleida Assmann, 'Zwischen Pflicht und Alibi', in Heimrod et al. (eds), *Denkmalstreit*, 503–7 (quote 504).

86 Assmann, 'Zwischen Pflicht und Alibi', 503.

87 Hillgruber, *Zweierlei Untergang*, 74.

88 Alfred Dregger, 'Nicht in Opfer und Täter einteilen', *Das Parlament* (17–24 May 1986).

89 The Neue Wache was used instead of Bonn after Berlin was to become the new capital. It had served as memorial place for the dead soldiers of the First World War since 1931, then during the GDR as memorial place for the 'victims of Fascism and Militarism'. Its current dedication to the 'victims of war and tyranny' lumps together soldiers, resistance fighters, victims of Stalinism and the victims of fascist race theory alike. It was heavily debated, not only for this ambiguous inscription, but also for the decision to use the enlarged version of a small (38cm) sculpture by Käthe Kollwitz of a mother holding a dead son. Despite the debate, the memorial was inaugurated in 1993. Holger Thünemann, *Holocaust-Rezeption und Geschichtskultur. Zentrale Holocaust-Denkmäler in der Kontroverse. Ein deutsch-österreichischer Vergleich* (Idstein: Schulz-Kirchner 2005), 34–53. See also 'Streit um Pieta in der Neuen Wache. Widerstand gegen Kohls Pläne für Zentrale Gedenkstätte in Berlin', *Berliner Zeitung* (30 June 1993), and Habermas's criticism in 'Eine Art Schadensabwicklung', *Die Zeit* (11 July 1986), published in English under the

title 'A Kind of Settlement of Damages (Apologetic Tendencies)', in *New German Critique*, 44 (1988), 25–39.

90 Assmann, 'Zwischen Pflicht und Alibi', 505.

91 'Chronik', in Heimrod et al. (eds), *Denkmalstreit*, 27.

92 The chronology of the project from 1988 until November 1997 and the official text of the competition can be found in Michael S. Cullen, *Das Holocaust-Mahnmal. Dokumentation einer Debatte* (Zurich/Munich: Pendo, 1999), a good summary of the difficult history of the monument. Much more extensive, with a detailed chronology is Ute Heimrod, Günter Schlusche, and Horst Seferens's *Denkmalstreit*. A controversy about the exclusion of other victims, in particular Roma and Sinti, started immediately and led to several heated debates between the Central Consistory of Jews and the Central Consistory of Roma and Sinti in the following years. See 'Roma und Sinti fordern eigene Gedänkstätte', *Der Spiegel* (30 July 1999), www.spiegel.de/kultur/gesellschaft/0,1518,33498,00.html (accessed 11 December 2012). In 2008, a monument to the homosexual victims of National Socialism, designed by Ingar Dragset and Michael Elmgreen, was inaugurated in Berlin's Tiergarten park.

93 'Künstlerischer Wettbewerb "Denkmal für die ermordeten Juden Europas"', Michael Jeismann (ed.), *Mahnmal Mitte. Eine Kontroverse* (Cologne: DuMont, 1999), 68f, and Heimrod et al. (eds), *Denkmalstreit*, 171ff. The twelve invited artists were Magdalena Abakanowicz, Christian Boltanski, Rebecca Horn, Magdalena Jetelova, Dani Karavan, Fritz Koenig, Jannis Kounellis, Gerhard Merz, Karl Prantl, David Rabinovitch, Richard Serra, and Günther Uecker.

94 A commission (all male) including art historian Werner Hofmann, architect Josef Paul Kleihues, and international experts such as James E. Young invited the following artists: Christian Boltanski, Eduardo Chillida, Peter Eisenman, Jochen Gerz, Zvi Hecker, Hans Hollein, Rebecca Horn, Dani Karavan, Daniel Libeskind, Markus Lüpertz, Gerhard Merz, David Rabinovitch, Ulrich Rückriem, James Turell, Gesine Weinmiller, and Rachel Whiteread. See Cullen, *Holocaust-Mahnmal*, 272–3. The site was also still contested at that point. The colloquium consisted of three panels, 'Why does Germany need the monument?', 'The site, its historical and political context', and 'Typology and iconography of the monument, ways of realisation', held on 10 January, 14 February and 11 April 1997, respectively. A protocol of these meetings was published by the Senatsverwaltung für Wissenschaft, Forschung und Kultur (ed.), *Colloquium. Denkmal für die ermordeten Juden Europas. Dokumentation* (Berlin, 1997). See also Manfred Sack, 'Noch mal, aber von vorn', *Die Zeit* (7 July 1995), 54. Sack does not 'shed any tears' for the cancelled project, and approvingly mentions a memorial in Berlin-Steglitz with names and dates etched into a mirror: 'Whoever reads the names, sees him/herself in strange company with the victims.' The echo of Maya Lin, both in architecture and reception, is striking.

95 James E. Young, 'Empfehlungen der Findungskommission', in Heimrod et al. (eds), *Denkmalstreit*, 939–40.

96 Though in a jury meeting of 31 October 1997 Gerz was eliminated from the competition, he was put back after another meeting that included the commissioning authorities, Lea Rosh, politicians, and others on 1 November 1997. See Günter

Schlusche, 'Protokoll der Sitzung der Findungskommission am 31.10.1997', and 'Protokoll der Sitzung des Beurteilungsgremiums am 1.11.1997', in Heimrod et al. (eds), *Denkmalstreit*, 920–1. Richard Serra was brought into the discussion early on: in April 1991, Harald Szeemann invited Serra to develop a concept for the monument. Harald Szeemann, 'Ein Denkmal für die ermordeten Juden Europas', in Heimrod et al. (eds), *Denkmalstreit*, 74–8.

97 Novelist Günter Grass and playwright George Tabori called for abandonment of the project in February 1998: 'Wir sehen nicht, wie eine abstrakte Installation von bedrückend riesigem Ausmaß einen Ort der stillen Trauer und Erinnerung, der Mahnung oder sinnhaften Aufklärung schaffen sollte.' Cullen, *Holocaust-Mahnmal*, 290. In 1998, Nobel Peace Price winner Elie Wiesel and writers Arthur Miller and Amos Oz also argued against the monument. Ibid., 293. See also 'Das engere Auswahlverfahren von 1997/98' and 'Der Entscheidungsprozeß vom November 1997', in Heimrod et al. (eds), *Denkmalstreit*, 919–1139.

98 'Der Platz existiert in zwei Zuständen, dem veränderbaren und dem endgültigen. Der endgültige Zustand ist erreicht, wenn er mit Antworten vollgeschrieben ist … Paradoxerweise aber ist der veränderbare Zustand des Denk- und Mahnmales der permanente, weil die Antworten der BesucherInnen auch nach der beendeten Beschriftung des Platzes gesammelt werden. Dieser fortdauernde Prozeß macht die zeitliche Dimension des Denk- und Mahnmales ähnlich unvorstellbar wie die Zahl der 6 Millionen Morde.' Jochen Gerz, 'Warum ist es geschehen? Denkmal für die ermordeten Juden Europas Berlin 1997.' Proposal, in Heimrod et al. (eds), *Denkmalstreit*, 884.

99 Ibid.

100 See Heimrod et al. (eds), *Denkmalstreit*, 920–1. The interactive element of the project was well received.

101 According to a press review, this question was raised very directly by an inter-locutor during a discussion in Berlin. Not perpetrators, but the victims, he argued, were entitled to ask 'Why?' Julia Naumann, 'Viel Beifall für Gerz' Provokation', *Die Tageszeitung* (19 January 1998), reprinted in Heimrod et al. (eds), *Denkmalstreit*, 984.

102 In contrast, Young had initially advocated an on-going debate about the monument, instead of actually building it. During the third colloquium, he 'admitted that until that moment, I had been one of the skeptics. Rather than looking for a central-ized monument, I was perfectly satisfied with the national memorial debate itself.' James E. Young, 'Germany's Holocaust Memorial Problem – and Mine', *The Public Historian*, 24:4, (Autumn 2002), 65–80, this quote from *At Memory's Edge*, 193. The text, which finally came out strongly for a physical monument, appeared in German as 'Gegen Sprachlosigkeit hilft kein Kreischen und Lachen. Wer an Vernichtung erinnnern will, muß die Leere gestalten; Berlins Problem mir dem Holocaust-Denkmal – und meines', in *Frankfurter Allgemeine Zeitung* (2 January 1998).

103 Eisenman architects with Richard Serra, Proposal text, reprinted in Heimrod et al. (eds), *Denkmalstreit*, 883–4.

104 James E. Young, 'Empfehlungen der Findungskommission', Heimrod et al. (eds), *Denkmalstreit*, 940 [I am retranslating what must have been an English original].

The press reactions were fairly positive after the presentation of the final proposals. See *Denkmalstreit*, 941ff. 'Uncanny' architecture as a spur to involvement is widely used in Holocaust museums: Daniel Libeskind's Jewish Museum in Berlin and the US Holocaust Memorial and Museum in Washington, D.C. are often interpreted thus. See James E. Young, 'Daniel Libeskind's Jewish Museum in Berlin. The Uncanny Arts of Memorial Architecture', *At Memory's Edge*, 152–83, and 'Memory and the Politics of Identity: Boston and Washington, D.C.', *Texture of Memory*, 323–49. Other Holocaust museums evoke fear in their display strategies (lights, narrow paths, unstable ground, etc.).

105 www.aksioma.org/sec/press.html. The quote is a paraphrase of claims in *At Memory's Edge* (accessed 2 June 2013).

106 For Halbwachs, history was opposed to memory due to its 'objectivity', a claim less common today. Maurice Halbwachs, *On Collective Memory* [*Les cadres sociaux de la mémoire*, 1925], edited, translated, and with an introduction by Lewis A. Coser (Chicago: University of Chicago Press, 1992). See also Aleida Assmann, 'Texts, Traces, Trash. The Changing Media of Cultural Memory', *Representations*, 51, Special Issue: The New Erudition (Autumn 1996), 123–34, and Jan Assmann, 'Collective Memory and Cultural Identity'. Aleida and Jan Assmann's mnemohistory is Halbwachsian in its emphasis on transmission.

107 Halbwachs, *On Collective Memory*, 38.

108 This conclusion may be more individualistic than Halbwachs himself would allow: see his 'Individual Consciousness and Collective Mind', *American Journal of Sociology*, 44:6 (May 1939), 812–22. See also the reconsideration of Halbwachs in Paul Ricoeur, 'L'Écriture de l'histoire et la représentation du passé', *Annales, Histoire, Sciences Sociales*, 55:4 (July–August 2000), 731–47, esp. 734. Ricoeur recounts how, after 'long embarrassment', he has become convinced that collective memory is grammatical fact, for 'I', 'you', 'he', 'she', etc. can all remember the same thing, as we can think the same thought. But note that this version of collective memory is of publicly available facts: no single subjective 'memory' is thus shared.

109 See 'Holocaust-Mahnmal: Richard Serra zieht sich zurück', *Der Tagesspiegel* (3 June 1998), in Heimrod et al. (eds), *Denkmalstreit*, 1053, and the interview with Peter Eisenman by Verena Lueken, 'Dem eigenen Unbewußten ins Gesicht schauen. Ein Mahnmal, das auf einen Bruch in der deutschen Geschichte deutet: Verena Lueken im Gespräch mit Peter Eisenman', *Frankfurter Allgemeine Zeitung* (22 September 1998); Jeismann, *Mahnmal-Mitte*, 270–6; and the interview with Richard Serra by Carsten Probst, 'Warum ist ein Holocaust-Mahnmal unmöglich, Mister Serra?', *Der Tagesspiegel* (25 November 1998), in Heimrod et al. (eds), *Denkmalstreit*, 1169–70. Serra claims to have left the project for personal reasons.

110 Eisenman architects, revised proposal, in in Heimrod et al. (eds), *Denkmalstreit*, 1114.

111 James E. Young, 'Die menschenmögliche Lösung des Unlösbaren', *Der Tagesspiegel* (22 August 1998), in Heimrod et al. (eds), *Denkmalstreit*, 1115–17.

112 Olaf Kuhlke, *Representing German Identity in the New Berlin Republic. Body, Nation, and Place* (Lewiston/Queenston/Lampeter: Edwin Mellen Press, 2004), 243–4.

113 The Minister of State designate, Naumann argued in 1998 for a branch of the Shoah Foundation instead of the monument. He became the most vocal advocate of an additional documentary centre. See *Mahnmal-Mitte*, 283f, and Heimrod et al. (eds), *Denkmalstreit*, 1143ff.

114 Jürgen Habermas, letter to Peter Eisenman (16 December 1998), in Heimrod et al. (eds), *Denkmalstreit*, 1185.

115 'Der Zeigefinger. Die Deutschen und ihr Denkmal', *Die Zeit* (31 March 1999), reprinted in Habermas, *Zeit der Übergänge* (Frankfurt am Main: Suhrkamp, 2001), 47–59, and in Heimrod et al. (eds), *Denkmalstreit*, 153–8. The text is published in English under the title 'The Finger of Blame: The Germans and Their Memorial', in Habermas, *Time of Transitions* (Cambridge: Polity Press, 2006), 38–50.

116 'Lösung im Streit um Holocaust-Mahnmal zeichnet sich ab', *Der Tagesspiegel* (16 January 1999) and Michael Naumann, 'Haus der Erinnerung und Holocaust-Mahnmal in Berlin', in Heimrod et al. (eds), *Denkmalstreit*, 1200ff.

5 Relations

A cheap holiday in other people's misery!

I don't wanna holiday in the sun
I wanna go to the new Belsen
I wanna see some history
'Cause now I got a reasonable economy.
(The Sex Pistols, 'Holiday in the Sun')

In 2006, Spanish artist Santiago Sierra (born 1966) produced one of the least-liked public artworks concerning the Holocaust (Figures 66 and 67). His project, *245 Kubikmeter* (Cubic Meters), installed in the former synagogue in Stommeln, Germany, consisted of the exhaust of six cars being discharged through tubes into the sealed building; visitors had to wear gas masks and were allowed inside the synagogue for five minutes each. Outcry promptly followed across the political spectrum, most outspokenly from the Secretary General of the Central Council of Jews in Germany, Stephan J. Kramer, who said the piece 'damaged the dignity, not only of Holocaust survivors, but of the whole Jewish community'.[1] The exhibition, planned to be open to visitors for several hours every Sunday, shut down prematurely. No doubt the installation was tasteless, and appalling if we see it as an attempt to submit the visitor to the experience that Holocaust victims lived through, or rather, to the experience of *death* by gassing. The vulgarity, beyond any question whether one should wish to simulate such an experience, is that this is not an experience that can be had: what one gets instead is the passive or voyeuristic frisson of having been tourist at a genocide.[2]

The shock value of *245 Kubikmeter* acquires its full significance, however, in the context of the statements concerning his intentions that Sierra released to the press. The work was, according to the artist, no act of commemoration but, rather, aimed at exposing the 'banalization of remembrance of the Holocaust'.[3] If his work is self-consciously unacceptable, the gist of Sierra's claim is that recent Holocaust commemoration has become a trivial abuse of history indistinguishable from the most traditional monuments. The

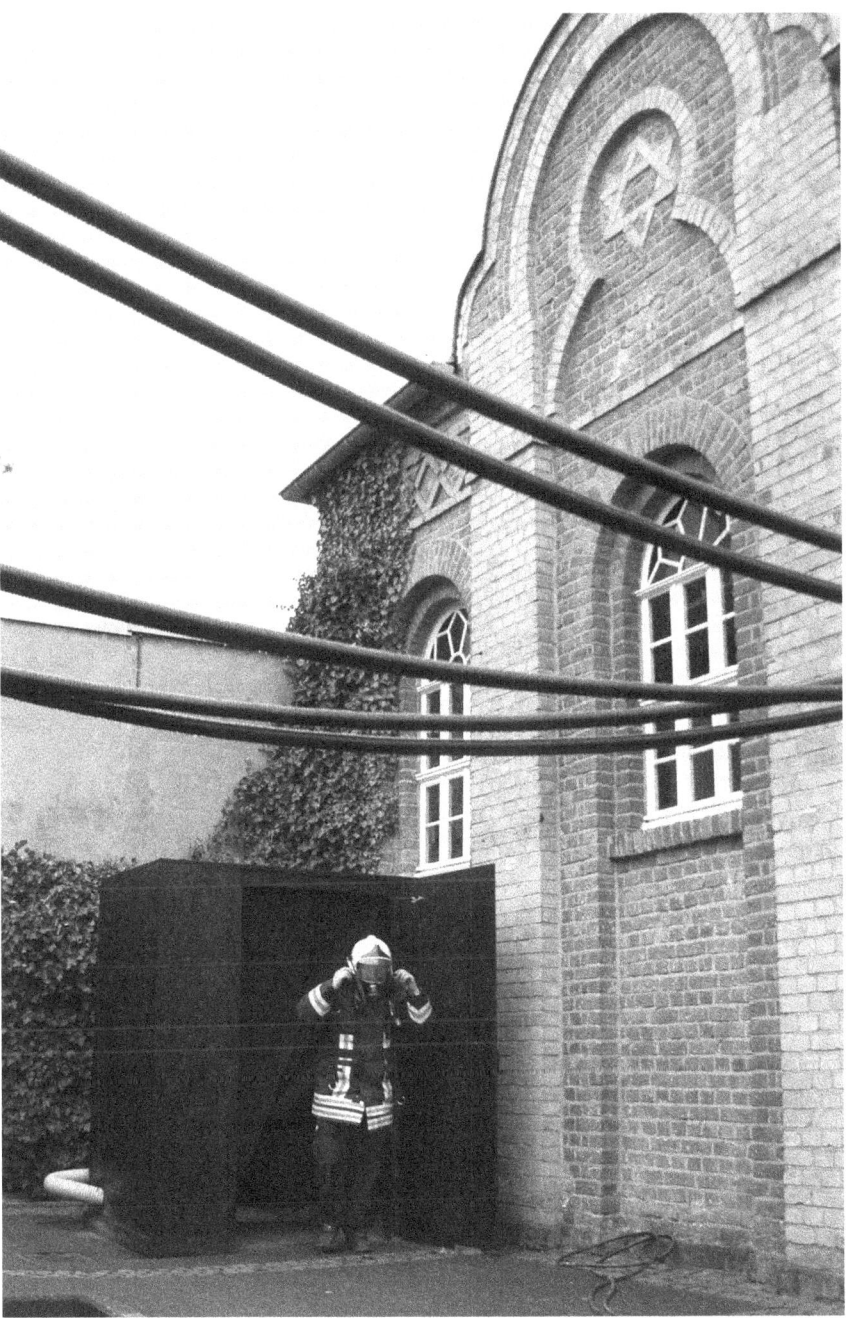

Santiago Sierra, *245 Kubikmeter*, 2006

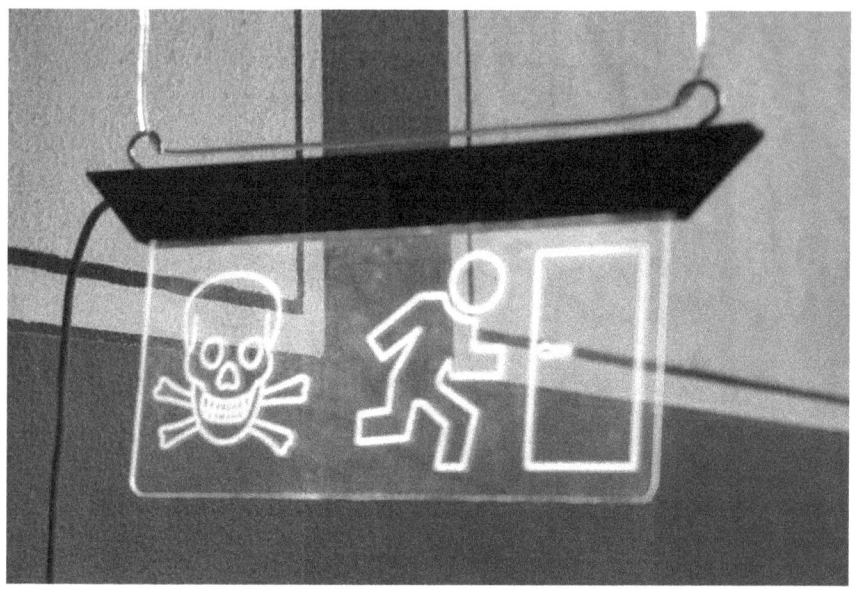

67   Santiago Sierra, *245 Kubikmeter*, 2006

venue does seem peculiarly well chosen for such a claim to strike home. The synagogue in Stommeln, near Cologne, has served as a medium for site-specific installations since the early 1990s, when the municipal Kulturverein began inviting prominent artists to exhibit in the only synagogue in the area to have survived National Socialism (the building was bought by the city in the 1970s). As a result, Stommeln gained an international reputation: to mention only one project, in 1998 Rebecca Horn executed *Spiegel der Nacht* (*Mirror of Night*), a poetic Holocaust memorial not unlike the proposal she submitted for the Berlin monument (Figure 68).[4] An experience both sensuous and literary, *Spiegel der Nacht* owes much to the German reception of Paul Celan, in which an imagery of night, mirrors, ashes, and desolate landscapes is taken as a melancholy form of subjective commemoration. In commenting on a general level on the subjective approach to Holocaust commemoration in Stommeln, Sierra launched an immanent critique of the memory boom. There had of course been voices raised against an exclusive emphasis on personal feelings and subjective memory in commemorative public art. Even Susan Rubin Suleiman, who pioneered a combination of poststructuralist literary criticism and autobiography in writing about the Holocaust, conceded that 'the emphasis on memory has been justly criticized because it can lead not only to dogmatism and kitsch but to political instrumentalization of every kind.'[5] But, Suleiman cautions, critics who oppose historical enlightenment to experiential approaches also 'miss the point'. The demand to experience the

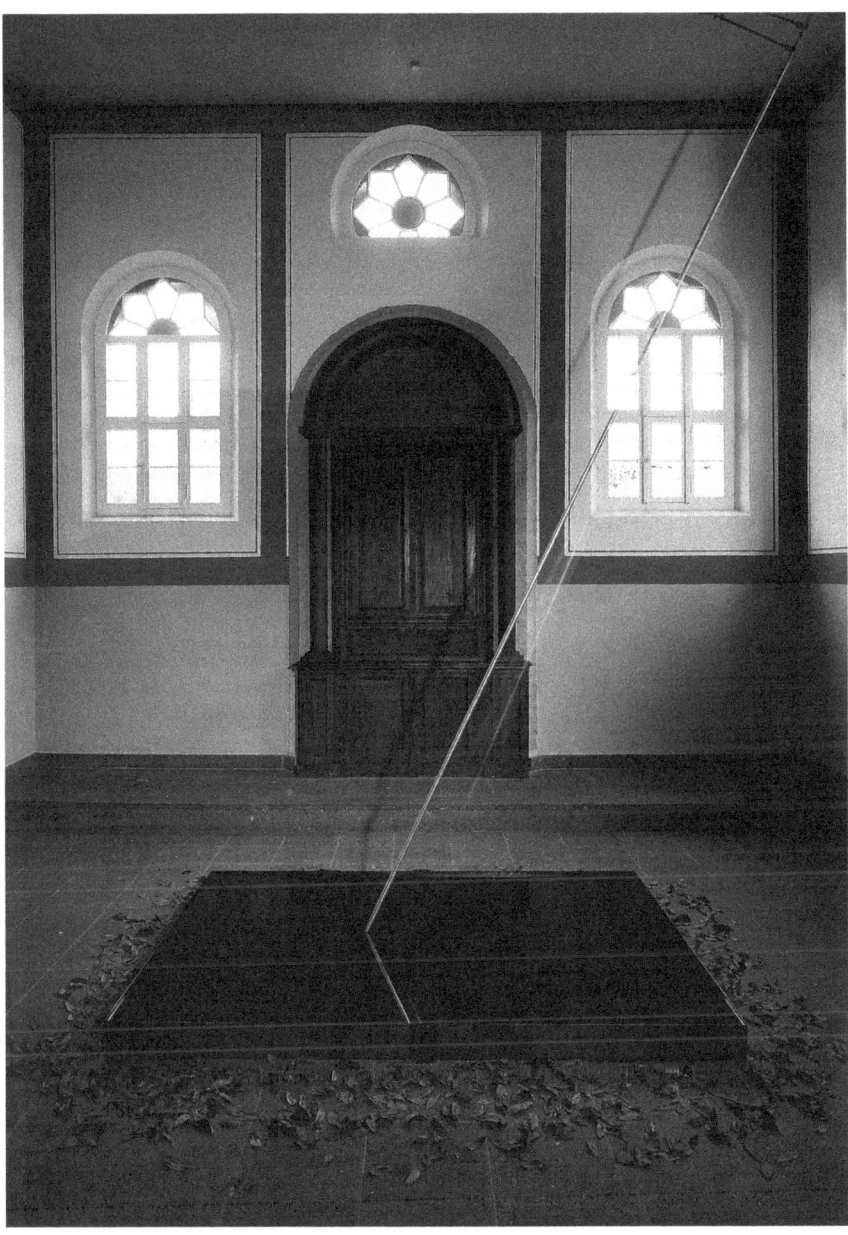

Rebecca Horn, *Mirror of Night*, 1998, Stommeln   **68**

past remains strong in individuals and institutions, so that as long as memoirs are being written and monuments commissioned, what is needed is aesthetically individual contributions, 'a poetics of memory, rather than a history or a politics'.[6] With Adorno, we are brought back to the hope that singular experience might lead us to critical self-reflection.

How would such an ascent from experience to self-reflection look in practice? One suggestion is the 1995 proposal for the *Memorial to the Victims of National Socialism at the Military Target Practice Range 'Feliferhof' in Graz*, Austria (competition 1995) by Hans Haacke. He proposed, below the military training ground, a passage 1.2 metres wide and 2.1 metres high, which visitors were to enter. Haacke expected visitors to

> feel trapped, isolated from the outside world, as if standing pinned against a wall oneself, threatened by an invisible firing squad … All these elements … could heighten one's psychological sensitivity to such an extent that, for a moment at least, a personal and initially unthinking identification may be possible with those whom the National Socialists murdered at Feliferhof. Such an experience could serve as a catalyst for a critical examination of the National Socialist past.[7]

At the site, the mass grave of 142 unknown persons was found in May 1945. Given this very sparse historical framework, it is difficult to see how the identification could lead to critical reflection. My exposition of these difficulties should not, however, be taken as a rejection of experience. A monument is not a historical treatise, precisely in its public political function, towards which the aesthetics of any piece of public art should be oriented. The difficulty of aesthetically tackling that limit of experience, absent historical knowledge, can also be seen in the winning entry at Feliferhof by Esther Shalev-Gerz and Jochen Gerz. They proposed that the soldiers were to conduct flag signals as part of their military exercises, the encoded texts of which, however, would bear such subversive slogans as 'Courage Brings Death', or 'Treason Against Your Country is Being Decorated'. Their project was not executed, due to resistance from the military.

What is interesting in this project is precisely that gap so tangible in Haacke between 'what the artist would like us to reflect on' and any possible experience to be had on site. Had the Gerz project been carried out, visitors would presumably be lulled into a sense of military routine on first seeing the flag signals, only to discover, on seeing a key to the signals, that what was being conveyed was anything but practical military communication or patriotic pomp. Indeed, the slogans would lead them to reflect on the questionable practice of officially instituted memorial art itself: a reflection, however, for which no encounter with live flag-pushers seems necessary or of much use. No wonder the military reacted.

The experience of the spectator, then, cannot be left out of public art (as with any art), any more than can its social consequences, for it makes them possible. The whole thrust of my discussion of performative monuments has not been that history trumps experience, but that the only way to link the latter to the former is by publicly available individual acts. Let us examine how such an interaction is offered up to the spectator and at the same time rendered obscene by Sierra. The visitor to Stommeln synagogue in 2002 was expected to walk into the gas-filled space with a gas mask that prevented injury. But there were no other means of access to the subject of commemoration. Though presumably it would have required some courage just to entrust oneself to the protection of the gas mask and step inside, one would then only be able peer through the visor at the synagogue, which presumably did not look very different filled with poisonous exhaust, and then leave. On-site discussion was pre-empted, as was any act besides the potentially suicidal one of taking off the mask.

What Sierra puts into question in Stommeln is, then, not commemoration in general, nor performative commemoration in particular, which he himself relied on. What he must be taken to be criticizing, rather, is the 'Holocaust sublime' mode of commemoration that seeks to put spectators in the victims' shoes and evoke emotional reactions on the basis of such experience. In this sense, *245 Kubikmeter* may in fact succeed in being a radical critique of the cathartic element in all commemoration, including itself. Insofar as the performative monument presupposes individuals making choices and not just serving as nodes of 'social relations', it does seem to always run the risk of reassuring these individuals in the present about a past that should not offer any reassurance. This is, at bottom, the same stricture as Adorno's in asserting the barbarity of 'poetry after Auschwitz'. As the older Adorno and, eventually the young Gerz came to realize, this critique is so uncompromising that it is in danger of undermining itself: if all discourse about the Holocaust is self-serving, so is all critique of discourse about the Holocaust. Sierra, with his scandalizing *245 Kubikmeter*, has concretized the instability of the critique of monuments. If even democratic commemoration is both authoritarian and self-serving, one is thrown back either into a return to some sort of traditional commemoration (which is at least honest about its political violence) or one must, with Nietzsche and the German new conservatives, say goodbye to the bleak past and embark on a project of therapeutic forgetting. Neither choice is particularly appealing.

Sierra's piece can at least, in its blunt negativity, be seen as a spur to action in the form of reflection. This takes the form of interior performances that should not be confused either with catharsis or with the contractual monuments of the 1980s. Over the course of this book I have shown the development of the performative monument from 1960s performance to the national Holocaust memorials and multimedia monuments of the 1990s and early twenty-first century. In narrating this development, I have focused on the work of one generation of European artists formed after the Second World War. Since then, performance art, some decades ago a marginal practice in artistic production, has successfully travelled into aesthetic theory, art production, and has even replaced older models of exhibiting.[8] 'Performativity' now stands for a whole range of aesthetic and political ideals. The term is often applied loosely to a new model of art production in which the audience is granted access to the art piece on ostensibly equal terms with the producer, if not indeed as co-producer. Most prominent in this respect has been the discussion around relational art, a term coined by Nicolas Bourriaud, who is also its theoretical and curatorial spokesperson. Relational art, according to Bourriaud, aims at producing 'sociability' in a positive sense or social interaction more generally, often on a symbolic level, but occurring directly in the world, of which the art world (gallery, studio, and museum network) is seen as one significant, strategically insulated subset.[9]

Relational art implicitly operates on assumptions similar to those of 1960s art, even though Bourriaud sees a clear distinction, principally that the event status of performance prevents the formation of hierarchies. Indeed, critical dichotomies have fallen away with the acceptance of the objects of performance, notably relics, photographs, and film: most obviously, what has been blurred is a dichotomy between the ephemeral and the permanent. And yet that dichotomy continues to operate subtly and to sanction much of the striving for the non-hierarchical in art. The permanence of the monument still serves as its antithesis or hidden referent. Thus Bourriaud: 'Present-day art has no cause to be jealous of the classical "monument" when it comes to long-lasting effects.'[10] He explains that relational art 'touches eternity precisely *because it is specific and temporary*'. In other words, as in Gerz's Berlin proposal, ephemeral events have chains of effects that last longer and are more socially effective than monoliths in public space. But if relational art is thus socially persistent, it cannot be divested of authority. Bourriaud is indeed cautious about advancing such a claim: contemporary art is 'marked by its non-availability', he claims, 'by being viewable only at a specific time', and is thus 'no longer presented to be consumed within a "monumental" time frame and open to a universal public'.[11] Bourriaud evades the common charge that relational art is elitist (because, say, only a handful of art world insiders get to attend a dinner by Rikrit Tiravanija) by identifying the 'universal public' of earlier art with a suspicious 'monumental' time-frame. But of course such a time frame-enters relational art in the form of documents for a reading audience: from Santiago Sierra's purposely cool monochrome photographs, meant to remind viewers of 1960s conceptualism, to Tiravanija's book of recipes by his art world friends, which no more records a single original experience than any other cookbook.

Individual experience and its mediation, however we measure their relative weights, remain indispensable in interpreting the memory debate, and also public art, into the twenty-first century. That this experience need not be based on being 'present' at the event experienced, I hope to have shown. Sierra seems to go one step further. By insisting on the crudest possible presence in Stommeln, he hints that the experience it generates may be radically misleading. If he is right, much contemporary public art is problematic. Even so, this would not mean the necessary failure of all attempts to engage the individual through experience. It would mean only that we must approach the idea of experience as carefully as that of presence. I have tried to show that a contemporary practice of monuments need not be purely negative, that important questions of political and historical responsibility in public space can be addressed through delegation of authority by a performatively equipped monument. And so aesthetics is not, as it appears in so much recent criticism, a mirror of political theory but, rather, a parallel investigation of the social world. Whether performative commemoration itself will persist, collapse into orthodox monumentality, or disappear in the interstices of an ever-expanding relational art practice, remains to be seen.

Notes

1 'Synagoge als "Gaskammer"'. Die Autos bleiben vorerst aus', *Frankfurter Allgemeine Zeitung* (13 March 2006).
2 One might consider in this connection several texts by John Lydon to music of the Sex Pistols in 1976 and 1977 ('Holiday in the Sun', 'Belsen was a Gas') that imagine the Holocaust through the eyes of an emotionally and politically sedate tourist. See also the discussion analysis of use of fascist symbols in punk in Dick Hebdige, *Subculture: The Meaning of Style* (London: Methuen, 1979), 116–17.
3 See 'Umstrittene Kunst. Synagoge wird zur "Gaskammer"', *Der Tagesspiegel* (12 March 2006).
4 Other artists who have used the space are Jannis Kounellis, Richard Serra, Georg Baselitz, Eduardo Chillida, Maria Nordman, Carl Andre, Lawrence Weiner, Rosemarie Trockel, Richard Long, and Sol LeWitt. Not all the works, but a good portion, deal directly or indirectly with the Holocaust.
5 Susan Rubin Suleiman, 'History, Memory and Moral Judgment in Documentary Film: On Marcel Ophuls's *Hotel Terminus: The Life and Times of Klaus Barbie*', *Critical Inquiry*, 28:2 (Winter 2002), 509–41, this quote 513. See also Charles S. Maier, 'A Surfeit of Memory? Reflections on History, Melancholy, and Denial', *History and Memory*, 5 (Winter 1993), 136–51
6 Suleiman, 'History, Memory and Moral Judgment'. Suleiman goes on: 'And, I would add, an ethics, too – not only how, but to what end?' I leave out this question, central to my last chapter, because it doesn't constitute an answer to the historians she is addressing (Charles S. Maier and Dominick LaCapra), who do after all criticize memory on ethical grounds.

7 Hans Haacke, 'Description of the Proposal', in Sabine Breitwieser (ed), *Hans Haacke, Mia San Mia* (Exh. Cat. Generali Foundation Vienna, 2001), 114–23.

8 From documenta to manifesta and the Venice Biennale, exhibitions are now proclaimed open structures, aiming at a non-hierarchical interplay between curators, artists, and audience. The 'platform' has become a favourite genre, most prominently in Okwui Enwezor's *documenta 11*, where the exhibition in Kassel was declared only one of many platforms of discussion and interaction in locations ranging from Vienna to Dakar.

9 Sierra is not discussed in in Bourriaud's *Relational Aesthetics* [*Esthétique relationelle*, 1998], translated by Simon Pleasance and Fronza Woods with the participation of Mathieu Copeland (Paris: Les Presses du Réel, 2002). Claire Bishop finds that Sierra and Thomas Hirschhorn are 'conspicuously ignored' by Bourriaud, and introduces them in the framework of Laclau and Mouffe's theory of antagonistic democracy. Claire Bishop, 'Antagonism and Relational Aesthetics', *October*, 110 (Autumn 2004), 51–79. Bourriaud discusses Hirschhorn in his second book, *Postproduction. Culture as Screenplay: How Art Reprograms the World* [2002] (New York: Lukas & Sternberg, 2005), 31. See also Hal Foster's very critical review of Bourriaud's two books originally published in the *London Review of Books* entitled 'Arty Party' (4 December 2004), reprinted as 'Chat Rooms' in Claire Bishop (ed.), *Participation. Documents of Contemporary Art* (Cambridge, Mass.: MIT Press, 2006), 190–5. Claire Bishop's new book, *Artificial Hells: Participatory Art and the Politics of Spectatorship* (London/New York: Verso, 2012), though it puts more emphasis on direct, disturbing experiences, again praises Sierra for making clear the relationship between delegated performance and economy (222ff). See my review on www.caarviews.org.

10 Bourriaud, *Relational Aesthetics*, 54. Bourriaud calls Félix Gonzáles-Torres's installations 'contemporary monuments'. The task of monumentality today is 'the commemoration of events, the continuity of memory, and the materialization of the intangible'. Gonzáles-Torres's installations consisting of sweets that visitors could take away lend themselves very literally to recollection by visitors who would make part of the work their own.

11 Bourriaud, *Relational Aesthetics*, 29. He goes on: 'The example of performance is the most classic of all. Once the performance is over all that remains is documentation that should not be confused with the work itself.' Despite this naïve presentism, Bourriaud does see a 'contractual' element in agreeing with the viewer on a specific time (and place) for a work.

Select bibliography

Numerous exhibition catalogues and newspaper articles, as well as archival sources, are cited in the chapter notes of this monograph.

Abel, Lionel. *Important Nonsense*. New York: Prometheus Books, 1987.

Abramović, Marina. *Biography*. Stuttgart: Cantz, 1994.

——. 'Cleaning the House. An Interview'. In Ric Allsop and Scott deLahunta, eds. *The Connected Body? An Interdisciplinary Approach to the Body and Performance*. Amsterdam: Amsterdam School of the Arts, 1996.

——. 'Interview'. In Michael Huxley and Noel Witts, eds. *The Twentieth-Century Performance Reader*. New York: Routledge, 1996.

——. *Performing Body*. Milan: Charta, 1998.

——. *Seven Easy Pieces*. Milan: Charta, 2007.

Adorno, Theodor W. *Prismen. Kulturkritik und Gesellschaft*. Munich: Deutscher Taschenbuchverlag, 1963.

——. *Erziehung zur Mündigkeit*, Frankfurt am Main: Suhrkamp, 1970.

——. 'What Does Coming to Terms with the Past Mean?' (1977). In Geoffrey H. Hartman, ed. *Bitburg in Moral and Political Perspective*. Bloomington: Indiana University Press, 1986.

Alberro, Alexander. *Conceptual Art and the Politics of Publicity*. Cambridge, Mass.: MIT Press, 2003.

Amanshauser, Hildegund, ed. *Der Überblick. Günter Brus*. Vienna/Salzburg: Residenz, 1986.

Anelli, Marco. *Portraits in the Presence of Marina Abramović*. Bologna: Damiani, 2010.

Arns, Inke, and Gabriele Horn, eds. *History Will Repeat Itself: Strategien des Reenactment in der zeitgenössischen (Medien-)Kunst und Performance*. Cat. Institute for Contemporary Art, Kunst-Werke Berlin. Frankfurt am Main: Revolver, 2007.

Art, David. *The Politics of the Nazi Past in Germany and Austria*. Cambridge: Cambridge University Press, 2005.

Askey, Ruth. 'VALIE EXPORT interviewed by Ruth Askey in Vienna 9/18/79'. *High Performance Magazine* (Spring 1981).

Assmann, Aleida. 'Texts, Traces, Trash. The Changing Media of Cultural Memory'. *Representations*, 51, Special Issue: The New Erudition (Autumn 1996).

——, and Ute Frevert. *Geschichtsvergessenheit – Geschichtsversessenheit*. Stuttgart: Deutsche Verlagsanstalt, 1999.

——. *Geschichte im Gedächtnis*. Munich: Beck, 2007.

——. and Sebastian Conrad, eds. *Memory in a Global Age. Discourses, Practices and Trajectories.* Houndmills, UK/New York: Palgrave Macmillan, 2010.

Assmann, Jan. 'Collective Memory and Cultural Identity' [published in German in 1988]. *New German Critique*, 65 (Spring/Summer 1995).

——. and Tonio Hölscher, eds. *Kultur und Gedächtnis.* Frankfurt am Main: Suhrkamp, 1988.

——. *Moses the Egyptian. The Memory of Egypt in Western Monotheism.* Cambridge, Mass./London: Harvard University Press, 1999.

Augstein, Rudolf. *'Historikerstreit'. Die Dokumentation der Kontroverse um die Einzigartigkeit der nationalsozialistischen Judenvernichtung.* Munich: Piper, 1987.

Auslander, Philip. *Presence and Resistance: Postmodernism and Cultural Politics in Contemporary American Performance.* Ann Arbor: University of Michigan Press, 1992.

——. *Liveness: Performance in a Mediatized Culture.* London/New York: Routledge, 1999.

——. 'The Performativity of Performance Documentation'. *Performing Arts Journal*, 84, 28:3 (September 2006).

Austin, J.L. *How to Do Things with Words.* Cambridge, Mass.: Harvard University Press, 1962.

——. 'Performative-Constative'. Translated by Geoffrey Warnock. In Charles E. Caton, ed. *Philosophy and Ordinary Language.* Urbana: University of Illinois Press, 1963.

——. *Philosophical Papers.* Oxford: Oxford University Press, 1979.

Ayer, Alfred J., Noam Chomsky, Robert S. Cohen, Dagfinn Follesdal, Jürgen Habermas, Jaakko Hintikka et al. Letter to Tito. *The New York Review of Books* (6 February 1975).

Bäcker, Heimrad, ed. *VALIE EXPORT. Körpersplitter.* Linz: Edition Neue Texte, 1980.

Badura-Triska, Eva, and Hubert Klocker. *Vienna Actionism. Art and Upheaval in 1960s Vienna.* Cologne: Walther König, 2012.

Battcock, Gregory, and Robert Nickas, eds. *The Art of Performance. A Critical Anthology.* New York: E.P. Dutton, 1984.

Becker, Christoph, and Annette Lagler, eds. *Biennale Venedig. Der Deutsche Beitrag.* Ostfildern: Cantz, 1995.

Benjamin, Walter. 'Theses on the Philosophy of History'. In Hannah Arendt, ed. *Illuminations.* New York: Schocken Books, 1969.

Berezin, Mabel, and Martin Schain, eds. *Europe without Borders. Remapping Territory, Citizenship and Identity in a Transnational Age.* Baltimore: Johns Hopkins University Press, 2003.

Berman, Russell. *Cultural Studies of Modern Germany: History, Representation and Nationhood.* Madison: University of Wisconsin Press, 1993.

Biesenbach, Klaus, ed. *Marina Abramović. The Artist is Present.* New York: Museum of Modern Art, 2010.

Biro, Matthew. *Anselm Kiefer and the Philosophy of Martin Heidegger.* Cambridge/New York: Cambridge University Press, 1998.

Bishop, Claire. 'Antagonism and Relational Aesthetics'. *October*, 110 (Autumn 2004).

——. *Artificial Hells: Participatory Art and the Politics of Spectatorship.* London/New York: Verso, 2012.

Bitter, Sabine, and Helmut Weber, eds. *Autogestion, or Henri Lefebvre in New Belgrade.* Berlin: Sternberg Press, forthcoming.

Bjelić, Dušan I., and Obrad Savić, eds. *Balkan as Metaphor: Between Globalization and*

Fragmentation. Cambridge, Mass.: MIT Press, 2005.

Blackson, Robert. 'Once More … With Feeling: Reenactment in Contemporary Art and Culture'. *Art Journal* (Spring 2007).

Block, René, ed. *In the Gorges of the Balkans. Europe's Art and Cultural Scene*. Kassel: documenta und Museum Fridericianum, 2003.

Blocker, Jane. *What the Body Cost: Desire, History, and Performance*. Minneapolis: University of Minnesota Press, 2004.

——. *Seeing Witness. Visuality and the Ethics of Testimony*. Minneapolis: University of Minnesota Press, 2009.

Bois, Yves-Alain. 'A Picturesque Stroll around Clara-Clara', *October*, 29 (Summer 1984).

Boorstin, Daniel. *The Image. A Guide to Pseudo-Events in America* [c. 1961] New York, Harper & Row, 1964.

Borejsza, Jerzy W., and Klaus Ziemer, eds. *Totalitarian and Authoritarian Regimes in Europe*. New York/Oxford: Berghahn Books, 2006.

Bourdieu, Pierre. *Esquisse d'une théorie de la pratique*. Gèneve: Droz, 1972.

Bourriaud, Nicolas. *Relational Aesthetics* [*Esthétique relationnelle*, 1998], translated by Simon Pleasance and Fronza Woods with the participation of Mathieu Copeland. Paris: Les Presses du Réel, 2002.

——. *Postproduction. Culture as Screenplay: How Art Reprograms the World*. New York: Lukas & Sternberg, 2005.

Breitwieser, Sabine, ed. *Hans Haacke, Mia San Mia*. Exhibition catalogue. Vienna: Generali Foundation, 2001.

Brus, Günter. *Unter dem Ladentisch*. Vienna: self-published, 1969.

Buchloh, Benjamin H. D. 'Beuys: The Twilight of the Idol'. *Artforum*, 5:18 (January 1980).

——. 'Hans Haacke: Memory and Instrumental Reason'. *Art in America*, 76 (February 1988).

——. 'Gerhard Richter's Work of Mourning'. *October*, 75 (Winter 1996).

——. 'Cargo and Cult. The Displays of Thomas Hirschhorn, *Artforum*, 40:3 (November 2001).

Burstow, Robert. 'The Limits of Modernist Art as a "Weapon for the Cold War": Reassessing the Unknown Patron of the Monument to the Unknown Political Prisoner', *Oxford Art Journal*, 20:1 (1977).

Burton, Johanna. 'Repeat Performance. On Marina Abramović's *Seven Easy Pieces*'. *Artforum*, 44:5 (February 2006).

Busch, Werner, ed. *Funkkolleg Kunst Eine Geschichte der Kunst im Wandel ihrer Funktionen*. Munich: Piper, 1987.

Buskirk, Martha. *The Contingent Object of Contemporary Art*. Cambridge, Mass.: MIT Press, 2003.

——. *Creative Enterprise: Contemporary Art between Museum and Marketplace*. New York: Continuum Press, 2012.

Buskirk, Martha, and Clara Weyergraf-Serra, eds. *The Destruction of Tilted Arc*. Cambridge, Mass.: MIT Press, 1991.

Butler, Judith. 'Performative Acts and Gender Constitution: An Essay in Phenomenology and Feminist Theory'. *Theatre Journal*, 40:4 (December 1988).

——. *Gender Trouble. Feminism and the Subversion of Identity*. New York: Routledge, 1990.

——. *Bodies That Matter. On the Discursive Limits of 'Sex'*. New York: Routledge, 1993.

——. *Excitable Speech. A Politics of the Performative.* New York: Routledge, 1997.

——, and Gayatri Chakravorty Spivak. *Who Sings the Nation State? Language, Politics, Belonging.* London/New York: Seagull Books, 2008.

Butt, Gavin. 'Happenings in History, or, The Epistemology of Memory'. *Oxford Art Journal,* Special Issue: 'On Installation', 24:2 (2001).

Calhoun, Craig, ed. *Habermas and the Public Sphere.* Cambridge, Mass.: MIT Press, 1992.

Carlson, Marvin. *Performance. A Critical Introduction.* London/New York: Routledge, 1996.

Choay, Françoise. *The Invention of the Historic Monument* [*Allégorie du patrimoine,* 1992]. Cambridge: Cambridge University Press, 2001.

Concannon, Kevin. 'Yoko Ono's Cut Piece. From Text to Performance and Back Again'. *PAJ: Performing Arts Journal,* 90, 30:3 (September 2008).

Craddock, Sacha. *L'Anti-Monument: les Mots de Paris de Jochen Gerz.* Paris/Arles: Paris Musées/Actes sud, 2002.

Crary, Jonathan. *Techniques of the Observer. On Vision and Modernity in the Nineteenth Century.* Cambridge, Mass.: MIT Press, 1992.

Cullen, Michael S. *Das Holocaust-Mahnmal. Dokumentation einer Debatte.* Zurich/Munich: Pendo, 1999.

Dawsey, Jill Christina. 'The Uses of Sidewalks: Women, Art, and Urban Space, 1966–1980'. Doctoral dissertation, Stanford University, 2008.

Debord, Guy. *La Société du spectacle.* Paris: Buchet/Chastel, 1967.

Deleuze, Gilles. 'Ecrivain non: Un noveau cartographe'. *Critique,* no. 343 (December 1975).

Derrida, Jacques. 'Signature, Event, Context'. In *Margins of Philosophy.* Translated by Alan Bass. Chicago: University of Chicago Press, 1982.

Deutsche, Rosalyn. *Evictions. Art and Spatial Politics.* Cambridge, Mass.: MIT Press, 1996.

Dimitrijević, Braco. *Braco Dimitrijević.* Zagreb: Galerija Suvremene Umjetnosti, 1973.

Djurić, Dubravka, and Misko Suvaković. *Impossible Histories: Historical Avant-Gardes. Neo-Avant-Gardes and Post-Avant-Gardes in Yugoslavia,* Cambridge, Mass.: MIT Press, 2003.

Doezema, Marianne, and June Hargrove. *The Public Monument and its Audience.* Cleveland: Cleveland Institute of Art, 1977.

Domhardt, Konstanze Sylva. *The Heart of the City. Die Stadt in den transatlantischen Debatten der CIAM 1933–1951.* Zürich: Verlag gta, 2012.

Durini, Lucrezia De Domizio. *Beuys Voice.* Milan: Electa, 2011.

Eiblmayr, Silvia, ed. *Sanja Iveković. Personal Cuts.* Vienna: Triton, 2001.

Elfert, Eberhard. 'Denkmalspraxis in Ost- und West-Berlin', in *Erhalten, zerstören, verändern? Denkmäler der DDR in Ost-Berlin. Eine dokumentarische Ausstellung.* Exhibition catalogue. Berlin: Neue Gesellschaft für Bildende Kunst, 1990.

Erić, Zoran, ed. *Differentiated Neighborhoods.* Belgrade: Museum of Contemporary Art, 2009.

EXPORT, VALIE. *VALIE EXPORT. Works from 1968–1975. A comprehension.* Paris, 1975.

——. *Das Reale und sein Double: Der Körper.* Bern: Benteli, 1987. English version in *Discourse,* 11 (Fall/Winter, 1988–89).

——. 'Aspects of Feminist Actionism'. *New German Critique*, no. 47 (Spring–Summer 1989).

——. *Split: Reality VALIE EXPORT*. Vienna: Museum Moderner Kunst Stiftung Ludwig, 1997.

——. *VALIE EXPORT. Ob/De+Con(Struction)*. Philadelphia: Moore College of Art and Design, 1999.

Famulla, Rolf. *Joseph Beuys: Künstler, Krieger und Schamane*. Giessen: Imago, 2008.

Fischer-Lichte, Erika. *Ästhetik des Performativen*. Frankfurt am Main: Suhrkamp, 2004.

——, and Kristiane Hasselmann, eds. *Performing the Future. Die Zukunft der Performativitätsforschung*. Munich: Fink, 2013.

Foucault, Michel. *The Archaeology of Knowledge*[*L'Archéologie du savoir*, 1969]. New York: Pantheon Books, 1972.

——. *Language, Counter-Memory, Practice*. Edited by Donald F. Bouchard. Ithaca: Cornell University Press, 1977.

Fraueneder, Hildegard. 'Körperrituale: Die Entmachtung des Repräsentativen in der Kunst VALIE EXPORTs und Friederike Pezolds'. Doctoral dissertation, University of Salzburg, 1988.

Freundeskreis des Kurhauses und Koekkoek-Haus Kleve, ed. *Joseph Beuys. Strassenbahnhaltestelle. Ein Monument für die Zukunft*. Kleve: Museum Kurhaus, 2000.

Fried, Michael. *Art and Objecthood: Essays and Reviews*. Chicago: University of Chicago Press, 1998.

Gallwitz, Klaus, ed. *Biennale 76 Venedig. Deutscher Pavillon. Beuys. Gerz. Ruthenbeck*. Stuttgart: Cantz, 1976.

Gardner, Anthony. 'The Idealizing Democracy. On Thomas Hirschhorn's Postsocialist Projects'. *ArtMargins*, 1:1 (February 2012).

Gehrman, Lucas, ed. *Judenplatz Wien 1996. Competition Monument and Memorial Site dedicated to the Jewish victims of the Nazi Regime in Austria 1938–1945*. Bolzano/Vienna: Folio, 1996.

George, Adrian, ed. *Art, Lies and Videotape. Exposing Performance*. Exhibition catalogue. Tate Liverpool. London: Tate Publishing, 2003.

Germer, Stefan. 'Intersecting Visions, Shifting Perspectives: An Overview of German-American Artistic Relation'. In *The Froehlich Foundation: German and American Art from Beuys and Warhol*. London: Tate Publications, 1996.

Gerz, Jochen. *Die Schwierigkeit des Zentauren beim vom Pferd Steigen. The Centaur's Difficulty When Dismounting the Horse.* Munich: Kunstraum München, 1976.

——, and Esther Shalev-Gerz. *The Harburg Monument against Fascism*. Edited by Achim Könneke. Ostfildern, Ruit: Hatje, 1994.

Getsy, David. 'Mourning, Yearning, Cruising: Ernesto Pujol's *Memorial Gestures*'. *Performing Arts Journal, no. 90* (2008).

——. 'Acts of Stillness: Statues, Performativity, and Critical Passivity', *Criticism,* 56:1 (forthcoming Winter 2014).

Giannachi, Gabriella, and Nick Kaye. *Performing Presence: Between the Live and the Simulated*. Manchester: Manchester University Press, 2011.

Giannachi, Gabriella, Nick Kaye and Michael Shanks, eds. *Archaeologies of Presence. Art Performance and the Persistence of Being*. London/New York: Routledge, 2012.

Giedion, Sigfried. *Architecture, You and Me. A Diary of a Development*. Cambridge,

Mass.: Harvard University Press, 1958.

Gillen, Eckhart, ed. *Deutschlandbilder. Kunst aus einem geteilten Land*. Cologne: DuMont, 1997.

Gilligan, Melanie. 'The Beggar's Pantomime'. *Artforum*,45:10(Summer 2007).

Gludovatz, Karin, Dorothea von Hantelmann, Michael Lüthy, and Bernhard Sieder, eds. *Kunsthandeln*. Zurich: Diaphanes, 2010.

Goffman, Erving. *The Presentation of Everyday Life*. New York: Anchor, 1959.

Goldberg, RoseLee. *Performance: Live Art from 1909 to the Present*. New York: Abrams, 1979 (revised under the title *Performance Art. From Futurism to the Present*. London: Thames and Hudson, 1988).

——. 'Performance: The Golden Years'. In Gregory Battcock and Robert Nickas, eds. *The Art of Performance. A Critical Anthology*. New York, 1984.

——. *Performance. Live Art since 1960*. New York: Harry N. Abrams, 1998.

Gorsen, Peter. *Zur Phänomenologie des Bewusstseinsstroms*. Bonn: Bouvier, 1966.

Grasskamp, Walter, ed. *Unerwünschte Monumente. Moderne Kunst im Stadtraum*. München: Schreiber, 1989.

Green, Malcolm, ed. *Writings of the Vienna Actionists*. London: Atlas Press, 1999.

Grosswiler, Paul. *Method is the Message. Rethinking McLuhan through Critical Theory*. Montreal: Black Rose Books, 1998.

Gržincić, Marina. *Fiction Reconstructed. Eastern Europe, Post-Socialism and The Retro-Avant-Garde*. Vienna: Edition Selene, 2000.

Gumbrecht, Hans Ulrich. *Präsenz*. Frankfurt am Main: Suhrkamp, 2012.

Habermas, Jürgen. 'Unruhe erste Bürgerpflicht'. *Diskus*, 8:5 (June 1958).

——. *Erkentniss und Interesse*. Frankfurt am Main: Suhrkamp, 1968.

——. *Technik und Wissenschaft*. Frankfurt am Main: Suhrkamp, 1968.

——. *Protestbewegung und Hochschulreform*. Frankfurt am Main: Suhrkamp, 1969.

——. *Knowledge and Human Interests*. Translated by Jeremy J. Shapiro. Boston: Beacon Press, 1971.

——, and Niklas Luhmann: *Theorie der Gesellschaft oder Sozialtechnologie: Was leistet die Systemsforschung?* Frankfurt am Main: Suhrkamp, 1971.

——. *The Theory of Communicative Action*. Translated by Thomas McCarthy. Boston: Beacon Press, 1984.

——. 'Concerning the Public Use of History" *New German Critique*, 44 (Spring–Summer 1988).

——. *The Structural Transformation of the Public Sphere. An Inquiry into a Category of Bourgeois Society*. Cambridge, Mass.: MIT Press, 1989.

Halbwachs, Maurice. *On Collective Memory* [*Les cadres sociaux de la mémoire*. Paris, 1925]. Edited, translated, and with an introduction by Lewis A. Coser. Chicago: University of Chicago Press, 1992.

——. 'Individual Psychology and Collective Psychology'. *American Sociological Review*, 3:5 (October 1938).

——. 'Individual Consciousness and Collective Mind'. *American Journal of Sociology*, 44:6 (May 1939).

Häni, Susanne, ed. *Der Hang zum Gesamtkunstwerk: Europäische Utopien seit 1800*. Frankfurt am Main: Sauerländer, 1983.

Hantelmann, Dorothea von. *How to Do Things with Art: The Meaning of Art's*

Performativity. Paris: Les Presses du Réel, 2010.

Hartman, Geoffrey H. *Holocaust Remembrance: The Shapes of Memory*. Oxford/ Cambridge, Mass.: Basil Blackwell, 1994.

Hapkemeyer, Andreas, ed. *Jochen Gerz. Res Publica. The Public Works*. Ostfildern, Ruit: Hatje, Cantz, 2000.

Heathfield, Adrian, and Amelia Jones, eds. *Perform, Repeat, Record: A Critical Anthology of Live Art in History*. Bristol: Intellect, 2012.

Hegy, Lóránd, ed. *50 Jahre Kunst aus Mitteleuropa*. Vienna: Museum Moderner Kunst, 1999.

Heimrod, Ute, Günter Schlusche, and Horst Seferens, eds. *Der Denkmalstreit – das Denkmal. Die Debatte um das 'Denkmal für die ermordeten Juden Europas'. Eine Dokumentation*. Berlin: Philo, 1999.

Henri, Adrian. *Total Art. Environments, Happenings and Performance*. New York/ Toronto: Oxford University Press, 1974.

Herf, Jeffrey. *Divided Memory: The Nazi Past in the Two Germanys*. Cambridge, Mass.: Harvard University Press, 1997.

Hillgruber, Andreas. *Zweierlei Untergang: Die Zerschlagung des Deutschen Reiches und das Ende des europäischen Judentum*. Berlin: Siedler, 1986.

Hirschhorn, Thomas. *Bataille Maschine*. Berlin: Merve, 2003.

——, ed. *Establishing a Critical Corpus*. With essays by Claire Bishop, Hal Foster, Sebastian Egenhofer, and others. Zurich: Ringier Kunstverlag, 2011.

Hohendahl, Uwe. 'Recasting the Public Sphere'. *October*, 73 (Summer 1995).

Hummel, Julius, ed. *Wiener Aktionismus. Sammlung Hummel*. Milan: Mazzotta, 2005.

Husserl, Edmund. 'Systematische Raumkonstitution'. In *Ding und Raum. Vorlesungen 1907*, Husserliana, vol. 16, ed. Ulrich Claesges. Den Haag : M. Nijhoff, 1973.

——. *Ideen zu einer reinen Phänomenologie und phänomenologischen Philosophie*. Vol. I: *Allgemeine Einführung in die reine Phänomenologie* [1913]. Tübingen: Niemeyer, 1980.

Husslein-Arco, Agnes, Angelika Nollert, and Stella Rollig, eds. *VALIE EXPORT. Time and Countertime* (Catalogue of the Österreichische Galerie Belvedere and Lentos Kunstmuseum Linz). Cologne: Walther König, 2010.

Huyssen, Andreas. 'In the Shadow of McLuhan: Jean Baudrillard's Theory of Simulation, *Assemblage*, 10 (December 1987).

——. Anselm Kiefer: The Terror of History, the Temptation of Myth'. *October*, 48 (Spring 1989).

——. *Twilight Memories. Marking Time in a Culture of Amnesia*. New York/London: Routledge, 1995.

——. 'Sculpture, Materiality and Memory in an Age of Amnesia'. In *Displacements. Miroslaw Balka, Doris Salcedo, Rachel Whiteread*. Toronto: Art Gallery of Ontario, 1998.

Iles, Chrissie, ed. *Marina Abramović. Objects performance video sound*. Oxford: Museum of Modern Art Oxford, 1995.

IRWIN, ed. *East Art Map. Contemporary Art and Eastern Europe*. London: Afterall, 2006.

Jappe, Elisabeth. *Performance – Ritual – Prozess. Handbuch der Aktionskunst in Europa*. New York/Munich: Prestel, 1993.

Jarzombek, Mark. *The Psychologizing of Modernity: Art, Architecture, and History*. Cambridge/New York: Cambridge University Press, 2000.

——, and Mechtild Widrich, eds. *Krzysztof Wodiczko, a 9/11 Memorial*. London: Black Dog, 2009.

Jaspers, Karl. *The Question of German Guilt* [*Die Schuldfrage*, 1946]. Translated by E.B. Ashton. New York: Dial Press, 1947.

Jeismann, Michael, ed. *Mahnmal Mitte. Eine Kontroverse*. Cologne: Dumont, 1999.

Johnson, Geraldine A., ed. *Sculpture and Photography. Envisioning the Third Dimension*. Cambridge: Cambridge University Press, 1998.

Jones, Amelia. 'Presence in Absentia. Experiencing Performance as Documentation'. *Art Journal*, 56:4 (Winter 1997).

——. *Body Art: Performing the Subject*. Minneapolis: University of Michigan Press, 1998.

——, and Andrew Stephenson, eds. *Performing the Body, Performing the Text*. London/New York: Routledge, 1999.

——. '"The Artist is Present". Artistic Re-enactmens and the Impossibility of Presence'. *TDR. The Drama Review*, 209, 55:1 (Spring 2011).

Jones, Caroline. *Machine in the Studio. Constructing the postwar American Artist*. Chicago: University of Chicago Press, 1996.

——. 'Staged Presence'. *Artforum*, 48:9 (May 2010).

Kaprow, Allan. *Essays on the Blurring of Art and Life*. Berkeley/Los Angeles/London: University of California Press, 1993.

Kaye, Nick. *Postmodernism and Performance*. Basingstoke: Macmillan, 1994.

——. *Site-Specific Art: Performance, Place and Documentation*. London/New York: Routledge, 2000.

Klein, Kerwin Lee. 'On the Emergence of Memory in Historical Discourse', *Representations*, 69 (Winter 2000).

——. *From History to Theory* (Berkeley, Los Angeles: University of California Press, 2012.

Klocker, Hubert, ed. *Viennese Actionism 1960–71*. Klagenfurt: Ritter, 1989.

Koselleck, Reinhart. *Kritik und Krise*. Freiburg: Alber, 1959.

Kotz, Liz. *Words to Be Looked At*. Cambridge, Mass.: MIT Press, 2007.

Koweindl, Daniela. *Ein Mahnmal für die Ermordeten Österreichischen Juden*. Master's thesis, University of Vienna, 2003.

Kramer, Mario. 'Joseph Beuys. Auschwitz Demonstration 1956–1964'. In Eckhart Gillen, ed. *German Art from Beckmann to Richter*. New Haven/London: Yale University Press; and Cologne: Dumont, 1997.

Krämer, Sybille, ed. *Performativität und Medialität*. Munich: Wilhelm Fink, 2004.

Krauss, Rosalind. 'Sculpture in the Expanded Field'. *October*, 8 (Spring 1979).

——. *Passages in Modern Sculpture*. Cambridge, Mass.: MIT Press, 1981.

Kröller-Müller Museum, ed. *Living Art on the Edge of Europe*. Bielefeld: Kerber, 2006.

Kunstwerke Berlin, ed. *A Little Bit of History Repeated*. Paris/Berlin: Edition Valerio/Kunstwerke Berlin, 2001.

Kwon, Miwon. *One Place after Another. Site-Specific Art and Locational Identity*. Cambridge, Mass.: MIT Press, 2004.

Lambert-Beatty, Carrie. *Being Watched: Yvonne Rainer and the 1960s*. Cambridge, Mass.: MIT Press, 2008.

——. 'Against Performance Art'. *Artforum*, 48:9 (May 2010).

Lee, Pamela. 'Public Art and the Spaces of Democracy. *Assemblage*, no. 35 (April 1998).

——. 'Bare Lives'. In Mathias Michalka, ed., *X-Screen: Film Installations and Actions in the 1960s and 1970s*. Cologne: Walther König, 2004.

Lefebvre, Henri. *Le Droit à la ville*. Paris: Éditions Anthropos, 1968.

——. *The Production of Space* [French 1974] Oxford: Blackwell, 1991.

Lippard, Lucy. *Six Years: the Dematerialization of the Art Object from 1966 to 1972*. New York: Praeger, 1973.

——. 'Art Outdoors, In and Out of the Public Domain'. *Studio International*, 193 (March–April 1977).

Lippmann, Walter. *The Phantom Public*. New York: Harcourt, Brace, 1925.

Loewy, Hanno, ed. *Holocaust: Die Grenzen des Verstehens. Eine Debatte über die Besetzung der Geschichte*. Reinbek bei Hamburg: Rowohlt, 1992.

Lorenz, Inge, ed. *Joseph Beuys Symposium Kranenburg*. Basel: Weise, 1995.

Louis, Eleonora, and Mechtild Widrich, 'Die Gelassenheit des Verräters. Zur Methodik in Jochen Gerz' Foto/Text Arbeiten'. In *Jochen Gerz, Daran denken. Texte in Arbeiten 1980–1996*. Düsseldorf: Richter, 1997.

Lütticken, Sven, ed. *Life, Once More. Forms of Reenactment in Contemporary Art*. Rotterdam: Witte de With Center for Contemporary Art, 2005.

Mackert, Gabriele, and Gerald Matt, eds. *Santiago Sierra*. Vienna: Kunsthalle Wien, 2002.

Magistrat der Stadt Wien, ed. *Der transparente Raum*. Vienna: MA 57 – Frauenförderung und Koordinierung von Frauenangelegenheiten, 2000.

Mai, Ekkehard, and Gisela Schmirbe, eds. *Denkmal, Zeichen, Monument: Skulptur und öffentlicher Raum heute*. Munich: Prestel, 1989.

Maier, Charles S. 'A Surfeit of Memory? Reflections on History, Melancholy, and Denial'. *History and Memory*, (Winter 1993).

Marcoci, Roxana, ed. *Sanja Iveković: Sweet Violence*. New York: Museum of Modern Art, 2011.

Marcuse, Herbert. *Eros and Civilization. A Philosophical Inquiry into Freud*. Boston: Beacon Press, 1955.

Martin, Randy. *Performance as Political Act*. New York/Westport/London: Bergin and Garvey, 1990.

Matzner, Florian. *Public Art. Kunst im öffentlichen Raum*. Ostfildern-Ruit: Hatje Cantz, 2001.

McLuhan, Marshall. *Understanding Media: The Extensions of Man*. New York: McGraw Hill, 1964.

——. Review of *Television: Technology and Cultural Form,* by Raymond Williams. *Technology and Culture*, 19:2 (1978).

Mehring, Christine. 'Continental Schrift: the Story of Interfunktionen'. *Artforum*, 42:9 (May 2004).

——. *Blinky Palermo: Abstraction of an Era*. New Haven: Yale University Press, 2008.

Meltzer, Richard. *The Aesthetics of Rock*. New York: Something Else Press, 1970.

Merleau-Ponty, Maurice. *Phénoménologie de la perception*. Paris: Gallimard, 1945.

Mersch, Dieter. *Ereignis und Aura. Untersuchungen zu einer Ästhetik des Performativen*. Frankfurt am Main: Suhrkamp, 2002.

——. *Was sich zeigt. Materialität, Präsenz, Ereignis*. Munich: Fink, 2002.

Mesch, Claudia. 'Problems of Remembrance in postwar German Performance Art'. Doctoral dissertation, University of Chicago, 1997.

——, and Viola Michely, eds. *Joseph Beuys. The Reader*. Cambridge, Mass.: MIT Press, 2007.

——. *Modern Art at the Berlin Wall: Demarcating Culture in the Cold War Germanys*. London: I.B. Tauris, 2009.

Meschede, Friedrich. *Marina Abramović*. Ostfildern, Ruit: Cantz, 1993.

Meyer, James. 'Der funktionale Ort'. In *Platzwechsel* (Kunsthalle Zurich, 1995); reprinted in *Springer*, 2:4 (1996). English: 'The Functional Site; or, The Transformation of Site-Specificity'. In Erika Suderberg, ed., *Space, Site, Intervention: Situating Installation Art*. Minneapolis: University of Minnesota Press, 2000.

Moderna Galerija Ljubljana, ed. *Body and the East. From the 1960s to the Present*. Cambridge, Mass./London: MIT Press, 1999.

Moravánszky, Ákos, ed. *Architekturtheorie im 20. Jahrhundert: eine kritische Anthologie*. Vienna: Springer, 2002.

Mosse, George L. *The Nationalization of the Masses. Political Symbolism and Mass Movements in Germany from the Napoleonic Wars through the Third Reich*. Ithaca/London: Cornell University Press, 1975.

Mueller, Roswitha. *VALIE EXPORT. Fragments of The Imagination*. Indiana University Press: Bloomington and Indianapolis, 1994.

Mulvey, Laura. 'Visual Pleasure and Narrative Cinema'. *Screen*, 16:3 (1975).

Mumford, Lewis. 'Monumentalism, Symbolism and Style', *Architectural Review*, 105 (1949).

Naef, Maya. *Joseph Beuys. Zeichnung und Stimme*. München: Fink, 2011.

Naginski, Erika. *Sculpture and Enlightenment*. Los Angeles: Getty Publications, 2009.

Negt, Oskar, ed. *Die Linke antwortet Jürgen Habermas*. Frankfurt am Main: Europäische Verlagsanstalt, 1968.

——, and Alexander Kluge. *Public Sphere and Experience. Toward an Analysis of the Bourgeois and Proletarian Public Sphere*. [1972] Minneapolis: University of Minnesota Press, 1993.

Neue Gesellschaft für Bildende Kunst, ed. *VALIE EXPORT: Mediale Anagramme*. Berlin: Akademie der Künste, 2003.

Nitsch, Hermann. *Das Orgien Mysterien Theater. Manifeste, Aufträge, Vorträge*. Salzburg/Vienna: Residenz, 1990.

——. *Das Orgien Mysterien Theater, Die Partituren aller aufgeführten Aktionen*. Napoli: Edition Morra, 1979–84.

Noack, Ruth. *Sanja Iveković. Triangle*. London/New York: Verso, 2013.

Nolte, Ernst. 'Die Vergangenheit, die nicht vergehen will'. *Frankfurter Allgemeine Zeitung* (6 June 1986).

——. *Das Vergehen der Vergangenheit: Antwort an meine Kritiker im sogenannten Historikerstreit*. Berlin: Ullstein, 1987.

Nora, Pierre. *Realms of Memory. Rethinking the French Past*. New York: Columbia University Press, 1996.

O'Dell, Kathy. 'Toward a Theory of Performance Art: An Investigation of its Sites'. PhD dissertation, City University of New York, 1992.

——. *Contract with the Skin: Masochism, Performance Art, and the 1970's*. Minneapolis: University of Minnesota Press, 1998.

Oettermann, Stephan. *The Panorama: History of a Mass Medium*. New York: Zone Books, 1996.

Ozouf, Mona. *Festivals and the French Revolution* [1976]. Cambridge, Mass.: Harvard University Press, 1988.

Palla, Rudi, ed. *Erinnerungsstätte Allentsteig – eine Dokumentation*. Vienna: Triton, 1999.

Petrović, Madeleine. *Der Wiener Gürtel: Wiederentdeckung einer Prachtstraße*. Vienna: Brandstätter, 2009.

Pejić, Bojana. 'Being-In-The-Body. On the Spiritual in Marina Abramović's Art'. In Friedrich Meschede, *Marina Abramović*. Stuttgart: Cantz, 1993.

——. 'Sozialistischer Modernismus und die Nachwehen'. In Lóránd Hegy, ed. *50 Jahre Kunst aus Mitteleuropa*. Vienna: Museum Moderner Kunst Stiftung. Ludwig, 1999.

Phelan, Peggy. *Unmarked: The Politics of Performance*. London/New York: Routledge, 1993.

Potyka, Alexander, ed. *Betrifft Anschluss. Ein Almanach*. Vienna: Arbeitsgemeinschaft Österreichischer Privatverlage, 1988.

Prammer, Anita. *VALIE EXPORT. Eine multimediale Künstlerin*. Vienna: Wiener Frauenverlag, 1988.

Pusch, Detlev, ed. *Gewalt/Geschäfte Eine Ausstellung zum Topos Gewalt in der künstlerischen Auseinandersetzung*. Berlin: Neue Gesellschaft für Bildende Kunst, 1994.

Puvogel, Ulrike. *Gedenkstätten für die Opfer des Nationalsozialismus. Eine Dokumentation*. 2 vols. Bonn: Bundeszentrale für politische Bildung, 1995 and 1999.

Rattemeyer, Volker, ed. *Jochen Gerz. Get Out of My Lies. 18 Installationen der siebziger Jahre*. Catalogue. Museum Wiesbaden. Nuremberg: Verlag für Moderne Kunst, 1997.

——, *Jochen Gerz. Performances, Installationen, und Arbeiten im öffentlichen Raum*. Oeuvre catalogue, vol. 1. Nuremberg: Verlag für Moderne Kunst, 1999.

Ray, Gene, ed. *Joseph Beuys. Mapping the Legacy*. New York: D.A.P., 2001.

Reithmann, Max, ed. *Joseph Beuys. Par la présente, je ne appartiens plus à l'art*. Paris: L'Arche, 1988.

Rendell, Jane. *Art and Architecture: A Place Between*. London: I.B. Tauris, 2006.

Riegl, Alois. *Der Moderne Denkmalkultus, sein Wesen und seine Entstehung*. Vienna: W. Braumüller, 1903, translated as 'The Modern Cult of Monuments: Its Character and Origin'. *Oppositions*, no. 25 (1982).

Roselt, Jens, and Ulf Otto, eds. *Theater als Zeitmaschine. Zur performativen Praxis des Reenactments. Theater- und kulturwissenschaftliche Perspektiven*. Bielefeld: Transcript, 2012.

Rosenberg, Harold. *The Tradition of the New*. New York: McGraw-Hill, 1965.

Rosenthal, Mark. *Anselm Kiefer*. Chicago: Art Institute of Chicago, 1987.

——. *Joseph Beuys. Actions, Vitrines, Environments*. Houston: The Menil Collection, 2004.

Roussel, Danièle. *Der Wiener Aktionismus und die Österreicher. Gespräche*. Klagenfurt: Ritter, 1995.

Rowe, Colin and Robert Slutzky. 'Transparency. Literal and Phenomenal'. *Perspecta*, 8 (1963).

Ruhl, Carsten, ed. *Mythos Monument. Urbane Strategien in Architektur und Kunst seit 1945*. Bielefeld: Transcript, 2011.

Saltzman, Lisa. *Anselm Kiefer and Art after Auschwitz*. Cambridge/New York: Cambridge University Press, 1999.

——. 'Readymade Redux: Once more the Jewish Museum'. *Grey Room*, 39 (Autumn 2002).

Salzburg Foundation, ed. *Kunstprojekt Salzburg. Moderne Kunst auf alten Plätzen.* Vienna: Brandstäter, 2008.

Santner, Eric L. 'The Trouble with Hitler: Postwar German Aesthetics and the Legacy of Hitler'. *New German Critique*, 57 (Fall 1992).

Santone, Jessica. 'Marina Abramović: Seven Easy Pieces. Critical Documentation Strategies for Art's Histories'. *Leonardo*, 41 (February 2008).

Sarrazin, Thilo. *Deutschland schafft sich ab: wie wir unser Land aufs Spiel setzen.* Munich: Deutsche Verlags-Anstalt, 2010.

Savage, Kirk. *Monument Wars. Washington D.C., the National Mall, and the Transformation of the Memorial Landscape.* Berkeley/London/Los Angeles: University of California Press, 2009.

Schimmel, Paul, ed. *Out of Actions: Between Performance and the Object, 1949–1979.* The Museum of Contemporary Art, Los Angeles. London/New York: Thames and Hudson, 1998.

Schjeldahl, Peter. 'The Hitler Show: The Jewish Museum Revisits the Nazis'. *The New Yorker*, 78:6 (1 April 2002).

Schneider, Rebecca. *The Explicit Body in Performance.* New York: Routledge, 1997.

——. *Performing Remains: Art and War in Times of Theatrical Reenactment.* New York: Routledge, 2011.

——. 'Performance Remains Again'. In Gabriella Giannachi, Nick Kaye, and Michael Shanks, eds. *Archaeologies of Presence. Art Performance and the Persistence of Being.* London/New York: Routledge, 2012.

Schütz, Sabine. *Anselm Kiefer – Geschichte als Material. Arbeiten 1969–1983.* Cologne: Dumont, 1999.

Schwarz, Dieter, ed. *Aktionsmalerei – Aktionismus. Wien 1960–1965. Eine Chronologie von Dieter Schwarz.* Zurich: Seedorn, 1988.

Scribner, Charity. *Requiem for Communism.* Cambridge, Mass.: MIT Press, 2003.

Senatsverwaltung für Wissenschaft, Forschung und Kultur, ed. *Colloquium. Denkmal für die ermordeten Juden Europas. Dokumentation.* Berlin, 1997.

Senie, Harriet F. and Sally Webster, eds. *Critical Issues in Public Art.* Washington, D.C.: Smithsonian Institution Press, 1992.

Sennett, Richard. *The Fall of Public Man.* Cambridge: Cambridge University Press, 1977.

Shanken, Andrew M. 'Planning Memory. Living Memorials in the United States during World War II'. *Art Bulletin*, 84:1 (March 2002).

Sohm, Hanns, ed. *Happening & Fluxus. Materialien.* Cologne: Kölnischer Kunstverein, 1970.

Solomon-Godeau, Abigail. 'Mourning or Melancholia: Christian Boltanski's Missing House'. *Oxford Art Journal*, 21 (1998).

Sontag, Susan. 'Fascinating Fascism'. In *Under the Sign of Saturn.* New York: Farrar, Strauss, and Giroux, 1972.

Stanek, Lukasz. *Henri Lefebvre on Space. Architecture, Urban Research and the Production of Theory.* Minneapolis: University of Minnesota Press, 2011.

Stevens, Quentin, Karen Franck and R. Fazakerley. 'Counter-Monuments: The Anti-Monumental and the Dialogic'. *Journal of Architecture*, 17 (2012).

Stierli, Martino. *Las Vegas im Rückspiegel. Die Stadt in Theorie, Fotografie und Film.* Zürich: gta, 2010.

——, and Mechtild Widrich. *Participation in Art and Architecture: Spaces of Interaction and Occupation*. London: I.B. Tauris, forthcoming.

Stiles, Kristine. 'Performance and Its Objects'. *Arts Magazine*, 65:3 (1990).

——, Klaus Biesenbach, and Chrissie Iles. *Marina Abramović*. London: Phaidon, 2008.

Stooss, Toni, ed. *Marina Abramović. Artist Body. Performances 1969–1997*. Milan: Charta, 1998.

Sturken, Marita. *Tangled Memories: The Vietnam War, the AIDS Epidemic, and the Politics of Remembering*. Berkeley: University of California Press, 1997.

Suderberg, Erika, ed. *Space Site Intervention. Situating Installation Art*. Minneapolis: University of Minnesota Press, 2000.

Suleiman, Susan Rubin. *Crises of Memory and the Second World War*. Cambridge, Mass.: Harvard University Press, 2006.

Susovski, Marijan. *The New Art Practice in Yugoslavia, 1966–78*. Zagreb: Gallery of Contemporary Art, Zagreb, 1978.

Thünemann, Holger. *Holocaust-Rezeption und Geschichtskultur. Zentrale Holocaust-Denkmäler in der Kontroverse. Ein deutsch-österreichischer Vergleich*. Idstein: Schulz-Kirchner, 2005.

Tisdall, Caroline, ed. *Joseph Beuys*. New York: Solomon R. Guggenheim Museum, 1979.

——. *Joseph Beuys*. London: Thames and Hudson, 1988.

Todorova, Maria. *Imagining the Balkans*. Oxford: Oxford University Press, 1997.

Ursprung, Philip. *Allan Kaprow, Robert Smithson, and the Limits to Art*. Berkeley/Los Angeles/London: University of California Press, 2013.

——, Mechtild Widrich, and Jürg Berthold, eds. *Presence. A Public Workshop*. Zurich: Lars Müller, forthcoming.

Vidler, Antony. *The Architectural Uncanny. Essays in the Modern Unhomely*. Cambridge, Mass.: MIT Press, 1992.

Virilio, Paul. *L'espace critique*. Paris: Christian Bourgeois, 1984.

Vischer, Theodora. *Beuys: Die Einheit des Werkes. Zeichnungen, Aktionen, Plastische Arbeiten, Soziale Skulptur*. Cologne: Walther König, 1991.

Von der Heiden, Anne, and Nina Zschocke, eds. *Autorität des Wissens. Kunst- und Wissenschaftsgeschichte im Dialog*. Zurich: Diaphanes, 2012.

Wagner, Anne. 'Performance, Video, and the Rhetoric of Presence'. *October*, no. 91 (Winter 2001).

Ward, Frazer. 'Some Relations between Conceptual and Performance Art'. *Art Journal*, 56:4 (1997).

Warner, Marina. *Monuments and Maidens*. New York: Atheneum, 1985.

Wechsberg, Joseph. 'Enemy of Gemütlichkeit'. *The New Yorker* (20 April 1963).

Weibel, Peter. *Kritik der Kunst. Kunst der Kritik*. Vienna/Munich: Jugend & Volk, 1973.

——, ed. *The Vienna Group*. Vienna/New York: Springer, 1997.

——, and VALIE EXPORT. *Bildkompendium Wiener Aktionismus und Film*. Frankfurt am Main: Kohlkunstverlag, 1970.

West, Richard. *Tito: And the Rise and Fall of Yugoslavia*. New York: Carroll & Graf, 1995.

Whitechapel Gallery, ed. *A Short History of Performance*. London: Whitechapel Gallery, 2003.

Widrich, Mechtild. 'Reperformances: Da capo oder Zugabe?' In Gabriele Mackert, ed. *Blind Date. Zeitgenossenschaft als Herausforderung*. Nuremberg: Institut für Moderne Kunst, 2008.

——. 'Locations and Dislocations. VALIE EXPORT's Media Performances'. *Performing Arts Journal*, no. 99 (September 2011).

——. 'Can Photographs Make It So? Several Outbreaks of Valie Export's Genital Panic'. In Hilde van Gelder and Helen Westgeest, eds. *Photography between Poetics and Politics: The Critical Position of the Photographic Medium in Contemporary Art*. Leuven: University Press Leuven, 2008, reworked as 'Can Photographs Make It So? Repeated Outbreaks of VALIE EXPORT'S Genital Panic since 1969'. In Amelia Jones and Adrian Heathfield, eds., *Perform, Repeat, Record: A Critical Anthology of Live Art in History*. Bristol: Intellect, 2012.

——. 'Process and Authority: Marina Abramović's Freeing the Horizon and Documentarity'. *Grey Room*, no. 47 (May 2012).

——. 'Ge-Schichtete Präsenz und Zeitgenössische Performance. Marina Abramovićs The Artist is Present'. In Uta Daur, ed. *Authentizität und Wiederholung. Künstlerische und kulturelle Manifestationen eines Paradoxes*. Bielefeld: Transcript, 2013.

——. 'Is the "Re" in Reenactment the "Re" in Reperformance?' In Thun-Hohenstein, Felicitas, and Carola Dertnig, eds. *Mapping Research and Teaching in Times of Performative Fine Arts*. Berlin: Sternberg Press, 2013.

——. 'Spatial Implications of the Monument to Freedom and Unity in Leipzig'. *Log*, no. 27 (Spring 2013).

——. 'The Informative Public of Performance: A Study of Viennese Actionism, 1965–1970'. *TDR. The Drama Review*, 217 (February 2013).

——. 'The Willed and the Unwilled Monument. Judenplatz Vienna and Riegl's *Denkmalpflege*'. *Journal of the Society of Architectural Historians (JSAH)*, 72:3 (2013).

Wiesenthal, Simon, ed. *Projekt: Judenplatz Wien*. Vienna: Zsolnay, 2000.

Wiles, David. *Theatre and Citizenship: the History of a Practice*. Cambridge: Cambridge University Press, 2011.

Wirth, Uwe, ed. *Performanz. Zwischen Sprachphilosophie und Kulturwissenschaften*. Frankfurt am Main: Suhrkamp, 2002.

Young, James E. 'The Counter-Monument. Memory against Itself in Germany Today'. *Critical Inquiry*, 18 (1992).

——. *The Texture of Memory. Holocaust Memorials and Meaning*. New Haven: Yale University Press, 1993.

——, ed. *The Art of Memory: Holocaust Memorials in History*. Catalogue. The Jewish Museum New York. Munich/New York: Prestel, 1994.

——. *The Changing Shape of Holocaust Memory*. New York: American Jewish Committee, 1995.

——. *At Memory's Edge. After-Images of the Holocaust in Contemporary Art and Architecture*. New Haven: Yale University Press, 2000.

——. 'Germany's Holocaust Memorial Problem – and Mine'. *The Public Historian*, 24:4 (Fall 2002).

Youngblood, Gene. *Expanded Cinema*. New York: Dutton, 1970.

Index

Note: page numbers in *italics* refer to illustrations; 'n' following a page reference indicates the number of a note on that page.

EU authorised representative for GPSR:
Easy Access System Europe, Mustamäe tee 50,
10621 Tallinn, Estonia
gpsr.requests@easproject.com